ETHNIC CONFLICT AND INDOCTRINATION

Irenäus Eibl-Eibesfeldt is Professor Emeritus, Max-Planck-Institute for Behavioral Physiology and Senior Fellow of the Center for Human Sciences, University of Munich. He is the author of innumerable scholarly papers and monographs, including the groundbreaking *Love and Hate* and *Human Ethology*.

Frank Kemp Salter is a researcher with the Max-Planck-Institute for Behavioral Physiology and the Center for Human Sciences, University of Munich, and the author of *Emotion in Command*.

ETHNIC CONFLICT AND INDOCTRINATION

Altruism and Identity in Evolutionary Perspective

❧

Edited by

Irenäus Eibl-Eibesfeldt

and

Frank Kemp Salter

Berghahn Books
New York • Oxford

Published in 1998 by **Berghahn Books**

www.BerghahnBooks.com

© 1998 Irenäus Eibl-Eibesfeldt and Frank Kemp Salter

Library of Congress Cataloging-in-Publication Data
Ethnic Conflict and Indoctrination : Altruism and Identity in
Evolutionary perspectives / edited by Irenäus Eibl-Eibesfeldt
& Frank Kemp Salter
    p.   cm.
   "Research Centre for Human Ethology in the Max Planck
Society, Andechs, Germany."
   Includes bibliographical references (p.   ) and index.
   ISBN 1-57181-923-1 (alk. paper).--ISBN 1-57181-766-2 (pbk.
alk. paper)
   1. Political socialization.   2. Ideology.   3. Ethnopsychology.
4. Dominance (Psychology).   5. Aggressiveness (Psychology).
I. Eibl-Eibesfeldt, Irenäus.   II. Salter, Frank K.   III. Forschung-
stelle für Humanethologie in der Max-Planck-Gesellschaft.
HM291.I537   1998
301--dc21   97-3888
                                           CIP

British Library Cataloguing in Publication Data

A catalogue record for this book is available
from the British Library.

CONTENTS

FIGURES AND TABLES

❧

FIGURES

TABLES

MAPS

ACKNOWLEDGMENTS

We wish to express our gratitude to the many people who contributed to organizing the meeting that formed the basis of this book, and to the meeting participants. After the meeting was conceived by the first editor, Karl Grammer and Johanna Uher laid much of the groundwork in 1991, and following some setbacks, the task was completed in 1994 by the editors with the invaluable assistance of Wulf Schiefenhövel. During the meeting Sven Klose donated valuable technical assistance. Participants not reflected in the volume's chapters made substantial contributions to discussion at Ringberg, and accordingly we thank Richard Byrne, Linnda Caporael, Daniel Freedman, Duane Quiatt, Victor A. Shnirelman, Al Somit, and Carmen Strungaru. Finally, the editors wish to thank the Max Planck Society for its generous support of this meeting, which they warmly hosted during a three-day blizzard at the Society's elegant Ringberg Castle beside Lake Tegern in Bavaria. Further, the editors wish to thank Prof. Dr. h. c. Berthold Beitz and the Alfried Krupp von Bohlen and Halbach Stiftung, Traudl Engelhorn-Vechiatto, the Doctors Günter and Anemarie Haackert and the Haackert Foundation and Dr. Rudolf Kerscher and the Fritz von Thyssen Stiftung for their continuing support, which allowed us to continue our studies on cultural ethology.

NOTES ON CONTRIBUTORS

Robert Boyd is Professor of Anthropology at the University of California, Los Angeles. He received his Ph.D. from the University of California, Davis in 1974 for research in ecology oriented toward economics. He and Peter Richerson began collaborating on the study of cultural evolution in 1975. Their 1985 book *Culture and the Evolutionary Process* is widely regarded as one of the major contributions to this field. Boyd has also published work on evolutionary game theory, and he and Joan Silk have recently published a biological anthropology textbook, *How Humans Evolved*.

Danielle Case received her B.A., summa cum laude, in 1994, and M.A. in 1997, from York University. Her masters thesis was an archival analysis of the role of ethnocentrism in recent genocidal movements, a follow-up to her coauthored chapter in this volume. In addition, she has a coauthored paper in press on parsing schizophrenia with neurocognitive tests. She was the recipient of the 1994 York University Scholarship, the 1994 Founders College Book Prize, and Ontario Graduate Scholarships in 1995/96 and 1996/97.

Hiram Caton is Professor of Politics and History at Griffith University, Brisbane, Australia, and a consultant in crowd management. He took his B.A. at the University of Chicago and his Ph.D. at Yale University. He has held appointments at the Pennsylvania State University, the Research School of Social Sciences, Australian National University, and Harvard University. He is presently writing *People Power: A Study of Collective Action*, for the Cambridge University Press.

Robert D. Deutsch is a consultant on public communications to government and corporate clients. His ethologically based methodology—Primalysis—uncovers the deep structure of the public's mood and mind and how these are embodied in behavior and thought. A graduate of the Albert Einstein College of Medicine, Dr. Deutsch was a member of the Human Ethology Workgroup at the Max Planck Institute in Germany and then an Advisor on public diplomacy to the U.S. government. He is a frequent contributor of opinions and editorials to major U.S. newspapers and TV news programs.

Irenäus Eibl-Eibesfeldt was born in Vienna, 15 June 1928. He is Professor of Zoology at the University of Munich. From 1951 to 1970 he was a research associate of Konrad Lorenz. From 1970 to 1996 he headed the Research Group for Human Ethology in the Max Planck Society. He conducts long-term research in several different cultures: San, Himba, Yanomami, Eipo, and Trobriands amongst others. In 1992 he founded the Ludwig Boltzmann Institute for Urban Ethology in Vienna and became its Honorary Director. He is now Head of the Film Archive for Human Ethology at Andechs. His major publications translated into English include: *Galápagos: Wonders of Noah's Ark in the Pacific* (1960), *Ethology, the Biology of Behaviour* (1970, 1975) *Love and Hate* (1970; 1996), *The !Ko Bushman Society* (1972), *The Biology of Peace and War* (1979), and *Human Ethology* (1989), a second English edition of which is in preparation.

Siegfried Frey was born in Stuttgart. He is Professor of Communications and Media Psychology and Head of the Human Interactions Laboratory at the Gerhard Mercator University in Duisburg. He previously worked at the Max Planck Institute for Psychiatry in Munich, at the University of California, San Francisco, and at the University of Berne, Switzerland. Over the past ten years he has been engaged in interdisciplinary communications research as *Directeur d'Études* at the École des Hautes Études en Sciences Sociales in Paris, as Harris German Dartmouth Distinguished Visiting Professor at Dartmouth College and as Alcatel-SEL Foundation Professor at the University of Stuttgart. For developing a movement notation system equivalent to the alphabetical notation of speech, he has been awarded the Research Prize for Technical Communication by the Standard Electric Lorenz Foundation.

Gebhard Geiger was born in Bensheim, Germany. After receiving his Ph.D. in physics in 1977, he studied philosophy of science and social science in Germany and the United States. In 1981 he received an M.A. in political science from UCLA and in 1987 a Ph.D. (*Habilitation*) in philosophy of science from the Technical University of Munich, where he currently teaches philosophy. His publications include *Evolutionary Instability: Logical and Material Aspects of a Unified Theory of Biosocial Evolution* (1990), and *Verhaltensökologie der Technik* (Behavioral Ecology and Technology) (1997).

Karl Grammer, born 1950 in Germany, received his Ph.D. in biology at the University of Munich and the Research Institute for Human Ethology, Max Planck Society, Andechs, in 1982 for a dissertation on child ethology. From 1983 to 1991 he served as Assistant Professor at the Research Institute. In 1991 he became joint Scientific Director (with Prof. Dr. I. Eibl-Eibesfeldt) of the Ludwig Boltzmann Institute for Urban Ethology in Vienna. He is widely published on the ethology of sexual behavior, and in 1993 published *Signale der Liebe* (Signals of Love: The Biological Laws of Partnership) (English translation in preparation). Prof. Grammer has served as Secretary of the International Society for Human Ethology since 1992. Currently he is researching communication at subliminal levels.

Kevin MacDonald is Professor of Psychology at California State University–Long Beach. His research has focused on developing evolutionary perspectives in history and developmental psychology. In addition to numerous journal articles, he has edited two books, *Sociobiological Perspectives on Human Development* (1988) and *Parent-Child Play: Descriptions and Implications* (1993). He has also authored two monographs, *Social and Personality Development: An Evolutionary Synthesis* (1988) and *A People That Shall Dwell Alone: Judaism As a Group Evolutionary Strategy* (1994). A second volume on Judaism within an evolutionary framework, *Separation and Its Discontents: Toward an Evolutionary Theory of Anti-Semitism*, is scheduled to be published in 1997. He is Secretary/Archivist of the Human Behavior and Evolution Society.

Roger D. Masters is Nelson A. Rockefeller Professor of Government at Dartmouth College and Chair of the Executive Committee of the Gruter Institute for Law and Behavioral Research. His publications include *The Nature of Politics* (1989), *Beyond Relativism: Science and Human Values* (1993), and *Machiavelli, Leonardo, and the*

Science of Power (1996). He also has coedited a number of volumes: *Primate Politics* (with Glendon Schubert, 1990; paperback edition 1994), *The Sense of Justice* (with Margaret Gruter, 1992), the first five volumes of *The Collected Writings of Rousseau* (with Christopher Kelly, 1990–1995), and *The Neurotransmitter Revolution: Serotonin, Social Behavior, and the Law* (1994). He is also general editor of the *Gruter Institute Reader in Biology, Law, and Human Social Behavior* as well as editor of the "Biology and Social Life" section of the journal *Social Science Information*.

Michael McGuire, M.D., is Professor of Psychiatry and Biobehavioral Sciences, a member of the Brain Research Institute, and Director of the Nonhuman Primate Laboratory at the University of California–Los Angeles. He was the founding editor of the journal *Ethology and Sociobiology* from 1979, and has published widely on evolutionary approaches to social behavior, including the books *The Saint Kitts Vervet, Reconstructions in Psychoanalysis, and Ethological Psychiatry* (with Lynn Fairbanks, also of UCLA). His latest book, *Darwinian Psychiatry* (coauthored with Alfonso Troisi of the University of Rome) is forthcoming with Oxford University Press. In addition, he is Research Director of the Gruter Institute for Law and Behavioral Research.

Detlev W. Ploog, Dr. med. Dr. phil.h.c., was born in Hamburg in 1920. He is Director Emeritus of the Max Planck Institute for Psychiatry, and Honorary Professor of Psychiatry. Originally trained in medicine and psychiatry, Professor Ploog's research interests broadened to include primatology. He was a Visiting Scientist with the NIMH, Bethesda, Maryland, working with Paul D. MacLean, from 1958 to 1960. From 1961 to 1988 he headed the Department of Primate Behavior, Max Planck Institute of Psychiatry, Munich, and from 1964 to 1988 was Director of that institute's clinical research institute and hospital. From 1964 to 1981 he was an Associate of the Neuroscience Research Program, M.I.T, Cambridge, Mass. Professor Ploog's fields of research include evolutionary psychiatry and psychopathology, the ethology and neuroethology of nonhuman and human primate behavior and communication, and the prerequisites of human speech.

Michael J. Raleigh, Ph.D., is Professor of Psychiatry and Member of the Brain Research Institute, University of California, Los Angeles. His major research interests include nonhuman primate behavior, central nervous system physiology, and physiology-behavior interactions.

Peter J. Richerson is Professor of Environmental Studies at the University of California, Davis. His collaborative work with Robert Boyd on the dual inheritance theory of gene-culture coevolution began in the mid 1970s. Their well-received book, *Culture and the Evolutionary Process*, was published by the University of Chicago Press in 1985, and continuing work includes theoretical papers on the evolution of reciprocal altruism and punishment in large groups, an empirical study of group selection, and an analysis of why complex culture is rare. He is a limnologist by training and also conducts research projects on lake ecology.

J. Philippe Rushton is Professor of Psychology at the University of Western Ontario in Canada. He holds two doctorates from the University of London (Ph.D. and D.Sc), is a Fellow of the John Simon Guggenheim Foundation, the American Association for the Advancement of Science, and the American, British, and Canadian Psychological Associations. His primary research interest is human altruism. His work in the 1970s focused primarily on social learning in children. In the 1980s he conducted a large twin study and found that the heritabilities for altruism, empathy, and nurturance are about 50 percent. Prof. Rushton has made important theoretical contributions to the sociobiology of human altruism, complementing kin-selection theory with genetic similarity theory, which offers an explanation of assortative friend- and mate-choice. He has also provided a controversial theory of the evolution of human race differences. Altogether he has published nearly two hundred articles and six books, the latest of which is *Race, Evolution, and Behavior* (1995).

Frank K. Salter was born in Sydney, Australia, and received his Ph.D. in humanities from Griffith University in Brisbane in 1990. After serving as a consultant with government departments in Australia, he took up a position as guest scientist at the Research Center for Human Ethology in the Max Planck Society, Andechs, Germany, where he remains. He is also an Associate of the University of Munich's Human Sciences Center. His ethological monograph (*Emotions in Command: A Naturalistic Study of Institutional Dominance*, 1995) analyzed the behaviors and social technologies activating command hierarchies. Present research extends social technology theory to the study of ethnic competition in the United States.

Wulf Schiefenhövel was born in 1943 in Siegen, Germany, and undertook his first field study in the New Guinea Highlands from

1965 to 1966. Subsequent ethnomedical, anthropological, and human ethological fieldwork has taken him to Melanesia and Indonesia, the results contributing to over two hundred publications. He completed his M.D. in 1970, and in 1974 to 1976 was Field Director of the Deutsche Forschungsgemeinschaft interdisciplinary project "Man, Culture and Environment in the Central Highlands of Irian Jaya, West New Guinea." Since 1977 Professor Schiefenhövel has been a Senior Research Fellow at the human ethology unit at the Max Planck Institute for Behavioral Physiology, Andechs, and in addition since 1991 Professor for Medical Psychology and Ethnomedicine at the University of Munich.

James N. Schubert is Professor of Political Science at Northern Illinois University and has research interests in the areas of biopolitics, political psychology, and the politics of public health. His innovative application of ethological field methods to political phenomena has been applied to a major study of Supreme Court oral argument. Present research includes a cross-cultural study of nonverbal dominance as a predictor of electability, based on data gathered during the 1996 Romanian elections.

Irwin Silverman received his Ph.D. in psychology from the University of Rochester in 1962 and has held professorial appointments at the State University of New York at Buffalo, the University of Florida, and York University in Toronto, where he is presently in residence. He is a Fellow of the Canadian Psychological Association and served as first Chairperson of the Division of Evolutionary Psychology. He has authored two books and more than one hundred scholarly publications and presentations.

Christa Sütterlin received her doctorate in art history and literature in 1977. Postdoctoral research concerned lateral asymmetry in aesthetic perception at the Institute of Medical Psychology, University of Munich. She was a member of the Reimers Foundation study group on "Biological Aspects of Esthetics," from 1979 to 1982 in Bad Homburg. Since 1983 Dr. Sütterlin has been located at the Research Group for Human Ethology in the Max Planck Society, Andechs, where she has investigated the ethology of aesthetic perception and art. In 1992 she coauthored with I. Eibl-Eibesfeldt *Im Banne der Angst: Zur Natur-und Kunstgeschichte menschlicher Abwehrsymbolik* (1992) (Frozen in Fear. The Natural and Art History of Apotropaic Symbols).

Lionel Tiger was born in Montreal and educated at McGill University and the London School of Economics. He is currently Darwin Professor of Anthropology at Rutgers University in New Brunswick, New Jersey, and has taught at McGill, the University of Ghana, and the University of British Columbia. With Robin Fox he wrote in 1966 "The Zoological Perspective in Social Science" (*Man: J. of Royal Anth. Inst.*, 1996) and was, with Fox, Research Director of the H. F. Guggenheim Foundation in New York from 1972 to 1984. Among his books are: *Men in Groups* (1969/1987), *The Imperial Animal* (1971/1989/1997—with Fox), *Women in the Kibbutz* (1975), *Female Hierarchies* (1978—edited with H. Fowler), *Optimism: The Biology of Hope* (1979/1995), *The Manufacture of Evil: Ethics, Evolution and the Industrial System* (1987/1989), and *The Pursuit of Pleasure* (1992). He lives in New York City.

Alfonso Troisi, M.D., is a Research Psychiatrist at the University of Rome Tor Vergatta. His major research interests include clinical psychiatry, human ethology, and primate behavior.

Johan M. G. van der Dennen, born in Eindhoven, the Netherlands, in 1944, studied behavioral sciences at the University of Groningen, and is at present a researcher at the Political Science Section of the Department of Legal Theory, formerly the Peace Research Institute, University of Groningen, the Netherlands. He has published extensively on all aspects of human and animal aggression, including intergroup competition in primates and preindustrial human societies, sexual violence, theories of war causation, and ethnocentrism. He is secretary of the European Sociobiological Society. In 1995 he published *The Origin of War: The Evolution of a Male-Coalitional Reproductive Strategy*, a two-volume report of his ongoing research of more than twenty years.

Polly Wiessner received her PhD. from the University of Michigan, Ann Arbor in 1977 and is currently a research associate at the Research Group for Human Ethology in the Max Planck Society, Andrechs. Between 1973 and 1977 she worked on reciprocity, exchange networks and style in artifacts among the !Kung San. Since 1985 she has been doing ethnohistorical work on environment, exchange networks, warfare and cults among the Enga of Papua New Guinea.

CHAPTER ONE

INTRODUCTION

Irenäus Eibl-Eibesfeldt
and Frank Kemp Salter

Arthur Koestler once remarked that it is not an excess of aggression but of loyalty that could ruin us. And indeed it was and is up to the present the identification with values of a community, be they religious, party-political or ethnonationalistic, that have led to the most atrocious bloodshed of our history.

In particular, ethnic nationalism seems to resist attempts at suppression. Our indoctrinability, our group loyalty, and our proneness to collective aggression are phenomena deserving attention. Why this loyalty and feeling of belongingness to a group characterized by shared language, cultural practices, beliefs and other symbols of identity? And why the diversity of cultures—why so many different ethnicities at all?

From an evolutionary point of view, the why-question aims at an understanding of the selection pressures responsible for a trait, whether a cultural practice or an innate motor pattern or disposition. We thus try to understand the function of a behavior in promoting survival or reproduction. More generally, we want to learn the ways in which phylogeny prepared us to act so as to enhance our fitness on the individual, kin, and even group level. Preparation can take the form of preadaptation, the fortuitous matching of a trait with some new environmental challenge. A case in point is natural selection at the level of groups, a concept now back in vogue after being banished from the realm of the plausible where it had been introduced by Darwin (1874), Keith (1949), and others. Humans' culturally enhanced ability to discipline group members and detect free-riders can be seen as a preadaptation for group selection (Eibl-Eibesfeldt 1982), in the manner formalized by Richerson and Boyd (1992; this volume).

Since evolution is a continuing process in a constantly changing world, adaptations lag behind the changes they have to cope with. This is particularly true for the human species, which for most of its history lived in small communities where individuals knew each other personally and in which each community set itself apart from similar others, usually by occupying and defending discrete territories. There could be no sharper contrast between this primordial environment and the technologically advanced civilizations of anonymous millions organized around megacities that we have created for ourselves. This is an environment for which we are less phylogenetically adapted than the intimate hunter-gatherer band. Our attempts to culturally adapt to this new situation include experiments with a diversity of social strategies of leadership, ideologies, and economic systems. Emotionally we are well prepared for a life in small face-to-face communities. The large anonymous society and the impersonality of technical civilization creates problems.

The trial-and-error "learning" by selection acting on variation, which has characterized our biological and much of our cultural evolution, is a painful process. Were we to rely on this process of "self organization" as recommended by nineteenth-century Social Darwinists and the economic liberal van Hayek, the pain would continue for some considerable time. And time is running short. Due to the success of our species we have probably outbred the long-term carrying capacity of our planet, and our descendants will be caught between the anvil of limited resources and the hammer of global pollution. Oil resources appear to have comprised the booty of two recent wars, and there is a disturbingly great potential for destructive international competition over strategic minerals and living space as the developing world flexes its newfound industrial muscles.

Is it possible to imagine societal life without institutionalized dominance? Small face-to-face communities do exist without institutions, but for anonymous mass societies institutionalized dominance seems to be inevitable (Salter 1995). In a democratic society the conditions for the application of repressive dominance must be well defined and accepted by the population. One condition is a degree of popular trust in those wielding power, combined with institutional checks and balances, including elections. Citizens expect those to whom they delegate power to use it to maintain the public goods of law and order and the regulation of the profit motive when it would lead to environmental degradation or exploitation. The trend in democratic states is towards a balance of administrative nurturance and authoritarian dominance. The demand for both is due to phylogenetically evolved dispositions, but in the anonymous society nurturance tends to have a lower priority to considerations of personal security and status competition. For those who would construct a nurturant society, special attention must be devoted to preventing the escalation of authoritarian dominance. The history of human social forms can be seen as attempts to strike a tolerable balance between authority and nurturance, a process that continues up to the present time.

Certainly we should not rely on the self-organizing tendency of institutions. Natural selection shows no mercy. If prey is abundant, predators multiply until they overshoot the carrying capacity of their resource, and a joint population collapse ensues, acting as a corrective. This allows for recovery of the prey animals and, with a little delay, of the predators, and so forth in endless tides of suffering. Booms and recessions follow this principle, and it seems as if democracy could finally endanger its existence should laissez faire be allowed to take its course. This risks an escalation of repressive dominance leading to rebellion. Do we want selection to act as a corrective in this way? Certainly not. It would hardly be appropriate for a species capable of reasoning. Surely, we are always under the scrutiny of natural selection. But we can actively seek and select the conditions under which to live, exposing ourselves to a variety of selective forces. We can learn much from nature, but its laws allow great freedom of maneuver over long spans of time. Wresting our destiny from the sorrows of natural selection does not avoid a degree of trial and error, but as already said above, we can combine this ability to strive for set goals with the readiness to correct mistakes in time. And this should become our second nature. We also noted that face-saving often blocks our readiness to admit error. But once we recognize this stumbling block of our heritage, we can cope with the situation (Eibl-Eibesfeldt 1988; 1995).

All organisms are in search of a better world, as Karl Popper used to say. That is, all life pushes ahead, exposing itself to new selective conditions as they arise. Our species is no exception, but we have one advantage not enjoyed by any other species: we can deliberate, debate, and plan ahead and thus can set ourselves goals toward which to strive. As long as we avoid dogmatic fixations and are prepared to learn from mistakes and correct our course in time, new paths are opened up to us. We could free our future course from being too erratic and painful, while speeding the process of cultural adaptation. We are not only intellectually but emotionally prepared for such an enterprise; our nurturant dispositions are the basis of our humanitarian concerns.

Humans' genetic outfit in many ways facilitates cultural adaptation to mass societies, but there are also innate dispositions that in particular situations hamper further development. Pitfalls may reveal themselves in certain situations if we are not aware of them. What were adaptive dispositions in the hunter-gatherer milieu can be destructive in the artificial environment of the modern state. Our striving for repressive dominance is one example. Another is our short-term thinking. All organisms throughout their history, dating back at least 2.5 billion years, have been bred for instant competition. Who won the race right now made it—or retained options for the future. This has also bred in us a basically opportunistic, exploitative disposition that seriously hampers the development of a long-term survival ethos predicated on the fate of future generations.

In evolutionary terms, individual survival means nothing if it does not contribute to the survival and reproduction of genetically related kin. The resulting patterns of loyalty and competition have traumatized our history. Yet as far back as the historical record allows us to infer, ever since humans first reflected upon the uniqueness of life they became concerned about the sufferings imposed by war, including the sufferings of those not belonging to their own communities. Is there a chance for peace in an overcrowded world? And can a sustainable peace be compatible with the preservation of ethnic diversity? It must if we are to avoid a global repressive regime, since the human tendency to experiment with new ways of group living is pronounced. Life has always tended to diversify—a tendency that has served as pacemaker of evolution. And after all, only through diversification has life continued and grown in richness on this planet.

The Book Plan

The burning issue of why humans are susceptible to indoctrination for ideologies which lead to intergroup hostility is overwhelmingly treated as a matter divorced from human evolution. Yet a biologist, confronted by this salient behaviour in another species, would know which questions to ask. What are the contours of this predisposition, and how can we understand it in the context of the species' evolutionary past? To what extent can the ethnonationalist conflicts that have so marred the twentieth century be attributed to an evolved trait of indoctrinability? How is this predisposition exploited by politicians, corporations, and cult leaders? We thought it would be a valuable and timely exercise to have these issues discussed by leading scientists from several fields. The resulting symposium was in keeping with the multidisciplinary orientation of modern evolutionary social science. While indoctrinability and processes of indoctrination were treated as biological phenomena, this was not seen as a reason to exclude ethnographic, physiological, psychological, political, and cultural aspects; not only because these fields provide important description, but because they have in part joined the biosocial project.

These were the underlying considerations motivating this volume. It is based on a symposium called by the first author and organized by both authors in collaboration with colleagues at the Max Planck Research Centre for Human Ethology in Andechs, Germany. The questions posed in the previous paragraph can be grouped under Niko Tinbergen's (1963) four basic questions of ethology: (1) How does a behavior develop? (2) What is its evolutionary history? (3) What are its immediate or "proximate" causes? and (4) What are its functions; how does it help an animal adapt or reproduce? This volume addresses all but the first of these in separate sections, the discussion of indoctrinability through various stages of the life cycle being distributed across several chapters, notably in Caton's remarks on infantilization and Eibl-Eibesfeldt's analysis of childhood xenophobia.

Part One, "Evolutionary precursors and models," devotes four chapters to the theme of phylogeny. These are different yet convergent approaches to the evolutionary history of indoctrinability. **Irenäus Eibl-Eibesfeldt** sets the agenda by stating his argument, developed over three decades of cross-cultural behavioral research, that ethnonationalistic ideologies owe their universal appeal to the way they hook into species-typical dispositions that evolved to elicit bonding and "we-group" identification between mother and child, and other family members. He elaborates the concept of indoctrinability, which he introduced in 1982, as a specific learning disposition analogous to the imprinting that bonds mothers and their babies in many species. More than analogous, the two processes, both of which establish a fixation or attachment, are probably *homologous* in some of the biological mechanisms involved. Certainly they resemble one another in being resistant to therapy ("Humans follow a flag like an experimentally imprinted duckling a ball") and in their dependence on sensitive learning periods during childhood. Indoctrinability facilitates acceptance and identification with a group's characteristics and thus serves we-group demarcation. Because of our evolutionary history, the we-group tends to coincide with tribe, ethnicity, or nation, groups whose supporting myths and ideologies deploy symbols of familial and kinship solidarity. The human tendency to "pseudospeciate" by fissioning along kinship lines is illustrated with recent observations of a Yanomami community in Venezuela. Without institutional mechanisms renewing communal bonds, the objective ethnic uniqueness of this people is not yet matched by a popular sense of ethnic identity, with the result that we-group demarcation is evident at the "micro" level of individual families splitting themselves off from long-term communities. Eibl-Eibesfeldt concludes by cautioning proponents of multi-culturalism about the risks posed to internal harmony by the propensity to form "us-group" identifications in situations of ethnic competition.

Detlev Ploog addresses the question of how far back in humans' evolutionary history the strategic assessment necessary for planning peace and war emerged. Is such assessment purely the result of cultural processes, or does it have phylogenetic underpinnings? To answer these questions he reports an experimental study of the relatively primitive New World squirrel monkey. He presents a graphic description of the aggression and appeasement involved in the fusion of two captive colonies and combines this with data on preschool children to argue that at the behavioral level of social signaling, the strategies employed in initiating or resolving disputes between groups are functionally homologous across the primate order, including man. Ploog's classical-ethological study suggests that a fully "humanized" approach to regulating conflict around the world cannot ignore cross-species universals in the art of making peace.

Pete Richerson and **Robert Boyd**'s chapter, "The Evolution of Human Ultrasociality," reviews the game theoretical literature on social behavior. By their very abstractness, mathematical models can be as readily applied to one species as another, and Richerson and Boyd begin by comparing *Homo sapiens* to the social insects and corals. Our species' unique evolution of cultural systems of social control have helped shape our genetic makeup and allowed us to surpass even ants and termites in the scale and complexity of society. That uniqueness may be due to group selection acting on culturally transmitted variation and then, as an effect, on gene frequencies. Cultural group selection appears more feasible than genetic group selection, Richerson and Boyd argue. In support they present a model grounded on the ethnography of the New Guinea highlands: selected cultural markers signify group boundaries, acting to instill cooperation between in-group members by manipulating humans' genetically inherited social repertoire, and facilitating discipline of would-be free-riders.

Lionel Tiger completes the section by arguing that what Robin Fox has called the "ethnographic dazzle" is quite consistent with genetic effects on social behavior if indoctrinability is seen as a species-specific adaptation. Our species' facility at adopting cultural solutions to group adaptive problems is a low-cost alternative to changing our body shape or neural wiring, the latter being costly somatic transformations. Indoctrinability serves cultural adaptation by homogenizing social values, facilitating cooperative group. Hence, cultural variation is evidence of a natural propensity for cultural adaptation, rather than support for the extreme "culturalist" position that humans have somehow freed themselves from their phylogeny and that culture is an autonomous realm immune to the discoveries of the natural sciences.

Part Two continues the phylogenetic theme, but less directly, by examining indoctrination in noninstitutionalized societies, affording a cross-cultural perspective to our theme. As urged by Darwin (1872) and subsequently put into practice by human ethologists and evolutionary anthropologists, the systematic comparison of diverse cultures is a powerful method for identifying species-typical traits.

Wulf Schiefenhövel describes indoctrination practices among the Eipo, a Highland Papuan culture, serving to cement loyalty within the village and its allies, while directing aggression towards outsiders. Indoctrination exaggerates group differences, "ethnicity indoctrination" being a major focus of instructional effort. But that effort is not made in isolated ceremonies. Schiefenhövel's insightful descriptions allow the reader to get a feel for the human realities of daily indoctrination as it occurred in one Eipo village, in which the drip-drip of examples, symbolism, and lessons forged a group united in its conceptions of gender, morality, warriorship, and cultural identity.

Polly Wiessner's ethnographical comparison of two egalitarian societies points to a reverse function of indoctrination and indoctrinability, namely the homogenization of aspects of the culture of neighboring communities as a means of facilitating exchange between socially defined kin. Wiessner offers an interesting definition of indoctrinability as "the predisposition to be inculcated with values or loyalties that run contrary to immediate individual interest." She hypothesizes that indoctrinability evolved due to individual, not group, selection, and that in its evolutionary setting this trait acted to *counteract*, not enhance, family solidarity. Wiessner argues that strong family loyalty can inhibit the formation of exchange networks. But these networks were, and are, the preindustrial version of "insurance policies," used by people with subsistence economies to guard against the ravages of famine and conflict. She makes this point in two brief case studies of social networking, child training and initiation in the !Kung San, hunter-gatherers of southern Africa, and the Enga, horticulturalists of Highland Papua-New Guinea. Wiessner shows how, in these two egalitarian but economically different societies, indoctrinability predisposes individuals to become culturally homogenized and standardized with a relatively large pool of family units, thereby opening new opportunities for social and economic networking.

Johan van der Dennen reviews the social mechanisms underlying peace and war in many preindustrial societies, concluding that indoctrination can serve both group activities. In the course of his argument, he notes that ecological exigency is a major factor shaping cultural adaptations, whether of peacefulness or warlikeness; that bellicosity is not the same as aggression; and that in traditional societies the destructive potential of warfare is mitigated by practices and rules, including exogamy, arbitration, trade, diplomacy, intercommunity rites and feasts, hospitality, war substitutes such as potlatch, personal bonds, formal declaration of war, fixing the time and place of battle in advance, and postbattle compensation. The breadth of this chapter reflects the massive documentation of its two-volume parent (1995, *The Origins of War*).

Part III examines proximate causation in four chapters on individual behavioral mechanisms. Authors develop and test hypotheses, quantitatively drawing on the latest methods in ethology and evolutionary psychology.

Siegfried Frey discusses the phenomenon of prejudice in the age of communication, in which we are flooded with visual images. Since Walter Lippmann proposed stereotyping as the core factor in the formation of prejudice, research in the field has followed a profoundly cognitivist path. According to that view, hostile attitudes toward people with different ethnic or cultural backgrounds are the result of prior conscious deliberation of biased information fed to persons who have no means to verify its validity. This conception also exerted a lasting impact on the way the issue was empirically approached: it made the sender, rather than the perceiver, the center of attention and it dealt almost exclusively with verbal behavior. Frey documents how in recent years there has been increasing evidence that the cognitive model can only partially explain the process of prejudice formation. Research on the perception of works of art, done in Frey's laboratory, has found that nonverbal stimuli can be employed as powerful tools in the experimental creation of stereotypes. This suggests that stereotypes can, in fact, develop in us all by themselves, without being mediated by some sender's verbal output, solely on the basis of an automatic type of visual information processing, which Hermann von Helmholtz (1867) introduced to the literature as *unbewußter Schluß* (unconscious inference). One fascinating finding is that firmly held prejudices about a person can develop after only a quarter-second exposure to his or her image. Recent research by Frey and colleagues has shifted the focus of research on prejudice from the sender to the perceiver and from verbal to nonverbal stimuli. To this end a technology was developed which permits the assessment of the cognitive response to nonverbal stimuli along with a detailed analysis of the reactions of the automatic vegetative system (based on simultaneous measures of pupil reaction, galvanic skin response, skin temperature, electrocardiogram, peripheral blood pressure, pulse, respiration, and motility). This system was applied in research with Roger Masters on how subjects in Germany, France, and the United States respond to televised pictures of political leaders.

Karl Grammer employs evolutionary theory of sexual selection to generate hypotheses about how we should expect advertisers to exploit images of men and women to indoctrinate consumers to buy products. Two possible broad strategies emerge: using opposite sex images to produce good feelings about a product (reinforcement), and "comparison with the normative self," in which the lesson is if you want to be like the attractive person in the advertisement, buy our product. The latter strategy is revealed to be most frequently used in a large-circulation, glossy Austrian magazine. Grammer reaches this finding using ethological methods of behavioral analysis applied to 357 advertisements. Women were presented as being friendlier, more submissive, and sexier than men, who are presented as of higher status but not aggressive. These results strongly confirm the evolutionary hypotheses. How could advertisers be so prescient? Grammer concludes that the behavioral sophistication of advertisements is due to cultural evolution, in which successful ads—those that are effective in manipulating consumers—proliferate while less appealing formats "die out."

Jim Schubert's chapter switches our focus to television in the United States. He reports a study of the "rally-round-the-flag" effect of presidential speeches announcing military action by United States' forces. A mix of ethological and social-psychological methods was used, and a pronounced sex difference in response was found. Females were more discriminating than males in supporting a call to arms, being most responsive to humanitarian concerns. Males were more responsive to justifications based on "vital national interests." The finding is consistent with evolutionary theory in which women's fitness is enhanced by a more "caring and nurturant" approach to social relations, a theory receiving growing support from ethological and feminist research. Women are not indiscriminate pacifists, but are more likely to consent to the use of force when it is portrayed as serving humanitarian purposes. Males conform to the *Realpolitik* ethos.

Which brain processes underlie our receptiveness to indoctrination? An expert assessment is provided by **Michael McGuire**, **Alfonso Troisi**, **Michael Raleigh**, and **Roger Masters**, who extend James Danielli's idea that religion promotes feelings of integration, control, and well-being by releasing endogenous neurotransmitters. Eating and sex give the same effects, but, according to McGuire and colleagues, so can information—hence our appetite for ideologies that soothe and stabilize. They explain Regulation-Disregulation Theory (RDT) to hypothesize that acceptance of an ideology "correlates with the degree to which embracing it increases the likelihood of attaining physiological homeostasis." The analysis links neural processes to personality and social function. Successful ideologies organize and prioritize thought, raise self-esteem, demarcate in-groups and out-groups, regulate in-group exchange and rituals, and promote desirable emotional states.

Part IV continues the proximate causation theme with two analyses of symbolism in the service of indoctrination via art and television. **Christa Sütterlin** discusses the use of art in indoctrination. An interesting, and to censors a perplexing, thing about art is that it conveys ethical and social norms through a medium that outflanks the verbal channel. A scientific understanding of how art has the effects that it does requires an approach to human aesthetic perception on the basis of behavioral, and especially evolutionary, concepts. Human sensitivity to certain visual and auditory "key stimuli" can be traced back to archaic biases built into our perceptual apparatus. These evolved as adaptations to our natural and human environment and served different functions. Art can use these biases to release simple aesthetic pleasures and different moods; it can also exploit the same mechanisms to trigger messages of a nonaesthetic but political or ideological character and thus manipulate our attitude towards norms and values. Regularity of form not only organizes an unstructured space, but in architecture can convey a sense of monumentalism conveying dominance, authority, control, and legal power. In different artistic constructions the figure of a half-dressed woman can serve an erotic appeal or can draw attention to the heroic figure of Freedom and its political message of Revolution. Other concepts and symbols of indoctrination are discussed within an ethological framework.

Robert Deutsch argues that indoctrination into joining one side in hostile intergroup relations is possible because people need to belong and feel powerful. Strategies of persuasion can be built into communications that can seize upon this emotional need, totally bypassing rational thought. Mechanisms of indoctrination have been with us since the time of early man. In postmodern society, characterized by mass media and simulated reality, these mechanisms have become hyperritualized. With television now the prime political "soapbox," forms of behavior that underlie indoctrinability have themselves become highly exaggerated and condensed. The result is that even the words of political propaganda we hear on TV are interpreted in the visual mode by the viewing audience. Television transforms order and meaning by eliminating all nuance and abstraction. We are left only with expressions and gestures—the essence of emotion. Personality dominates. Ideology and the actions it would explain are super-seded by the image of those embodying them. Using examples from televised press conferences, speeches, interviews, and news broadcasts during international crises (e.g., the Gulf War), and from political advertisements during presidential campaigns (e.g., Reagan), Deutsch describes the general process by which world leaders gain ascendancy in public opinion.

Part V on "Group processes" moves onto Tinbergen's final theme, that of function. In animal ethology, the function of a behavior is the way it serves survival or reproduction. With the advent of the neo-Darwinian synthesis, the reproductive function was reinterpreted as genetic fitness. As a group-living species, humans have a basic set of adaptations that equip us to integrate into groups, accommodate to their internal social structure, and, if the group selectionists are right, perform as a cooperative member in a manner that strengthened the group as a unit of selection in the evolutionary past. For humans and other group-living species, an understanding of how a behavior or predisposition affects group integration supplies vital information about its survival value. The four chapters address this question by taking both a "disposition's-eye view" and a "group's-eye view."

Hiram Caton begins by challenging the negative connotations of indoctrination, pointing out that it serves positive functions of integrating individuals into work and social groups. People crave indoctrination because it instills "pride, energy, commitment, a sense of power and well being, and operational competence." Yet to onlookers indoctrination is childish. The process involves infan-tilization because this facilitates imitation and learning of new social scripts. Indoctrination allows the individual to change sociopolitical and psychosocial identity, and this is usually a rewarding experience, at least subjectively and for the time being. To illustrate, Caton presents two snapshot case studies: Patty Hearst's abduction and conversion by the Symbionese Liberation Army in the 1970s; and the motivation movement, whose gurus transmit, for a price, the secrets of positive/lateral thinking, and of how to win friends and influence people. These polished "spin doctors" have made an industry out of indoctrinability by mass producing infantilization and the therapy-dependency that goes with it. Looking at the techniques involved, Caton finds a com-mon denominator in the T-group devised by Kurt Lewin.

Kevin MacDonald contributes to the resurgent interest in group selection with a case study of traditional Judaism as a "group evolutionary strategy." The analysis draws on Boyd and Richerson's (1992) argument that culturally based strategies are more plausible locomotives of group selection than are genetically based strategies. Using cultural devices, humans are able to create and maintain groups that impose high levels of altruism on their members and punish or exclude cheaters. An evolutionary group strategy is thus an "experiment in living," rather than a deterministic outcome of natural selection. Group strategies differ along a number of independent dimensions, including degree of altruism among members, extent of sanctions against cheating, degree of genetic and cultural segregation, degree of biological relatedness of members, extent of within-group egalitarianism, and extent of ecological specialization. Highly cohesive group evolutionary strategies, such as traditional diaspora Judaism, tend to be characterized by intense socialization pressures (i.e., indoctrination) directed at producing within-group altruism and economic cooperation.

The final two chapters in this section present an interesting debate between Philippe Rushton on the one hand, and Irwin Silverman and Danielle Case on the other. Rushton offers a mass of evidence and theoretical models supporting the view that humans are genetically predisposed to ethnocentrism—including racism and nationalism—by a primordial tendency to mate with and otherwise discriminate in favor of similar others. Silverman and Case reject this view based on previous theoretical work and, in this volume, on an experimental psychological study. The differences between these two views are made more significant by their similarities—both are biosocially oriented, accepting that biology has important effects on social behavior. Yet within this shared approach there is considerable room for disagreement.

Philippe Rushton's chapter approaches the issue of group selection from the perspective of genetic similarity theory, which he and colleagues named in the 1980s. His argument is as follows. As previously reviewed (Rushton 1989), much evidence exists that genetic similarity mediates human relationships, both within and between families. Across a wide range of traits, including anthropometric, psychological, and cultural indicators, people tend to marry and befriend similar others. Rushton argues that this has implications for the study of social behavior in small groups and even in large ones, both national and international. The genetic mechanisms underlying the findings may constitute a biological substrate of ethnocentrism, enabling group selection to occur.

Social attitudes and ideologies can be expected to follow lines of genetic and ethnic similarity, Rushton surmises. This would occur if indoctrinability were biased to accept ideas and practices disseminated by genetically (e.g., ethnically) similar indoctrinators.

Irwin Silverman and **Danielle Case** reject similarity theory, maintaining that preferential treatment between genetically related individuals is restricted to direct kin. Beyond the family, they contend, interpersonal and intergroup relations are determined by pragmatism. Ethnocentrism appears ubiquitous because outgroup prejudices, which are constantly shifting, serve as rationalizations, means of preserving self-images of fidelity and fairness in the face of the perennial pursuit of situationally optimal intra- and intergroup alliances. Silverman and Case present data in support of this view. The first section of the paper describes a survey-type study, designed to ascertain the salience of ethnocentric motives when confronted by pragmatic considerations. Various hypothetical scenarios were presented to subjects, for which they were required to decide whether they would favor a member or members of their own self-defined ethnic group or some other ethnic group, under conditions of nil, little and significant cost/risk if the subject favored his or her own ethnic group. The second section analyzes two contemporary so-called "ethnic wars" to determine whether perceived ethnic dissimilarity could more reasonably be considered a cause or effect of the conflict. Silverman and Chase discuss the recent wars in ex-Yugoslavia and in the Central African republics of Burundi and Rwanda, both of which involved so-called ethnic cleansing. They conclude that both studies point to pragmatism rather than ethnocentrism as the more compelling motivating force in human affairs.

Part VI is an assortment of synthetic approaches dealing with the political implications of indoctrinability. People's predisposition to become indoctrinated into the identity and values of groups has been exploited by institutional techniques and in turn has helped shape those techniques through cultural evolution.

Gebhard Geiger reinterprets the sociologist Max Weber's theory of charismatic authority in ethological terms. He finds many parallels between Weber's description of charisma and the face-to-face ritualized cues used by animals, including humans, to negotiate informal rank. For example, Weber contended that charisma is the emotional stimulus to voluntary submission under the command of a person who is believed to possess extraordinary qualities. The resemblance between charisma and prestige or dominance is striking. Geiger makes the important point that becoming indoctrinated to bureaucratic or military regimes in industrial societies is not necessarily or usually adaptive. He concludes that indoctrinability is an evolved predisposition to ritualized submission transplanted to novel sociocultural contexts. Indoctrinability is a preadaptation that allows integration in large social units, even though it may not be adaptive in reproductive terms for the individual being indoctrinated. But certainly the organization or social efficiency benefits. Furthermore, and contributing to this, beliefs in the legitimacy of a given social order or action are, fundamentally, the outcome not of cognitive processes, but of authority interactions. Their dependence on noncognitive attitudes makes them particularly susceptible to ideological manipulation and indoctrination. This underlies the argument that ideological mobilization exploits human biobehavioral dispositions even for purposes for which they have not been shaped by natural selection. For instance, ideological indoctrination may make the social order of modern large-scale societies look legitimate. Or it may elicit voluntary compliance with planned and purposely organized violent mass action, such as war.

Frank Salter reviews several methods of indoctrination to test the hypothesis of a universal trait, a disposition, of indoctrinability. He defines indoctrination as the purposive inculcation of an identity or doctrine. It is thus the opposite of imprinting, since the former requires repetition, deception, and often coercion, while the latter can occur on one exposure to a releasing stimulus. Cultural evolution has concentrated indoctrination methods around functional doctrines and practices that are not readily adopted. Hence, indoctrinability with regard to a particular doctrine or practice should be negatively correlated with the power of techniques directed at inculcating it. A good example is Chinese Communist "brainwashing," which was successful at indoctrinating highly resistant subjects. Salter's approach is to examine the techniques used to indoctrinate as one would examine a template to discern the shape, in negative, of the object being molded. Based on a review of the literature on Chinese Communist brainwashing, totalitarian indoctrination, cult recruitment, "deprogramming" from cults, traditional initiation, and political advertising, he finds that these techniques are highly transferable across cultures and eras, and repetitive in the subroutines they deploy. There appear to be some relatively fixed species-typical principles of indoctrination. The lack of variety of effective paths to indoctri-

nation tends to confirm the hypothesis that the means of indoctrinating humans, no matter how technically developed, are constrained by the necessity of keying into the human sensory and
cognitive apparatus, which is itself a product of phylogeny that is
effectively constant on the historical time scale.

Roger Masters presents a mathematical model (yet understandable to laymen) of the evolutionary underpinnings of indoctrinability to the symbols and myths of "the State." These symbols
and myths are all types of "recognition markers" that draw forth
cooperation and investment in public goods, such as public education. The five types of markers identified by Shaw and Wong
(1989) are kinship, phenotypic similarity (see also Rushton this
volume), language, religion, and territory. "It is not typical for
mammals, or even for humans, to help strangers indiscriminately;
the institutions of the centralized State, which require such helping behavior of the citizen, taxpayer, and soldier, are relatively
recent and surprisingly fragile events in the broad scope of human
history. Only when this fact is fully understood do we realize how
mythical recognition markers—such as the fictive kinship of the
modern nation—serve as a basis for the development of economic
and social infrastructures...." This model is applied to the phe-
nomenal rise of ethnonationalism in Eastern Europe coinciding
with the breakup of the Soviet Union in the late 1980s. Masters'
contribution is a fitting way to end this volume, since it exploits
the abstracted power of the neo-Darwinian calculus, yet combines
this with examples drawn from suburbia and noninstitutional
society, thus keeping the analysis in touch with human values and
behaviors with which we can all identify.

Conclusion

The various perspectives on indoctrinability and its implications
for ethnic ideology presented in this volume all take seriously the
potential of the life sciences, including evolutionary models, to
contribute to our understanding of these most important subjects.
Yet as a close reading of the above summaries will indicate, we do
not pretend at a monolithic consensus in the face of such complex
phenomena, at least at this stage of development of the social sciences. We have already discussed the theoretical dispute between
Rushton and Silverman and Case over the issue of whether ethnic
ideologies play on a general principle of "similars attract," or

whether the behavioral raw material is much more constrained, consisting only of familial loyalties. Let us conclude by pointing the reader to two more fission points.

There is a polite yet yawning gap between those who contend that indoctrination in premodern societies has served to weld groups with a loyalty so tight that they might even serve as units of selection (Eibl-Eibesfeldt; Schiefenhövel) and those who take such loyalty to be a self-organizing one, requiring indoctrination to *overcome* the natural tendencies of groups to conflict (Wiessner).

Then there is the matter of basic definitions. The nexus of ideology, group solidarity and other shared characteristics, and a trait of indoctrinability will remain blurred until it is agreed whether indoctrination serves to promote strong tendencies or to overcome them. And that debate will remain inconclusive until indoctrination is clearly defined. Is indoctrination any formal or informal process leading to socialization, as Eibl-Eibesfeldt, the first editor, would have it? Should we include self-inculcation as a type of indoctrination, in agreement with Caton? Or is it more correct to define indoctrination as closer to political socialization, performed in a purposive manner by an external, specialized institution or staff as contended by Salter, the second editor? These issues were discussed at the conference at Ringberg in January 1995 but were not resolved. Further research and debate are needed.

References

Boyd, R. and Richerson, P. J. (1992). Punishment allows the evolution of cooperation (or anything else) in sizable groups. *Ethology and Sociobiology*, **13**, 171–95.

Darwin, C. (1874). *The descent of man and selection in relation to sex*. Murray, London.

Eibl-Eibesfeldt, I. (1982). Warfare, man's indoctrinability and group selection. *Ethology (Zeitschrift für Tierpsychologie)*, **60**, 177–98.

———. (1988). *Der Mensch, das riskierte Wesen. Zur Naturgeschichte menschlicher Unvernunft*. Piper-Verlag, Munich.

———. (1995). *Wider die Mißtrauensgesellchaft. Streitschrift für eine bessere Zukunft*, 2d ed. Piper-Verlag, Munich.

Keith, A. (1949). *A new theory of human evolution*. Philosophical Library, New York.

Rushton, J. P. (1989). Genetic similarity, human altruism, and group selection. *Behavioural and Brain Sciences*, **12**, 503–59.

Salter, F. K. (1995) *Emotions in command. A naturalistic study of institutional dominance*. Oxford University Press, Oxford.

Shaw, R. P. and Wong, Y. (1989). *Genetic seeds of warfare: Evolution, nationalism, and patriotism*. Unwin Hyman, London.

Tinbergen, N. (1963). On the aims and methods of ethology. *Zeitschrift für Tierpsychologie*, **20**, 410–33.

PART I

**EVOLUTIONARY PRECURSORS
AND MODELS**

CHAPTER TWO

US AND THE OTHERS

THE FAMILIAL ROOTS OF ETHNONATIONALISM

Irenäus Eibl-Eibesfeldt

Ever since the transition of face-to-face communities into larger anonymous societies, human beings have been confronted with the problem of developing loyalties towards people unknown to them. Since then human beings have experimented with ways to deal with this situation, which in evolutionary terms is new to our species. For most of their existence, humans have lived in small, individualized communities, an arrangement to which they seem fairly well adapted.

I will argue that familial dispositions are the basis of humankind's prosociality. Furthermore, I will discuss the phylo-genetic origin of our nurturant motivations and behaviors, includ-ing the propensity to become fixated on symbols and values with a permanence that resembles imprinting. And I shall argue that this propensity is the basis of our indoctrinability. In summary, familial adaptations constitute preadaptations for living in certain larger anonymous communities, such as ethnicities, nation-states, and multinational federations. But these preadaptations had to be welded by cultural experiments—deliberate attempts at adapta-tion. The ultimate goal of these attempts was the formation of larger communities capable of self-defence and relatively free of internal strife, the members identifying with or at least obeying their rulers and communicating among themselves in a coopera-tive way not limited to the family and kinship ties.

The variety of social techniques employed in these cultural experiments ranges from repressive and nurturant dominance to nurturant leadership and the various combinations of the three. These techniques tap into existing social dispositions, which in part derive from our species' vertebrate heritage. However, not all of our predispositions serve as preadaptations for large group formation. Some, at least in certain contexts, also act as obstacles (*Problemanlagen*, Eibl-Eibesfeldt 1994).

Us and the Others

All over the world a resurgence of tribalism and ethnic conflict is evident. We are confronted with worldwide manifestations of ethnocentrism and xenophobia. One might define ethnicity as a mere construct to be deconstructed, but that in practice will not do away with the problem. Kurds will nonetheless define themselves as Kurds. Armenians as Armenians, Bosniaks as Bosniaks, and Serbs as Serbs. And many indeed are ready to sacrifice their lives to preserve their identity. They are misled, one might argue. But this invites at least the question: Why are people all over the world so easily misled?

Us against them—this certainly constitutes one of our major problems. How did this distinction come into the world? There are turning points in evolution: *Sternstunden*, to borrow a term coined by Stephan Zweig. They are events that switch the rails in new directions. The evolution of nurturant maternal care constitutes such a turning point in the evolution of the land vertebrates.

In January 1954 I had a "key experience" on the remote Galapagoan island of Narborough. Stepping ashore I found the surf-beaten rocks literally covered with hundreds of marine iguanas. They were tightly packed side by side and evidently seemed gregarious, but in contrast to the mammals and birds, which I had studied so far, they did not interact in any prosocial way. There was no mutual grooming to be seen, no mutual feeding, nor the bonding rituals derived from those nurturant activities. The social interactions of these large iguanas consisted in patterns of ritualized fighting with dominance displays, headbutting, and submissive postures of the loser (Fig. 2.1). Even their courtship behavior consisted of dominance displays by the males. Females ready for copulation accepted these overtures by assuming a submissive posture, lying flat on their bellies. I realized that there was a basic difference in the social behavior of reptiles on the one hand and birds and mammals on the other. Reptilian social behavior is based upon dominance and submission. Furthermore, reptiles do not form groups bonded by individual acquaintance. They aggregate but do not discriminate between individuals on the basis of "us" and "others."

In contrast mammals and birds often live in pairs or even in larger groups of bonded individuals that clearly distinguish group members from others. Furthermore, in addition to patterns of dominance and submission, a rich repertory of affiliative nurturant behaviors can be observed.

Comparative studies in the years to follow revealed that the capacity for such affiliative bonding evolved with the development of nurturant individualized care of the young, involving feeding, cleaning, warming, and defending, as well as the motivation for infant care. Conversely, the young evolved the motivation to seek protection and care, as well as signals triggering caretaking behaviors from the parents. In addition, in mother and offspring

Fig. 2.1 *The ritualized fighting of marine iguanas. Above: After an introductory display, the opponents measure their strength by headbutting. Below: If the weaker realizes that he has no chance of winning, he assumes a submissive posture by lying flat on his belly. The winner stops further aggression and waits for the rival to leave (after Eibl-Eibesfeldt 1955).*

the capacity of mutual individual recognition and for individualized bonding evolved.

Once present, these adaptations were available for bonding
between adults. If we investigate courtship behaviors in birds and
mammals as well as the behaviors by which established bonds are
nursed and reinforced (Figs. 2.2 and 2.3), we realize that the patterns employed are derived from the nurturant behaviors and the
infantile appeals originally developed in the service of child care
(Eibl-Eibesfeldt 1970; 1971).

During courtship many birds, such as sparrows, act alternately
in the role of the nurturer and the nurtured. The courting female
sparrow may behave like a fledgling, uttering begging calls and
engaging in begging behaviors such as gaping and wing flutter-
ing, upon which her male partner may feed her. Shortly afterwards the male may in turn take on the infantile role. Both sexes
of the black-headed gull exhibit a black face mask, a signal that
triggers aggressive responses. When a female lands in the territory
of a male in response to his beckoning call, she runs the risk of
being attacked. To avoid this she approaches the male with the
food-begging behaviors typical of the young and thereby triggers
feeding responses. Another appeasement behavior of black-

Fig. 2.2 *Parental behaviors (left) and derived courtship patterns (right). Above:
Common tern feeding its young and an adult male offering a fish to the begging
female during courtship. Below: Raven feeding its young and a pair of adult
ravens courtship feeding each other (from Eibl-Eibesfeldt 1970).*

Fig. 2.3 *Courting female black-headed gull begging for food (from a photograph by N. Tinbergen).*

headed gulls is "headflagging," characterized by a demonstrative turning away of the face mask from the mate. Both exhibit to each other the back of the head, thus concealing the trigger signal for attack. These "formalities" are only needed during the first stages of courtship, however, for once the mates know each other well, they need little appeasement to get along. Personal acquaintance neutralizes the fear- and aggression-releasing qualities of the signals which otherwise trigger agonistic responses.

Likewise, in mammals nurturant behaviors such as grooming, mutual licking, feeding, and defending, as well as infantile behaviors, serve to establish and maintain a bond. Aggression between group members can be blocked by infantile behavior. A wolf approaching a high-ranking pack member and in fear of being attacked will crouch submissively and push with his snout against the corner of the lip of the high-ranking individual, just as puppies do when begging for food. And if during a fight among pack members one individual loses, he can submit by rolling on his back like a puppy presenting itself to its mother for cleaning. The loser may even urinate, an apparent signal to elicit cleaning, since even an attacker may cut short his attack and start licking the surrendering individual. What started as a fight may finally end up in friendly social play. Infantile signals may induce a change of mood from agonistic to affiliative behavior. We may thus say that the evolution of nurturant individualized broodcare constitutes a turning point in the evolution of vertebrate social behavior, since it paved the way for long-lasting, truly affiliative friendly interaction and love between individuals (Eibl-Eibesfeldt 1970; 1971).

In humans, the capacity for individualized bonding is also familial in origin. Patterns expressing affection, such as caressing,

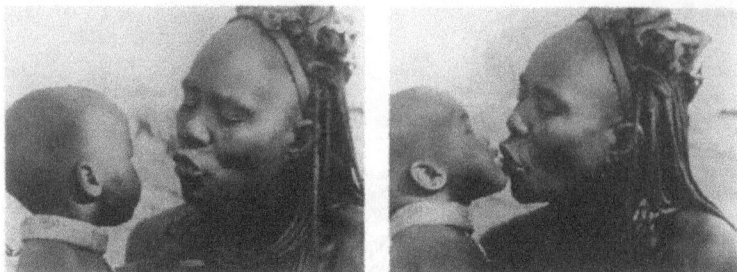

Fig. 2.4 *Kiss-feeding between a Himba granddaughter and grandmother. The grandmother had passed a candy to the child. Now she wants her turn and with protruding lips she invites her granddaughter to pass the candy. Upon lip contact the child opens the mouth and pushes the candy into the grandmother's mouth (from a 16 mm film taken by the author).*

are clearly derived from maternal behaviors, as are embracing, kissing (derived from kiss-feeding, see Figs. 2.4 and 2.5) and baby talk in a voice raised by one octave. Feeding, which is at the base of hosting, is also rooted in maternal nurturance (Figs. 2.6 and 2.7). Crying is another of the primary infant signals. Some forms of crying seem irritating, but others trigger sympathetic responses

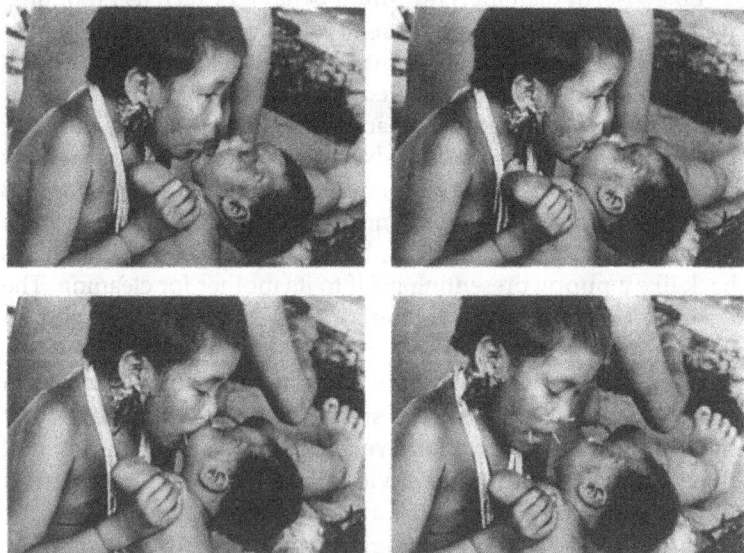

Fig. 2.5 *Kiss-feeding as an expression of tender affection in a Yanomami girl who kiss-feeds her little sister with saliva (from a 16 mm film taken by the author).*

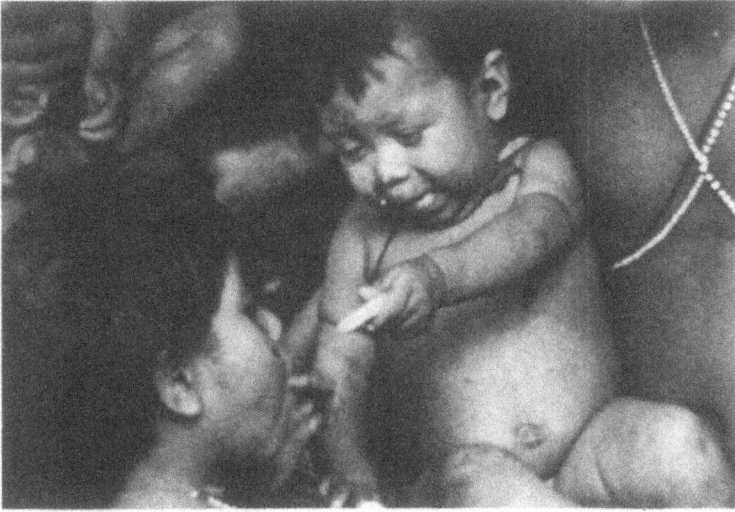

Fig. 2.6 *Offering food by hand is another nurturant behavior used already by small children in an effort to establish friendly relations, here in a Yanomami baby toward her elder sister (from a 16 mm film taken by the author).*

in children as well as in adults. Sagi and Hoffmann (1978) found clear empathic distress in newborns as a response to tapes of crying. Other sound recordings of equal stimulus strength but different quality did not trigger empathic responses.

It also holds true for humans that individual acquaintance creates a relationship of trust, whereas a stranger is met with distrust. The first manifestation of distrust of strangers appears early in life and is well known as the phenomenon of "stranger awareness" or "fear of strangers." Every healthy baby demonstrates during its first months of life basic trust: any approaching human

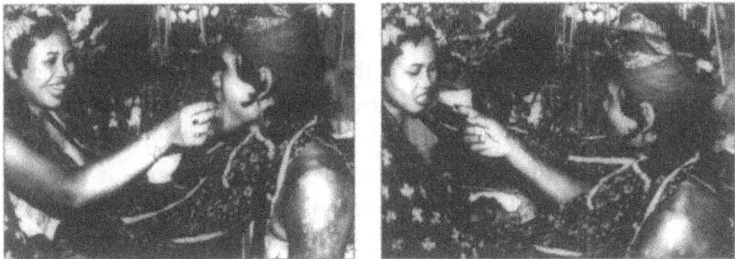

Fig. 2.7 *Mutual feeding in a Balinese couple: at the end of the initiation ritual of tooth filing the adolescents are pair-wise bonded around their necks by a scarf. They feed each other in turn with delicacies (photograph: Eibl-Eibesfeldt).*

Fig. 2.8 *Childhood xenophobia: a visitor attempts to hug a baby, which protests and seeks protection with his father. Yalenang, Western New Guinea (from a 16 mm film taken by the author).*

being will be greeted with a smile. From approximately the age of six months onwards, the baby then distinguishes between persons it knows and strangers, the latter releasing now ambivalent responses. The baby may smile at a stranger, but usually after a few seconds it will turn toward its mother and hide its face. It will fluctuate between approach and withdrawal responses or show superpositions of these two behaviors (Figs. 2.8 and 2.9). Should the stranger be insensitive to the baby's fear and continue to approach, the baby usually shows strong fear and clings to its mother in clear avoidance. This is a universal pattern and does not depend on prior bad experiences with strangers. It persists throughout life as stranger awareness, and it finds its clear expression in ambivalent behaviors (Fig. 2.10). It can be regarded as the first manifestation of an "us two" versus perceived "others." It evolved to secure the mother-child bond in a species dependent on particularly long child care, but it also provided new potential

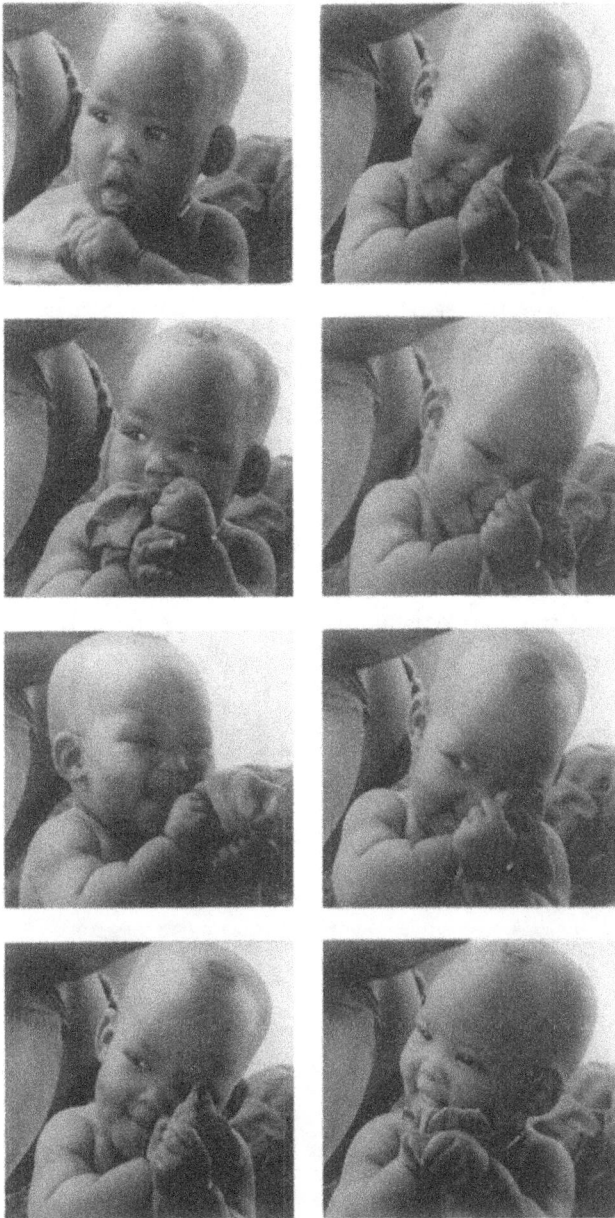

Fig. 2.9 *The ambivalence of a G/wi baby (Central Kalahari San) toward a stranger. Upon eye contact she fluctuates between repeated gaze aversion and eye contact with smiling (from a 16 mm film taken by the author).*

Fig. 2.10 *Ambivalence towards a male stranger as demonstrated by an Agta woman (Philippines) (from a 16 mm film taken by the author).*

for larger group formation. By "familiarization" with others, behavior shifts along a continuum from mistrust to trust.

Extended families and small individualized groups, in which everybody knows each other, were then formed. They demarcated themselves from other similarly organized "in-groups." Behavior patterns of bonding thus spread by kin selection and proved so effective that members of the individualized groups not directly belonging to a family were able to bond by means of additional cultural institutions in such a way that the group could, in certain situations, such as war, act as a unity. Arguably, this allowed hunter-gatherer groups to become a unit of selection (Eibl-Eibesfeldt 1982). Bonding at all levels in humans is reinforced by relationships of mutual sharing and reciprocity, often called reciprocal altruism. The literature on the evolution of reciprocal altruism in ethology and its current expressions in anthropology is vast and beyond the scope of this chapter. Social networks based on delayed reciprocal altruism, which serve the function of social security, certainly constitute one of the most important cultural inventions in the social evolution of our species. They are already found in kin-based societies living in small group communities. One of the best analyzed is the Xharo system of the Kalahari !Kung (Wiessner 1977; 1982). There, each adult male and female cultivates relations with 16 exchange partners on average, spread over a wide area 20 to 200 kilometers from their exchange partners. The exchange partners receive presents and reciprocate with a certain delay. This cements an unwritten contract that allows the exchange partners to visit each other and, in times of emergency, to hunt and collect in the territory of the partner. Mutual aid is thus secured. Wiessner was able to study the effectiveness of this sort of social security during a famine in 1974. The presents exchanged are bracelets made of beads, arrowheads, and in recent times objects such as blankets. The cost of their purchase and the amount of work invested in their production or to get the means for their acquisition is considerable. Wiessner calculated that a person spent on average fifteen days per year producing or acquiring exchange items.

Exchange networks of this type serving social security as well as trade were found in a variety of forms all over the world in kin-based societies. When larger societies emerged, the networks became elaborated in order to integrate expanded populations into solidarity groups.

The ability to form such networks is based upon a number of universal predispositions, such as the motivation and affiliative behavior patterns evolved in the service of bonding, the ability to symbolize, and in the special case of giving, the norm of possession, the ability for delayed reciprocity, and the ability to extend familial behaviors to distant relatives and nonrelatives—in particular, to establish fictive-kinship relationships by marriage.

One striking characteristic of human social organization concerns male group solidarity, a phenomenon discussed by Tiger (1969). An interesting precondition for the evolution of this male group solidarity might have been virilocality. In the majority of kin-based societies males usually stay within their local group and territory, while females migrate. A similar pattern is found with chimpanzees, where males stay within the territory in which they were born. Only females migrate during their first rut to other groups, and in doing so change their affiliation group. Males of one local chimpanzee group are therefore closely related by blood, and male solidarity thus enhances inclusive fitness. In early man the situation might have been similar. Even today human males tend to stick to their natal group, while females more often than not change location on marrying. However, the solidarity that persists in humans between females and their natal groups allows for the instrumental use of female kinship ties to establish reciprocal relations with members of other groups. Such alliances, which frequently serve to reduce a wide variety of risks in the natural and social environment, are an important precondition for the establishment of intragroup alliances (Wiessner 1977; Cashdan 1980; Wiessner 1982; Winterhalder 1986; Smith 1988; among many others).

With the distinction of "us" versus "others," a new quality of social behavior came into the world as well as a potential for further evolution. Members of the same species became distinguished according to their relatedness as friend or foe. Agonistic behavior is certainly old. In reptiles, rivals fight each other, the latter being mainly members of the same sex. But reptiles know only "others," such as potential mates or rivals. The capacity to distinguish "us" from "others" developed in the societies of birds and mammals. This new ability found a variety of expressions in the pair-bond, the family, in human individualized groups, and even in anonymous mass societies such as nations. The nurturant affiliative behaviors of bonding and the exclusivity coupled with it established a new evolutionary potential.

In humans, ties of friendship and belonging bind members of the individualized group together in an atmosphere of basic trust. By contrast, strangers are met with suspicion. It is well known that xenophobia is a universal phenomenon (Reynolds et al. 1986; Eibl-Eibesfeldt 1989), but I want to emphasize that fear of strangers is not to be confused with hatred of strangers, which is a result of indoctrination. We should be aware, however, that due to the basic mistrust of strangers our perception is biased in such a way that one negative experience usually has greater impact than a multitude of positive experiences. Another characteristic of the relationship with members of other groups is that the human inclination to establish a dominance-submission relationship is accentuated. Ethics toward strangers is certainly different from ethics toward own-group members.

Human social behavior is thus characterized by a fundamental ambivalence toward conspecifics. Agonistic and affiliative behaviors are simultaneously aroused. The former are the older vertebrate heritage, which control dominance and submissive sociality. The reptilian brain still forms a structure in the human brain as large as a fist (Bailey 1987). The old dominance-submission mechanism continues to operate in humans, and the achievement of repressive dominance in fight and competition is rewarded, as in other mammals, by a hormonal reflex. Tennis and chess players experience an increase in the blood testosterone level after victory and a drop after defeat (Mazur and Lamb 1980; Mazur et al. 1992). The winner thus experiences an ego boost. This disposition is not without problems, since success rewarded at every step is positive feedback and can lead to escalation of competitiveness.

Tendencies toward repressive dominance are ever present. Within bonded face-to-face communities they are, however, tabooed, and group pressure among others acts against them. Affiliative behaviors predominate, and leaders are chosen according to their ability to act in a socially integrative way. Individuals who are able to protect the weak, who comfort the distressed, who share—in short, who have nurturant dispositions and who in addition demonstrate special skills, such as spokesmen, war leaders, horticulturists, healers—individuals with these characteristics become leaders. The others approach them for help, seeking protection and advice. If people lose their social and special skills competence, they lose their status. Interestingly enough, children choose their playgroup leaders according to the same criteria (Hold 1976).

Repressive dominance, however, is a pattern often observed in use by individuals or groups toward strangers, which in traditional societies means nongroup members. Members of other groups not bonded by alliance contracts or other reciprocal ties may be exploited, robbed, driven away, and even killed, if this can be done without endangering the security of one's own group members. The ruthless rivalry between groups over scarce resources, such as land, constituted one of the factors that drove the evolution of modern humans. For a while it was thought that war came into the world with horticulture and animal husbandry, but there is substantial evidence of warfare in the Paleolithic and among contemporary hunter-gatherers prior to European contact. Warfare, unfortunately, is a long-standing cultural achievement (Eibl-Eibesfeldt 1979; van der Dennen and Falger 1990). Warfare is not in our genes, but primary agonistic dispositions are culturally fostered while prosocial dispositions are suppressed toward humans who are defined as enemies. War does have to do with our genes, inasmuch as it is the genes of the victorious that are passed on. As a cultural mode of competition, war allows for group selection (Eibl-Eibesfeldt 1982). This was recently confirmed by an investigation of warfare in New Guinea by Soltis, Boyd, and Richerson (1995). The group extinction rates reported appear fairly high to me, though the authors emphasize that many of those defeated and expropriated of their lands became absorbed as refugees. In any case, we can take it for granted that the loss of their resources did not enhance their fitness. We know furthermore that massacres committed by the victorious cause substantial victimization in New Guinea as well as in other parts of the world, in tribal societies as well as in those that call themselves "civilized," and in ancient times as well as modern. Richerson and Boyd in this volume argue that it is cultural group selection that takes place in the case of warfare. I see no real difference since the outcome remains the same. The routes of selection are of course intrinsically interesting but the biological result is differential survival of the members of competing groups according to loss or victory.

Until recently, the concept of group selection has had a cool reception, the main counterargument being that it is mathematically unlikely (Hamilton 1964; Wilson 1975). However, it was not discarded as a possibility. Wilson (1975, 562) pointed out that conformity created by indoctrination could serve to bond groups in such a way that they could become units of selection. When conformity becomes weak, Wilson said, groups become extinct. In this version selfish, individualistic members gain the upper hand and multiply at the expense of others. But their rising prevalence accelerates the vulnerability of the society and hastens its extinction. "Societies containing higher frequencies of conformer genes replace those that disappear, thus raising the overall frequency of the genes in the metapopulation of societies.... The genes might be of the kind that favors indoctrinability, even at the expense of the individual" (Wilson 1975, 562). Indoctrination, however, according to Wilson, could also come about by individual selection since "the ability to conform permits them to enjoy the benefits of membership with a minimum of expenditure and risk." Finally, group and individual selection could be mutually reinforcing. The ethological study of human behavior from a cross-cultural perspective and of animal behavior from a cross-species perspective reveals a number of behavior patterns derived from mother (parent)-child behaviors serving the function of nurturance, individualized bonding, and defense, which came about by individual and kin selection, allowing groups to become so tightly cemented that they could act as units of selection. Indoctrination is one such behavior pattern, assumed as having evolved from behaviors such as the infantile following response that can be imprinted to crude parent substitutes. Humankind's identification via symbols bears much resemblance to these imprinting phenomena.

With humans we can observe competing groups in trade and war and gauge the results of winning and losing on populations large and small. We can examine how populations are spaced or even driven to dispersion or extinction. Losing certainly does not enhance fitness. Through individual and kin selection, characteristics evolved that allowed groups to bond so effectively that further cultural evolution could tap into these adaptations to bond very large anonymous groups, such as ethnic nations, which in turn acted as units in situations of group competition such as war (Eibl-Eibesfeldt 1982; 1989).

Perhaps it is politically undesirable to face such facts. But blinding ourselves to reality will not contribute to solving the problem of maintaining the peace in an ever more crowded and rapidly changing world. In human phylogeny, warfare has worked in a group-selective way. We owe a part of what we are—patterns of affiliation as much as of aggression—to this activity. But we are not bound to follow primordial dictates. War is a culturally elaborated form of destructive group aggression open to cultural control, provided we find alternate means for fulfilling functions so far performed by warring—competition and the protection of one's land, identity, and other resources.

Indoctrinability and Anonymous Societies

With the cultural evolution of animal husbandry and agriculture, higher population densities became possible and competition over land, property, and other resources became better organized and thus more destructive, as history teaches us. Groups able to recruit more manpower for attack and defence had an advantage over smaller groups. Of course, there were other factors involved, such as technological advantage, but from this stage onward there was a definite tendency for the formation of larger anonymous societies.

Among the cultural mechanisms that enhance the biologically given predispositions for kinship affiliation and reciprocity, ideology is of paramount importance. Our indoctrinability, in this context, plays an important role. Through indoctrination a fixation to culture-specific standards of behavior, ethical concepts, values, symbols, and other characteristics takes place, seemingly similar to the learning processes called "imprinting" by ethologists. Like imprinting, indoctrination proves to be quite resistant to therapy. Again, a predisposition for the evolution of this capacity first appeared in the mother-child relation where it served to strengthen the bond by mutual fixation of both mother and child on individual characteristics of the other. This trait proved to be preadapted to bonding kin and then distant kin and finally other group members.

In ungulates, seals, many rodents, and other mammals, intensive mother-child interaction can be observed immediately after birth. Mothers lick their babies and vocalize, and the babies respond with orientation toward the mother and vocalizing in turn. Thus, individual characteristics of the offspring, such as particular smells or vocalizations, are mutually acquired in an imprinting-like fashion during a short sensitive period. We know that in sea lions mother and young recognize each other individually by their voices, which they distinguish from those of the many other individuals in their colonies (Eibl-Eibesfeldt 1984; Trillmich 1984). Once formed, the mutual attachment is exclusive.

Mothers will accept only their own young and reject approaches of others.

The physiology of this individual bonding has been investigated in sheep in more detail. If a newborn lamb is left with her mother for five minutes following birth, then separated for an hour, and afterwards presented to the ewe together with another lamb, the mother will accept her young and chase the foreign lamb away. However, should the newborn be removed immediately after birth and presented together with another lamb to the ewe an hour later, she will chase both away and accept none. Her sensitive period for adopting a lamb has passed. We know that a hormonal reflex is responsible for the short sensitive period. When during birthgiving the cervix becomes extended, oxytocin is released and induces the readiness to accept a young. If the cervix is mechanically extended in a ewe who has never given birth, the readiness to accept a young can be experimentally induced. If a lamb is presented to such a female immediately following this experiment, she will act like a mother, adopt the lamb, and chase others away in the experimental situations just described. During the period after birth or in the experiment just mentioned, intensive interaction between the female and her young can be observed. Ewes lick their babies, and both interactants bleat. Later, mother and child recognize each other by individual features of voice and odor.

In humans, too, mutual fixation to individual characteristics like smell, vocalization, and visual cues takes place within the first day after birth. Immediately following birth the baby is very alert in orienting toward its mother. Mothers, too, show affectively tuned interest in their newborn, provided the birth was a normal one without complications and medical sedation. Oxytocin seems one factor of importance in bonding. The hormone is released during birthing and later during nursing. In this context, it is interesting to note that oxytocin is not only triggered in the mother-baby context, but also in adult heterosexual interactions. Manipulation of the nipples releases oxytocin, as well as affecting vaginal stimulation during intercourse and orgasm, further evidence confirming the theory that adaptations evolved in the mother-child context are secondarily employed to strengthen the adult pair bond (see Eibl-Eibesfeldt 1995 for further references and discussion).

The indoctrinability of our species seems to be a special learning disposition to form an affective attachment to symbols and values characterizing the quasi-familial we-group. Again, this learning is characterized by affective attachment and resistance to therapy. Once acquired, individuals seem substantially fixated to their religious, political, and other values and to the symbols typical for the we-group. The readiness to attach and adhere to such values takes place during the juvenile period, and I hypothesize that the physiological mechanisms (brain chemistry) involved with symbol identification are derived from those that secure familial attachment of the child. Humans follow a flag like an experimentally imprinted duckling, a ball.

It seems, however, that humans' indoctrinability is nursed from several roots and that the process of cultural indoctrination taps into several genetic predispositions. Besides those securing family solidarity, those underlying sex identification seem of paramount importance since they enhance male bonding. Boys identify themselves with their fathers and other males, and girls with female models—in many cultures apparently without cultural pressure. A bias in perception enhances this preference. Given the choice between schematized drawings of male and female frontal view body contours (which do not show any other sex characteristics), prepuberal boys and girls alike show a clear preference for the same-sex body schema. With puberty, a dramatic reversal of preference takes place. Now the shape of the other sex is preferred. The prepuberal preference guides attention to the appropriate model (Fig. 2.11). Boys gang up in same-sex groups, and there is little doubt that male bonding, which becomes culturally reinforced by symbols of identification and by shared ideologies, is of paramount importance for group identity and group defense. At political rallies when people are identifying with the "sacred" symbols and hymns of their religious or political community, altered states of mind are induced. People experience these as trance-like states that come upon them somehow beyond their control, as described by the terms "zeal" and the German *Begeisterung*. It is as if God or the spirits have taken possession of them. At the same time people often experience the shudder of being deeply touched. This feeling is caused by the contraction of the muscles that raise the hair on the back, shoulders, and arms, an archaic response of social defense, which in our primate ancestors caused the fur to stand on end. It would be worthwhile to investigate the ethophysiology of this response.

Humans' indoctrinability as a specific learning disposition was enhanced by the advantage it brought about in cementing existing

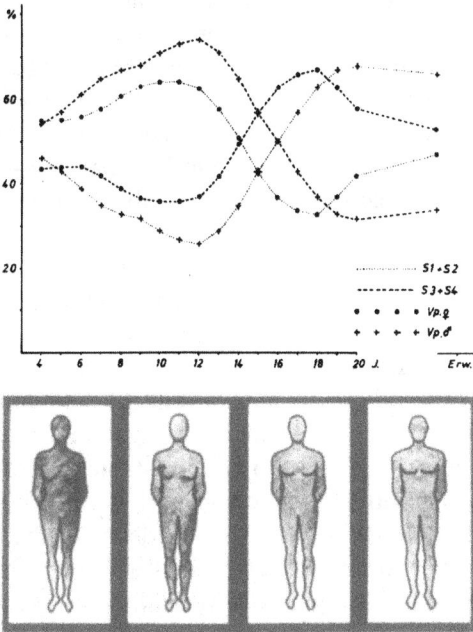

Fig. 2.11 *Model choice study with human silhouettes: selection of female (...) and male (- - -) body contour features by female (•) and male (+) test subjects of various age classes. Abscissa: % of choices. Ordinate: age classes (at least 100 subjects per year and sex). Below: The female and male silhouette models are shown (pp. 1–4). The frequency curves indicate that a change in preference occurs at puberty, with the same sex preferred before puberty and the opposite sex thereafter (Erw. = adult) (after Skrzipek 1978).*

bonds and cultural institutions, thus supporting the social, economic, and political institutions necessary for preserving harmony within the group (conflict management, rules for sharing, and the like). This was accomplished by strengthening a sense of togetherness, building up loyalties, and emphasizing contrasts to others often by creating images of enemies. Such bonding was to the advantage of both the individual and the group, for in the face of fierce intergroup competition an individual had few chances outside of a strong group. Indoctrinability is a special learning disposition that allows acceptance and identification with group characteristics and thus serves we-group demarcation. Once learned, these aspects of group identity seem to be resistant to eradication.

Characteristics of group tradition are acquired early. Dialect stands out in this context, since the intonation and melody of voice remains for a lifetime and allows insiders to distinguish us- and other-group membership. It is very difficult to acquire such characteristics later in life. Identification with one's own family during childhood lies at the roots of human indoctrinability—small local groups acting as quasi-family units. But this is certainly not the whole story.

The bond to a native land is another affective disposition contributing to humans' indoctrinability. This bonding to our home country is a type of "imprinting" that may well be rooted in territoriality. Whether the affective bonding to home and country are of different origin and quality than the affective bonding to family and group, however, needs further investigation. In Western culture, people who grow up in a certain stable environment get "homesick" when moving for longer periods, which is a highly peculiar state of affection. We found evidence for homesickness also in traditional societies, such as in the Trobrianders. People who change their home repeatedly in childhood seem not to form this attachment, thus achieving a certain ability to be mobile. The matter of a critical period for territorial attachment needs investigation. Cultural indoctrination imprints group identity and love of one's native land in principle by the same means in tribal societies as in our Western culture (Eibl-Eibesfeldt 1989).

Human beings are in particular open for value imprinting around puberty when adolescents seek group values with which to identify. Accordingly, it is at this time that initiation combined with indoctrination of group values occurs in most societies.

Since values supporting group interest were advantageous when groups were competing in war, selection favored the disposition for indoctrination (Eibl-Eibesfeldt 1982). Young males, indeed, often willingly fight and risk death in combat for their group. Nonetheless, the bond to the family usually remains stronger. In our modern nation-states family also comes first, and nepotism is still a problem in society. Attempts to dissolve the family in modern times have failed. It is possible, however, to indoctrinate individuals to such an extent that their loyalty to the extended family is overruled by loyalty to the larger group, as represented by the head of the tribe, the monarch, or by the symbols of a nation. Indoctrination intends to counteract nepotism by putting tribe or state ethos above family ethos in the scale of values. Loyalty to the symbolic head of state is supposed to come first, particularly in times of emergency.

With the formation of the early state, ideologies as promoted by political and religious leaders took on the additional function as pacemaker of evolution by setting new goals and thus initiating new ways of acting and thinking. Ultimately, though, ideologies are measured against the yardstick of fitness.

Cultural Pseudospeciation

As previously noted, the pressures that selected for large group formation derived from intergroup competition. (Here, amongst other things, sheer manpower counted.) Depending upon the subsistence strategy and the carrying capacity of the land, groups in pre-state societies ranged from a few dozen to a few hundred. In these societies, most groups split when they reach the size of 300 to 600. They usually split along kinship lines, assuming that it is their closest kin whom they would help (Chagnon 1979). Humans show a strong inclination to form such subgroups, which eventually distinguish themselves from others by dialect and other subgroup characteristics and go on to form new cultures. Erikson (1966) aptly spoke of this process as "cultural pseudospeciation." As a result, the two tendencies are in conflict with each other, fissioning most likely to occur where kin ties are weakest, and fusion where individuals or groups need one another, whether for spreading economic risk or for joint security.

Which of the two tendencies dominated in certain societies depended on many factors, such as the subsistence strategy and the war pressures to which the groups were exposed. Thus, due to a relaxation of the war pressure among the Yanomami, splitting tendencies have increased during the last two decades. For example, in the early 1970s the Patanoeteri lived as a large local group of about 200 people at Patanoe in Venezuela. In the second half of the 1970s they moved to Sheroana. In 1983, a group of 130 people separated from the others and moved to Thorita. The group of 96 remaining at Sheroana split again in 1988, and a group of 41 people moved to a place called Hapokashita. And even within this small group further splitting tendencies became visible during my last visit in 1996. Yet only three years before they were living in the traditional way under a communal sheed roof surrounding a central square. Now, by early 1996, two families have started to shield themselves off from the central square and thus from the others by constructing a wall from branches covered with clay. Similar developments can be observed in other places, particularly in areas closer to the missions, where even separate individual houses have been constructed. This process of individualization will surely have strong repercussions on future communal life. In order for a communal society to survive, new institutions such as communal housing and ceremonies, and perhaps new forms of institutionalized chieftainships, must develop, not to mention the need to develop a feeling of identity on a higher level, if cultures like the Yanomami are to survive ethnically. So far no trace of such institutional development is visible, and a sense of ethnic identity does not exist. However, institutions for communal bonding could be developed from the communal male *Hekuramous*, which serve to fight the evil spirits believed to cause illness, and from traditional feasting, which so far has served to establish and strengthen alliances between local groups. And there is reason for optimism. In 1996 I witnessed for the first time the preparation of a feast in Hapokashita, held just for the enjoyment of the local population.

The tendency for cultural pseudospeciation, whereby larger groups tend to split or smaller groups parcel themselves off through custom and dialect, initiates ethnocultural diversification, which in turn can serve as pacemaker for further biological evolution. Large group formation sometimes allows for rapid cultural change but inhibits cultural diversification, as the increasing uniformization of our world civilization shows. It also endangers existing ethnic groupings, which may be one source of increasing unrest on our globe.

Cultural markers that set groups apart are often deviations in cultural practice based upon the same belief. Thus, the closely related Etoro, Onabasulu, and Kaluli in the Bosavi area (Papua-New Guinea) share the belief that boys become physically mature men only if they are inseminated by men during initiation. The three groups distinguish themselves from each other only by method. The Etoro achieve insemination through oral intercourse, the Kaluli through anal intercourse and the Onashbasulu through masturbation, smearing the semen over the initiates (Kelly 1977). The Etoro consider the practices of the others as totally disgusting, and each group views the other as fundamentally different.

If we look at the mechanisms employed to bond members or groups who are not close kin, we find that they tap into the existing phylogenetic adaptations already mentioned. In kin-based societies one common means of bonding is by extending kinship principles (terminology and accompanying behavior) beyond the circle of close kin to more distant kin and in some cases nonkin. This is done by the creation of segmentary lineage systems and other systems of descent: groups can thus trace themselves to a common ancestor. These groups are held together on the basis of both kinship and reciprocity.

In segmentary kinship societies, bonding ideologies thus call on the metaphor of kinship to create fictive descent from mythical ancestors and creators. Such beliefs bond all as quasi-blood relatives. Indeed, terms to address persons who are not blood relatives are often derived from those that characterize a familial relation, for example, sibling, sibling-in-law, or, if the person is much older, "older sibling." "Father" or "mother" are widely used as forms of polite address. By a fictive relationship, distant kin are reclassified as close kin, and the person is accepted as a member of the we-group. For example, the Mek speakers of Highland Irian Jaya (New Guinea) to which the Eipo belong are composed of approximately 10 clans, each tracing its origin to a mythical ancestral figure. The clans are spread widely over the home range of the language group, and clan members are obliged to assist each other as if they were relatives, even if they come from distant villages and do not know each other. By special greeting formulae, they document clan membership. Due to hostile relations between two different valleys of the Mek speakers at the time of our arrival in the area, the obligations between clan members within the valley were limited to certain smaller areas only. With the pacification of the Mek area, the network of obligations was extended farther as travel to other valleys became safer. In addition to the segmentary lineage system, other kinds of networks exist: the Eipo initiate their young men at intervals of several years, and accordingly the uninitiated young men and boys of several age classes and from various villages, even outside the valley, are initiated as a group. The members belonging to such an initiation group are bonded by ties of friendship, and they are obliged to help each other. Further ties are created by marriage.

Familial ties are, of course, stronger than the ties between village members, which are in turn stronger than intervillage ties within the one valley. The feelings of obligation and loyalty are graded in accordance with an inherited family bias.

Myths also help establish fictive kinship. The Eipo have myths that refer to their origin from a common ancestor or a bringer of culture. This creates a feeling of shared descent and belongingness for all group members. This did not prevent the splitting up of the Mek into warring subgroups. However, with pacification, the shared myth of origin became a medium of further unification. In addition, there are myths specific to certain villages or localities. The people of Dingerkon used to call out the name of the sacred sites from which certain ancestral figures or founders of the village came. Referring to a certain mountain in the vicinity, they called out "Kataua!" when fighting, in a formalized appeal to the ancestors.

When planting the Cordyline—the sacred plant used to mark boundaries and sacred places (Schiefenhövel 1976)—around the men's house, the Eipo reenact the creation of habitable land by the culture heroes who inserted rocks in the primordial mud to provide solid ground on which humans could live. Along with the plants, stones are planted into the ground (Eibl-Eibesfeldt and Heeschen 1995; Eibl-Eibesfeldt et al. 1989).

It is interesting to note that the neighboring Yale and Dani tribes use two types of symbolic stones—sacred ones, which are kept hidden in the men's house and handled only by important men at certain ceremonies, and profane ones used as "exchange stones" during funerals for display to placate the ghosts. The Dani receive these stones from the Yale (Heider 1970). The exchange stones are decorated with a miniature female grass skirt and yellow orchid strings that males use for decoration, indicating that these stones represent a bisexual humanoid being. This interpretation is supported by the fact that the terms for parts of the stone are anthropomorphic: one end is addressed as the head, the other as the anus; one side as the face, and the other as the back (Fig. 2.12a).

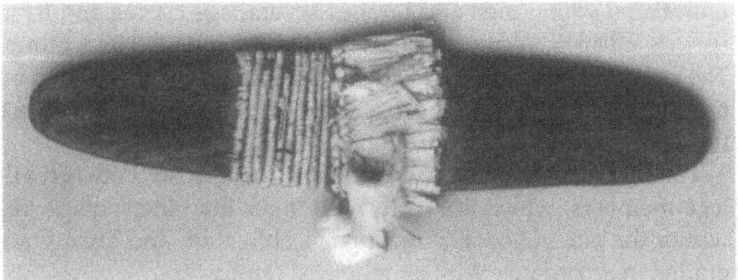

Fig. 2.12a *Exchange stone of the Dani decorated with female and male characteristics.*

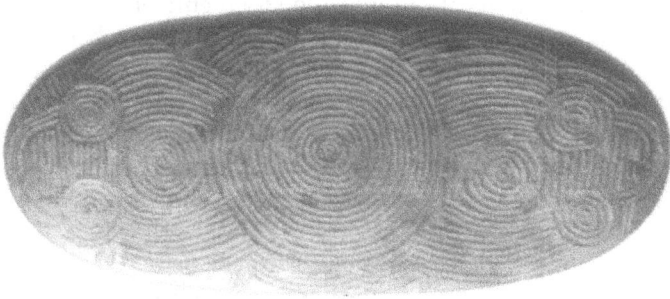

Fig. 2.12b *Stone Juringa of the Honeyant clan of the Walbiri near Mt. Allen. The large central circles represent a claypan northeast of Yuendumu. This was where the totemic ancestor lived. The other symbols (semicircles and circles) represent the ways and the camps the totemic ancestor traveled (photographs Eibl-Eibesfeldt).*

Fig. 2.13 *Pawlow landscape engraved in a 25,000-year-old mammoth tooth. The waves refer to a river, the parallel lines to slopes and hills of the area, where the tooth was found. The symbolism resembles that of a Juringa (from Häberlein 1990).*

I see here a connection with the stone cult of the Eipo, the sacred stones being images of the ancestral culture heroes who made the land habitable. The Eipo also harbor sacred stones in their net bags, but these are less elaborately decorated. They consist of shale slabs painted with several dark transverse bands. They also consider the clubheads that they find in the ground while building houses or gardens as sacred and store them away in their net bags.

Interestingly, the idea that stone slabs can be used as symbolic representations of ancestors also occurs in Australia. The Stone Juringas of the Walbiri are slabs in which the journeys and activities of the totemic ancestors within the territory of the group are engraved in a symbolic form (Fig. 2.12b). It would be intriguing to know whether this parallel comes from a common cultural heritage or from independent invention. In this context, it is interesting that this symbolism is already found in Paleolithic artifacts of Europe (Fig. 2.13). In addition to shared myths and sacred rituals, styles of body ornamentation, ways of dancing, and feasting, as well as other particularities of everyday life, allow the perception of similarities that creates a feeling of togetherness.

Repressive and Nurturant Strategies of Governing Populations

Human sociality is characterized by the conflicting behaviors of dominance and nurturance. The patterns of the former realm are the various forms of aggression (physical violence and the many forms of threat display), as well as the behaviors that serve flight or submission. All these are usually contrasted as agonistic behaviors as opposed to the prosocial behaviors that in mammals and birds are derived from parental nurturance.

Dominance can be achieved in a variety of ways. *Repressive dominance* is usually achieved by agonistic behaviors such as physical attack or threat, the dominated being subjugated, displaced into lower status or out of a previously held territory, or even killed (see Salter 1995 for a review and observational study of dominance techniques deployed by governments and other organizations).

Interestingly enough, nurturant behaviors can also serve the function of dominating. Giving can be used as a weapon, since reciprocity is felt as an obligation. We know of rituals in which host and guests in a sequence of reciprocal invitation try to outdo each other in the generosity of giving, until one, finally, is unable to reciprocate. This brings him into the subordinate position of a debtor. The potlatch of the Kwakiutl is one famous example.

Repressive dominance is usually suppressed in individualized, face-to-face communities, where high-ranking individuals are those with prosocial competence. Thus, by means of prosocial behavior individuals can also achieve high-ranking positions, such as community leader. And all gradients from nurturant leadership to nurturant dominance can be found. Children normally submit to the nurturant behaviors of their mothers or caretakers. It is, after all, comforting to be cared for. The motivation to nurture can be so strong that efforts to that effect are continued against the resistance of the nurtured (Fig. 2.14). Such overcaring can hamper emancipation of the individual and keep it in infantile dependence. Nurturant leadership is primarily a behavior characteristic of small, individualized communities.

Societies numbering in the many thousands or even millions, such as (ethnic) nations, share history, descent, language, and a set of cultural beliefs and practices. These signs of relatedness, if entrained, help create feelings of solidarity. Nonetheless, the prob-

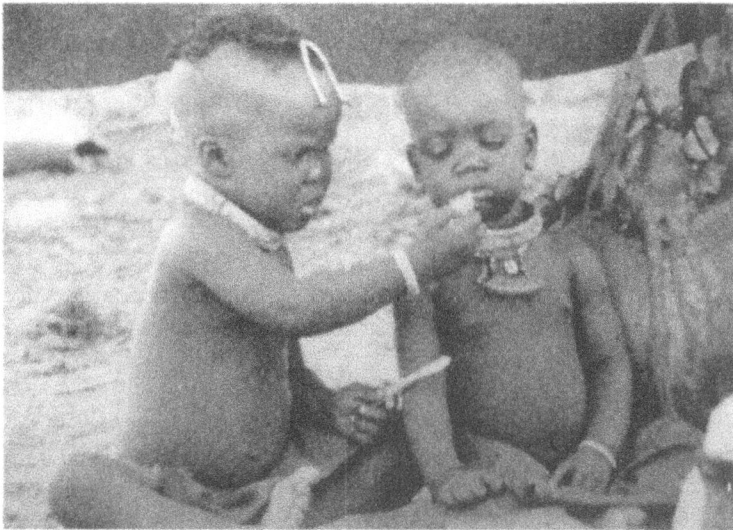

Fig. 2.14 *The phenomenon of nurturant dominance: a Himba girl (4 ½ years old) pressing her little cousin to accept food (from a 16 mm film taken by the author).*

lem exists that in anonymous societies people are not bonded with equal strength, but rather demonstrate clear preferences along family and kinship lines. In the other direction, the inclination to establish repressive exploitative dominance relations toward persons not known and therefore not bonded in a personal way is less inhibited (*Ellbogengesellschaft*). It was probably this fact that caused Thomas Hobbes to assume that human beings, due to their egoistic nature, could be induced to live in harmony only by the coercive rule of a supreme sovereign. And in fact, repressive dominance by a king or a ruling caste was and still is a widely employed technique of government. Human beings are prepared to submit to repressive dominance if they cannot resist. However, they remain ready to revolt, vigilant for signs of weakness in the ruling elite, awaiting the chance to rid themselves of their oppressors or even to turn the tables on them.

The readiness to submit to command is strong, as demonstrated by the now classical experiments of Stanley Milgram (1974), but repressive dominance, for reasons just explained, does not secure stability of government. History, however, shows that sometimes it works for generations, in particular if those who rule by intimidation also present themselves as protectors, since fear arouses protection-seeking in the vicinity of the strong, even if fear and protection derive from the same source. Closer examination reveals that infantile behaviors of flight to the parent are activated (Eibl-Eibesfeldt 1989). It seems that in particular early civilizations, such as those of ancient Europe and Central America (Aztec, Maya), the rulers used repressive dominance to induce fear while at the same time offering protection. The rulers were often considered divine and ruled in cooperation with priests by means of terrifying rituals and terrifying gods. Their political architecture is awe-inspiring but certainly lacked any friendly appeals (Sütterlin in this volume). Repressive dominance does not want closeness. The rulers keep distance from those ruled, and they employ high-low symbolism in their political architecture.

Often High Gods serve to support group morals. Roes (1995) found a clear, positive correlation between size of societies and the belief in High Gods. Repressive dominance strategies have again and again been supplemented by nonrepressive nurturant governing styles. The ancient Romans knew even then that bread and circuses help preserve internal peace. In modern times, absolute rulers have been replaced by the parent figure of leaders who protect and nurture. Modern dictators as well as democratic rulers combine these two roles in their strategies of government, and this seems to accord more with human nature. What governments have sought in their many experiments of ruling is the right balance at the appropriate time. In times of emergency, stricter strategies of government are certainly required more than in times of abundance and peace. Where people are fortunate to select their leaders by vote, the political elites seek nurturant closeness to the voter, in an attempt to establish quasi-personal nurturant relations that conform with humans' primary disposition for life in individualized groups.

From the many experiments of history, the democratic concept seems to provide the best solution tried so far, since political rulers must present themselves to the voters and can be stripped of their power if they fail to fulfill expectations. Democracy also seems to be the most nurturant form of government yet devised, but sometimes to the extent of nurturing the people into a state of dependency (nurturant dominance). On other occasions the wish to avoid any repression sometimes prevents governments from exercising legitimate power, such as when needed in order to keep internal peace and to check criminality. This derives in part from misconceptions about the meaning of freedom and tolerance. Tolerance is the readiness to understand others with deviating opinion, but not necessarily the acceptance of every deviation; and liberty does not mean that everything should be permitted since that would always be at the cost of the liberty of others.

In anonymous societies, internal peace and harmony are constantly threatened by conflicting interest groups. This is particularly the case in multiethnic states where in times of emergency the different ethnic groups tend to compete in their efforts to dominate each other in order to secure access to scarce resources. More attention should be given to this cause of internal conflict. Some well-meaning philanthropists believe they are serving peace and opposing racism by encouraging the development of multicultural societies in formerly fairly homogenous nation-states. "Bold experiments" (Lack and Templeton 1995) like this could easily prove disastrous, the results being contrary to expectations, the more so since some proponents even of Caucasian stock seem to act in clear hostility to their own group (for a discussion of the pros and cons of multicultural stability see Brimelow 1995; D'Souza 1995; Olzack 1992).

Peaceful coexistence of different ethnic groups within one state is certainly possible if none of the groups need fear the domination of others, more generally if none finds itself in a situation of interethnic competition. This is best achieved when each group owns its own land and enjoys sovereignty over its own affairs as is the case in Switzerland.

At the basis of the liberal laissez faire is often the evolutionary concept of selection. Among others, Friedrich von Hayek (1979) expressed the opinion that we should rely on the regulating power of selection. But selection is a crude and certainly not human regulatory device. The prey-predator relationship is a classic example of the corrective principle of nature: if prey is abundant, the predator population increases. Finally, the prey population, suffering from overexploitation, diminishes, and starvation of the predators ensues, leading to an abrupt die-off. This gives the surviving prey population the chance to recover, and, with a delay, predators can start to thrive again and so forth. Certainly, we cannot want selection to shape our fate this way. We can set ourselves goals and plan ahead, and, provided we are ready to correct mistakes in time, this gives our species unique opportunities for rational and human planning. Laissez faire is not enough. At a certain point disorder and chaos may cause the pendulum to swing in an authoritarian direction and endanger liberal democracy. Open society was Karl Popper's demand. By this he meant open to new ideas regardless from where they come. The Open Society should not be interpreted to mean the complete dismantling of barriers and acceptance of everything and everyone without regard to numbers, with consequent social unrest and environmental degradation.

Conclusion

Ethnocentrism and tribalism are universal phenomena rooted in primordial familial dispositions. The first manifestation of "us" versus "others" is the individualized mother-child dyad. With the evolution of individualized nurturant maternal care, caring motivations, behaviors and mother-child signals evolved and became available for adult bonding. They proved so effective that members of individualized face-to-face groups not directly belonging to a family were able to bond in such a way that the group could, in certain situations, such as war, act as a unit. Intergroup competition selected for large-group formation. If we look at the mechanisms employed to bond members of groups who are not close kin, we find that they tap into existing phylogenetic adaptations of familial sociality. Culturally developed symbols of identification enhance similarity, and entrained shared values make the behavior of group members predictable for each other. Thus, mistrust of the unfamiliar is counteracted. Indoctrinability is a special learning disposition allowing acceptance and identification with group characteristics, which thus serves bonding and we-group demarcation.

References

Bailey, K. (1987). *Human paleopsychology. Applications to aggression and pathological processes.* Lawrence Erlbaum Associates, London.

Berghe, P. L. van den (1981). *The ethnic phenomenon.* Elsevier, New York.

Brimelow, P. (1995). *Alien nation.* Random House, New York.

Cashdan, E. A. (1980). Egalitarism among hunters and gatherers. *American Anthropologist*, **82**, 116–20.

———. (1983). Territoriality among human foragers: Ecological models and an application to four Bushman groups. *Current Anthropology*, **24**, 47–55.

Chagnon, N. A. (1979). Mate competition, favoring close kin, and village fissioning among the Yanomamö indians. In *Evolutionary biology and human social behaviour: An anthropological perspective* (ed. N. A. Chagnon and W. Irons), pp. 86–132. Duxbury Press, North Scituate, Mass.

Dennen, J. van der and Falger, V. (1990). *Socio-biology and conflict.* Chapman & Hall, London.

D'Souza, D. (1995). *The end of racism. Principles for a multiracial society.* Free Press, New York.

Eibl-Eibesfeldt, I. (1955). Der Kommentkampf der Meerechse (Amblyrhynchus cristatus Bell) nebst einigen Notizen zur Biologie dieser Art. *Zeitschrift für Tierpsychologie*, **12**, 49–62.

———. (1970). *Liebe und Haß. Zur Naturgeschichte elementarer Verhaltensweisen.* Piper (Piper Series **113**, 1976), Munich.

———. (1971). *Love and hate. The natural history of behavior patterns.* Holt, Rinehart & Winston, New York.

———. (1975). *Krieg und Frieden aus der Sicht der Verhaltensforschung.* Piper, Munich.

———. (1979). *The biology of peace and war.* The Viking Press, New York.

———. (1982). Warfare, man's indoctrinability and group selection. *Zeitschrift für Tierpsychologie*, **60**, 177–98.

———. (1982). Patterns of parent-child interaction in cross-cultural perspective. In *The behaviour of human infants* (ed. A. Oliverio and M. Zappella), pp. 177–217. Plenum Press, London.

———. (1984). *Die Biologie des menschlichen Verhaltens.* 4th ed., 1997. Piper, Munich.

———. (1989). *Human ethology.* Aldine de Gruyter, New York.

———. (1990). Dominance, submission, and love: Sexual pathologies from the perspective of ethology. In *Pedophilia–biosocial dimensions.* (ed. J. R. Feierman), pp. 150–75. Springer, New York, Berlin, etc.

———. (1994). *Wider die Mißtrauensgesellschaft.* 2d ed., 1995. Piper, Munich.

Eibl-Eibesfeldt, I. and Heeschen, V. (1994). Eipo (West-Neuguinea, Zentrales Hochland) Demonstration des rituellen Pflanzens einer Cordyline. Film E 3037 von I. Eibl-Eibesfeldt, Publ. Wiss. Film, Ethnol., Sonderband 9: Humanethologie (1994), pp. 13–25.

Eibl-Eibesfeldt, I., Schiefenhövel, W., and Heeschen V. (1989). *Kommunikation bei den Eipo. Eine humanethologische Bestandsaufnahme.* D. Reimer, Berlin.

Erikson, E. H. (1966). Ontogeny of ritualization in man. *Philosophical Transactions of the Royal Society,* London, **B251,** 337–49.

Goffman, E. (1963). *Behavior in public places: Notes on the social organization of gatherings.* Free Press, Macmillan, New York.

Häberlein, R. (1990). Kartenähnliche Darstellungen im Eiszeitalter. In *Kartographische Nachrichten,* 5, 185–7.

Hamilton, W. D. (1964). The genetic evolution of social behavior. Parts 1 and 2. *Journal of Theoretical Biology,* **7,** 1–51.

Heider, K. G. (1970). *The dugum dani.* Aldine, Chicago.

Hold, B. (1976). Attention structure and rank specific behaviour in pre-school children. In *The social structure of attention.* (ed. M. R. A. Chance and R. R. Larsen), pp. 177–201. Wiley, London.

Kelly, R. C. (1977). *Etoro social structure. A study in structural contradiction.* The University of Michigan Press, Ann Arbor.

Lack, J. and Templeton, J. (1995). *Bold experiment. A documentary history of Australian immigration since 1945.* Oxford University Press, Melbourne.

Lorenz, K. Z. (1985). My family and other animals. In *Leaders in the study of animal behavior. Autobiographical perspectives.* (ed. D. A. Dewsbury), pp. 259–87. Bucknell University Press, Lewisburg.

———. (1992). *Die Naturwissenschaft vom Menschen. Eine Einführung in die vergleichende Verhaltensforschung. Das "Russische Manuskript."* Piper, Munich.

Mazur, A. and Lamb, Th. (1980). Testosterone, status and mood in human males. *Hormones and Behavior,* **14,** 236–46.

Mazur, A., Booth, A., and Dabbs, J. (1992). Testosterone and chess competition. *Social Psychology Quarterly,* **55,** 70–77.

Milgram, St. (1974). *Obedience to authority: An experimental view.* Harper and Row, New York.

Olzak, S. (1992). *The dynamics of ethnic competition and conflict.* Stanford University Press, Stanford.

Ortiz, S. R. de (1973). Uncertainties in peasant farming. A Colombian case. *Monographs on Social Anthropology,* **46,** The Athlone Press, London; Humanities Press Inc., New York.

Reynolds, V., Falger, V., and Vine, I. (1986). *The sociobiology of ethnocentrism.* The University of Georgia Press, Athens.

Roes, F. L. (1995). The size of societies, stratification, and belief in High Gods supportive of human morality. *Politics and the Life Sciences,* **14,** 73–77.

Sagi, A. and Hoffmann, M. L. (1978). Emphatic distress in the newborn. *Developmental Psychology,* **112,** 175–6.

Salter, F. K. (1995). *Emotions in command. A naturalistic study of institutional dominance.* Oxford University Press, Oxford.

Schiefenhövel, W. (1976). Die Eipo-Leute des Berglands von Indonesisch-Neuguinea. *Homo,* **24,** 263–75.

Skrzipek, K. H. (1978). Menschliche "Auslösermerkmale" beider Geschlechter I. Attrappenwahluntersuchungen der Verhaltensentwicklung [The characteristics of the human releaser of the sexes I. Experiments on the development of behavior with dummies]. *Homo,* **29,** 75–88.

Smith, E. A. (1988). Risk and uncertainty in the "original affluent society": Evolutionary ecology of resource-sharing and land tenure. In *Hunters and gatherers: Property, power and ideology* (ed. T. Ingold, D. Riches, and J. Woodburn), pp. 222–51. Berg, Oxford.

Soltis, J., Boyd, R., and Richerson, P. J. (1995). Can group-functional behaviors evolve by cultural group selection? *Current Anthropology,* **36,** 473–94.

Tiger, L. (1969). *Men in groups.* Random House, New York.

Trillmich, F. (1984). The Galápagos seals. Part 2. Natural history of the Galápagos fur seals. In *Galápagos. Kea environments.* (ed. R. Perry), pp. 215–24. Pergamon Press, Oxford.

Wiessner, P. (1977). *Hxaro: A regional system of reciprocity for reducing risk among the !Kung San,* Ph.D. dissertation. University of Michigan, university microfilms. Ann Arbor.

————. (1982). Risk, reciprocity and social influences on !Kung San economies. In *Politics and history in band societies* (ed. E. Leacock and R. Lee), pp. 61–84. Cambridge University Press, Cambridge, London.

Wilson, E. O. (1975). *Sociobiology: The new synthesis.* Harvard University Press, Cambridge, MA.

Winterhalder, B. (1986). Diet choice, risk and food sharing in a stochastic environment. *Journal of Anthropological Archaeology,* **5,** 369–92.

CHAPTER THREE

WAR AND PEACEMAKING

THE FUSION OF TWO NEIGHBORING CAPTIVE MONKEY COLONIES

Detlev W. Ploog

My contribution deals with nonhuman primate behavior. Is it permissible to use terms like "war" and "peace" in the context of aggressive and affiliative behavior, i.e., as parts of the social behavior, of animals? The claim that warfare and peacemaking are purely cultural phenomena can be supported by good arguments. For instance, wars are planned and the chances of losing and winning are weighed against the likely gains and losses. Peacemaking can also require assessment of the likely outcome of an encounter. This seems purely humanlike—a result of cultural evolution. However, observations and research on pongids, foremost on chimpanzees, conducted during the last decade have demonstrated that these animals are capable of strategic thinking. Various forms of deceptive behavior in chimpanzees are good examples. The question is whether the evolutionary roots of warfare and peacemaking reach far back in the natural history of animals, thereby forming the basis for the culturally determined behavior in humans that leads to war and peace.

Our results from observations of the fusion process of two neighboring captive monkey groups indicate that even New World monkeys—squirrel monkeys in our case—exhibit behavior patterns that are basic for the resolution of human conflict behavior. When living in neighboring territories without the possibility of exploring each other closely, emotional behavior, mostly aggressive vocal expressions, is directed from members of one group to members of the other group, and vice versa. The two groups have different social structures formed by social signaling. Although the set of social signals, the communicative repertoire, is species-specific and genetically determined, the distribution of signals is socially determined, according to the formula *who does what to whom how often at what time*. This distribution is responsible for group dynamics and group formation. In principle, intragroup signaling is the same as intergroup signaling. The animals direct the "language" they have learned in their group to foreign groups. Thus, the outcome of group encounters and the formation of a new group structure and hierarchy is determined by the distribution of social signals over time.

The claim of this chapter is that the basic pattern of conflict resolution in nonhuman primates as well as in the human primate is functionally homologous and phylogenetically determined. As long as this part of our nature is not generally recognized by our society, the efforts to develop "humanized" ways and means of resolving conflict around the globe will remain doubtful.

I shall proceed stepwise, first considering encounters of individuals and then analyzing an encounter between two groups.

If we take a reductionistic view in regard to behavior patterning, we might postulate that in the beginning the simplest modes of intraspecific encounters were nothing but approach and avoidance of members of the same species. The outcome of such encounters must have been rather unpredictable and dependent on the conspecific's readiness to act, which, as we know from ethology, depends not only upon external stimuli but also upon the internal state of the individual. We speak of the motivation of an animal. As the theory goes, because communication between conspecifics was advantageous, social signals evolved and signaling resulted as a more flexible mode of encounter with a greater degree of information about the outcome. Social signaling has two facets: the signal carries the message to the recipient and simultaneously expresses the sender's motivational state. The near ubiquity of these signaling functions in the animal kingdom can be demonstrated by the encounter of two stalk-eyed flies (*Cyrtodiopsis whitei*) during ritualized fighting (Fig. 3.1). The more rivals a male can drive away by this display, the greater will be his chance of mating with as many females as possible in the harem he has won (de la Motte and Burkhardt 1983).

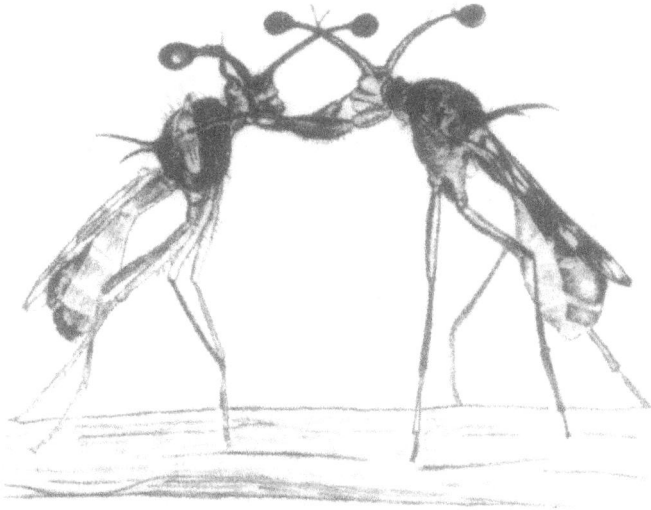

Fig. 3.1 *Stalk-eyed flies during ritualized fighting (de la Motte and Burkhardt 1983).*

Turning to the social signaling of primates, when we began our studies on squirrel monkeys in the early 1960s very little was known, let alone about the brain mechanisms involved. The general opinion was that basic ethological findings were hardly applicable to nonhuman primates, whose social life was governed by social learning and experience. There was very little emphasis on innate behavior. Instead of going into the now obsolete nature-nurture debate I want to give just one example of social signaling, which will lead directly into my topic of war and peacemaking.

While observing a captive colony of squirrel monkeys, we found, among other social signals, one that is best described as genital display (Ploog and MacLean 1963; Ploog et al. 1963). This signal is used in various types of agonistic, dominance, and courtship behaviors. It consists of several components: penile erection, lateral positioning of one leg with the hip and knee bent, and marked supination of the foot and abduction of the big toe. Here without a doubt we have a classic ritualized social signal. Fig. 3.2 shows four variations of this genital display: (a) in the open position, the displaying dominant animal looking at the partner to be subdued from a distance; (b) in the closed position, sometimes seen as counterdisplay in rival males—think of the rival stalk-eyed flies; (c) a 49-day-old male displaying at his mirror

Fig. 3.2 Genital display of squirrel monkeys in four variations (Ploog 1967).

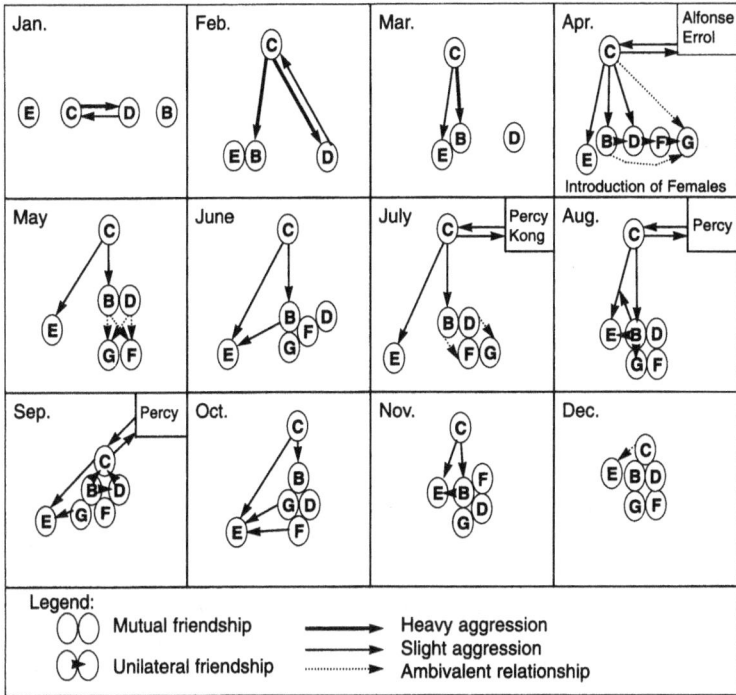

Fig. 3.3 *Group formation of a squirrel monkey colony over a one-year period (Ploog et al. 1963).*

image and vocalizing; and (d) a newborn on the second day of life displaying at a conspecific from his mother's back.

This signal, among others, is widely employed during group formation and the establishment of group hierarchy. In Fig. 3.3 the dynamics of group formation over a one-year period are depicted monthly. The diagram is based on sociometric data, with four males (E, B, C, D) and two females (F, G); the group has an abnormal gender composition. C establishes himself as the alpha male; B is second and attains the mediating role; D is a male in puberty opposing C from the beginning by genital display, which is an "undue" signal towards a superior of this age and rank; F and G are mature females, close to B and D, but never to C; and E is the omega animal, often the scapegoat of the group but sometimes protected by B (see August section). You will note that C as the alpha male defended the group against strange males (April and August sections).

If one changes the group composition, the group dynamics will change, as shown in Fig. 3.4. The group just described is charac-

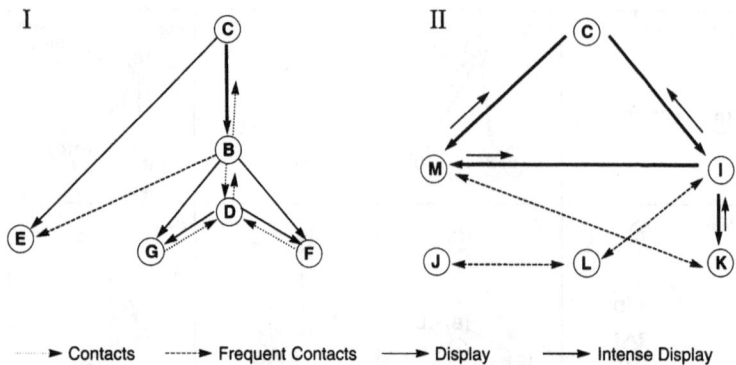

► Contacts   ----► Frequent Contacts   ──► Display   ──► Intense Display

Fig. 3.4 *Group dynamics depending upon group composition (Ploog et al. 1963; Ploog 1963).*

terized on the left. In the second group, on the right, C again establishes himself as the alpha male, having I as a male rival, and four females (K, L, M, J) as cagemates. Whereas the first group is rather stable and quiet, the second group is rather dynamic and eventful. C has to act toward his rival I and toward the female M, who receives frequent and intensive genital displays from I and from C. The forces that mold the group structure and lead to a temporary equilibrium, a social homeostasis as we have called it, are mainly expressed by social signals such as genital display. How a specific hierarchy and the roles of individuals therein are specified depends also on the idiosyncrasies of the individuals making up the group.

With this in mind, the reader is probably sufficiently prepared to critically follow the main issue of this contribution: an experiment involving the fusion of two neighboring groups of different composition. The purpose of such an experiment is to study the social transformation processes that are observable during the fusion of two groups with different structures into one group with a new structure. It is not hard to think of comparable processes in human life—in school, in sports, after a long separation between parts of countries, encounters between large groups of different ethnicity, etc.

The scenario before fusion was the following. There were two outdoor areas separated in part by an opaque wall and in part by a rail fence, 1.40 m apart. This was the place where the observer sat and the area in which the neighboring animals could not only hear but also see each other from a distance. The two territories

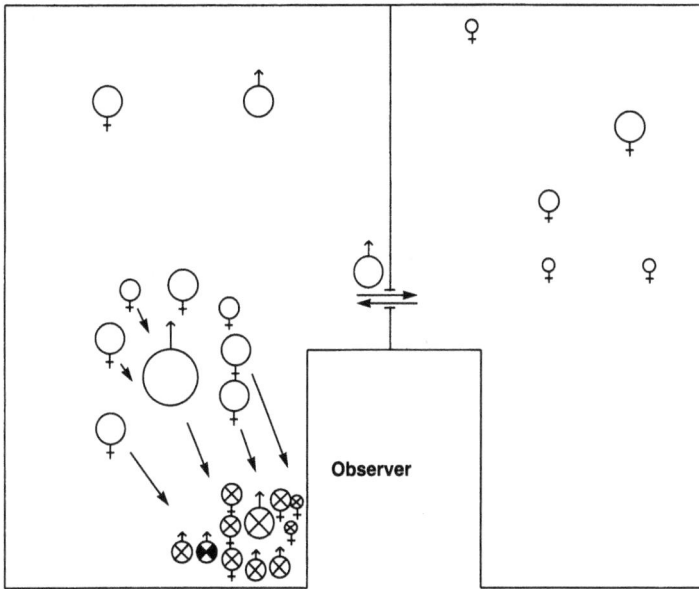

Fig. 3.5 *The fusion process: the Y-group (in blank circles) invaded the territory of the B-group (in crossed circles). The black and white circle depicts the rival of the alpha male of the B-group (Castell and Ploog 1967).*

could be connected by a small sliding door measuring 26 by 16 cm (see Figs. 3.5 and 3.6). As before, the sex ratios of the two groups were different. The Y-group in the right-hand compartment, with head hair stained yellow, was composed of 3 males and 13 females; the top male (alpha male) was heavier than the other two males. The B-group in the left-hand compartment, with head hair stained black, consisted of 5 males and 6 females. In the following two figures the members of the B-group are marked by crossed circles, the members of the Y-group by open circles.

Before fusion of the groups, each group was observed for a total of 30 hours in numerous time samples over several weeks. Fourteen agonistic and affiliative behavioral units of the squirrel monkeys' behavioral repertoire (Ploog et al. 1963; Ploog et al. 1967; Hopf et al. 1974) were recorded according to the rule, who does what to whom and in what order. It was noted that the Y-group with Y1 as the alpha animal had a stable hierarchical order with very few quarrels and no fights, whereas the B-group's behavior was much more dynamic. There were more quarrels and several fights, which always occurred between the alpha animal B1 and his rival B2 (black and white circle) who challenged B1 in his alpha position.

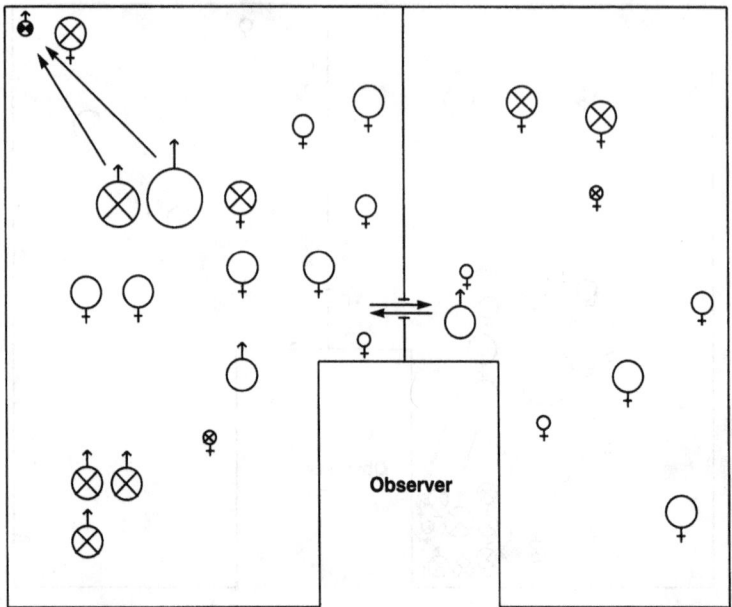

Fig. 3.6 *A new coalition is formed (Castell and Ploog 1967).*

During this phase of the investigation, it was noted that agonistic signals, mainly vocal ones, were exchanged between members of the two groups. It was quite obvious that animosities were
building up between the two groups.

On day X, about eight weeks after the beginning of the study, the
sliding door was opened, and the fusion of the two groups began
immediately. In almost no time most members of the Y-group
invaded the territory of the B-group (Fig. 3.5). Half of the Y-group
females joined Y-alpha, mainly by shrieking, whereas Y-alpha exhib-
ited genital display towards B-alpha and the other B males, who
counterdisplayed. The display duel lasted more than a minute. The
B-group was cornered, and only after a few minutes it was evident
that the Y-group was superior to the B-group. After 8 minutes the first
bite-fighting occurred between 3 Y-females and 2 B-females. After 40
minutes the first peacemaking gesture was performed by Y-alpha,
who approached the B-group, rolled on his back and developed
penile erection. Thereupon a B-female inspected his genitals with her
nostrils. This conspicuous behavior, which we have studied experimentally (Castell et al. 1969), has a clear appeasement function.

After 24 hours Y-alpha attacked B2 and B-alpha assisted his former rival by biting Y-alpha in the neck. Two weeks later, on day 15

of the fusion process, the situation had drastically changed (Fig. 3.6). Y-alpha and B-alpha attacked B2 severely. From then on B-alpha was submissive to Y-alpha, who became the boss of the fusioned groups, whereas the former B2 never gained back his rank, was the target of further attacks by Y-alpha, the former B-alpha and Y-females, became inactive, and sank to the bottom of the new hierarchy.

Fig. 3.7 depicts the fusion process over 40 days. On the left, threatening (crosses) and fighting behavior (columns) is depicted. In the left upper segment the behavior of the Y-group and in the left lower segment the behavior of the B-group is plotted. The open parts of the columns represent fights between the groups, the hatched parts represent the fights between B1 and B2 of the B-group, and the solid parts represent the fights between the Y-group and B2 of the B-group. All these agonistic behavioral frequencies decreased over time. Turning to the right part of the figure, avoidance behavior and contact behaviors of various kinds as well as huddling behavior (i.e., sitting together with fur contact) is plotted over time. The members of the two groups avoided each other in the beginning, the B-group, in the lower segment, showing

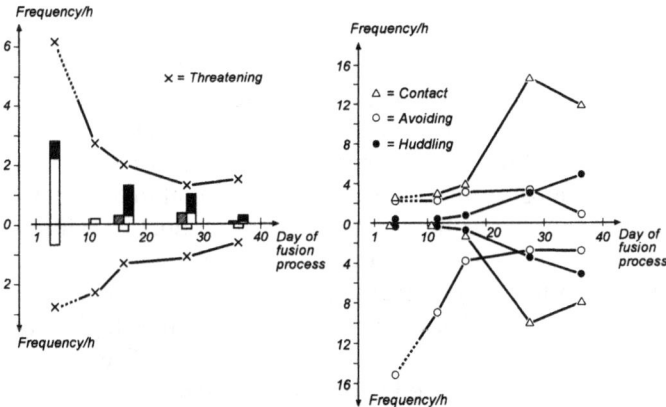

Fig. 3.7 *The fusion process over a period of 40 days. Left: The columns depict the number of fights of the Y-group against the B-group (upper quadrant) and of the B-group against the Y-group (lower quadrant). The black proportion depicts the frequency of fights of the Y-group against No. 2 of the B-group, and the hatched proportion the frequency of fights of No. 1 against No. 2 of the B-group. Right: Frequencies of contact, avoiding, and huddling of the Y-group (upper quadrant); same behaviors of the B-group (lower quadrant) (Castell and Ploog 1967).*

a much higher frequency of avoidance behavior than the Y-group, in the upper segment. In contrast to the avoidance behavior, the contact behavior between the members of the two groups increased over time, with more coming from the Y-group than from the B-group. Finally, the huddling behavior, a sign of intense affiliation, increased in both groups over time. At the end, after 40 days, the social homeostatic processes had stabilized. The two groups had formed a new hierarchy with alpha Y1 as the boss.

Besides fighting, threatening, contact, avoidance, and huddling behavior, sexual behavior such as genital inspection, genital display, and copulatory behavior were registered. These behaviors increased over time and contributed to the formation of the new group structure. Both males and females of the intruding Y-group were much more active in sexual behavior than the members of the B-group.

From the evidence I have presented here we can conclude that social signaling between nonhuman primates is instrumental in establishing a social order in a group of animals. This order is hierarchical. There are stable and unstable hierarchies. The latter tend to create social unrest and in-group fighting. The same means of social signaling that is employed in group formation is employed in intergroup encounters. Even before any physical contacts have taken place, animosities between groups may build up. The reasons for such animosities are usually not obvious to a human observer. Observations of chimpanzees seem to suggest that strangers are considered to be potential intruders and therefore dangerous. In this sense, chimpanzees are territorial. In quite the same vein, most primates seem to be territorial in that they don't accept strangers into their groups without strain. In our first squirrel monkey group we saw signs of such behavior: the alpha animal C defended the group against intruders (Ploog et al. 1963).

In the encounter between two monkey groups, highly aggressive behavior was mixed with cohesive behavior. The affiliation of the two groups progressed over time and resulted in a new group forming with a new hierarchical order after a new equilibrium, a social homeostasis, had been reached.

At this point I want to make a jump in my contribution and give you a glimpse of the ontogeny of agonistic and cohesive behavior in young human children. This behavior has been investigated ethologically in preschool children. Barbara Hold (1992), a member of the Eibl-Eibesfeldt research group, was one of the first to investigate social status in preschool children. She found that the attention structure (Chance 1967) proves to be the best index of social status. This means that subordinate children within a group pay much more attention to dominant ones than vice versa.

The question, then, is how a child becomes dominant or subordinate. A Canadian study of 134 French-speaking preschool children between 17 months and 5.5 years of age who were observed from an ethological perspective revealed the following behavioral development over a period of two years. In the youngest group (mean age 18 months) almost all of the interactions were agonistic. In Fig. 3.8, upper left, the child on the right hits the child on the left; in the lower left, the child on the left cowers and makes a cry face. It loses this encounter. In Fig. 3.8, upper right, a girl tries to get at an object in the possession of a boy. The boy retains the object (middle), counterattacks, and pushes the girl over (lower right). The boy is the winner of this encounter.

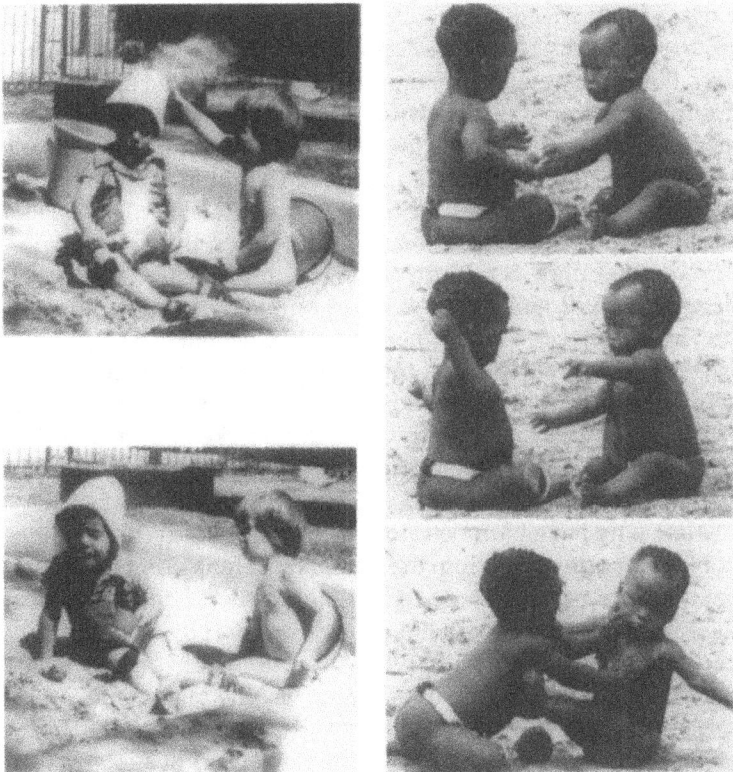

Fig. 3.8 *Agonistic behavior in preschool children (2 photos at left: Lauer 1992; 3 photos at right: Eibl-Eibesfeldt 1984).*

In the groups of 2- and 3-year-olds there is a transitional phase. Agonistic behaviors decrease proportionally and affiliative interactions increase in proportion to all registered behaviors. This tendency continues at age 3 and is clearly established at ages 4 to 5, where affiliative or cohesive behavior outweighs agonistic or aggressive behavior by far. Thus, between 1 and 5 years of age children become increasingly prosocial. The only exception to the clear distinction of agonistic and affiliative activity involved the behavioral category of competition, which remained significantly correlated with both dimensions of social participation throughout the latter three years of the preschool period (Strayer 1992).

Under the conditions of a community daycare center, these children form a hierarchy in their groups that is established by aggressive and affiliative interactions, whereby the relative rate of affiliative activity far exceeds the rate of agonistic activity. However, the ratio of initiated agonistic activity to initiated affiliation varies systematically as a function of age. Analyses of the total receipt of affiliative acts showed that in each group certain children obtained significantly more than their expected share of the group's total cohesive activity. These children were chosen more often as preferred social partners by other group members. These popular children appeared to be more central in the group network, whereas others assumed peripheral or isolated roles. Here again there was an age-dependent difference in regard to preferred social partners. In the youngest groups there was a tendency for children to choose lower-ranking group members as preferred social partners, whereas among the older groups there was an increasingly evident trend for choices to be directed preferentially toward higher-ranking group members. These results, which were obtained by Strayer and coworkers, corresponded with Barbara Hold's "attention structure" as a measure of social status in groups of children.

Now why have I jumped from the communicative behavior of nonhuman primates—from the formation of rank orders and combat over ranks—to preschool children? Preschool children, even in their prelinguistic phase of life, form rank orders by means of nonverbal agonistic and affiliative interactions. The same can be demonstrated in nonhuman primates. Competing over rank and role is a substantial part of a primate's life, whether human or nonhuman. The competition is exerted by means of agonistic and affiliative interactions. The same categories of behavior that are exercised in families and groups from childhood on are employed in communicating between members of groups unfamiliar or unknown to each other. In many species, groups communicate vocally over long distances and thereby stay out of each other's way. If they come into view, a large part of the repertoire of displays is employed. Whether such groups steer clear of each other or set out for an attack depends upon several internal and external conditions.

I have given but one example of such a battle followed by a gradual fusion process in which agonistic and affiliative acts resulted in the establishment of a new rank order. Only then was there peace. Among the internal conditions that can be critical for war or peace is the degree of social stability within a group. A stable and an unstable group were involved in our example. The stable group won. Among the external conditions involved, the size of the groups may be important. In our case, the winning group outnumbered the losing group even though the latter had two more males, the dominant sex in this species. Two other external conditions could have been decisive. The invaded territory was about 8 percent larger so that the winners gained more space. The invaded territory also had more sunshine per day, and squirrel monkeys love the sun. Unfortunately, the design of this study does not allow us to infer that these territorial attractions influenced the animals to pick a fight or, if one wishes, to start a war.

Conclusion

Social signaling is the major means of establishing rank order in primate societies, including man. The communicative signals can be divided into agonistic or aggressive acts on the one hand and cohesive or affiliative acts on the other. In forming rank orders, both categories of communication are used.

The communicative repertoire of a given primate species is used in intra- as well as intergroup interactions. Each encounter between groups is a challenge to the social homeostasis in one group, i.e., a threat to the established rank order.

Whether a group encounter amounts to fighting or yielding, to war or peace, depends on certain internal factors within each group and to circumstantial external factors that can be decisive for war and peace.

It is, of course, a strong claim that the basic behavioral patterns employed in making war or peace are functionally homologous in

Fig. 3.9 *Thor-Donar, the god of thunder and war, at warfare. Neolithic petroglyph, Sweden (Kühn 1963).*

nonhuman primates and man. It is also a potentially significant claim for those who would promote peaceful resolution of conflict across and between cultures, and is thus worth debating.

The last figure (Fig. 3.9) illustrates my central point. This painting on the wall of a rock shelter was made in the late Stone Age. Two groups are fighting with each other. What we see looks like genital display. Both groups are using weapons. The god Thor-Donar, symbolized by crosses in the shield, is portrayed as being involved. The ships in the rear may symbolize the resources of the two parties.

References

Castell, R. and Ploog, D. (1967). Zum Sozialverhalten der Totenkopf-Affen (*Saimiri sciureus*): Auseinandersetzung zwischen zwei Kolonien. *Zeitschrift für Tierpsychologie*, **24**, 625–41.

Castell, R., Krohn, H., and Ploog, D. (1969). Rückenwälzen bei Totenkopfaffen (*Saimiri sciureus*): Körperpflege und soziale Funktion. *Zeitschrift für Tierpsychologie*, **26**, 488–97.

Chance, M. R. A. (1976). Attention-structure as the basis of primate rank orders. *Man*, **2**, 503–18.

Eibl-Eibesfeldt, I. (1984). *Die Biologie des menschlichen Verhaltens*. Piper, Munich.

Hold, B. C. L. (1976). Attention-structure and rank-specific behaviour in preschool children. In *The social structure of attention* (ed. M. R. A. Chance and R. R. Larsen), pp. 177–201. Wiley, London.

Hopf, S., Hartmann-Wiesner E., Kühlmorgen B., and Mayer, S. (1974). The behavioural repertoire of the squirrel monkey (*Saimiri*). *Folia Primatologia*, **21**, 225–49.

Kühn, H. (1963). *Vorgeschichte der Menschheit*, Vol. 2: Neusteinzeit. Fig. 164. Dumont Schauberg, Cologne.

Lauer, C. (1992). Variability in the pattern of agonistic behaviour in preschool children. In *Aggression and peacefulness in humans and other primates* (ed. J. Silverberg and J. P. Gray), pp. 172–88. Oxford University Press, New York.

Motte, I. de la and Burkhardt, D. (1983). Portrait of an Asian stalk-eyed fly. *Naturwissenschaften*, **70**, 451–61.

Ploog, D. (1963). Vergleichend quantitative Verhaltensstudien an zwei Totenkopf-affen-Kolonien. *Zeitschrift für Morphologie und Anthropologie*, **53**, 92–108.

———. (1967). The behaviour of squirrel monkeys (*Saimiri sciureus*) as revealed by sociometry, bioacoustics, and brain stimulation. In *Social communication among primates* (ed. S. A. Altmann), pp. 149–84. The University of Chicago Press, Chicago.

Ploog, D. W. and MacLean, P. D. (1963). Display of penile erection in squirrel monkey (*Saimiri sciureus*). *Animal Behaviour*, **11**, 32–39.

Ploog, D. W., Blitz, J., and Ploog, F. (1963). Studies on social and sexual behaviour of the squirrel monkey (*Saimiri sciureus*). *Folia Primatologia*, **1**, 29–66.

Ploog, D., Hopf S., and Winter P. (1967). Ontogenese des Verhaltens von Totenkopf-Affen (*Saimiri sciureus*). *Psychologische Forschung*, **31**, 1–41.

Strayer, F. F. (1992). The development of agonistic and affiliative structures in preschool play groups. In *Aggression and peacefulness in humans and other primates* (ed. J. Silverberg and J. P. Gray), pp. 150–71. Oxford University Press, New York, Oxford.

Chapter Four

The Evolution of Human Ultrasociality

Peter J. Richerson and Robert Boyd

Introduction

Human sociality in comparative perspective

E. O. Wilson (1975) described humans as one of the four pinnacles of social evolution. The other pinnacles are the colonial invertebrates, the social insects, and the nonhuman mammals. Wilson separated human sociality from that of the rest of the mammals because, with the exception of the social insect-like naked mole rat, only humans have generated societies of a grade of complexity that approaches that of the social insects and colonial invertebrates. In the last few millennia, human societies have even begun to exceed, in numbers of individuals and degree of complexity, the societies of ants, termites, and corals.

Human social complexity is based on quite different principles than the ultrasociality of any other species. In all other known cases, the constituent individuals of societies are either genetically identical, as in the colonial invertebrates, or closely related, as in the social insects and nonhuman mammals. In the prototypical social insect colony, elaborate societies are built around a single reproductive queen, who suppresses the reproduction of workers in the colony. The offspring of the queen are siblings that share many genes in common, and they make up the work force of the colony. W. D. Hamilton (1964) argued in his famous pair of papers that worker sterility and relatedness to each other and the queen are fundamental to insect sociality. It is interesting to note (Wilson and Hölldobler 1988) that the phylogenetic rarity of eusociality in insects is in sharp contrast to its ecological ubiquity. Ants and termites are among the most abundant insects, and social bees and wasps are by no means rare. As with other social animals, the range and adaptive diversity of the human species has increased, and our population densities have exploded, as our societies have grown more sophisticated. Thus, the cooperation, coordination, and division of labor that characterize ultrasocial animals appear to be highly adaptive in many contexts. At the same time, evolutionary processes can rarely overcome the conflicts between individual reproductive success and the cooperation and self-sacrifice required to produce the colony-level benefits that ultrasociality produces.

Humans are, arguably, a new page in the natural history of animal cooperation (Campbell 1983). Our reproductive biology is similar to that of other social mammals. Among our close relatives, the apes and monkeys, genetic relatedness and reciprocal altruism support a diverse array of small-scale societies, but no other spectacular ones. Humans have built extremely complex societies using some mechanism or mechanisms different than any other known highly social species. At the same time, there are remarkable parallels between human and ape social behavior (deWaal 1982) and material culture (McGrew 1992), not to mention many convergences between humans and other social and tool-using species. Consistent with classical comparative anatomy and modern molecular studies, human behavior is clearly recently derived from ape behavior. There is room for only relatively few modifications of the behavior of the last common ancestor of chimpanzees and humans.

In this chapter, we draw together the results of some of our own theoretical work on the role of the processes of cultural evolution in the evolution of human sociality, the contributions of human sociobiologists, the general comparative data on the form of human societies, and some critical experimental data from psychology to develop a hypothesis about how human ultrasociality might have arisen by the Darwinian coevolution of culture and genes. We believe that evidence from several independent theoretical and empirical domains support the hypothesis.

The argument in outline

Our basic claim in this chapter is that cultural evolutionary processes drove the evolution of human ultrasociality. The cultural transmission of ordinary adaptive information has advantages in the highly variable environments of the Pleistocene, and the hominid line diverged from the last common ape ancestor in developing a massive dependence on adaptive social and technological traditions. Some of these processes have the effect of making group selection *on cultural variation* possible and the use of *cultural cues to structure populations* common. As cultural group selection began to produce primitive patterns of in-group cooperation and out-group hostility, human cognitive capacities and emotional responses, presumably coded in large measure by genes, responded to adapt people to living in culturally defined cooperative groups.

Cultural transmission is a little like the haplodiploidy of the social insects. It tweaks the evolutionary process in a way that happens to make the evolution of ultrasociality possible. It is quite unlike haplodiploidy in that it leaves the genetic system of inheritance itself unaltered. Thus human ultrasociality arose by adding a cultural system of inheritance to a genetic one that normally supports small-scale societies based on kinship and reciprocity.

Our account is a modernization of Darwin's (1874) argument in Chapters 3 to 5 of the *Descent*, in which he outlines his theory of the evolution of the psychological basis of human ultrasociality. His account turns on a mixture of what we would call today reciprocity based on foresight of consequences, aided by group selection (see also Alexander 1987, 93ff.). For the usual reasons, genetic group selection is likely to be weak in humans (but see Wilson and Sober 1994, and commentators). Group selection on *cultural* variation is a different story.

Kin Selection, Reciprocity, and Punishment in Human Societies

Most evolutionary biologists believe that all known cases of nonhuman animal cooperation can be explained by kinship and reciprocity. Both are certainly important in human societies.

Kin selection is fundamental to the evolution of cooperation in many animal societies. Not only is the eusociality of the social insects built upon kinship, but so are the much more modest social systems of the nonhuman primates. In the case of our closest relatives, the chimpanzee, the core of the social system is a set of related males (Goodall 1986). A population composed of relatively small, relatively exogamous kin groups with limited reproductive suppression of subordinate members of societies is a rather typical pattern for social mammals.

There is little doubt that cooperation with kin is deeply ingrained in human psychology. One excellent body of evidence comes from the seemingly tangential literature on incest avoidance. Westermarck (1894) suggested that there is an innate avoidance of inbreeding. If so, humans must have an innate kin recognition system. The operation of this device is nicely illustrated by the rarity of marriage among Israeli kibbutz age-mates (Shepher 1983) and the poor success of Taiwanese minor marriages (Wolf 1970). In these famous examples, potential husbands and wives are raised in close companionship as children, much as siblings normally are, even though unrelated in fact. Coresident age-mates apparently have an innate algorithm that invokes a mating avoidance mechanism. The kin recognition system fails in the rather unusual circumstances discovered by Shepher and Wolf, but in normal families will function properly as an incest avoidance mechanism.

Daly and Wilson (1988) explore a useful set of data on patterns of homicide. Family members living in close proximity have the maximum opportunity to kill one another, and family homicides are a large fraction of the total. Nevertheless, there is a striking tendency for consanguineal relatives to refrain from killing each other, compared to affinal family members. For example, child abuses and child murders are very disproportionately committed by stepparents. The homicide data, like that from incest avoidance, strongly suggest that humans have deep-seated psychological mechanisms for kin recognition and for kin appropriate behavior, as predicted by Hamilton's theory of inclusive fitness. One famous example of human altruism argued to contradict the theory, Polynesian adoption practices, turns out to strongly support it (Silk 1980). Kin altruism no doubt has deep roots in the vertebrate order, and human examples of nepotistic behavior can be multiplied at will.

Trivers (1971) described a mechanism whereby long-continued interactions between partners might lead to the development of sufficient trust in reciprocation of acts of aid to make such acts routine. Axelrod and Hamilton (1981) analyzed the case of pair-wise interactions of players of "prisoner's dilemma" in their important contribution to the theory of reciprocity. In their model, the interaction has a given probability of continuing for another turn. In this situation, it is easy for strategies like "tit-for-tat," ("cooperate on the first round of the game, and then do whatever your partners did on the previous round of the game") to evolve. If two players of this strategy meet, they cooperate from the first. If tit-for-tat players play against an unconditional noncooperator, they receive the worst possible sucker's payoff on the first round of the game, but are only victimized once. If payoffs to coopera-tion are relatively high and games go on for many rounds, then selection can prevent unconditional defectors from invading a population of tit-for-tat strategists.

Most important for our purposes here, Alexander (1987) has proposed that Axelrod's and Hamilton's result can be extended to very large societies by what he calls indirect reciprocity. If one of us helps you, you may help some third person who in turn helps the other of us. Rather than being restricted to pairwise interac-tions, perhaps reciprocity can encourage cooperation among large, diffuse networks of reciprocators. Primatologists (Byrne and Wit-ten 1988; Dunbar 1992; Kummer et al., in press) provide some sup-port for this idea in the form of what is called the "social intelligence hypothesis." Perhaps primate encephalization is gen-erally an adaptation to managing more complex societies, and humans are merely the most extreme case. Dunbar's data suggest that brain size is correlated with group size in nonhuman pri-mates. Intuitively, the trouble with supposing that intelligence alone can increase cooperation is that smart individuals can com-pute selfish advantage and learn sophisticated deceptive tactics just as readily as they can compute their enlightened self-interest via cooperation. Intelligence may be necessary to manage human cooperation, but is it sufficient to produce it?

We have studied mathematical models of the effects of group size on the evolution of strategies like tit-for-tat. In one series of models, we considered unstructured groups in which all individ-uals in the group simultaneously played repeated turns of pris-oner's dilemma (Boyd and Richerson 1988). We generalized the idea of tit-for-tat to large groups by studying rules of the form "cooperate if k out of the other n individuals cooperated on the last iteration of the game." The tit-for-tat results do not generalize to large groups. As group size increases, it rapidly gets very hard to get reciprocity to increase when rare in a population dominated by unconditional defection. This makes sense. In a situation where interacting groups are of size ten and your rule is cooperate if five others do, it is highly improbable that the five others obeying the same rule will be in any given group when rare overall. Alexander's idea involves indirect reciprocity flowing along fairly stable networks (what goes around eventually comes around). Adding a ring structure to groups to organize reciprocity in larger groups helps, but not much (Boyd and Richerson 1989).

It is often suggested that punishment of rule-breakers plays an important role in the maintenance of cooperation. The defection of tit-for-tat strategists when their partners defect is a kind of punishment, but in large groups it is very inefficient since it leads to the breakdown of cooperation for cooperators as well as defectors. It should be much more efficacious to punish defectors by discriminating retribution and by continuing to cooperate with other cooperative individuals. We used the repeated prisoner dilemma system to model how punishment might evolve (Boyd and Richerson 1992). Each round of the game is divided into two parts. In the first part, individuals in a group of size n either cooperate or defect. In the second stage of the round, some strategies will, at some cost, punish those who defected in the first part of the round. The results of this theoretical investigation suggest that a division of labor can arise in which a few punishers can induce a larger number of reluctant cooperators to cooperate. At equilibrium, under a range of conditions, a group tends to have one punisher, just the number needed to induce cooperation in most groups. This result is reminiscent of the famous "big-man" political systems of New Guinea, and common in tribal societies elsewhere. We need not imagine that "punishers" are brutal thugs dictating cooperation by physical coercion. "Big-men" may be, as Eibl-Eibesfeldt has remarked (personal communication), prosocial leaders who pay the costs of persuading and cajoling to induce cooperation from others, with perhaps the distant threat of physical harm.

Punishment suggests the possibility of the evolution of "moralistic" strategies in which punishers punish reluctant cooperators not only if they defect, but also if they do not punish others who fail to cooperate and even those who fail to punish those who don't punish. Such strategies can certainly induce cooperation, but they can also make any arbitrary behavior an evolutionary stable strategy (ESS) that happens to become the target of a moralistic strategy.

This effect is in turn only an extreme example of the way games of coordination arise in models of cooperation. In games of coordination, it is best to do whatever everyone else is doing. You may hate daylight savings time, but it is quite inconvenient to arrange life around standard time when everyone else begins work an hour earlier. As models of cooperation become more complex, there are typically many ESSs, introducing a coordination effect. Moralistic strategies can potentially make even absurd things, like wearing neckties to work, evolutionarily stable. Cultural evolution is perhaps rapid enough to evolve to different coordination equilibria in different local populations, leading to group selection among societies with different equilibria. It is likely that genetically determined variation in coordination equilibria exists only at the species level, making interdemic group selection on the basis of different coordination equilibria unlikely.

There is no doubt that humans are capable of using rules about appropriate behavior in partners as a basis for social decisions and actions. Cosmides (1989) conducted a series of experiments to test the hypothesis that at least one of the kinds of problems that people evolved to solve involves social contracts. She supposed that human cognition includes the rule "if you take the benefit, then you must pay the cost." Of the many simple rules that humans might use in social or more general decision-making this one is uniquely suited to detecting defection in games like repeated prisoner's dilemma. She then tested the subjects' ability to solve a logical problem when couched as a social contract compared to when it was couched as some simple nonsocial problem. For example, the rule "if a man eats cassava, he has a tattoo on his face" can be framed as a social rule (only men who have undergone the painful ritual of tattooing can eat cassava) or as a mere contingent empirical fact (tribes that eat cassava also happen to practice tattooing). When framed as a cheater detection problem, success rates were in excess of 70 percent, while less than 25 percent solved the problem in its empirical form. Cosmides interprets these results to mean that people have an innate decision-making module devoted to detecting cheaters on social contracts. Whatever one might think of the innate interpretation of the experiment, it would certainly appear that humans are very efficient decision-makers when it comes to detecting defectors on social contracts.

In addition to recognizing cheaters in social games, people seem psychologically prepared to exact retribution. Daly and Wilson (1988) report high rates of spousal homicide in some modern communities. Suspicion of infidelity and sexual rivalry are very common motives for murder. Knauft (1987) notes that in small-scale communities lacking any formal authority, murder is quite common. In the absence of a satisfactory rule of law (that poor people can't afford, and some simple societies don't have), individuals are certainly capable of costly acts of punishment. Of course, the ultimate threat of physical coercion backs up formal law.

The capacity of people to behave as reluctant cooperators is strikingly demonstrated in experimental settings such as those constructed by Milgram (1974) and Nuttin and Beckers (1975). In one of Nuttin and Beckers' experiments, Belgian college students (male) were asked by Beckers (an attractive young woman experimenter) to give a speech in *favor* of a hated exam system, to which they were subjected. A strenuous protest movement *against* the system was supported by virtually all students. In the most extreme experimental condition used, all 11 students assigned to experimental treatment requesting students to give a television speech favoring the exam system complied with Beckers' request for cooperation. When 22 fellow students were asked how many students would comply with such a request, the majority replied that less than 5 percent would do so, and the most cynical guessed only 30 percent!

Kin Selection, Reciprocity, and Punishment Are Not Enough

There is no doubt that kinship, reciprocity, and punishment—family, friends, and righteous anger—are important components of human social life. There is little doubt that they account for the eusociality of insects and the small-scale cooperation of nonhuman primates. However, it is hard to imagine how to make a case for these processes—unaided—creating human ultrasociality.

The comparative evidence strongly suggests that the conventional mechanisms aren't sufficient. If kin selection, reciprocity, and punishment were sufficient to create ultrasociality in local populations with open mating and without reproductive suppression of workers, then ultrasociality ought to be common in our relatives, given its ecological success in our case. Unusual adaptations suggest unusual environments or unusual evolutionary processes.

The common theoretical problem that afflicts all three processes is that they all inherently favor small groups, absent special mechanisms like sterile worker castes. Kin altruism should favor the most closely related individuals differentially. Sibships and even first or second cousinships are composed of relatively few people. All else being equal, it is much easier to organize reciprocal cooperation in smaller groups than in larger ones. Even if cooperation in large units somehow gets started, the relative ease of organizing nepotistic cooperation and small cabals of reciprocators will tend to subvert larger scale organizations. It would seem that socially intelligent individuals might organize many pairwise reciprocal arrangements, but not engage in much indirect reciprocity.

Punishment by leaders is limited because individuals can monitor and punish only so many reluctant cooperators. Also, the cooperation produced by leaders creates a public good for all participants. If leaders can control group size in their own interest, they are not likely to select the group size that maximizes overall benefits. If the marginal cost of having more than a few individuals in the group exceeds the benefits, leaders will keep groups small. In fact, in the classic iterated prisoner's dilemma model to which we added punishment, the per capita benefits do not increase as a function of group size, and potential leaders would prefer to be loners and have to coerce no one. The asocial heroes that Clint Eastwood often plays in films illustrate this result. His characters can coerce cooperation from whole towns, but they do so only when circumstances make exit impossible. At the other extreme, it is easy to imagine situations in which punishment is cheap, and in which punishers can reward themselves disproportionately from the fruits of cooperation. Leaders would then be motivated to assemble a large number of exploitable retainers. In this situation, coerced individuals will exit if they possibly can. What is lacking in the punishment system, and in related moralistic strategies, is any obvious internal mechanism to regulate them in the group interest, even approximately. The comparative evidence (Eibl-Eibesfeldt 1989, 297ff.) is not supportive of the idea that coercion can generate ultrasociality. Coercion and deference to coercion are very widespread in animal societies in the form of dominance hierarchies and similar principles of social organization. Dominant animals sometimes act as prosocial leaders. Human dominance behavior shows many continuities with animal dominance, and if dominance behaviors alone could build large societies, they ought to be common in other social animals.

Our hypothesis, then, is that these conventional mechanisms for the evolution of cooperation in humans act quite strongly, but only to favor the same small-scale cooperation that they do in other mammals. They are a major source of *conflict* in human societies (Campbell 1983). Processes of cultural group selection build large-scale ultrasocial institutions that very frequently compete with kinship and friendship for the loyalties of people. This conflict has no easy resolution because the culture-driven institutions and psychological mechanisms that support ultrasociality have been appended to a mating system, family system, and face-to-face reciprocity system that derive directly from life in small primate troops, as zoologists have noted (Harcourt 1992).

Microsociological data seem to support the conflict hypothesis. Predatory crime, fraud, embezzlement, antitrust violations and the like, when they are cooperative at all, are typically organized on a small scale. Pairs of robbers may engage in their enterprises with *some* confidence that they have solved the prisoner's dilemma problem. Larger-scale criminal enterprises, like the Mafia and the Colombian drug cartels, resemble legal ultrasocial institutions. They use principles of recruitment like ethnicity and ritualistic resocialization to extend their scale of organization far beyond what a single kin group or band of close friends can accomplish. Olson (1982) gives evidence that the postwar economic success of the countries defeated in World War II can be explained as the result of the temporary absence of small-scale organizations exploiting large-scale institutions. In Germany and Japan, the prewar totalitarian regimes destroyed or coopted many small-scale social organizations. Then, denazification and demilitarization destroyed the organizations created by the totalitarian regimes. The constitutions imposed on the two countries by the Allies reconstructed national-scale organizations, and for some period of time these operated free of the influence of a multitude of small-scale interest groups. The economies of the Allied victors grew more slowly because "special interest" organizations remained intact, demanding expensive and inefficient subsidies and other aid at the expense of the nation as a whole.

Genetic Group Selection Implausible

Several prominent modern Darwinians (Hamilton 1975; Wilson 1975: 561–2; Alexander 1987: 169; and Eibl-Eibesfeldt 1982) have given serious consideration to group selection as a force *in the special case* of human ultrasociality. They are impressed, as we are, by the organization of human populations into units that engage in sustained, lethal combat with other groups, not to mention other forms of cooperation. The trouble with a straightforward group selection hypothesis is our mating system. We do not build up concentrations of intrademic relatedness like social insects, and few demic boundaries are without considerable intermarriage. Moreover, the details of human combat are more lethal to the hypothesis of genetic group selection than to the human participants. For some of the most violent groups among simple societies, wife capture is one of the main motives for raids on neighbors. In precontact New Guinea, warfare typically results in the social breakup of a defeated group and the dispersal of its members to other groups where the defeated have bonds of friendship and kinship (Soltis et al. 1995). Pastoralists in Eurasia generated complex intermarrying confederations across ethnic lines to the extent that it takes considerable detective work to be reasonably certain that groups like Attila's Huns were mainly a Turkic group (Maenchen-Helfen 1973). The human groups that compete are demographically very open, and violent conflict increases migration rates. It is hard to see how genetic differences can be maintained in the face of such migration rates.

Cultural Evolutionary Processes and Ultrasociality

Are there cultural evolutionary processes that can support the evolution of norms and sentiments that permit people to live in large cooperative groups, even in the teeth of small-scale loyalties based on kinship and reciprocity? Humans are unique in the scale of their use of learning from others as a mode of adaptation. Cultural transmission is like genetic transmission in many respects, although the differences are just as important (Cavalli-Sforza and Feldman 1981; Boyd and Richerson 1985). Humans are also unique among vertebrates in the scale of our social cooperation— the degree to which social groups are marked by symbolic means—and apparently unique among all animals in the mode by which we construct those means. Thus, it is worth pursuing the hypothesis that the association of culture and cooperation is not accidental. We think there is good evidence that cultural evolutionary processes did play a role loosely analogous to haplodiploidy and reproductive suppression of workers in engendering human ultrasocial institutions.

Cooperation and cultural group selection

Theoretical models. Intuitively, group selection on culturally transmitted variation is more plausible than in the genetic case because of differences in the way culture is transmitted. One such difference is that humans may survey several individuals in the course of acquiring a cultural trait. We can have more than two cultural "parents." In variable environments with migration between subpopulations, there are liable to be many erroneous ideas introduced into the population by outsiders whose behavior is appropriate for a different environment. We can expect the adaptive forces—even natural selection—to act on culture to keep advantageous traits in high frequency so long as the amount of migration is not overwhelming. Theoretical models show that using a conformist transmission rule of the form "when in Rome, do as the Romans do" is advantageous in this circumstance. Individuals benefit by using the information about the commonness or rarity of a cultural trait to bias their adoption choice. This transmission rule in turn has the effect of reducing variation within populations and protecting between-population difference. Even with fairly substantial migration rates and relatively weak conformity, the differences between groups are maintained in the models (Boyd and Richerson 1985: Ch. 7). Cultural group selection meets the test of theoretical plausibility, a test that most evolutionary biologists believe genetic group selection flunks.

In addition to between-group differences stabilized by conformity, games of coordination, the coordination element in many games of cooperation, and moralistic punishment all lead to multiple evolutionarily stable equilibria. If cultural evolution is generally more rapid than genetic evolution—and there is reason to assume that this is one of the basic adaptive advantages of learning by imitation (Boyd and Richerson 1985: Ch. 4)—then cultural meta-populations may find more alternative equilibria than meta-populations without culture, and there will be more variation at the group level on which selection might play.

Empirical data. The cultural group selection hypothesis predicts that social units that are cosocialized should be the groups that cooperate. Some evidence supports this prediction. Otterbein's (1968) cross-cultural study of warfare revealed that societies engaged in internal warfare had small-scale fraternal interest groups composed of related males as the dominant element of social organization. Societies that suppressed internal warfare and conducted mostly external warfare emphasized socialization of warriors into age sets, police societies, or other military institutions that crosscut units of male relatedness. When the cultural group that is cosocialized is restricted to genetic kinsmen, we recover, approximately, as expected, the pattern predicted by ordinary kin selection theory. When a larger group is the focus of socialization for military virtues, larger-scale fighting units emerge.

Elsewhere we have reviewed the psychological evidence that humans actually use conformist rules in cultural transmission. Despite a large amount of literature on conformity, more work is needed on the extent to which we actually use it in cultural acquisition (Boyd and Richerson 1985: 223–7).

It is also possible to test the empirical plausibility of the cultural group selection process with a direct microevolutionary analysis. Soltis et al. (1995) used information on group extinctions by warfare in Highland New Guinea to provide an estimate of the plausibility and power of group selection. The New Guinea data provide relatively extensive and sophisticated ethnographic accounts for a series of simple tribal societies before contact with colonial powers. Although they are horticultural rather than hunting and gathering societies, the sorts of processes operative in Highland New Guinea are roughly similar to those that might have operated on simple societies generally over the long period of time during which human ultrasociality arose.

To work effectively, cultural group selection by the conformity mechanism requires a number of conditions to be effective. For example, new groups must be formed mainly by the splitting of old groups, not by drawing random samples of migrants to a new group. The former mode of group multiplication preserves variation between groups, whereas the latter destroys it.

Group extinctions due to chronic warfare between village communities are quite common in New Guinea. For the five populations for which quantitative estimates could be derived from the literature, rates ranged from 1.6 percent to 31.3 percent per generation. Taking into consideration the quality of the data used in the estimates, the long-term, area-wide rate was probably between 10 percent and 20 percent. The New Guinea data strongly support the model's assumed group reproduction processes. New groups always arise by the fissioning of existing groups—usually large, successful ones. There is ample evidence for cultural differences between groups, although there is little evidence in Highland New Guinea ethnography documenting differences that persist for long periods of time or that are directly connected to extinctions. Other sets of data do strongly suggest that group differences in competitive ability are common (e.g., Barth 1981; Knauft 1985; 1993).

Taking the New Guinea rates at face value, our calculations suggest that cultural group selection can cause an initially rare, favored institution to become common in about a millennium. This rate is fast on the time scales of genetic macroevolution, and is roughly consistent with rates of evolution of human political institutions under pre-state conditions. The archaeological and linguistic evidence from Western North America, where hunting and gathering subsistence is the rule, suggests that major events causing population displacements did indeed have approximately millennial time scales (Bettinger and Baumhoff 1982). If this process began working sometime back in the Pleistocene, then there will have been some tens of millennia, perhaps as many as a few hundred, for this process to have affected human social cognition by genetic coadaptations to life under group-selected cultural adaptations.

We know from simpler cases that cultural evolution can drive a genetic response in cases like the evolution of adult lactose absorption in dairying populations on the millennial time scale (Durham 1991: Ch. 5). If a process like cultural group selection worked over substantial periods of time, and especially if it recruited coercive strategies to effectively punish defectors from social contracts, it is reasonable to expect that human decision-making strategies should be adapted to life in a prosocial world.

Batson's (1991) experimental studies of the psychology of human altruism provide good evidence that our cognitions and emotions have been molded by some form of group selection. His studies address the structure of motivations that produce helping behavior using laboratory experiments. The experiments were designed to distinguish between an empathy-altruism hypothesis and various forms of covertly egoistic motives for helping behavior. According to the empathy-altruism hypothesis, once a potential helper's empathy for a sufferer is engaged, helping behavior is motivated, at least in measurable part, by a genuinely unselfish desire to actually relieve the victim's suffering. Rational actor theorists propose that instead of a desire to help for its own sake, apparent altruists give aid in the expectation of some form of personal reward. Egoistic hypotheses are numerous. Individuals may help another in need because they seek to gain rewards or avoid punishment. These expected rewards and punishments may be external or internal. That is, people may expect others to give rewards or administer punishments, or it may be a matter of conscience, with self-administered rewards and punishments. Expected external rewards or punishments may be material (soldiers' pensions) or social (enhanced prestige). Of course, actual human motivations may be complex, and egoistic motivations of several kinds may jointly act with altruistic ones. Batson's question is whether any significant nonegoistic motivation can be demonstrated.

The experiments elicited an empathetic response on the part of some experimental subjects, for example, by asking them to take the point of view of the experiment's victim, while nonempathetic controls were asked to view the situation objectively. Then, the experimental conditions were manipulated to control for one or another egoistic motivation and to test whether subjects in the empathy condition were still willing to provide aid to the experiment's victim. For example, one egoistic motivation for aiding a victim might be to relieve one's own suffering at having to watch the victim suffer. To test this possibility, "Elaine," the sham victim in one experiment, was to suffer a series of moderately painful shocks. The experimental subjects were told at the beginning of the sham experiment that Elaine is unusually sensitive to shocks due to a traumatic childhood experience, and finds them exceedingly uncomfortable. The experimenter expresses concern about this, and offers the real subjects the chance to continue the "experiment" in place of Elaine. The shocks will be uncomfortable for them, but not nearly so painful as for Elaine. If helping is motivated by the desire to avoid viewing someone else suffering, Batson reasoned that allowing the experimental subjects to escape (watch only two trials of the experiment on Elaine instead of all ten) should reduce the tendency to help, whereas if subjects had a genuine desire to help Elaine, even subjects allowed escape should offer to help. In this experiment, difficult escape had a dramatic effect on helping in the low empathy case, raising the proportion helping from about 0.2 to 0.6. In the high empathy condition there was no significant difference in helping; in the easy escape condition the proportion offering to help was 0.9, and in the difficult escape, 0.8. While the egoistic motivation clearly had some effect, the helping in the empathy condition is consistent with the empathy-altruism hypothesis.

Batson even produced evidence that people's desires to aid others go beyond conscience and pride—internal psychological punishments and rewards for helping. In experiments in which the desire to help was aroused and then frustrated by someone else being chosen to help, an internal reward system would elevate the mood of those who got to help, but not those who did not. Contrary to this hypothesis, subjects who saw help provided, but didn't have to provide it themselves, had the greatest mood increase, and those that were prevented from helping when no one else did had the lowest mood. Once empathy is engaged, people apparently have a genuinely unselfish desire to help.

A skeptic about the effects of group selection does have rejoinders to these experiments. Genuine proximal altruism could be part of a strategy of advertisement of one's willingness to engage in acts helping kin and reciprocal partners, and perhaps be made consistent with some form of the social intelligence hypothesis. However, the cultural group selection hypothesis provides the most natural evolutionary explanation for Batson's results. If cultural groups have long been subject to group selection, then fellow group members ought to engage in empathy-altruism even when kinship is remote and expectations of reciprocity limited. The question is, what arouses our empathy?

Ideology and symbol system evolution: In-group marking

It is a striking feature of human ultrasociality that groups are explicitly defined and marked by symbolic boundaries. Some of these marks are relatively simple badges, such as body ornamentation and dialects. Others are complex ritual systems accompanied by elaborately rationalized ideologies. It is a commonplace that social relations are regulated by norms embedded in a group's sanctified belief system (Rappaport 1979). Even in simple hunting and gathering societies, the groups so marked are rather large, as we already noted. In this section we argue that symbolic cultural marks are potent factors dividing in-groups from out-groups, sharpening the boundaries between social units subject to cultural group selection, and regulating empathy and hence altruism.

Theory. We have studied models of a process we term "indirect bias" (Boyd and Richerson 1985: Ch. 8; 1987). In indirect bias, individual imitators use one trait in potential cultural models to weight that individual in the socialization process. Young people picking adult role models on the basis of charm, prestige, power, or whatever is a commonplace example. Once a role model is chosen, youngsters may pick up a number of other ideas, norms, skills, and attitudes without further bias. If any of these other traits happen to correlate with indices of prestige or charm that youngsters are using to choose role models, then the correlated variants will increase in frequency.

The evolution of symbolic, stylistic markers of group boundaries is an interesting special case of cultural evolution under indirect bias. We (Boyd and Richerson 1987) investigated a model of the evolution of "ethnic" markers motivated by these observations. Suppose that there are two episodes of transmission. In the first episode, children learn some neutral marker trait, like a speech dialect, from their parents and other local adults. In the second, they learn a subsistence trait and modify their dialect by selecting among a broader set of adult models. In the first episode there is just blind copying. In the second, models are weighted by both their symbolic trait and their subsistence success. Juvenile imitators prefer models with a dialect similar to that learned as children, but also prefer successful models. The broader set of models in the second episode is meant to mimic the effects of cultural diffusion from one environment to another. The question is, in an environment in which the best subsistence strategy is variable from place to place, can a symbolic marker reducing the effect of cultural diffusion of locally maladaptive traits from neighboring environments arise? The answer is yes. If there is a sharp environmental gradient, a dialect difference will emerge and continue to get more extreme until the degree of cultural isolation is sufficient to allow the population to optimize the mean subsistence behavior. Thus, to the picture of a culturally group-selected hominid from the previous section, we can also, in theory, imagine that the boundaries between groups are formally marked by symbol or style changes.

Empirical evidence. Archaeological evidence suggests that the acquisition of a fully symbolic cultural system led to a considerable increase in human adaptive sophistication (Bettinger 1991: 203–8). One notable feature of the human species, increasingly apparent throughout the Pleistocene, is our very wide geographical range. In Europe, stylistic features of culture that mark apparent ethnic differences first appear at the Upper Paleolithic Transition, about 35,000 ybp. Upper Paleolithic peoples apparently had more regionally differentiated subsistence strategies and greater population densities than the Middle Paleolithic populations they replaced. Upper Paleolithic peoples also extended the human range into such isolated land areas as Australia and the Americas.

There is a fair amount of data on the microevolutionary properties of indirect bias. First, it is highly plausible that people use indirect bias effectively for everyday culture acquisition. This is quite well documented in the applied literature on the diffusion of innovations (Rogers 1983). It also seems that in many societies, culturally defined prestige, which people use as indicators for indirect bias judgments, is correlated with wealth and reproductive success (Irons 1979; Borgerhoff Mulder 1988). As the theory suggests, everyday fitness advantages can be obtained by using indirect bias. Second, ethnographic investigations suggest that symbolic, stylistic markers in the form of body adornment and the like are used to communicate and negotiate personal and social identities relative to others. Wiessner (1984) makes a strong case for such usage in the Kalahari San. These data, together with the appearance of stylistic artifacts at the Upper Paleolithic Transition, argue that expressive symbolic displays have been part of human strategies for managing cultural transmission, among other problems of social life, for a respectable period. Third, there is also evidence—again Wiessner's (1983) San data is an example—that ethnolinguistic boundaries are symbolically marked, and that stylistic marks of group membership are highly salient. Wiessner collected arrow points from a number of Bushmen groups, including groups unknown to the Kalahari San and in fact ethnically rather different from them, and asked San men for comments on the distinctive styles. Confronted by points of an unknown style, Kalahari San guess that their makers are very different people from themselves. Within groups, on the other hand, exchange of stylistically familiar beadwork and other valuables is used to build up a notion of the Kalahari San social universe and to build a web of relationships that link people within ethnolinguistic units.

At the proximal psychological level, the "minimal group" experimental system developed by Tajfel (Tajfel et al., 1971) is interesting regarding the cognitive mechanisms involved in the use of symbols to demarcate groups and the actions people take based on group membership. It is a common finding in social psychological experiments, as in real life, that members of groups favor one another and discriminate against out-groups. The social psychologists in Tajfel's tradition were interested in separating the effects of group membership *per se* from the personal attachments that form in groups. Turner (1984) contrasts two sorts of hypotheses to explain group-oriented behavior. It could be that functional social groups are composed entirely of networks of individuals that are linked by personal ties, objective shared fate, or other individual-centered ties, much as in the social intelligence hypothesis. Groups, according to this hypothesis, are "some collection of individuals characterized by mutual interpersonal attraction reflecting some degree of interdependence and mutual need-satisfaction." The contrasting hypothesis is that identity symbols alone are sufficient to induce humans to accept membership in a group, acting positively toward in-group members and negatively toward out-groups.

In his prototypical experiments, Tajfel et al. (1971) told subjects that they were participating in a test of aesthetic judgment. They were shown pictures of paintings by Klee and Kandinsky, and asked to indicate which they preferred. Then the subjects were divided into two groups, supposedly on the basis of their art preference, but in fact at random. The subject's task was then to divide a sum of money among members of one's own group or the other group. Subjects discriminated in favor of the sham in-group members. The interpretation of these results was that indications of membership, even in a new, externally imposed, and very abstract group, was sufficient to motivate in-group favoritism on the part of subjects.

Turner et al. (1983) were interested in an extreme case of categorization generating group-oriented cooperative behaviors. Could such behavior be motivated by an external categorization of a group in which the group was categorized as that which everyone, including group members, disliked? Children were shown their picture paired with others and asked to rate the others as liked or disliked. Then children were ostensibly placed in groups by explicitly random criteria, or on the basis of liking or on the basis of disliking in different treatments. In still other treatments, children were not explicitly placed into groups. Then children had to make private decisions about rewards to allocate to others. Being explicitly assigned to a group had a marked effect, as in the classic Tajfel design. The most striking contrast was: In the ungrouped condition, disliked children favored liked others.

However, when they were explicitly grouped as to liked or disliked, disliked subjects, led to believe that they were now members of a group of pariah, disliked others, discriminated almost as much as liked-group members in favor of their fellow pariahs (recall classic films like *The Seven Samurai* and *The Dirty Dozen*, where the plot turns on the bonding among a group of initially hostile outcasts). Turner (1984) argues that such experiments show that shared membership even in a group of unattractive others can induce a commitment to the group. Categorization per se does have a strong effect, independent of interpersonal bonds.

Other social psychologists have objected that Tajfel and Turner have overemphasized the raw categorization effect in interpreting their experiments. Rabbie (1991) argues that no experimental system implying that people belong to a group can control away people's expectation that the group membership imposed by experimenters implies instrumental interdependence. From an evolutionary point of view, Rabbie's point is well taken; people presumably only react to symbolic badges of group membership because in the evolutionary past they generally signaled politically important social units. In the politically complex world outside the lab, where many groupings are abstractly possible, people no doubt attempt to make sensible decisions about which to take seriously in any given circumstance. Nevertheless, it is striking in humans how a rather abstract, large, impersonal, marked group (Protestant Irish, Serb, Jew, German, etc.) can attract great emotional salience and motivate desperate deeds of great risk to participants. Long periods of relative dormancy seem to leave largely intact the potential emotional power of groups that can plausibly claim deep historic roots. Individual decision-makers must also contend with the awful possibility that an aggressive out-group may suddenly, for reasons of its own, target them as belonging to a previously weakly relevant group, as has happened recently to Bosnian Muslims.

Conclusion

A considerable amount of evidence from several domains ranging from comparative natural history to psychology suggests that the processes of cultural evolution permitted group selection on cultural variation and the marking of group boundaries by cultural symbols. Archaeological evidence suggests that symbolic behavior is at least a few tens of thousands of years old. The residential bands of hunting and gathering societies were very small, overlapping with typical primate troops in size. However, ethnographic studies show that bands themselves are typically quite fluid, and that "tribal" ethnolinguistic units of 500 to 1,500 people (Birdsell 1968) are an important part of the human social adaptation. Hunting and gathering societies of the ethnographic record appear to expend considerable effort to maintain the ethnolinguistic tribe as an institution. Yengoyan (1968) noted that Australian marriage systems were most complex in the arid, sparsely populated interior. He argues that the complex section systems of the interior ensured that people sought mates from geographically great distances, which kept the dispersed tribe a functional demographic and ceremonial unit. In the harsh, variable environment of Central Australia, the ties at the tribe level were used to gain aid in times of emergency. Although tribal politics among hunters and gatherers is usually quite simple, some cooperation at the level of the ethnolinguistic tribe is very common. While kinship, reciprocity, and dominance organize higher primate troops into units as large as hunter-gatherer *bands*, there is in the nonhuman species no social unit corresponding to the ethnolinguistic *tribe*.

We suppose that the symbolically marked, cooperating in-group adaptation was based on a psychological decision-making system analogous to Chomsky's view of language as an innate set of algorithmic principles, whose parameters are set culturally by the specific language learned (Pinker 1994, 111–2). The propensity to cooperate with sympathy inspiring in-group members, and to use symbolic markers to define in-groups, is like the innate principles of language. The specific markers, size of group(s), and internal structure of the group(s) to which individuals belong are culturally variable parameters that generate a specific functioning instance of the innate propensities. Like innate language structures and adult lactose absorption, the social decision-making principles most likely coevolved as adaptations to an emerging cultural environment in which cooperation within culturally marked groups was becoming important. Success in intergroup competition came to depend upon within-group cooperation; an evolutionary arms race arose. The scale of cooperation-to-compete might escalate until ecological rather than evolutionary constraints bring a halt. Once the barriers of scale imposed by kinship and reciprocity are breached by cultural group selection, it is not

clear what the next natural evolutionary limit to scale of cooperation is. This picture squares with experimental evidence, such as
Batson's and Tajfel's, that perhaps gives us a look at the innate
principles of human social action, and it explains how human
societies can organize cooperation on a far larger scale than our
primate relatives.

It can be objected that the subjects of these experiments already
have considerable cultural sophistication when they participate
in such experiments. The same objection applies to the experiments by Cosmides on cheater detection. Fair enough—some
human universals probably do involve conservative cultural features as well as genetic elements. But it is also true that chimpanzees would not behave in the same way in any of these
experiments no matter how hard experimenters tried, nor would
our Australopithecine ancestors of five million years ago. Even if
we cannot yet be exactly sure what the innate principles are that
divide us from other apes, we can be sure that they exist, as
remarkably human-like as chimp behavior is in so many ways.

Human populations grew explosively in the Holocene when
the development of food plant production removed previously
tight constraints on human densities. With ecological constraints
removed, the cooperation-to-compete arms race renewed its
progress. Very large, hierarchically organized societies grew up in
the agricultural regions of the world. This phase of social evolution is still an ongoing process. The last ten thousand years have
witnessed the repeated emergence of ever more powerful societies, but so far no sign of any perfected equilibrium adaptation.

Complex societies make lavish use of symbolic boundary
marking and are capable of impressive feats of cooperation, such
as road nets, irrigation systems, and, unfortunately, armies. The
tendency of ethnic identities to retain great importance in even
the most modern societies was a surprise to many social scientists
(Glazer and Moynihan 1975). But complex societies also require
(or at any rate, always have had) a substantial degree of organized
coercive control. Ethnographically known hunting and gathering
societies have only the weakest forms of leadership and little tendency for leaders to be able to lead lives of privilege at the expense
of followers. Human social instincts are certainly not adapted to
living in societies numbering in the millions, organized by elites
that establish a great social distance between themselves and ordinary citizens. The means by which ancient social instincts and
modern cultural institutions conspire to create the impressive

coordination, cooperation, and division of labor of complex societies remains to be told. We suggest that a close examination of the mechanisms will reveal a series of only partially successful workarounds of social instincts deriving from adaptation to life in much simpler, but still highly cooperative, symbolically marked groups. The post-Pleistocene social institutions of complex societies add another layer of determinants of behavior to the conflicts between the small-group altruism normally favored by selection on genes and the in-group altruism that coevolved with culture in the Pleistocene. That new layer frequently conflicts with all our innate social instincts.

Acknowledgments: We thank the organizers of the Ringberg conference, Irenäus Eibl-Eibesfeldt and Frank Salter, for the opportunity to participate in this project. Sam Boles, Sandy Harcourt, Mary Jackman, Michael McGuire, Lore Ruttan, Dan Sellen, Joseph Soltis, Jonathan Turner, and David Wilson provided most helpful comments on the manuscript. This work was supported in part by a grant from the Alfred P. Sloan Foundation

References

Alexander, R. D. (1987). *The biology of moral systems.* Aldine de Gruyter, New York.

Axelrod, R. and Hamilton, W. D. (1981). The evolution of cooperation. *Science,* **211,** 1390–6.

Barth, F. (1981). *Features of person and society in Swat: Collected essays on Pathans.* Routledge and Kegan Paul, London.

Batson, C. D. (1991). *The altruism question: Toward a social psychological answer.* Lawrence Erlbaum, Hillsdale NJ.

Bettinger, R. L. and Baumhoff, M. A. (1982). The Numic spread: Great Basin cultures in competition. *American Antiquity,* **47,** 485–503.

Bettinger, R. L. (1991). *Hunter-gatherers: Archaeological and evolutionary theory.* Plenum, New York.

Birdsell, J. B. (1968). Some predictions for the Pleistocene based on equilibrium systems of recent hunter-gatherers. In *Man the hunter* (ed. R. B. Lee and I. DeVore), pp. 229–40. Aldine, Chicago.

Borgerhoff Mulder, M. (1988). Behavioural ecology of traditional societies. *Trends in Ecology and Evolution,* **3,** 260–4.

Boyd, R. and Richerson, P. J. (1985). *Culture and the evolutionary process.* University of Chicago Press, Chicago.

———. (1987). The evolution of ethnic markers. *Cultural Anthropology,* **2,** 65–79.

———. (1988). The evolution of reciprocity in sizable groups. *Journal of Theoretical Biology,* **132,** 337–56.

———. (1989). The evolution of indirect reciprocity. *Social Networks,* **11,** 213–36.

———. (1992). Punishment allows the evolution of cooperation (or anything else) in sizable groups. *Ethology and Sociobiology,* **13,** 171–95.

Byrne, R. and Whiten, A., eds. (1988). *Machiavellian intelligence: Social expertise and the evolution of the intellect in monkeys, apes, and humans.* Oxford University Press, Oxford.

Campbell, D. T. (1983). The two distinct routes beyond kin selection to ultrasociality: Implications for the humanities and social sciences. In *The nature of prosocial development: Theories and strategies* (ed. D. Bridgeman), pp. 11–39. Academic Press, New York.

Cavalli-Sforza, L. L. and Feldman, M. W. (1981). *Cultural transmission and evolution: A quantitative approach.* Princeton University Press, Princeton.

Cosmides, L. (1989). The logic of social exchange: Has natural selection shaped human reason? Studies with the Wason selection task. *Cognition,* 31, 187–276.

Daly, M. and Wilson, M. (1988). *Homicide.* Aldine de Gruyter, New York.

Darwin, C. (1874 [1902]). *The descent of man,* 2d ed. American Home Library, New York.

de Waal, F. B. M. (1992). *Chimpanzee politics.* Jonathan Cape, London.

Dunbar, R. I. M. (1992). Neocortical size as a constraint on group size in primates. *Journal of Human Evolution,* 22, 469–93.

Durham, W. H. (1991). *Coevolution: Genes, culture, and human diversity.* Stanford University Press, Stanford.

Eibl-Eibesfeldt, I. (1982). Warfare, man's indoctrinability, and group selection. *Zeitschrift für Tierpsychologie,* 67, 177–198.

———. (1989). *Human ethology.* Aldine de Gruyter, New York.

Glazer, N. and Moynihan, D. P. (1975). *Ethnicity: Theory and experience.* Harvard University Press, Cambridge MA.

Goodall, J. (1986). *The chimpanzees of Gombe: Patterns of behavior.* Harvard University Press, Cambridge MA.

Hamilton, W. D. (1964). Genetical evolution of social behaviour I, II. *Journal of Theoretical Biology,* 7, 1–52.

———. (1975). Innate social aptitudes of man: An approach from evolutionary genetics. In *Biosocial anthropology* (ed. R. Fox), pp. 133–55. Malaby, London.

Harcourt, A. H. (1992). Cooperation in conflicts: Commonalities between humans and other animals. *Politics and the Life Sciences,* 11, 251–9.

Irons, W. (1979). Cultural and biological success. In *Evolutionary biology and human social behavior* (ed. N. A. Chagnon and W. Irons), pp. 257–72. Duxbury Press, North Scituate, MA.

Knauft, B. M. (1985). *Good company and violence: Sorcery and social action in a Lowland New Guinea society.* University of California Press, Berkeley.

———. (1987). Reconsidering violence in simple human societies: Homicide among the Gebusi of New Guinea. *Current Anthropology,* 28, 457–500.

———. (1993). *South Coast New Guinea cultures: History, comparison, dialectic.* Cambridge University Press, Cambridge.

Kummer, H., Daston, L., Gigerenzer, G., and Silk, J. (1997). The social intelligence hypothesis. In *Human by nature* (ed. P. Weingard, S. Massen, S. Mitchell, and P. Richerson), pp. 157–179. Lawrence Erlbaum, Hillsdale, NJ.

Maenchen-Helfen, O. J. (1973). *The world of the Huns.* University of California Press, Berkeley.

McGrew, W. C. (1992). *Chimpanzee material culture: Implications for human evolution.* Cambridge University Press, Cambridge.

Milgram, S. (1974). *Obedience to authority: An experimental view.* Harper and Row, New York.

Nuttin, J. M., Jr. and Beckers, A. (1975). *The illusion of attitude change: Towards a response contagion theory of persuasion*. Academic Press, London.

Olson, M. (1982). *The rise and decline of nations: Economic growth, stagflation, and social rigidities*. Yale University Press, New Haven.

Otterbein, K. F. (1968). Internal war: A cross-cultural study. *American Anthropologist*, **70**, 277–89.

Pinker, S. (1994). *The language instinct: How the mind creates language*. William Morrow, New York.

Rabbie, J. M. (1991). Determinants of instrumental intra-group cooperation. In *Cooperation and prosocial behaviour* (ed. R. A. Hinde and J. Groebel), pp. 238–62. Cambridge University Press, Cambridge.

Rappaport, R. A. (1979). *Ecology, meaning, and religion*. North Atlantic Books, Richmond, CA.

Rogers, E. M. (1983). *Diffusion of innovations*, 3d ed. Macmillan, New York.

Shepher, J. (1983). *Incest, the biosocial view*. Academic Press, New York.

Silk, J. B. (1980). Adoption and kinship in Oceania. *American Anthropologist*, **82**, 799–820.

Soltis, J., Boyd, R., and Richerson, P. J. (1995). Can group-functional behaviours evolve by cultural group selection? An empirical test. *Current Anthropology*, **36**, 437–94.

Tajfel, H., Flament, C., Billig, M. G., and Bundy, R. P. (1971). Social categorization and intergroup behaviour. *European Journal of Social Psychology*, **1**, 149–75.

Trivers, R. L. (1971). The evolution of reciprocal altruism. *Quarterly Review of Biology*, **46**, 35–57.

Turner, J. C. (1984). Social identification and psychological group formation. In *The social dimension: European developments in social psychology*, vol. 2 (ed. H. Tajfel), pp. 518–38. Cambridge University Press, Cambridge.

Westermarck, E. (1894). *The history of human marriage*. Macmillan, London.

Wiessner, P. (1983). Style and social information in Kalahari San projectile points. *American Antiquity*, **48**, 253–76.

———. (1984). Reconsidering the behavioral basis for style: A case study among the Kalahari San. *Journal of Anthropological Archaeology*, **3**, 190–234.

Wilson, D. S. and Sober, E. (1994). Reintroducing group selection to the human behavioural sciences. *Behavioral and Brain Sciences*, **17**, 585–654.

Wilson, E. O. (1975). *Sociobiology: The new synthesis*. Harvard University Press, Cambridge.

Wilson, E. O. and Hölldobler, B. (1988). Dense heterarchies and mass communication as the basis of organization in ant colonies. *Trends in Ecology and Evolution*, **3**, 65–67.

Wolf, A. P. (1970). Childhood association and sexual attraction: A further test of the Westermarck hypothesis. *American Anthropologist*, **72**, 503–15.

Yengoyan, A. A. (1968). Demographic and ecological influences on Aboriginal Australian marriage systems. In *Man the hunter* (ed. R. B. Lee and I. DeVore), pp. 185–99. Aldine, Chicago.

CHAPTER FIVE

NOTIONS OF NATURE, CULTURE, AND THE SOURCES OF INDOCTRINABILITY

Lionel Tiger

A long-standing heuristic in the social and psychological sciences, as well as in theology and common sense, is that there is a conflict between the inner, turbulent, instinctive life of human beings and the socialized arrangements that discipline and restrict the forces of raw nature. Conventional distinctions such as between nature and culture, or the painfully simple Freudian map of id, ego, and superego, or the endlessly reiterated contest between genetics and environment—all reveal one of the profound judgments human beings have made about themselves. This is that in some real sense we all suffer—either actually or potentially—from some behavioral original sin. And of course when judgments about good and evil must be made about particular behaviors or people engaged in them, it is largely thought that malign behavior or people represent the heart of darkness that is nature. At the instinctive human core is the turbulent reservoir of potential mayhem.

This is not an altogether pure conception. At least two caveats must be entered immediately. One is that when nature refers to other animals or to natural settings, it is often regarded as noble and desirable, a pastoral purity not to be violated by the actions of people. Here nature is the value, and human behavior is its defiler. (It is also interesting that often the same people committed to the protection of animal rights and the natural environment most ardently oppose assertions such as the biosocial about the impact of human evolution on contemporary behavior.) The second caveat is that there is often supposed to be great artistic and psychological value in expressing one's deep inner nature, for example in the sexual or sensual sense developed by D. H. Lawrence, Freud himself, and the actor and teacher Stanislavsky. These and other protagonists championed liberating colorful inner appetites from the restrictions of lackluster conventional society. In boisterous expressiveness lay true aesthetic honesty. Here is the common somewhat operatic theme, at least in Euro-American society, of the contest between the sharp, ardent artist and the muffled containment of bourgeois society.

Nature Is Grubby, Culture Prestigious

Nevertheless, the effective impact of the broad weight of opinion, both social-scientific and lay, is that "culture" bears the prestige and function of circumscribing "nature." In one sense this is no more than to acknowledge that children must be socialized by communities. Apart from the feral children of legend and rare fact, there is no alternative model than that the potentially intractable child by inducement and well-meaning *force majeure* is rendered fit for capable conduct of the life cycle.

This masks a strong assumption that in turn masks an important function of culture pertaining directly to indoctrinability. We can begin with the conventional meaning of the word "cultured." This is commonly thought to describe an individual capable of appreciating and participating in an elegant manner in an array of artistic, intellectual, and judgmental issues. The cultured person has an expansive and probing sense of the possibilities of human endeavor and interaction. A cultured person has explored the varieties of human experience and creativity and has somehow achieved a balanced posture of both immersion in such activity and generous judgment about their quality. A cultured person by definition suspends total consent to the ambient demands of a cultural system—he or she has "taste." Yet the person with "tasteful" culture is a vigorous proponent and consumer of it. So this meaning of culture contains both a positive judgment about it and at the same time a sense that an expert in cultural matters is somehow adept at individualist apartness, being elegantly within the culture but also able to step outside it.

How Many Exceptions Prove the Rule?

I want to make a contrary assertion about the relationship between culture and independence, within a broad biological context. This begins by adapting to social science the zoological law known as Romer's rule. Romer was one of E. O. Wilson's predecessors at the Harvard Zoological Museum, and his rule in effect claimed that the prevailing adaptive strategy of animals in response to changing conditions was to make small changes in order to avoid making large ones. So if the climate changed and a green habitat became brown, a bird could make the relatively minor adjustment of the coloration of its plumage rather than the far more demanding one of becoming terrestrial and perhaps a burrowing creature to avoid attracting the attention of predators. Similarly, humans may have adjusted with shifts in skin color that affected heat transfer at the external level rather than adjusting to climatic variations with alterations in basal body temperature, metabolic rates, and the like, which obviously involves very substantial and costly changes.

Can we not adapt Romer to social behavior? Is cultural variation the societal equivalent of the feather or skin-color response? Human groups adapt to changing conditions, either environmental or social, by altering the way they behave. The immense number of different cultural groups in the human species may reflect more the skill of the species in conforming to Romer's rule than that there are behaviorally effective genetic differences between these different groups. Given the array of habitats, climates, densities, ambient fauna, and other societies in which people are immersed, it is hardly surprising that human beings found ways to confront such diverse challenges with a variety of strategies—a variety that can be called cultural variation.

So as a first result of this story we can dispense with the most extreme environmentalist notion, which in various forms and intensities continues to characterize much thinking concerning the link between behavior and the human genotype. This is that cultural variation illustrates that the human genotype cannot and does not have effect at the level of social behavior. What my colleague Robin Fox has called "ethnographic dazzle" has frequently induced social scientists to conclude that there cannot possibly be any major genotypically linked consistency in the social behavior of our species. Surely, it is argued, "culture" is an autonomous realm, uncontaminated by primordial restrictions. Alexander

Argyros of the University of Texas has described such a view of culture as a creationist position, but one without God. Derek Freeman has described amusingly, if despairingly, his experience with American anthropologists who bitterly resented his challenge to the assertions of the paradigmatic figure Margaret Mead about the autonomy of human culture. These were in part based on her Samoan ethnography, which Freeman saw fit to revisit and fundamentally query (Freeman 1966; Caton 1990). Carl Degler has provided a sober account of the intellectual history at the root of this surprisingly fervent dialogue (Degler 1991) that Roger Masters has positioned specifically in political science (Masters 1989) and the variegated description of which is a discrete academic industry all on its own.

Destructive Deconstruction

The "culturalist" point of view, though seemingly extreme to anyone even minimally aware of the complex lessons of modern biology, has now surprisingly found a generous homestead in American social and cultural science. There, the deconstructionist perception continues to claim primacy, or at least confident respectability. It boasts the conclusion that both reality and the perception of it by those who call themselves scientists are highly conditional because science is itself a fatally flawed cultural form. At base, it is just one of the ongoing intellectual fashions. Thus self-critical linear science is a baroque folkway largely of mainly white males who sustain self-reinforcing and mutually rewarding norms of conduct, to say nothing of often guaranteed salaries. Partial explanation and even partisanship is inevitable, goes the invulnerable claim, because all persons reflect only their own biographical particularities—national, class, sexual, political, disciplinary, etc. Even the lens of the microscope shows different things to different people. Individuality is a perceptual and conceptual prison. The envelope of the self is also a fortress of inevitable prejudice in which each person's cognitive apparatus is as distinctive as his or her fingerprints—an intellectual version of fundamental Protestant individuality and responsibility. A genuine community of openly self-critical perception on which science claims it must depend is remarkably unlikely in this account. In effect, this means that even the unusually rigorous socialization (or indoctrination) of the scientist cannot overcome the radical impact of individual differences. And, perhaps most peculiarly, even the enormous power of the skills in communication of *Homo sapiens* is insufficient to overcome this central perceptual loneliness.

As if that were not defeatist enough, reality is also clouded, the earnest claim continues, by the inevitable impact of the observer on the situation observed. This is a corruption of the Heisenberg principle from which it appears to derive its intellectual ancestry. Heisenbergian effects are important to the behavior of subatomic particles, but they do not influence the behavior of larger entities, such as organisms. Apples continued to fall down while Newton was watching, but his watching did not precipitate their fall.

Such are some elements of the frail intellectual foundation of the common notion that cultural variation illustrates the absence of genotypical regulation of human behavior. Now let's turn this around in the service of our overall intellectual project. The very ubiquity of the pattern surely compels this proposition: there is something naturally human in the ability to generate variable cultural patterns. A quarter of a century ago, following Chomsky's proposal of an inherent cortical capacity to acquire human language, the universal grammar (Chomsky 1968), Robin Fox and I proposed there was a "culture acquisition device" that was the basis for the readiness with which people acquired and sought to maintain the special character of their particular group (Tiger and Fox 1971, 1987, 1998). If there could be a genotypically available mechanism for learning language—a relatively recent phylogenetic capacity—surely it was parsimonious to predicate the possibility of a similar kind of readiness for learning the more ancient forms of social interaction such as mate choice, political order, cooperative food-gathering, and socialization of the young.

Natural Culture

But why would we need such a device? The next step of my claim, which bears on indoctrinability, is that it is precisely this great intrinsic biological variability among people that necessitates some unifying capacity in order to coordinate socioeconomic, political, and military behavior. There has to be some way to link the different bits of the normal curve of variation.

In essence, a central function of cultural patterning is to reduce the inherent biological diversity among people.

For example, in appearance, choice of clothing, size, body movement, and the like, even members of very coherent cultures vary considerably. The intrinsic function of culture as a phenomenon is to limit the range of operation of a set of individuals who have inherited an extremely broad range of aptitudes, enthusiasms, and resistances. Without some restriction of these variations, coordinated social activity could become relatively problematical. For example, in what is perhaps the most sharply sculpted of cultures—military groups—a stringent dominance hierarchy, constant repetitive drill, and a set of narrowly defined procedures are necessary to ensure some coordinated and circumscribed behavior among individuals who may be otherwise able and adventurous in their privately chosen behavior (Salter 1995). The historian William O'Neill has even argued that the capacity for marching and rhythmic dancing has been central to the evolution of human organizational competence (O'Neill 1994). What is military training if not the reduction of phenotypical variety in the demanding name of cultural focus? Also, there is another form of behavior—religion—in which otherwise precarious survival is regarded as an outcome of successful coordinated action. Incoming practitioners may be subjected to a mandatory regimen involving emotional and cognitive control comparable to the physical emphasis of military training. Perhaps because of the ubiquity and political influence of claims about the sacred, there has in fact been something of a resurgence of interest in the biological elements of religious observance, such as from Irons (manuscript), Hartung (1995), Alexander (1987), Barkow et al. (1991), MacDonald (in this volume), and my own 1987 publication on the subject.

But military and religious organizations are only extreme forms of more general patterns of social coherence that emerge in human groups.

My simple point is that the culture acquisition device has evolved as a mechanism for relatively quick and reliable inculcation of social values.

Again, this is not necessarily to impose conformity for its own sake but to reduce the inherent variability of human beings given the complexity and lack of fixity of our genotypical system. In his critically helpful formulation, David Hamburg saw more than thirty years ago the poverty of the either-or conception of the links between genotype and behavior. He claimed that there are some patterns of animal and human behavior that are "easy to learn" (Hamburg 1963). This ease-of-learning hypothesis helps clarify why it is that the culture acquisition device can operate as effectively as it does. And with ease, also, it defuses the traditional confusion about the roles of genotype and ongoing experience in affecting the stream of behavior. It also begins to account for what may be considered excesses of the ease-of-learning process, in the form of moderate indoctrinability or its Orwellian extreme.

And here we are at the core of our issue: while political and other leaders may find it attractive to indoctrinate their subordinates to accept convenient pictures of the world, these subordinates are also available for the process.

Ease of learning is easily ease of indoctrinability. When the Leader speaks, the ears have it. While indoctrination may be imposed with ruthless cynicism, it is met halfway by human beings prepared by the natural evolution of cultural skill to accept and join the glistening ambient social scheme in which they find themselves. This may after all be the only world they know or can share or envisage. And while indoctrination may deprive a person of an ample portion of human and political rights, membership in a community with beliefs, rights, and obligations may also be a human right to enjoy. Presumably, this is why solitary confinement is usually a punishment, not a reward.

Biological Radicals

I want to turn now to examples of the evasion of the central tendencies of culture, in the form of radicalism, free speech, academic freedom, and the like.

My colleague Irving Louis Horowitz, in an anguished review of the sharp limits on free thought in the world, notes that in no more than twenty communities are there genuine principles of academic freedom which reliably operate to protect individuals who challenge existing notions of reality and human possibility (Horowitz 1995). Perhaps they challenge the comforting certainties of the world as Galileo did; or perhaps they envisage utopian communities that threaten the stability of society, such as the Shakers, or messiah-ridden cults like the one at Waco, Texas, or countless others in recorded knowledge. One of my first senior colleagues, the sociologist Kaspar Naegele of the University of British Columbia, said, "The clearing is very small." He meant that the room for maneuver of genuinely free thinkers was very restricted. These souls must confront a potent combination of the culture acquisition device alloyed with the earnest enthusiasm of those in power to use it. And this can and does make working life difficult for those who question the foundations of the community or even specific features of its operation.

This becomes extreme in wartime when those who question the leadership can be viewed as traitors. But it is obvious at other times, too, especially when insecure political or military leaders concoct or exaggerate outside threats the better to restrict opportunities for internal challenge to their world-view and maintenance of power. The flag becomes a blanket on free speech and contemplation. The use of the in-group/out-group distinction to cement internal systems of control is universal and a relatively obvious and reliable mechanism. It is as common as it is because it mobilizes and depends on a biosubstrate that is itself at the heart of the process of social organization and the conduct of politics. Perhaps also pertinent here is Colin Irwin's observation that it is characteristically difficult for people to learn foreign languages without an accent after puberty—a biogenic disability that he has suggested is related to the need of persons choosing mates and their kinfolk to be able to identify legitimate members of their community, not interlopers and impostors (Irwin 1990).

So even at the level of language acquisition, it is possible there are some ongoing controls over the distinction between in-group and out-group. This reflects the power of indoctrination to maintain existing structures and threaten outsiders. It is also useful in parsing the power and nature of indoctrination to consider the links between politics and exogamy; "sleeping with the enemy" is obviously a reproductive version of the political traitor. A striking biomilitary innovation was unveiled in the Balkan struggle of the mid-1990s when captive women were raped and then held prisoner beyond the availability of abortion so that they would be compelled to bear the offspring of enemy males. This graphically parsimonious strategy is presumably cousin to less dramatic techniques of group assertion.

The Effects of Pseudospeciation

It is thirty years now since Erik Erikson reflected on his concept of "pseudospeciation" at that pivotal meeting on ritualization which Julian Huxley organized at the Zoological Society of London in 1965. In effect, Erikson suggested that humans were capable of defining members of hostile or foreign groups as other species

(Erikson 1966). Hence, they could be subject to predation rather than aggression—a distinction commonly observed, for example, in the detailed neurophysiological studies of feline behavior. Through symbolic management, people can redirect emotional energies of intrahuman conflict into those available for prey animals. This is important for a hunter-gatherer for whom human enemies are much more easily and efficiently damaged or liquidated if they are defined as impersonal, nonhuman prey. New and improved tutorial methods to accomplish this translation have been recently described by the American army officer David Grossman (Grossman 1995). An informal study of death cries in wartime children's comic books that I conducted sometime after the ritualization conference reveals that characteristic death calls and other vocalizations differed between opposing sides, more or less as if they were different species (Tiger 1969/1987).

These mechanisms are, broadly speaking, the work of the higher cortical and symbolic faculties, those most proudly reflected in the diagnostic *sapiens* humans have applied to themselves. They are not mainly or even partly the result of endocrinological or other similarly primordial secretions, though as Kemper (1990) among others has shown, secretions such as testosterone may affect thought and behavior as literally as alcohol or other substances. Rather, the organic system responsible for the *sapiens* element of our self-description is the enabling facility. It is the capacity for cultural denotation and symbolic sorting of people into groups that underlies hostilities. The contrast between the complexity and subtlety of notions of free speech and academic freedom with the behavior in the Balkans or the sudden murderousness of the Rwandans suggests which behavioral system is the easiest to learn, particularly when social and economic pressures escalate.

An Irish ambassador to the UN once too whimsically noted: "The most dangerous place in the world is under men's hats." Here is a serious proposal that requires inspection from natural scientists.

References

Alexander, R. (1987). *The biology of moral systems*. Aldine de Gruyter, Hawthorne, NY.

Barkow, J., Cosmides, L., and Tooby, J. (1991). *The adapted mind: Evolutionary psychology and the generation of culture*. Oxford University Press, Oxford.

Caton, H. P. (1990). *The Samoa reader: Anthropologists take stock*. University Press of America, Lanham, MD.

Chomsky, N. (1968). *Language and mind.* Harcourt, Brace and World, New York.

Degler, C. (1991). *In search of human nature.* Oxford University Press, Oxford.

Erikson, E. (1966). Ontogeny of ritualization in man. Philosophical Transactions of the Royal Society of London, **B251**, 337–49.

Freeman, D. (1966). The debate, at heart, is about evolution. In *The certainty of doubt: Tributes to Peter Munz* (ed. M. Fairburn and W. H. Oliver). Victoria University Press, Wellington.

Grossman, Lt. Col. D. (1995). *On killing: The psychological cost of learning to kill in war and society.* Little, Brown, New York.

Hamburg, D. (1963). Emotions in perspective of human evolution. In *Expression of the emotions in man* (ed. P. Knapp). International Universities Press, New York.

Hartung, J. (1995). Love thy neighbor: The evolution of in-group morality, *Skeptic*, **3**, 4.

Horowitz, I. L. (1995). Social science as a calling. Scanticon Center, Princeton, NJ, September 23.

Irons, W. (1995). Morality, religion, and human evolution. In *Building bridges between theology and the natural sciences* (ed. W. Mark Richardson and Wesley Wildman). Manuscript.

Irwin, C. (1990). Conference on the sociobiology of conflict, European Sociobiological Society, Jerusalem, 1987. Cognate paper published in *Sociobiology and conflict* (ed. J. van der Dennen and V. Falger). Chapman and Hall, London.

Kemper, T. D. (1990). *Social structure and testosterone.* Rutgers University Press, New Brunswick, NJ.

Masters, R. (1989). *The nature of politics.* Yale University Press, New Haven.

O'Neill, W. (1994). Plenary address. Human Behaviour and Evolution Society Meeting, Ann Arbor, June.

Salter, F. K. (1995) *Emotions in command. A naturalistic study of institutional dominance.* Oxford University Press, Oxford.

Tiger, L. (1969/1987). *Men in groups.* Random House, New York; Marion Boyars, New York and London.

———. (1987/1989). *The manufacture of evil: Ethics, evolution, and the industrial system.* Harper & Row, New York; Marion Boyars, London and New York.

Tiger, L. and Fox, R. (1971, 1987, 1998). *The imperial animal.* Holt, Rinehart and Winston, New York: Holt, New York: Transaction Press, New Brunswick, NJ & London.

PART II

❧

TRADITIONAL CULTURES

CHAPTER SIX

INDOCTRINATION AMONG THE EIPO OF THE HIGHLANDS OF WEST-NEW GUINEA

Wulf Schiefenhövel

Introduction

Introspection, not the worst way to form hypotheses about psychological mechanisms in ourselves, can tell us something about indoctrination's power—how we, as children and juveniles, are influenced by doctrines. Ideologies received from our parents, teachers, and peers are potent mixtures of beliefs and deep emotions. It seems that our physiology has at its disposal specific reward mechanisms reinforcing such ideologies in certain contexts (see McGuire, this volume). Take, for example, the beliefs and rituals developed by the Catholic Church. Blending the sacred and the inexplicable, the congregation's synchronicity in movements, praying, singing, and feeling—all enhanced by the limbically powerful smell of incense—might move one to tears. A similar reaction might attend the hearing of a heroic story, preferably one of sad or tragic love or of true friendship and loyalty that does not flinch even at the threat of death.

I remember well how my reward physiology reacted to being accepted by whom I believed was an important leader figure and to the feeling of being united in thought and action—as an altar boy and as a participant in a student's protest trying to wake up the sleepy city of Erlangen in Franconia to political awareness.

We know very little about the presumably neurobiological mechanisms involved; some critics of evolutionary biology may claim that such mechanisms do not exist at all or that present knowledge does not justify assuming their existence a priori—or that if they do exist, they are brought about by early and later socialization. Indeed, much research is still needed to obtain solid knowledge of how indoctrination works. In this paper I shall focus on the phenomenology of indoctrinating actions and on their possible functions, especially with regard to gender differences, an aspect of moral behavior, male martial powers, and ethnicity. The analysis will be based on two years of fieldwork among the Eipo, a group of mountain Papuans in Irian Jaya, an Indonesian province making up the western half of the island of New Guinea.

At the time we began our research in June 1974, the Eipo had rarely met foreigners and still lived in the traditional way, that is to say, in a manner very similar to neolithic conditions. This was the case not only in the material sense of tools made of stone, bone, and wood, and a mixed subsistence strategy combining simple digging-stick horticulture with collecting and hunting, but, most importantly, with a social life in small, tightly knit communities. The Eipo, in my view, can be seen as "modern models of the past"; how indoctrination functions in their primordial society should be close to the basic mechanism by which specific thoughts are transferred into the brains of a whole community or a demographic group.

The Eipo, Modern Models of the Past

The Eipo and their neighbors of the Mek family of languages and cultures live in the Daerah Jayawijaya region. The term "Mek" (water, river) was introduced to designate the rather uniform languages and cultural traditions in this area (Schiefenhövel 1976). The culture and behavior of the Eipo are here described in the past tense, as a number of (mostly mission-induced) changes have occurred since our fieldwork began (1974–80). Despite this caveat, many of the data and observations could be replicated today.

The Eipo proper inhabit approximately 150 square kilometers in the southernmost (upper) section of the Eipomek valley in a mountainous-to-alpine region at altitudes between 1,600 and 2,300 m above sea level, just north of the central mountain range (see Map 6.1). The lowest passes through this impressive mountain range are about 3,700 m high, yet they were frequently crossed by the Eipo and by their trade and marriage partners. The inhabited sections of the valleys are mostly steeply incised. Anthropogenic grassland (secondary vegetation) was found in a circle around the villages. Rain forest existed between the garden areas and, exclusively, on the mountains above approximately 2,400 m. In 1976 two severe earthquakes destroyed large areas of garden land and some villages. A number of inhabitants were killed or injured. It is likely that similar catastrophes have occurred in the past.

The Eipo proper numbered close to 800 people in 1980; the Mek may be estimated to range between 20–25,000. Indications are that the population is growing. The activities of a fundamentalist Christian mission (UFM), which started work in 1976, have contributed to this, particularly their banning of female infanticide (Schiefenhövel 1988), as has the periodical availability of modern medicine.

The Eipo language (Heeschen 1978; Heeschen and Schiefenhövel 1983) is one of the Mek languages and thereby belongs to the large phylum of Papuan languages spoken by the old population of New Guinea, whose members arrived on the shores of this island about 50,000 years ago. As in the other areas of this region

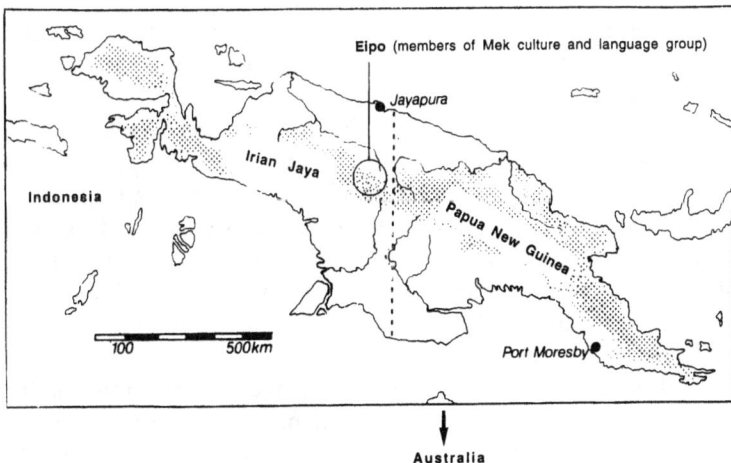

Map 6.1 *New Guinea is divided into independent Papua New Guinea and the Indonesian province Irian Jaya.*

of the highlands, no archaeological data are available for the Mek region. Ethnohistoric surveys are missing as well. It is, however, probable that parts of the Mek area, like those of comparable areas in Papua New Guinea, have been inhabited for more than 10,000 years. Comparison of religious beliefs indicates that important concepts (e.g., that of a mythical ancestral creator) have traveled from east to west. To date it is unknown at which time the sweet potato (*Ipomoea batatas*) was introduced, though this probably occurred between 200 and 300 years ago. Going by the significance of taro (*Colocasia esculenta*) in ceremonial-religious contexts, one can conclude that this crop was central in pre-Ipomoean times.

The first known contact between outsiders and a group of Mek people was made early in this century by a team of Dutch survey-ors who met some people near Mount Goliath at the southern edge of the central mountain range, far away from the home of the Eipo (de Kock 1912). Members of an interdisciplinary German research team of which I was a member conducted research in the Eipo valley and some adjacent areas mainly between 1974 and 1980.

The villages of the Eipo and their neighbors in the Mek area were usually built on spots that facilitated defense. They had between 30 and 250 inhabitants. One or more men's houses (*yoek aik*, see below), which often had sacred functions, occupied conspicuous places, either in the center or at the end of the village. The women's seclusion houses (*barye eik*, see below) were usually situated at the periphery of the village. The much smaller and less well-built family houses were the places of family-centered activities.

Descent was patrilineal. The origin of the clans was dated back to mythical times. Animals, sun, or moon were the respective fore-fathers and were worshipped as totems. Patriclans and patrilin-eages were exogamous, a rule that was strictly adhered to, even when choosing premarital or extramarital lovers. Consanguinal and affinal ties were the all important bases for most bonds and transactions. Children knew surprisingly many details of the intri-cate kinship network.

With increasing complexity and decreasing consanguinality, the following social levels existed: nuclear family, extended family, lineage/clan, men's house community, village, and politi-cal alliance of a number of villages. Loyalty was usually high among members of the same clan/lineage. Men's house communities, led by specific clans but consisting of members of several clans, played an important role as units of work and political decision-making.

On the basis of their intellectual, oratorical, social, and physical skills, "Big men" or "Great men" (as Godelier 1982 and others name them; the Eipo term is *sisinang*) led the village communities as persons who took initiatives and pursued plans. They also respected rules and traditions while using them to their own advantage. Men who took the role of war leader (*mal deyenang*, see below) were particularly respected. In this protomeritocracy, leadership was dependent on the actual power of the leader; persons who showed signs of losing competence lost their positions, too.

"Big men" exercised a certain amount of social control, but more important was the process of enforcing social norms through public opinion, which, in turn, was shaped by gossip and the discussion of disputed issues and, particularly, through belief in extrahuman powers, such as harmful spirits in nature or "black magic," the latter allegedly performed by female or male "witches" (see below). In this way, disease functioned as punishment for social wrongdoing and, thereby, as an executive power.

The visible world was also thought to be inhabited by numerous beings—souls of the deceased, zoomorphic spirits of the forests, and rivers, and powerful shapers of nature or bringers of culture who since mythical times had influenced people's lives. Yaleenye ("the one coming from the East") was the most prominent such cultural hero. In the sacred men's houses these mythical powers, symbolized by holy relics, were housed and honored. Various ceremonies pervading everyday life were performed to ensure the well-being of humans, domestic animals, and crops.

The first and most important initiation (*kwit*) of boys between approximately 4 and 15 years of age was a major event, involving participants from other valleys. It was held at intervals of about 10 years, depending on how many boys were available for this costly ceremony. Coinitiates kept a lifelong bond, addressing each other with a special term (*kwitnang*) and rallying for mutual support. Second and third stages were the bestowing of the cane waistband and penis gourd, and the *mum*, the typical male back decoration hanging down from the head.

Large, opulent ceremonial dance feasts for visitors strengthened ties, particularly with trade and marriage partners from the southern side of the mountains. Rare grand ceremonies, bringing together inhabitants from distant, sometimes inimical valleys,

were held to ensure the fertility of the soil; their inherent potential
to transcend ethnic boundaries, which were, at normal times,
solidified by we-group indoctrination, can be seen as a weak
counterforce to those mechanisms leading to the small-scale ethnicity that is so typical for New Guinea.

Gender Indoctrination

The culture of the Eipo was characterized by marked gender differences, even antagonism. Eipo males wore, after their second
initiation as adolescents, a belt (*deyatenga*) made of spliced rattan
fibers wound tightly around the waist. They also wore a conspicuous penis gourd (*sanyum*) held in place by a string looped
around the scrotum and a waist string attached to the tip of the
calabash holding it permanently in a quasi-erect position. The rattan belt compressed the lower abdomen, thus causing the width of
the shoulders to appear bigger (Fig. 6.1). Girls and women, in contrast, wore small grass skirts that accentuated the roundish

Fig. 6.1 *Eipo men, especially when*
they are younger, wear tightly wound
rattan belts. Their stated ideal is to
have a small waist and broad shoulders
(photo by Schiefenhövel 75/244/8).

Fig. 6.2 *Eipo women wear short,*
bushy grass skirts giving more volume
to the middle of their bodies (photo by
Schiefenhövel 74/78/8).

appearance of the pelvic region (Fig. 6.2). Male and female shapes among the Eipo can thus be seen as a triangle standing on the apex (broad shoulders, small waist) for men, versus one resting on its base (waist broader than shoulders) for women, as has been described by E. Jessen for European and African cultures (1981). Even from a distance, men and women were unmistakably different in appearance, and this outward difference was reflected in more symbolic realms of their culture as well.

The penis gourd can best be understood as a "frozen dominance erection" that has phylogenetic precursors in some infrahuman primates (Wickler 1966; Eibl-Eibesfeldt and Wickler 1968). The phallocrypts can thus be interpreted as cultural signs of the martial prowess of their bearers and of male supremacy in general.

The Eipo and other Papuan cultures further enhanced the differences between women and men through social institutions such as men's and women's houses, male initiation, gender-specific work tasks, and food taboos, as well as the mythically founded fear of men vis-à-vis the vagina with its fluids and female sexuality in general. To come in contact with menstrual blood was seen as extremely dangerous for males in the Eipo society as well as in many other highland groups. Men declined to sit on a piece of timber we had fastened to our house so that the medical and dental patients could be seated. They said that women had sat there before and that they would thus be harmed by the forces emanating from vulva and vagina. An empty rice bag placed over the seat and reserved strictly for males solved the problem.

Whereas girls and boys of all societies clearly identify with members of their own sex (cp. Skrzipek 1983), which can be seen as a biopsychological basis for intragender group formation and solidarity, cultures have considerable leeway in constructing gender relationships. The Eipo and many Papuan cultures go, as it were, back in phylogenetic time and create, through phallocrypts versus grass skirts, female versus male worlds, a cultural parallel to the marked sexual dimorphism which was typical for our Australopithecine ancestors, where males were up to double the size of females. In this sense then, the Eipo-type gender indoctrination produces a very archaic concept of male and female as basically two different entities, which cooperate in production and reproduction but which are also separated by clear boundaries.

Boys were separated from their mothers in order to be transformed into real men. The Eipo felt that while boys had to be shaped into real men through exposure to male culture, girls could become women and mothers by just growing up naturally. This antithesis is possibly true for all Papuan cultures and seems to be missing in the (more "modern") Austronesian cultures (Schiefenhövel 1992). In the men's house, boys, male juveniles, and unmarried men had their place and often spent the nights there, in the circle of other male members fanned out around the fire. Here, boys and male adolescents watched adult men perform the functions of the *sisinang*, the ones who had a say in society. In the men's house they witnessed the intricate, skillful, and some-

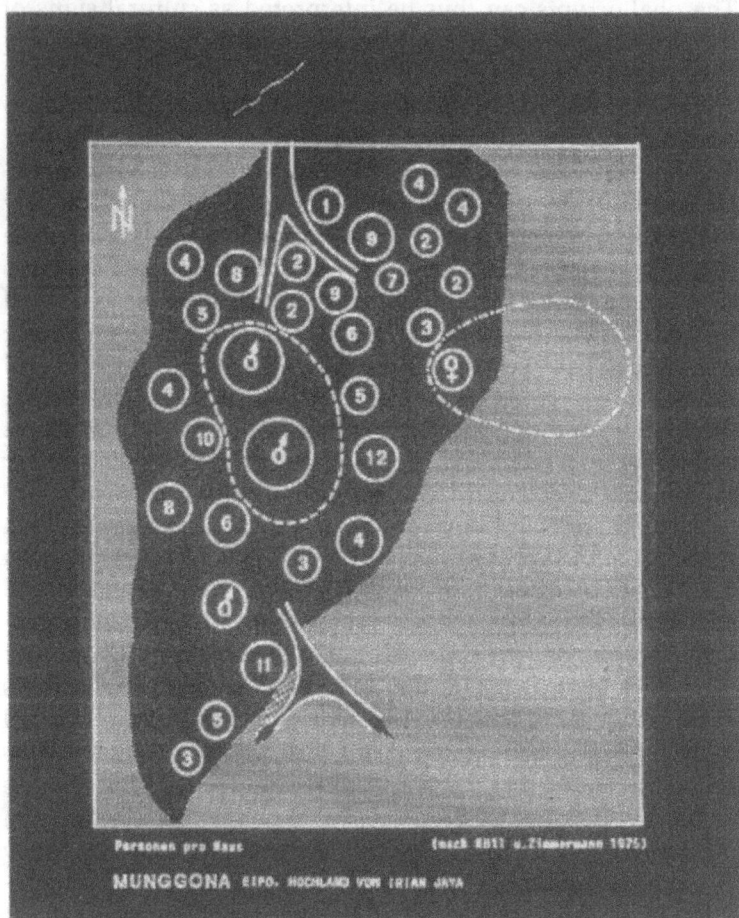

Map 6.2 *Map of the village of Munggona with male and female sector (adapted from Röll and Zimmermann).*

times daring schemes to host large feasts for allied villages or to conduct prominent religious ceremonies.

Women had a *pendant* to the men's house, the *barye aik*, a house, usually at the fringe of the village, where they spent the days of their menstrual cycle, and where, assisted by other women, they gave birth and spent the *puerperium*. They could also stay here when they were very sick or when they had serious disagreements with their husbands. Men were not allowed to enter the women's house, except in cases when they were called to conduct, as mediators to the extrahuman world, religious-therapeutic rites to help parturients in difficult childbirth. Access to the men's house and the sacred village ground around it was taboo for women; the latter was, however, used by both men and women during the ritual dances (*mote*). The division of Eipo society into female and male sectors also becomes quite evident through the ground plan of their villages (see Map 6.2). Why the Papuan gender concept has to be backed up by such strong sexual and gender antagonism and corresponding indoctrination remains an open question. Other traditional cultures and modern northern cultures have different strategies. In the matrilineal society of the Trobriand islanders (Malinowski 1922; 1929; 1935; Weiner 1976; Bell-Krannhals 1990), the biological difference between women and men is diminished, e.g., through a kind of "unisex" dress for certain dances connected to the *milamala* harvest ceremonies and through close contact of the sexes in everyday life. Also, Trobriand men do not harbor, as do men in Papuan societies, the horror of menstrual blood and other vaginal fluids as possibly fatally harmful substances. Trobriand women perform a socially and politically important ceremony connected to the chain of mortuary rites (*sagali*)—the exchange of banana fiber skirts (*doba*), which takes place on the village ground and where men are bystanders, impressed by this demonstration of female industriousness, social skill, and personal power. Girls in Austronesian Trobriand society are indoctrinated to be, as is true for Papuan societies, caring givers of and providers for life, but they are also encouraged to excel in the sociopolitical arena. In Papuan cultures this is an aspiration reserved only for males.

Morality Indoctrination

While there was some degree of fair play and ritualization in intra-alliance fights, and even in warfare against an external enemy (see below), the torturing and killing of "witches" of either sex and the behavior towards their corpses was characterized by outright brutality and an almost total absence of empathic feelings. One such event was documented (Fig. 6.3).

Gumgum, a man of the Munggona village, was left by his wife who returned to her native village of Moknerkon when their son was about two to three years old. This boy died. His death was immediately attributed to "black magic" (kire) assumed to have come from Moknerkon. Burang, a woman born in a village quite far in the northwest of the central Eipo area and widowed in Moknerkon, came to visit the central village Munggona one day. At the same time, a man of Moknerkon who was believed to have the power of a seer (asing ketenenang) came to Gumgum and told him that he had found in the house of Burang a bundle hanging

Fig. 6.3 This woman was killed and her corpse was dragged to a stream because she was believed to have caused the death of a child through "black magic" (photo by Schiefenhövel 76/39/28).

over her fireplace, that he knew it contained food remains of Gumgum's dead boy, and that this bundle was therefore a magic bundle (*kirto*) used to inflict harm and death to people. He handed over this corpus delicti. The verdict was thus spoken. Gumgum shot Burang near the women's house. The body of the dead woman was dragged to the river, stoned, and shot at. Many of the participants were apparently highly aroused, even on the second day, when the brutal acts against the corpse continued. A few, mostly female, spectators showed concern in their faces and did not take part in the physical or verbal attacks. But the other villagers, including children, seemingly enjoyed being part of the scene.

It was obvious that Burang had no support in Moknerkon where she had been married. Her eldest but still juvenile son symbolically shot some arrows towards Munggona village; nobody attempted revenge against her killers. The opposite would have been the case if she had had strong and influential male relatives. In my view, Burang was sacrificed by the people of Moknerkon in order to make peace again with the powerful village of Munggona, whose inhabitants had blamed Moknerkon for the boy's death.

I had recorded reports of brutal torturing and killing of "witches" before but had tended to see them as gross exaggerations. What we witnessed after the death of Burang (Dieter Heunemann documented this on film) was shocking for us who knew the Eipo as spontaneous and at times aggressive, but not as people who would behave in such a seemingly unnecessary, brutal manner. Knauft (1985), in his account of "good company and violence" among the Gebusi, lowland Papuans in Papua New Guinea, has described similar behaviors towards "sorcerers" who had been "convicted."

This form of violence is relevant to the present chapter for the following reason. The Eipo knew that their lives were in almost constant danger. An arrow sent from the bow of an enemy or a covillager could carry death, as did the many, basically noncontrollable superhuman forces of nature. These threats could even enter the inner sphere of one's house. One such threat was that of being harmed or killed by a human "witch" or "sorcerer," who was believed to have the power of inflicting disease and death through kire. The reasons for this dreaded act were basically twofold. Either the person in command of *kire* bore a grudge against his or her victim, or somebody paid the "sorcerer" to punish somebody in this way. The process involved what is termed magic of personal leavings: the "sorcerer" secures, clandestinely, something of the body of the future victim, whether discarded food, cut-off hair or fingernails, feces, sperm, or menstrual blood. The "magic," involving the heat of fire and sacred formulae, was performed, pars pro toto, on these substances.

Whereas disease and death thought to be sent by the ancestors or, more often, by some of the powerful spirits of nature were usually accepted fatalistically as retaliation for some social or religious wrongdoing, the Eipo deemed the act of *kire* as particularly horrible. The "witch" had placed himself or herself outside the solidarity of normal life. That is why they, once found out (usually by some form of divination, cp. Knauft 1985) were tortured and killed with so much brutality by the relatives of the deceased. One can perhaps best describe the motivational background for these kinds of acts as "moralistic aggression" (Trivers 1971).

Morality is essential to every culture because it enhances, through its religiously founded norms and rules, uniformity of behavior, predictability of actions, "we-feeling," and other elements that are important in the competition of cultural groups with each other.

The example of what one Eipo village did to a suspected "witch" shows that they were particularly adamant in this area of moral behavior: humans should not send, via "black magic," disease and death to other humans. That is the message of the brutal killing and treatment of the corpses of "witches." One can see these spectacular public events of moralistic aggression as a culturally interesting form of indoctrination. Its function seems to be to ensure that life is not threatened more than it already is and that people should not become the source of harmful magic. The message of the savage sanctions could be described as "See what we do with persons who stand outside the rules of our lives and who send *kire*! They will be pursued, tortured, and killed without mercy."

Tragically, the persons who were accused of having performed *kire* were, most likely, perfectly innocent, even in the emic sense. I have never heard of anybody who boasted to have *kire* powers (as is not uncommon in other parts of Melanesia); that would, in light of the sanctions, be rather suicidal. It seems that these unfortunate women and men became victims of political plots. Fabricated accusation and indoctrination go hand in hand, from Stone Age society to the present.

Warrior Indoctrination

Despite the fact that the Eipo were usually friendly and controlled, the potential for aggressive acts was quite high and did not need much triggering. In both intra-alliance fights and interalliance warfare, approximately 3 persons per 1,000 inhabitants died of violence per year during the time of our documentation; every fourth male was likely to be killed rather than to die of natural or accidental causes (Table 6.1).

Ethnosemantically, the Eipo distinguished two major forms of aggressive encounter (Table 6.2). *Intragroup aggression* (*abala*, "fight") was that type of confrontation resulting from often trivial disagreements between persons in one village or between members of different but friendly and allied villages. Verbal quarrels, physical attacks, including the use of sticks, stone adzes, and the like, and (exclusively by males) shooting arrows were the usual stages of escalation. In one case, three warriors died because one man thought his dog had been killed by a man from a neighboring village. *Intergroup aggression* (*male fey bin*, literally: to go around having one's bow pulled; also called *ise mal*, literally: the arrow of the spirits—"warfare") in this case involved enemies who were, apparently since time immemorial, the inhabitants of a number of villages in the valley of the Fa river, two to three hours walk west of the valley of the Eipo river. Ceremonial cannibalism was occa-

Table 6.1. Homicide Rate Compared to All Deaths per Year in Some Papuan Cultures

	Women	**Men**	**Total**
Eipo			
Deaths	8	17	25
Homicide	1 (13%)	4 (24%)	5 (20%)
(Observed cases)			3/1000/year
Gebusi			
(Knauft 1985)			
Homicide	(29%)	(35%)	(32%)
(Anamnestic data)			7/1000/year
Nalumin			
(Bercovitch 1989)			1/1000/year
Kunimaipa (McArthur 1971)			5/1000/year
Etoro (Kelly n.d.)			
10/1000/year			

sionally involved, reflecting the hatred and violence directed against the enemy.

How important it was that a man did not diverge too much from the image of a reliable, good fighter is illustrated by a story capturing an incident that happened while we were in the Eipomek valley and that was recorded by V. Heeschen (1990, pp. 208–10; summary of the narrative, translation of the quoted passages into English and additions in brackets by W. Sch.).

Ningke, Mangat and Babum were in a garden digging out sweet potatoes. Ningke and Babum were filling them into string bags while Mangat went down to the *Min*-stream to look for something. He discovered a group of enemies from Marikla and warned Ningke and Babum. The enemies shot at Mangat who was closest to them and wounded him with five arrows [Mangat was severely injured and suffered an almost complete pneumothorax, i.e. collapse of both lungs; he showed no signs of panic, however, received traditional religious plus modern medical treatment and survived]. Ningke fought back shooting at the Marikla men. Babum hid in the grass, keeping still so that the enemy did not dis-

Table 6.2. Concepts of Aggression Among the Eipo, Highland West-New Guinea

	Abala (fight)	*Ise Mal* (war)
Type	intragroup/interkin	intergroup
Constellation	changing	"hereditary" enemy
Cause	spontaneous/individual	spontaneous/historic
Participants	small groups	villages, alliances
Duration	days to months	months to years
Ritualization	high	medium
Indoctrination	none	marked, dehumanizing
Truce	yes	no (?)
Homicide rate	1–2/1000/year	1–2/1000/year
Reaction to death of opponents	feeling of success, sometimes regret	triumph, official dance feast
Cannibalism	none	in certain cases
Mortuary rites	normal exposure in tree	ditto, if no prior cannibalism
Termination	peace treaty, usually lasting	peace treaty, temporary
Function	"residue" of human aggression in akephalic societies	indoctrination-enhanced aggression = motor for cultural pseudospeciation

cover him. When the men from Marikla had left, Babum shouted: "Damn it! They were shooting at us and have tried to kill us!"...

When Mangat had been brought to the village [Fig. 6.4] and a group of warriors had unsuccessfully tried to follow the men from Marikla to take revenge, the Eipo men said: "We are coming back with Babum but he hid out of fear ... and when he claims that we were fighting back together, then he is lying. He is a woman through and through because he hid in the grass. He is no man."... And to Babum they said: "You went with your cuirass {Babum was the only one wearing this rather effective protection made of rattan}. For what then did you go out there with your cuirass on? To wound an *orong* lizard or a *bal* lizard or to wound a grasshopper? That you took your bow, that you already compared yourself with somebody who shouts 'We would fight, oh, could we just fight!' Did you behave this way so that the women would see you? Did you put your cuirass on because of this?...

"We have Mangat lying here, whom they have riddled with arrows. You are not one of those who take a bow. A small children's bow you have and because you have not learned to do something proper with it you hide in the grass. Because you are a woman you are behaving this way. Because you have the soul of a ghost, because you have your heart only for yourself, because you are of a different kind your friends

Fig. 6.4 *The man in the foreground was ambushed by a group of enemies and hit by eight arrows. The man sitting behind him hid in the deep grass during the attack. Back in the village he was violently attacked for not having defended his friend (photo by Schiefenhövel 75/237/33).*

Fig. 6.5 *Boys shooting arrows into a rolling target. To be a good marksman is a male ideal (photo by Schiefenhövel 74/68/3).*

were about to hit you … You squatted there deep in the grass. You need only have shown yourself fighting and retreating from the enemy. For the two others had no cuirass but the same skin as you. They are your people. But while they were moving and trying to flee you were hiding. In the meantime your friend was shooting arrows against the enemy. If you two, Ningke and you Babum had done something together, had moved aiming and shooting, then the enemy would have retreated. The whole thing happened only because you are a woman." Babum kept silent.

This story will probably be told for many generations to come, despite the fact that the Eipo enjoy, for the time being, a kind of *pax christiana*. The indoctrinating power of this report of an actual event and other such accounts is strong and long-lasting. Babum, who was, incidentally, unmarried, certainly did not figure as a role model for the boys and juveniles.

Living with the Eipo it was evident how highly martial qualities in men were valued. Boys, as soon as their socialization shifted from the family to the peer group, i.e., at an age of 3 to 4 years, trained to be good marksmen (Fig. 6.5) and engaged in long and enthusiastically fought war games, either throwing the rather solid stalks of high *Mischanthum floridulum* grass at each other or shooting at opponents with blunt, but still dangerous, arrows. A number of male juveniles and adults had only one eye because of this sort of warrior socialization. But no parent ever attempted to stop their boys from getting involved in these games. On the contrary, going to or coming from the gardens they often stopped to watch their offspring attacking and ducking in the grassland around the village. Their commentaries featured praise for the brave and admonishment for the less accomplished.

The man who started an armed conflict involving at least several fighters on each side and lasting for weeks or months was called *mal deyenang*, the one who is at the base of the arrow, the war leader. All people killed on the side of the enemy were attributed to him because he was responsible for the outbreak of violence and for the consequences, including having to make compensatory payments for killed allies.

This institution of a formally responsible war leader had basically two effects. First, it reduced the likelihood of individual revenge, the natural outcome should a marksman whose arrow had actually killed somebody be known, which was often the case. Secondly, it enhanced the fame of the *mal deyenang*; the more successfully his war raged, the more frequently his name was mentioned. Personal revenge against him was not so easy to achieve for the enemy because the *mal deyenang* was usually a very powerful, martially skilled man who had enough male relatives to protect him.

It should be noted that Babyal, the leader of the Eipo in the renewed war against their enemy in the Famek valley, was not only a muscular, physically very powerful man, but also very intelligent and personable, combining sensitivity, accomplished social skills, and concern for others. War leaders in these primordial, akephalic communities cannot be criminals with nothing but great lust for murder. If they are not backed by the community, all their martial aspirations lead to nothing.

Eipo war leaders were not necessarily men with successful polygynous marriages. That seemed to depend more on other qualities, particularly that of diplomatic skill, since it was seemingly difficult to control two potentially antagonistic wives plus their families. It remains uncertain, then, whether being a great Eipo warrior yielded a bonus in inclusive fitness (as was described for the Yanomami by Chagnon 1968), but it is still true that there was a high social bonus for being a good and brave fighter, and it is perfectly plausible that being a powerful and skillful warrior could have helped in getting attention from women. At least that is probably what most Eipo men believed. Knauft (1990) has presented a theoretical discussion of the various elements and motors of Papuan warfare that sheds light on the intriguing question of why the men in these societies were so martial and why they conducted so many fights and wars.

Indoctrination towards warriorhood in Eipo society is intrinsically linked to the perception that one's own community is in danger of being attacked by the enemy; as a matter of fact, taking the lead in warfare against these "others" provided powerful identity to one's own group. Ethnicity is thus strongly stressed in the small-scale Papuan societies. Among all types of indoctrination, that directed to the maintenance of group differences was possibly the most intense—perhaps because the objective differences between the Eipo and their enemies were, in fact, very small.

Ethnicity Indoctrination

In 1974 a man of Munggona, the central village of the Eipomek valley, was killed by men of the Famek valley. The war that had been dormant for some time started anew. The motivation was akin to that which led Menelaus and Agamemnon to attack Troy. The Eipo Helen was a widow, a 28-year-old vital woman (Fig. 6.6) who had fallen in love with a man from the enemy valley and moved to his village. Her two brothers, Babyal (see above) and Irim, both in the prime of life, did not tolerate their sister's elopement and took her back to Munggona. The men in the Famek valley were enraged and renewed the war, which lasted for almost one year.

Several men on both sides were killed. One of the warriors from Munggona, Basing, was eaten by the enemy in the typical ceremonial act of cannibalism (for oral accounts of such occurrences see Heeschen 1990). The emic rationale for eating a person is neither hunger for protein nor the incorporation of the strength or spirit of the dead person. My informant Kwengkweng expressed it like this: "We so much hate the enemy that we eat one of them in case we can carry his body to our village. When we eat him, we destroy him completely; nothing will be left of him. That is why we eat people." Cannibalism, in its spectacular violation of ordinary human behavior (this is also the view of the Eipo themselves) is thus another tool of indoctrination towards ethnicity.

During the year of warfare, in which seven warriors on both sides were killed, some behaviors changed markedly. Whereas it

Fig. 6.6 *Oleto, the Eipo woman in the foreground, was a young widow. She had an affair with a man from the enemy Fa group and went to stay with him in his village. Her brothers took her back, thereby rekindling the war between the two groups—Helen of Troy in neolithic New Guinea (photo by Schiefenhövel 76/17/23).*

was quite acceptable to talk about the people in the Famek valley in normal times, my interaction partners now invariably stopped me in such situations and said: "Isenang, mem!"—they are ghosts, forbidden (to talk about them). In many other ways, too, the enemy was dehumanized.

Only sometimes were real "battles" fought with rows of armed men shooting at each other from a certain distance, usually across the Eipo river. Mostly the warriors were engaged in a kind of guerrilla tactic, trying to ambush or otherwise surprise the enemy (Fig. 6.7). Each time the Munggona fighters returned from what

Fig. 6.7 *Eipo warriors usually fight in small groups or alone in a kind of guer-rilla tactic (photo by Schiefenhövel 75/150/21).*

they (sometimes mistakenly) believed to have been a successful day, with an enemy wounded or killed, they performed the impressive dance spectacle (*mote*) which was also carried out during visiting feasts among friends.

K. F. Koch (1974), in his account of conflict and its management among the Yali, just west of the Mek, has provided an explanation for the many lives lost in the revenge systems typical of Papuan (and many other) cultures: since all interactions are dyadic, conflicts cannot be transferred to a third party, and unless one side chooses to give in and be dominated or flee and abandon territory, both must resort to the law of retaliation with its well-known Old Testament principle. Warfare and ethnicity indoctrination, then, serve a defensive function, in that one's own group does not give in, is not conquered by the enemy, and thereby belongs to "those who held onto home" as Robbins (1982) termed it for the Auyana in the eastern highlands of Papua New Guinea.

During this period, people going about their everyday chores, whether working in or returning from the garden, were under a continuous threat of attack. The warriors carried out a silent ceremony, *mal tekene* (standing with arrows). They assembled in one broad row on one of the hills easily visible from Munggona and the other villages of the alliance, holding their shining yellow arrows and their bows high up in the air. Our informants explained that this was to remind every warrior that he is at war, that he must not slacken in the group's defense, that every man must come to fight the enemy. Elsewhere (Schiefenhövel 1995), I have described these acts of propaganda as essential elements of traditional warfare. Without this appeal, the war would probably not have lasted so long, because the men and their families would have tired of fighting, would have been eager to return to cultivating their gardens, and would have worried about the rising death toll.

Mal tekene also served to build up the difference between "us" and "the others," thereby promoting the process of cultural diversification, which is so pronounced in Melanesia with its more than 700 languages and cultures. The ethological concept of "character enhancement" (*Kontrastbetonung* is the German term) originally was used to describe the evolution of distinct populations of animals and, eventually, of new species from a once sympatric homogeneous population. The same concept can serve to explain the cultural process of pseudospeciation (Ericson 1966), which is so typical for all human populations and which is dependent on the feeling and the principle of ethnicity, one of its driving forces.

Eipo ways of seeing their enemy-neighbors, with whom they rarely intermarried but from whom they were only fractionally different, were channeled through indoctrination. "Isenang, mem!"—do not talk about these "ghosts" over there; they are not real people and we should not have anything in common with them. My conclusion from 30 years of fieldwork in this part of the world is that the history of Melanesia, with its vast number of languages and its small-scale jigsaw puzzle of cultures, has been shaped decisively by cultural speciation in which warfare and its underlying indoctrinations, especially that defining the good warrior and the alien enemy, have played an important part.

Conclusion

Indoctrination in quasi-Stone Age New Guinea works toward in-group differentiation, toward making dead sure that everybody knows exactly to which group she or he belongs. Ethnicity indoctrination in remote New Guinea as well as in the heart of Europe, as we learn painfully every day, is a very powerful mechanism.

As Feil (1987), Merlan and Rumsey (1991), and Wiessner (this volume) show for other highland Papuan cultures, one form of indoctrination can be directed to partially overcoming ethnicity to build larger alliances, traditionally aimed at creating large-scale networks that serve the ambitions of powerful males (see also Strathern 1971; Meggit 1972; Feil 1987), who very skillfully direct the risky transactions involving enormous amounts of valuables like pigs, shells, and, nowadays, money. As has been said above, the Eipo and their neighbors were also connected by one such overarching ceremony, which ensured, more than other rites, the continuing fertility of the earth. But on the overall scale, this ideology did not have the same everyday effect as the one stressing ethnicity.

In other highland societies, cultural character enhancement through group indoctrination and warfare was equally strong, as is described in the monographs by Gardner and Heider (1969) and Heider (1970) for the Dani, by Hylkema (1974) for the Nalum and adjacent eastern neighbors of the Mek, and by Koch (1974) for the Jalé (Jalî, Yali), their direct western neighbors. As with many evolutionary traits in us humans, the biopsychology underlying indoctrination seems to be a rather versatile instrument, allowing different solutions to a multitude of ecocultural challenges.

Everywhere enculturation relies on indoctrination. It promotes learning of what is good and bad, or only forbidden and permitted, of what should be aspired to and what should be shunned. Indoctrination occurs in the constant process of shaping the individual to become a reliable, predictable member of the group.

Indoctrination among the Eipo did not take place during special occasions, except in a few highlighted instances like cannibalistic rites or the triumphant dance feasts after the killing of an enemy. It happened on a day-to-day basis and in a rather inconspicuous and unspectacular way. The "phatic commune," in Malinowski's term, which was, of course, also a nonverbal commune, was thus constantly exposed to the values and priorities founded in sacred tradition. This form of low-key, ever present indoctrination seems to be rather effective, probably not only under conditions similar to those of the Environment of Evolutionary Adaptedness, but also in our times. In our cultures, where individualism is more pronounced than it has probably ever been in history, the uniformity of this process and its goals are dissolved and have given room to a host of in-group/subculture ideals, which, again, are achieved by massive indoctrination—partly of the neolithic kind found in Highland New Guinea, partly through modern mediums such as video clips.

It seems an extremely difficult task to nicely separate good indoctrination from bad indoctrination, but it is also clear that there will not be any cultural values without it. The European ethnic wars of the early 1990s, in a subcontinent many believed was immunized against this type of destruction by two world wars, have resurrected the ethic: "My country, right or wrong." Clearly, the Eipo are also following this motto, albeit "my people" in their perspective. One possible way out of the indoctrination dilemma is perhaps to indoctrinate children to be vigilant so that the forces of indoctrination do not overpower them. With this kind of built-in indoctrination brake we might be able to make a step forward from the neolithic conditions that characterize the life of the Eipo and in which Western societies are still so much embedded.

References

Bell-Krannhals, I. (1990). *Haben um zu geben. Eigentum und Besitz auf den Trobriand-Inseln, Papua Neuguinea.* Basler Beiträge zur Ethnologie, Monograph No. 31.

Chagnon, N. (1968). *The fierce people.* Holt, Rinehart & Winston, New York.

de Kock, M. A. (1912). Eenige ethnologische en anthropologische gegevens omtrent een dwergstam in het bergland van Zuid Nieuw Guinea. *Tijdschrift van de Aardrijkskundige Genootschap*, **29**, 387–400.

Eibl-Eibesfeldt, I. (1989). *Human ethology.* Aldine de Gruyter, New York.

Eibl-Eibesfeldt, I. and Wickler, W. (1968). Die ethologische Deutung einiger Wächterfiguren auf Bali. *Zeitschrift für Tierpsychologie*, **25**, 719–26.

Erikson, E. H. (1966). Ontogeny of ritualization in man. *Philosophical Transactions of the Royal Society, London*, **251**, 337–49.

Feil, D. K. (1987). *The evolution of highland Papua New Guinea societies.* Cambridge University Press, Cambridge.

Gardner, R. and Heider, K. G. (1969). *Gardens of war. Life and death in the New Guinea stone age.* A. Deutsch, London.

Godelier, M. (1982). *La Production des Grands Hommes.* Fayard, Paris.

Heeschen, V. (1978). The Mek languages of Irian Jaya with special reference to the Eipo language. *Irian*, 7(2), 3–46.

———. (1990). *Ninye Bun. Mythen, Erzählungen, Lieder und Märchen der Eipo im zentralen Bergland von Irian Jaya (West-Neuguinea), Indonesien.* Reimer, Berlin.

Heeschen, V. and Schiefenhövel, W. (1983). *Wörterbuch der Eipo-Sprache. Eipo-Deutsch-Englisch.* D. Reimer, Berlin.

Heider, K. G. (1970). *The Dugum Dani. A Papuan culture in the highlands of West New Guinea.* Aldine, Chicago.

Hylkema, S. (1974). *Mannen in het Draagnet. Mens- en Wereldbeeld van de Nalum (Sterrengebergte).* Nijhoff, 'S-Gravenhage.

Jessen, E. (1981). Untersuchungen zur Geschlechtererkennung. Die Zuordnung einfacher geometrischer Formen zu Mann und Frau in verschiedenen Alterstufen und Kulturen. Dissertation. University of Munich.

Knauft, B. M. (1985). *Good company and violence. Sorcery and social action in a lowland New Guinea culture.* University of California Press, Berkeley.

———. (1990). Melanesian warfare. A theoretical history. *Oceania*, **60**, 250–311.

Koch, G. (1984). *Malingdam. Ethnographische Notizen über einen Siedlungsbereich im oberen Eipomek-Tal, zentrales Bergland von Irian Jaya (West-Neuguinea), Indonesien.* D. Reimer, Berlin.

Koch, K. F. (1974). *War and peace in Jalémo.* Harvard University Press, Cambridge, Mass.

Malinowski, B. (1922). *Argonauts of the Western Pacific. An account of native enterprise and adventure in the archipelagoes of Melanesian New Guinea.* Routledge & Kegan Paul, London.

———. (1929). *The sexual life of savages in North-Western Melanesia.* Routledge & Kegan Paul, London.

———. (1935). *Coral gardens and their magic. A study of the methods of tilling the soil and of agricultural rites in the Trobriand Islands.* 2 Vols. Reynolds, New York.

Meggit, M. J. (1972). System and subsystem. The Te exchange cycle among the Mae Enga. *Human Ecology*, **1**, 111–23.

Merlan, F. and Rumsey, A. (1991). *Ku Waru. Language and segmentary politics in the Western Nebilyer Valley, Papua New Guinea.* Cambridge University Press, Cambridge.

Robbins, S. (1982). *Auyana. Those who held onto home.* University of Washington Press, Seattle & London.

Schiefenhövel, W. (1976). Die Eipo-Leute des Berglands von Indonesisch-Neuguinea. *Homo*, **24**(4), 264–75.

———. (1988). *Geburtsverhalten und reproduktive Strategien der Eipo. Ergebnisse humanethologischer und ethnomedizinischer Untersuchungen im zentralen Bergland von Irian Jaya (West-Neuguinea), Indonesien.* D. Reimer, Berlin.

———. (1992). Zwischen Patriarchat und Matrilinealität. Melanesische Antworten auf ein biopsychologisches und soziokulturelles Problem. In *Interdisziplinäre Aspekte der Geschlechterverhältnisse in einer sich wandelnden Zeit* (ed. K. F. Wessel and H. A. G. Bosinski), pp. 144–64. Kleine, Bielefeld.

———. (1995). Aggression und Aggressionskontrolle am Beispiel der Eipo aus dem Hochland von West-Neuguinea. In *Töten im Krieg* (ed. H. v. Stietencron and J. Rüpke), pp. 339–62. K. Alber, Freiburg/Munich.

Skrzipek, K. H. (1983). Stammesgeschichtliche Dispositionen der geschlechtsspezifischen Sozialisation des Kindes. *Homo*, **34**(3/4), 227–38.

Strathern, A. (1971). *The rope of Moka. Big-men and ceremonial exchange in Mount Hagen, New Guinea.* Cambridge University Press, London.

Trivers, R. L. (1971). The evolution of reciprocal altruism. *The Quarterly Review of Biology*, **46**, 35–57.

Weiner, A. (1976). *Women of value, men of renown: New perspectives in Trobriand exchange.* University of Texas Press, Austin.

Wickler, W. (1966). Ursprung und biologische Bedeutung des Genital-Präsentierens männlicher Primaten. *Zeitschrift für Tierpsychologie*, **23**, 422–37.

CHAPTER SEVEN

INDOCTRINABILITY AND THE EVOLUTION OF SOCIALLY DEFINED KINSHIP

Polly Wiessner

Indoctrinability, the predisposition to be inculcated with values or loyalties that run contrary to immediate individual interest, is a universally found characteristic of humans. Examples of individuals sacrificing their lives for country or crusade fill the annals. Nonetheless, indoctrinability poses problems for evolutionary explanations: how could such a tendency spread in a population if those who are susceptible to indoctrination risk their lives for a cause that benefits others? Some evolutionary models turn to group selection (e.g., see Eibl-Eibesfeldt 1982), and as a logical correlate the evolution of indoctrinability becomes linked to intergroup competition in the form of warfare.

Here I will propose an alternate hypothesis for the evolution of indoctrinability that does not invoke group selection:

- That a strong selection pressure for indoctrinability came from the evolution of socially defined kinship, which allowed humans to construct effective networks for reducing risk outside the group.
- That the major thrust of indoctrinability was originally to counteract "natural" in-group loyalties of small, closely related family-based units. This was achieved by culturally homogenizing

and standardizing a relatively large pool of these family units, thereby opening new social and economic opportunities.

This is not to say that indoctrination was or is not also used to close boundaries and bind competing social groups. Once in existence, its use for the latter purpose could have led to the strengthening of a tendency that came into being via individual selection by selection at the group level.

Socially Defined Kinship

Socially defined kinship, sometimes called "fictive kinship,"[1] is the extension of kinship terms and relationships of mutual support to affinal relatives, distant kin, or even nonkin through cultural classification. All human societies have systems to classify kin by social means, and the number of elementary systems of kinship classification systems is finite (Lévi-Strauss 1969).

The evolution of socially defined kinship, a topic often neglected in evolutionary biology, is a critical adaptation of *Homo sapiens*. It permitted the construction of broad social security networks for risk reduction by granting access to human and natural resources lying outside the group. Losses due to fluctuations in natural resources, inability to find mates, conflict, and so on, could then be absorbed by a broader population. There is little doubt that it was the construction of such networks that has allowed humans to inhabit so many harsh niches (Cashdan 1985; Wiessner 1977; 1981; 1982; 1986; Yengoyan 1976; Myers 1986; Smith 1988; Testart 1982).

Cognitive and behavioral prerequisites for establishing socially defined kinship include abilities to: (1) categorize and symbolize; (2) engage in relationships of reciprocal altruism; and (3) treat less familiar individuals as if they were family members, even though their habits, behavior or ideas may seem foreign or even repellent. The last point is a source of tension in human societies, for people often are not inclined to treat those defined as kin in the same way as they treat close family members or group members with whom they have grown up. Consequently, most societies have a variety of cultural mechanisms to mediate, for example, the many pre-

---

1. I shall avoid the term "fictive kinship" because it conveys a false impression. Most socially defined kin are affinal relatives or distant consanguineous relatives.

scriptions and proscriptions attached to the mother-in-law relationship. The creation and functioning of social kinship systems is thus facilitated by the homogenization of behavior and values and by the establishment of culturally accepted means by which positive identity can be transmitted. It is in response to these needs that I propose that indoctrination/indoctrinability evolved hand in hand with socially defined kinship.

In this chapter I briefly review some archaeological studies of the Middle and Upper Paleolithic to argue that the evidence is compatible with the above hypothesis. Then, ethnographic examples from two very different societies will be used to illustrate the point that the opening of networks based on socially defined kinship generally requires more support from indoctrination than does closure. That is, due to a long evolutionary history of kin selection, in-group behaviors are instilled quite naturally, while those which open boundaries in the process of extending kinship must be constantly reinforced through indoctrination.[2] The ethnographic examples used will be taken from !Kung San (Ju/'hoansi) of southern Africa, the legendary example of low-density, peaceful, flexible hunter-gatherers, and the Enga of the New Guinea Highlands, a high-density agricultural population of renowned warriors with clearly defined group identities and social structure.[3]

Archaeological evidence for the evolution of social kinship networks

Systems of socially defined kinship cannot, of course, be detected directly in the archaeological record. However, indirect evidence for their evolution and that of supporting indoctrination can be obtained from several types of material remains. The first is the presence of artifacts with certain forms or decorations indicating that their makers had the capacity to symbolize. Certainly, the ability to define members of other groups as kin and maintain relationships of reciprocity over distance would be difficult without such capacity. The second is the appearance of body orna-

2.   Salter, this volume, makes essentially the same point by arguing that much indoctrination is directed at inculcating beliefs and behavior for which subjects show low indoctrinability.

3.   The material presented here is based on two years of fieldwork among the !Kung San between 1973 and 1975 and a ten-year project on oral history among the Enga.

mentation and stylistic expression in artifacts, which are universally used by humans in information exchange to negotiate personal and social identity (Hodder 1982; Wiessner 1983, 1984; Strathern and Strathern 1971; Wobst 1977). The third is evidence for regular long-distance exchange, testifying to the fact that broad-ranging social networks involving reciprocity were in action. The fourth is the appearance of certain art forms that are likely to have been used in the service of indoctrination (see Eibl-Eibesfeldt 1989).

Until the past few decades, many authors have viewed the transition from the Middle to the Upper Paleolithic (between ca. 30,000 and 40,000 BP) as abrupt and revolutionary, with the sudden appearance of modern humans and the development of the capacity for sophisticated manipulation of symbols and complex language (Klein 1973; Mellars 1973; White 1982). Recent work has supported a much longer and more gradual transition from the Middle to Upper Paleolithic (Hayden 1993; Lindley and Clark 1990; Rigaud 1989). For example, there is increasing evidence from the Lower and Middle Paleolithic indicating that hominids long had the capacity to symbolize (Marshack 1990; see also Bednarik 1995 for a good, though controversial, summary). Nonetheless, the examples of symbolic behavior in material remains that do exist from the Middle Paleolithic occur at a very low frequency, suggesting that it was not a regular part of Neanderthal adaptation. Furthermore, artifacts found exhibit little continuity or redundancy in form (White 1993), an indication that the social matrix in which symbolic behavior could flourish had not yet developed.

It is only in the Early Upper Paleolithic (Aurignacian) that stylistic expression in nonlithic artifacts and pierced pendants used for self-decoration are found in larger quantities and on a regular basis (Taborin 1993; White 1989; 1993). Apparently, it was at this time that such objects began to be used to transmit social information regarding personal or social identity. Because such expression would hardly be needed within small family-based camps where members knew each other well, it is reasonable to propose that this development was associated with the formation of relationships with those outside the group, in other words, the expansion of networks of socially defined kinship.[4]

---

4. See Crook (1981) for an interesting discussion of the projection of personal and social identity and reciprocal altruism.

Analyses of stylistic variation in mobile art from the Early Upper Paleolithic that reveal homogeneity over vast areas suggest that socially defined kin networks were used to create open systems and expand ties between groups (Gamble 1982). Only later at the height of the Magdalenian period of the Late Upper Paleolithic does one find stylistic evidence for the closure of groups and clear expressions of sociocultural boundaries (Joachim 1983; Barton et al. 1994; Pfeiffer 1982).

Further indications that such social kinship networks were in operation during the Early Upper Paleolithic come from a very substantial body of data from both western and eastern Europe concerning the increase in the long-distance movement of goods and valuables (see Gamble 1986, 331–38 for an excellent summary). Though results vary by area, the general trend is from a virtual absence of imported raw material in the Lower Paleolithic to the regular importation of stone and shells in significant proportions from sources 100 to 300 km away during the Upper Paleolithic. In short, the flourishing of style and personal ornamentation, long-distance trade, and population growth during the Upper Paleolithic have led numerous archaeologists to draw a conclusion similar to that reached by Barton et al. (1994, 201):

> Prior to the last glaciation, human populations appear to have displayed a very different response to environmental stress and loss of land area than is seen in the late Pleistocene. Europe, and presumably other middle latitude temperate regions of the Old World, was largely abandoned by human populations during glacial maxima in the Middle Pleistocene. In the Upper Paleolithic, however, social mechanisms evolved that permitted the maintenance of higher population densities and that resulted in the appearance of extra-familial corporate groups.

The evolution of indoctrination is a more elusive topic of research. One might argue that certain figurines project standardized conceptions of ideal types and that bead ornamentation gave a common denominator for projecting positive social identity, though this requires several assumptions. More substantial evidence comes with the advent of rich cave paintings, some of which are so awesome, both in location and aesthetic impression, that it seems most likely that they provided the context for initiation or group indoctrination. Because most of these sites are dated to the Late Upper Paleolithic, some authors have argued that they were imprinting for "relatively closed social networks" (Jochim

1983) in the face of increasing population density. This may indeed have been the case. However, studies by Conkey (1980)—showing that the impressive painted cave site of Altamira had the greatest diversity of styles of engraved antler rods when compared to other sites—indicate that it was an aggregation site for many different social groups and thus perhaps associated with the opening of social networks. Furthermore, the recent discovery of the magnificent cave art at Chauvet in Ardeche pushes the date for such works back to the Early Upper Paleolithic (ca. 27–30,000 BP),[5] a time when networks of socially defined kinship appear to have been forming and before there is any stylistic evidence for the closure of social networks.

In summary, the amount of material on the above-mentioned topics is vast, and interpretations are controversial due to the difficulty of extracting information on social relations from material remains. However, the foregoing brief review of archaeological evidence is compatible with the hypothesis that the first evidence for indoctrination appears hand in hand with the formation of social networks outside the group and that these networks granted access to the resources and assistance of other groups. This innovation, together with accompanying economic and technological ones, allowed modern humans to sustain relatively high population densities in Europe during the height of the last glaciation compared to those preceding it. Indoctrination at this time would have served to counteract the narrow in-group orientation of family-based units by standardizing and opening relationships of mutual support within a broader population. Let us now turn to ethnographic examples to illustrate the latter point.

The !Kung San (*Ju/'hoan*)

The !Kung San, who inhabit northwestern Botswana and northeastern Namibia, are among the best-studied hunter-gatherer populations (Marshall 1976; Lee 1979, 1984; Lee and DeVore 1976; Biesele 1993; Wilmsen 1989; among many others). In the 1950s to 1970s, when the most extensive research took place, their subsistence largely came from hunting and gathering resources from the natural environment, from neighboring agropastoralists, and from border police and administrators in Bushmanland of Namibia.

---

5. At the moment, there is some debate over these dates.

Their camps of 25 to 40 were composed of one or more cores of siblings, who maintained strong land rights to a certain water hole and surrounding land (*n!ore*), and attached affinal or consanguineous kin. Relations were strongly egalitarian, and leadership, based largely on respect and persuasion, was weakly defined. Few problems were solved by the group as a whole: the most common response to food shortage or conflict was for group members to "vote with their feet"—to disperse and live with relatives in other areas until the problem subsided.

The social resources of !Kung camps and the natural resources of their *n!ore* met the needs of the average year, but were insufficient to sustain a band through longer term environmental fluctuations and social problems. Thus each !Kung man and woman constructed his or her own network of social kinship ties underwritten by a formal exchange relationship called *hxaro* that permitted partners mutual access to the resources and assistance of their exchange partners whenever need arose.

A study of the *hxaro* networks of 81 !Kung men, women, and children (Wiessner 1977; 1981; 1982; 1986) revealed that adults had an average of 16.5 *hxaro* partnerships with individuals who were well distributed across the sexes, across different age categories and ways of making a living, as well as being spread geographically. The geographical spread of partners extended from camps within a 5 km radius to those up to 200 km away. When food shortage, conflict, or other problems arose, individuals or families traveled to the camp of a partner and remained for days, weeks, or months, hunting and gathering on their partner's land until trouble subsided. The average !Kung spent 2.2 months a year "visiting" *hxaro* partners and enjoying the benefits of their kin and country.

Hxaro relationships were constructed along the lines of both biological kinship and socially defined kinship. Lee (1986), in an extremely perceptive analysis of !Kung kinship, identified three principles for designating kin:

Kinship 1. This is the standard kinship system that assigns kin terms to those related to ego, distinguishing nuclear family from collaterals and, in most cases, collaterals from affinal kin.[6] Standard !Kung kinship terms are structured by relative age and generation, and each term carries with it a relationship of joking or

---

6. Only spouses' siblings and siblings' spouses are given terms that do not distinguish them from collateral kin.

respect that delimits eligibility for marriage and a range of permitted behavior.

Kinship 2. This is the name relationship (Marshall 1976) through which the sharing of personal names allows !Kung to extend terms of close kinship to distant relatives, if desired. The name relationship thus destroys the logic of standard kinship, and continues to do so as demographic events add new names to the Kinship 2 universe.

Kinship 3. The *"wi"* relationship allows elders to choose among possibilities afforded by standard kinship and the name relationship for terms that they wish to apply to juniors. In doing so, they resolve the discrepancy between Kinship 1 and 2.

After these three principles, *hxaro* comes into play activating the responsibilities of kinship and specifying those kin with whom a person wants to have more firm commitments. As with kinship, a !Kung's sphere of *hxaro* unfolds with age (Wiessner 1982).

The !Kung San are reputed to be some of the most unindoctrinable people on earth, for with so many opportunities afforded by kinship and *hxaro*, people tend to rely on individual solutions to problems. Anthropologists have marveled at how the movement of an entire camp can be paralyzed by the tantrum of a small child, development workers have despaired at unwillingness to work for long on cooperative group projects, and missionary after missionary has pulled out of the region after finding the !Kung friendly but difficult to convert. Upon closer scrutiny, however, it becomes apparent that rather intensive indoctrination does occur in at least three contexts, instilling values that assure the functioning of the !Kung's risk-sharing networks.

First, children are taught systematically and repetitively at an early age to exchange with kin situated outside their immediate families and to build networks of social kinship. Symbolic socialization for *hxaro* begins at six months to a year when an infant's beads are removed, the child is washed, and the beads are put in the child's hand to give to a relative outside the nuclear family. From this point on, whether the child agrees or not, parents or grandparents periodically remove a child's beads and give them to a more distant relative who takes an interest in the child, explaining carefully the kin term for that relative, how he or she cares about the child, how generous or beloved he or she is, and so on. It is often only in adolescence that children begin to give to more distant kin on their own initiatives. In this manner, the foundation of a social kinship network is laid during childhood, and the principles of reciprocity with those outside the camp instilled.

The next instance of indoctrination comes during male initiation. Young men were gathered from a wide region, for it was considered important that young men be initiated together with a pool of others whom they do not know well. After having gone through trials of hunger, thirst, exposure to severe climactic conditions, tattooing, and introduction to the sacred bull-roarer, young men were then instructed in the ways of !Kung life by an adult whom they hardly knew before or, preferably, who was a stranger to them. When asked what they were taught verbally, the men replied, "Everything that we already knew except that each teaching was prefaced by the statement, 'I am not your mother, I am not your father, but still I tell you this: we Ju/'hoansi (!Kung) do things this way.'" In brief, the !Kung explain their male initiation as a process of standardization and homogenization, of making young men aware that they belong to a much broader population that shares certain standards, practices, and values. It is an opening, not a closure. Furthermore, certain tattoos attest to other San that a man has been through initiation and shares certain values and norms of behavior.

A third and most prominent recurrent event involving indoctrination takes place during the trance dance, the only community response to a problem in San society performed on a regular basis. Trance dances are called when a community member is stricken with illness or when social tension is high. To the rhythmic clapping and singing of the women, the men dance, some falling into trances and journeying to combat spirits of the dead who try to take the stricken with them (Lee 1968; Katz 1976; Biesele 1993). At the same time, they circulate among all participants, touching or massaging each as a form of preventative medicine. The entire community thus participates—whether through song, dance, or trance—to heal and to keep their members well, the dance providing the ideal model for broad-based sharing within San society. The trance is not exclusive to a specific group: at the first sound of song, !Kung and neighboring agropastoralists travel from nearby camps to participate, providing the support of a very broad community. As an event embodying inclusiveness, egalitarianism, and above all caring for the broader community, the trance dance continually reinforces networks of social kinship.

In short, though relatively little indoctrination takes place in !Kung society, that which does is aimed at standardizing and inte-

grating individuals into the broader population, providing open-
ings rather than closures. And the !Kung system is far from unique
in foraging societies; similarly far-flung social security networks
(Cashdan 1985; Damas 1972; Myers 1986; 1993; Spencer 1959; Yengoyan 1976) and supporting rituals involving indoctrination
(Turnbull 1982; Myers 1993; Hayden 1987) are common in foraging societies throughout the world.

The Enga

The Enga inhabit the Highlands of Papua New Guinea at altitudes
between 1,500 and 2,500 m and densities up to 150 to 200 people
per sq. km. They have been the subject of a number of major
ethnographic works (Meggitt 1958; 1964; 1974; 1977; Feil 1984;
Wohlt 1978; Lacey 1975; Talyaga 1982; Waddell 1972; among many
others). Their staple crop, the sweet potato, is cultivated in an
intensive system of mulch mounding to feed large human and pig
populations. Throughout Enga great value is placed on pigs, the
major social and political currency. Politics, which center around
land and exchange, occupies much of men's time and effort, while
women devote themselves primarily to family, gardening, and pig
raising. While frequent and destructive warfare creates sharp divisions between clans (Meggitt 1977), ceremonial exchanges of pork,
live pigs, shells, salt, oil, foodstuffs, and other goods forge
alliances and are used to reestablish peace, among other things. As
members of a society in which egalitarianism embodies the ideal,
all men can potentially make names for themselves and become
big-men (*kamongo*) through displaying skill in mediation, organization, public oratory, and the manipulation of wealth. However,
competition in this arena is fierce, and should they fail, their
demise is rapid.

Two axes of kinship based on agnatic and affinal relationships
embed each person in a supportive network. Clan membership,
based primarily on descent from a common ancestor, defines
social and spatial boundaries, furnishing a pool of people who
cooperate in such activities as agricultural enterprises, defense of
land, procurement of spouses, and the performance of ancestral
cults. It assures security from the net bag in which babies are carried to the grave, so to speak—whether individuals' actions are
right or wrong, they are supported and defended. The affinal axis
of kinship, that established by marriage, has to be created and

maintained. It opens boundaries and is virtually the only path to resources or assistance from outside the clan. Efforts to build and maintain networks based on affinal/maternal kinship depend on family enterprise as well as social and economic competence. While all clan members can reap similar benefits from within the group, ability to successfully manipulate maternal and affinal relationships is the key to furthering the social, economic, and political standing of the family. Clan membership, with its accompanying strong loyalties, thus constitutes a centripetal force toward closed groups, and affinal/maternal kinship a centrifugal one, forging strong ties and loyalties outside the clan.

Land, the basis for sustenance, is prized and defended as the source of wealth, pride, and independence. It is defended through means of social boundary maintenance (Peterson 1973)—displaying resources to those related through marriage and giving them access to those resources—and through the physical means of warfare. Warfare took the lives of about 25 percent of men between 1900 and 1955 (Meggitt 1977).

The situation in Enga at the time of first contact in the 1930s did not represent a long-established situation, either ecologically or socially. Substantial changes occurred throughout the New Guinea Highlands beginning some 250 to 400 years ago when the sweet potato was introduced, releasing many constraints on production and making possible for the first time regular surplus agricultural production in the form of pigs. A rich and factual oral history records the changes that took place after the introduction of the sweet potato (Wiessner and Tumu 1996). The most significant of these changes were:

1. Population growth in Enga from some 10–20,000 persons (estimated from genealogy) about 240 years ago to 150,000 in 1980, which represents about 1.1 percent per annum growth.
2. Substantial population shifts and reorganization to take advantage of new opportunities provided by the sweet potato.
3. A gradual change from a prestige economy based on the trade of nonagricultural trade goods (salt, axes, cosmetic oil, shells, plumes, etc.) to one based on agricultural production in the form of pig exchange.
4. The formation of very large networks of ceremonial exchange in response to problems and opportunities that arose after the introduction of the sweet potato. The most significant problems mentioned in Enga oral history include struggles over control

of trade in the face of population redistribution and the ineffectiveness of warfare to solve problems as the population grew. While in pre–sweet potato times and shortly after its introduction warfare had served to relieve tensions by spacing groups, as the land filled it was no longer effective. New approaches to making peace and repairing ties were sought, so that boundaries could once again be maintained by social means. The upshot was the rise of large ceremonial exchange systems, the *Tee* Ceremonial Exchange Cycle and the Great Ceremonial Wars (Wiessner and Tumu 1996), in which large numbers of pigs and valuables were exchanged. The largest of these, the *Tee* Ceremonial Exchange Cycle, grew so rapidly that by the 1950s to 1970s some 40–70,000 participants were involved, and tens of thousands of pigs exchanged.

To help bring about change by setting new parameters for competition—who competes, for what, how, when, and with whom—and to mediate the effects of competition, an extensive "cult trade" took place during this time of rapid change. In this trade, ancestral and bachelors' cults were constantly imported, exported, and altered and used as a "social technology"[7] (Wiessner and Tumu 1998). Big-men sought cults from neighboring dialect or linguistic groups that would steer their followers in directions beneficial to themselves and their clans, and then arranged for their purchase and performance. If a cult was deemed successful and was accepted into a clan's repertory of cults, then the new owner could export it to other clans, thereby creating homogeneity in ritual life.

Notable among exchanged cults was the *Sangai* bachelors' cult, which was apparently imported into Enga from the south shortly after the arrival of the sweet potato. In subsequent generations, innovations were made that set the pace of change. When it was adopted, the *Sangai* bachelors' cult involved symbolic marriage to a spirit woman who would transform the bachelors into mature, handsome, and socially competent young men provided they remained chaste and faithful to her for some 5 to 10 years while they periodically attended bachelors' cults. The rites for the spirit woman instituted an age-grade hierarchy putting young men well in the grips of their seniors for education and delaying the time of first marriage. The next addition was a public emergence cere-

---

7. For elaborations on social technology theory and related concepts, see Caton (1988, re. "political technology") and Salter (1995, re. "control infrastructures," and this volume).

mony for the bachelors after completing secret rites that displayed the strength of the upcoming generation and drew crowds to planned events of ceremonial exchange. Finally, just prior to first contact with Europeans, rituals of courtship were added during emergence ceremonies, facilitating the arrangement of marriages between areas that formed the basis for the extension of ceremonial exchange networks. These innovations were initiated or adopted at a time when people of central Enga were changing subsistence and settlement patterns, reorganizing for larger scale military campaigns, and/or attempting to devise new ways to absorb mounting competition between groups through ceremonial exchange.

Within the above context of increasing intergroup competition in the form of both warfare and exchange, one might expect strong indoctrination for group loyalty and closure, particularly in the bachelors' cults that educated the future generations. Surprisingly, this is not the case—the bachelors' cults were virtually devoid of any in-group education or indoctrination for warfare. To summarize the rites:[8] a seclusion hut was built deep in the forest to which the young men of a clan would retire. Before coming into close contact with the spirit woman, who was represented by sacred objects, rites were performed to purge the bachelors' bodies and senses of all that was considered impure. Only then were they permitted to enter the cult house, where they were disciplined by a strict dietary and behavioral regime and required to speak in measured, symbolic language. Senior bachelors presided over all events.

During the four days that followed, they tended the sacred objects by day, performed rites for physical growth, and prepared wigs and other ceremonial attire for their emergence. Mental capacities were sharpened by a number of exercises, for example, evening sessions to comprehend and memorize the *Sangai titi pingi*, a lengthy praise poem relaying information about the origin, transmission, and effects of the sacred objects. This was told in obscure metaphor, taxing the very keenest of minds. These poems laid down the ideal by citing the qualities of heroes of the past. Ideals were framed in terms of lush gardens tended, fences built, pigs raised, participation in ceremonial exchange, and the creation of trade networks that crossed many clan boundaries. The following verse taken from a *Sangai* praise poem of central Enga puts

8. See Kyakas and Wiessner (1992); Meggitt (1964); Schwab (1995) for more detailed descriptions.

forward the qualities of a past leader who was transformed through the *Sangai* rites:

> Ameane's physical and mental capabilities were always there,
> His influence and renown were always there,
> People keep saying the long horizontally laid (garden) fencing is Ameane's,
> People keep saying the long picket (garden) fencing is also Ameane's,
> The long-leafed pandanus palm is also Ameane's,
> The sweet potato garden ready to harvest is also Ameane's,
> What makes Ameane as popular as he is?
> That huge, untamed and slit-eared pig is also Ameane's,
> He keeps saying that he has been alone at a funeral feast,[9]
> He keeps saying that he has been a major force in organizing the distribution of live pigs and butchered pork [in Tee exchange].

Note that fighting prowess and warfare do not enter into the ideal image.

Nights were spent by lapsing into short periods of sleep followed by discussion and dream interpretation. Most dreams were read as having implications for warfare or ceremonial exchange, and so young men were taught to reflect on broader politics. Verbal skills were trained by turning these dreams into metaphor and song. The young men, who emerged to parade majestically on the ceremonial grounds, to present predictions made from dreams through song, and to be courted by young women, were not warriors, but those indoctrinated to produce, orate, and succeed in exchange that opened a wide network of social kinship and with it access to the wealth and resources of others. This is not to say, however, that the bachelors' cults had nothing to do with group solidarity, for certainly those who went through the cults together felt strong loyalties for life. However, this result was the product of joint action and experience, not active indoctrination.

In short, few if any formal rites of Enga education teach young men group loyalty—such loyalty develops quite naturally in the process of maturation. Boys grow up in the men's house hearing clan history and stories of battle by night. From a very young age they attend events of ceremonial exchange in which the clan as a whole participates. By the time they come of fighting age, most are more eager to try their hands in battle, often as allies for other clans, than to knuckle down to the drudge of agricultural production and the intellectually taxing education for oratorical and

---

9. This means that he has provisioned a funeral feast with his own resources.

political skills. Formal education/indoctrination was thus aimed at restraining young men from violence, giving them a broader view, and instilling as the highest values production, intellectual acumen, and social skills. These would allow them to expand their networks of social kinship outside the clan and thereby acquire wealth for themselves and their clan. Those who wished to enhance their fighting skills had to do so through the private purchase of magic formulae, and when it was necessary to rally the clan for war, spirits were raised through songs that insulted or dehumanized the enemy and through rituals of unity held immediately prior to or during battle.

Conclusion

Despite very different programs and contexts of indoctrination among the !Kung San and Enga, the primary thrust of more formal indoctrination for both was to counteract in-group tendencies by standardizing and opening boundaries. Parochial loyalties that formed quite naturally during childhood through familiarity, sharing, and mutual support within the local group were thereby overridden, and the way was opened for the formation of broad networks of social kinship outside the group.

In closing, it should be noted that though the predisposition for indoctrinability appears to have a biological basis, its content is culturally stipulated. Once in existence, socially defined kinship and supportive indoctrination can be molded to suit the contexts and needs of each society, whether this be to open or close boundaries, or to form larger units of competition. The examples given here are of the former, but certainly other ethnographic examples illustrate the latter. It is precisely this flexibility that made socially defined kinship and supporting indoctrination such important factors in human evolution.

References

Barton, C. M., Clark, G., and Cohen, A. (1994). Art as information: Explaining Upper Paleolithic art in western Europe. *World Archaeology*, **26**, 185–207.

Bednarik, R. (1995). Concept-mediated marking in the Lower Paleolithic. *Current Anthropology*, **36**, 605–34.

Biesele, M. (1993). *Women like meat. The folklore and foraging ideology of the Kalahari Ju/'hoan.* Indiana University Press, Bloomington.

Cashdan, E. (1985). Coping with risk: Reciprocity among the Basarwa of northern Botswana. *Man*, **20**, 454–76.

Caton, H. P. (1988). *The politics of progress: The origins and development of the commercial republic, 1600–1835*. University of Florida Press, Gainesville.

Conkey, M. (1980). The identification of prehistoric hunter-gatherer aggregation sites: The case of Altamira. *Current Anthropology*, **21**, 609–30.

Crook, J. H. (1981). The evolutionary ethology of social processes in man. In *Group cohesion. Theoretical and clinical perspectives* (ed. H. Kellerman), pp. 86–108. Grune & Stratton, New York.

Damas, D. (1972). The copper Eskimo. In *Hunters and gatherers today* (ed. M. C. Bicchieri), Holt, Rinehart and Winston, New York.

Eibl-Eibesfeldt, I. (1982). Warfare, man's indoctrinability and group selection. *Ethology (Zeitschrift für Tierpsychologie)*, **60**, 177–98.

———. (1989). *Human ethology*. Aldine, New York.

Feil, D. (1984). *Ways of exchange: The Enga Tee of Papua New Guinea*. University of Queensland Press, St. Lucia.

Gamble, C. (1982). Interaction and alliance in palaeolithic society. *Man*, **17**, 92–107.

———. (1986). *The Paleolithic settlement of Europe*. Cambridge University Press, Cambridge.

Hayden, B. (1987). Alliances and ritual ecstasy: Human responses to resource stress. *Journal for the Scientific Study of Religion*, **26**, 81–91.

———. (1993). The cultural capacities of Neanderthals: A review and re-evaluation. *Journal of Human Evolution*, **24**, 113–46.

Heinz, H. J. (1966). The social organization of the !Ko Bushmen. M.A. thesis. University of South Africa.

Hodder, I. (1982). *Symbols in action*. Cambridge University Press, Cambridge.

Jochim, M. (1983). Paleolithic cave art in an ecological perspective. In *Hunter-gatherer economy in prehistory* (ed. G. N. Bailey), Cambridge University Press, Cambridge.

Katz, R. (1976). Education for transcendence: !Kia-Healing with the Kalahari !Kung. In *Kalahari hunter-gatherers* (ed. R. B. Lee and I. DeVore), Harvard University Press, Cambridge, Mass.

Klein, R. (1973). *Ice-age hunters of the Ukraine*. University of Chicago Press, Chicago.

Kyakas, A. and Wiessner, P. (1992). *From inside the women's house: Enga women's lives and traditions*. Robert Brown, Brisbane.

Lacey, R. (1975). Oral traditions as history: An exploration of oral sources among the Enga of the New Guinea Highlands. Unpublished Ph.D. thesis. University of Wisconsin.

Lee, R. B. (1968). The sociology of !Kung Bushman trance performances. In *Trance and possession states* (ed. R. Prince), R. M. Bucke Memorial Society, Montreal.

———. (1979). *The !Kung San: Men, women and work in a foraging society*. Cambridge University Press, Cambridge.

———. (1984). *The Dobe !Kung*. Holt, Rinehart and Winston, New York.

———. (1986). !Kung kin terms, the name relationship and the process of discovery. In *The past and future of !Kung ethnography: Critical reflections and symbolic perspectives. Essays in honour of Lorna Marshall* (ed. M. Biesele, R. Gordon and R. Lee), pp. 77–102. Helmut Buske Verlag, Hamburg.

Lee, R. B. and DeVore, I., eds. (1976). *Kalahari hunter-gatherers*. Harvard University Press. Cambridge, Mass.

Lévi-Strauss, C. (1969). *The elementary structures of kinship*. Eyre and Spottiswoode, London.

Lindley, J. and Clark, G. (1990). Symbolism and modern human origins. *Current Anthropology*, **31**, 233–61.

Marshack (1990). Early hominid symbol and the evolution of the human capacity. In *The emergence of modern humans: An archaeological perspective* (ed. P. Mellars), Edinburgh University Press, Edinburgh.

Marshall, L. (1976). *The !Kung of Nyae Nyae*. Harvard University Press, Cambridge.

Meggitt, M. (1958). The Enga of the New Guinea Highlands: Some preliminary observations. *Oceania*, **28**, 253–330.

———. (1964). Male-female relationships in the highlands of Australian New Guinea. *American Anthropologist*, **66**, 204–24.

———. (1965). *The lineage system of the Mae-Enga of New Guinea*. Barnes and Noble, New York.

———. (1974). "Pigs are our hearts!" The *Te* exchange cycle among the Mae-Enga of New Guinea. *Oceania*, **44**, 165–203.

———. (1977). *Blood is their argument*. Mayfield, Palo Alto.

Mellars, P. (1973). The character of the Middle-Upper Palaeolithic transition in south-west France. In *The explanation of culture change: Models in prehistory* (ed. C. Renfrew), Duckworth, London.

Myers, F. (1986). *Pintupi country, Pintupi self: Sentiment, place and politics among Western Desert Aborigines*. Smithsonian Institution Press and Australian Institute of Aboriginal Studies, Washington and Canberra.

———. (1993). Place, identity, and exchange in a totemic system: Nurturance and the process of social reproduction in Pintupi society. In *Exchanging products: Producing exchange*, vol. 43 (ed. J. Fajans), University of Sydney, Sydney.

Peterson, N. (1975). Hunter-gatherer territoriality: The perspective from Australia. *American Anthropologist*, **77**, 53–68.

Pfeiffer, J. (1982). *The creative explosion*. Harper and Row, New York.

Rigaud, J.-P. (1989). From the Middle to the Upper Paleolithic: Transition or convergence? In *The emergence of modern humans* (ed. E. Trinkhaus), pp. 142–53. Cambridge University Press, Cambridge.

Robbe, P. (1989). Le Chasseur Arctique et son Milieu: Stratégies individuelles et collectives des Inuit d'Ammassalik. Unpublished Doctorat d'État et Sciences thesis. Université Pierre et Marie Curie, Paris.

Salter, F. K. (1995). *Emotions in command. A naturalistic study of institutional dominance*. Oxford University Press, Oxford.

Schwab, J. (1995). The Sandalu bachelor ritual among the Laiapu Enga (Papua New Guinea). *Anthropos*, **90**(1/3), 27–47.

Smith, E. A. (1988). Risk and uncertainty in the "original affluent society": Evolutionary ecology of resource-sharing and land tenure. In *Hunters and gatherers: Property, power and ideology* (ed. T. Ingold, D. Riches, and J. Woodburn), pp. 222–51. Berg, Oxford.

Spencer, R. (1959). *The North Alaskan Eskimo: A study in ecology and society*. Bulletin no. 171. Bureau of American Ethnology, Washington.

Strathern, A. and Strathern, M. (1971). *Self-decoration in Mt. Hagen*. Duckworth, London.

Taborin, Y. (1993). Shells of the French Aurignacian and Perigordian. In *Before Lascaux: The complex record of the Upper Paleolithic* (ed. H. Knecht, A. Pike-Tay, and R. White), CRC Press, Boca Raton, Florida.

Talyaga, K. (1982). The Enga yesterday and today: A personal account. In *Enga: Foundations for development*, Enga Yaaka Lasemana, vol, 3. (ed. B. Carrad, D. Lea, and K. Talyaga), pp. 59–75. Dept. of Geography, University of New England, Armidale.

Testart, A. (1982). The significance of food storage among hunter-gatherers: Residence patterns, population densities, and social inequalities. *Current Anthropology*, **23**, 253–530.

Turnbull, C. (1982). The ritualization of potential conflict between the sexes among the Mbuti. In *Politics and history in band societies* (ed. E. Leacock and R. Lee), Cambridge University Press, Cambridge.

Waddell, E. (1972). *The mound builders: Agricultural practices, environment and society in the Central Highlands of New Guinea*. University of Washington Press, Seattle.

White, R. (1982). Rethinking the Middle/Upper Paleolithic transition. *Current Anthropology*, **23**, 169–92.

———. (1989). A social and technological view of Aurignacian and Castelperronian personal ornaments in SW Europe. In *El Origen del Hombre Moderno en el Sudoeste de Europa* (ed. V. Cabrera Valdés). Ministerio de Educacion y Ciencia, Madrid.

———. (1993). Technological and social dimensions of "Aurignacian-Age" body ornaments across Europe. In *Before Lascaux: The complex record of the Upper Paleolithic* (ed. H. Knecht, A. Pike-Tay, and R. White), CPR Press, Boca Raton, Florida.

Wiessner, P. (1977). *Hxaro: A regional system of reciprocity for reducing risk among the !Kung San*. University Microfilms, Ann Arbor.

———. (1981). Measuring the impact of social ties on nutritional status among the !Kung San. *Social Science Information*, **20**, 641–78.

———. (1982). Risk, reciprocity and social influences on !Kung San economics. In *Politics and history in band societies* (ed. E. Leacock and R. B. Lee), pp. 61–84. Cambridge University Press, Cambridge.

———. (1983). Style and social information in Kalahari San projectile points. *American Antiquity*, **48**, 253–76.

———. (1984). Reconsidering the behavioral basis for style: A case study among the Kalahari San. *Journal of Anthropological Archaeology*, **3**, 190–234.

———. (1986). !Kung San networks in a generational perspective. In *The Past and future of !Kung ethnography: Critical reflections and symbolic perspectives. Essays in honour of Lorna Marshall* (ed. M. Biesele, R. Gordon and R. Lee), pp. 103–36. Helmut Buske Verlag, Hamburg.

Wiessner, P. and Tumu, A. (1998). *Historical vines: Enga networks of exchange, ritual and wafare in Papua New Guinea*. Smithsonian Institution Press, Washington, D.C.

Wilmsen, E. (1989). *Land filled with flies*. University of Chicago Press, Chicago.

Wobst, M. (1977). Stylistic behavior and information exchange. In *Papers for the director*. Anthropological Papers No. 61 (ed. C. Cleland), University of Michigan Museum of Anthropology, Ann Arbor.

Wohlt, P. (1978). *Ecology, agriculture and social organization: The dynamics of group composition in the Highlands of New Guinea*. University Microfilms, Ann Arbor.

Yengoyan, A. (1976). Structure, event and ecology in Aboriginal Australia: a comparative viewpoint. In *Tribes and boundaries in Australia* (ed. N. Peterson), pp. 133–55. Australian Institute of Aboriginal Studies, Canberra.

Chapter Eight

The Politics of Peace in Primitive Societies

The Adaptive Rationale Behind Corroboree and Calumet

Johan M. G. van der Dennen

Peace: a period of cheating between two periods of fighting
Ambrose Bierce, *Devil's Dictionary*

Introduction

Peaceable preindustrial (preliterate, primitive, etc.) societies constitute a nuisance to most theories of warfare, and they are, with few exceptions, either "explained away," denied, or negated. Contending theories have also tended to severely underestimate the costs of war to the individuals as well as to the communities involved.

Materialist theory, as formulated by Ferguson, is one such exception: "[I]n contrast to the Hobbesian view, we should find nonwar, the absence of active fighting, in the absence of challenges to material well-being" (Ferguson 1984). Where the costs of initiating violence outweigh the benefits, war is expected to be absent (Durham 1976; Ferguson 1984; 1990; 1994). There is no theoretical reason to deny the possibility of peaceful societies. Indeed, "there may be alternative peaceable and militaristic *trajectories* of evolution" (Ferguson 1994).

The capability to make peace (peaceability) and the readiness to make war (warlikeness) are, it will be argued, not Platonic essences but rather the outcomes of a rational (Realpolitik) cost/benefit calculus (though the benefits of war or peace to the warrior-participants are not always *prima facie* obvious) and an adaptive response (in the Darwinian sense) to particular sociopolitical ecologies. Most peoples seem to prefer peace *when they can afford it*, i.e., when they can solve the internal problem of the "male fierce warrior syndrome" (especially prevalent when the warrior role is rewarded with social status and/or sexual privileges), and the external problem of being "left in peace" by other peoples.

The ecological roots of peace may be as complex as, or even more so than, the roots of violence and war. There may be as many reasons for peaceability as there are for belligerence: intercommunity nonviolence may be a response to overwhelming odds; it may be the taming effect of defeat; it may be enforced by colonial or imperial powers; it may be the result of isolation and/or xenophobia; it may be due to a negative cost/benefit balance of war, making peace more opportune under the given circumstances; it may be due to a voluntary decision to abstain from or abandon violence, or to a nonviolent ethic or pacifistic ideology; or some combination of all these factors. As Dentan (1992) reminds us: "[P]eaceability is not disability, not a cultural essence unrelated to a people's actual circumstances." Thus, warlike people are quite capable of peacefulness, while peaceable peoples are perfectly capable of intergroup violence *under altered circumstances*.

If war is so universal and ubiquitous as has been claimed by advocates of the "universal human belligerence" theorem (see van der Dennen 1990), the mere fact of peace constitutes a problem, and we would have to develop a theory of peace as an abnormal, anomalous condition. Gregor (1990) has actually proposed such a perspective: "Comparative research on the cause of war and peace is based on the hidden premises that peace is an expectable state of affairs in human relationships were it not for conflict. Peace is the absence of conflict, and it is conflict that needs to be explained (Cf. Haas 1990)." Gregor's perspective is the reverse: "Political systems are so volatile and war is so contagious that its existence should occasion little surprise. It is peace that needs special explanation" (Gregor 1990).

In this contribution I shall argue that the claim of universal human belligerence is grossly exaggerated; and that those students who have been developing theories of war, proceeding from the premise that peace is the "normal" situation, have not been starry-eyed utopians; and that peace—the continuation of potentially conflictive interactions between discernible groups of human beings with nonviolent means (to paraphrase the famous Clausewitzian dictum)—in primitive peoples is just as much a deliberate and rational political strategy, based on cost/benefit considerations and ethical judgments, as is war.

The Security Dilemma

General Robert E. Lee is reported to have said that "it is a good thing that war is so horrible or else we would grow too fond of it." The statement by Davie (1929) that "Men like war" is as apodictic as it is general (referring to *all* men), and obstinately reiterated to the present day. Lately, van Creveld (1991) stated (with a similar universal pretense): "However unpalatable the fact, the real reason why we have wars is that men like fighting, and women like those men who are prepared to fight on their behalf."

Jane Goodall (1986) observed a great eagerness in young prime male chimpanzees for the behaviors involved in "lethal male raiding" parties, but she also pointed out quite emphatically that there are distinct individual differences in this eagerness.

Fox (1991; Cf. Klineberg 1964) seems to advance what may be called a "bad seed" or "rotten apple" theory of war: one rotten apple soon spoils the whole basket. Similarly, one or a few percent of hyperaggressive or belligerent males distributed more or less at random throughout the megapopulation would be sufficient to create a rampant war complex among all the demes involved. The "potentials for aggressivity are not uniform but are normally distributed in any population. Thus, in any naturally occuring population, only about 1% of the individuals will be hyperaggressive" (Fox 1991). But this 1 percent might be responsible for the horrors of internecine wars.

There is a much more "tragic" variant of this theory in which no one actually has to harbor ill will. The expectation or suspicion thereof is in itself sufficient for a rampant war complex to develop.

Virulent war complexes do not have to be explained by some evil streak in human nature, but can be understood—at least in part—as the result of a war trap (Tefft 1988; 1990) from which nobody can disengage on penalty of annihilation.

Richerson (1995) advances what he calls the "evolutionary tragedy" hypothesis: warfare is liable to evolve even if it makes everybody worse off. It results from the perversion of the situation (the perfidious logic of the war "game") rather than that of the actors involved. The only practical way to avoid victimization by aggressors is to deter attack by being conspicuously prepared to fight, and to display a credible ability and will to inflict unacceptable damage on would-be attackers.

Primitive societies, like modern nation-states, are trapped in a security dilemma (e.g., Elias 1978). Simple game-theoretical analysis reveals why such a situation most of the time results in an equilibrial stalemate of mutual deterrence (assuming short-term rational choices of actors) even if none of the actors harbors evil intentions or sinister motives (or is equipped with aggressive/violent/belligerent drives, urges, or instincts).

The security dilemma in which (primitive) peoples find themselves has the formal structure of a "prisoner's dilemma" (PD) in which individual, short-term rational behavior leads to a collectively irrational outcome: all parties involved defect and lose (in terms of casualties, destruction of property, costs of war preparations, opportunity costs, etc.).

In a relatively stable socioecological environment (in which each society knows its and others' place, numerical strength, retaliatory capacity, etc.), to be on the alert and to be prepared to defend oneself may be a beneficial strategy resulting in a kind of peace through insulation with only sporadic and incidental flareups of overt violence.

In this case, which has the formal structure of an *iterated* PD, diplomacy and peace become viable options. In such an iterated PD situation, when both parties know each other more or less intimately and expect future reciprocal or mutually beneficial interactions, mutual suspicion and xenophobic fear can be converted to mutual caution and diplomatic maneuvering, but probably only if there is also a higher (e.g., tribal) authority to stop the private-enterprise revenge raiding, or to relax the obligations of the blood feud and the concomitant male ideal of the macho warrior, and the material rewards and social privileges attached to the warrior role.

"The Mohave Indians of the Colorado River valley are by reputation a warlike tribe," Stewart (1947) relates, "although my informants insisted that the people as a whole were pacifically inclined. It was asserted that, while war was disliked by a majority of the Mohave, battle was the dominant concern of the kwanamis ('brave men'), who were responsible for the recurrent hostilities and over whom there was no effective control."

As Goldschmidt (1994) points out, the problem of internal dissatisfaction with existing peace treaties among preindustrial societies is a recurrent one. The problem is caused partly by (a) distrust and fear; and (b) inability to restrain the entrepreneurial raiding of the warriors. "Even when the population is war weary," Goldschmidt concludes, "even when there is a genuine need for peace, the peace is fragile precisely because there remain those who feel that their masculinity, by which we mean their social identity, is lost if they do not press their cause," that is, the hatchet will not be ceremonially buried when there is no acceptable face-saving device (peace with honor) for the "fierce" warriors.

Nevertheless, even in a situation of chronic insecurity, the acceptance of mitigating rules of combat, of a common law of war and peace, is in accordance with enlightened self-interest: "Die Annahme bestimmter Kampfesregeln entspricht schließlich einem wohlverstandenen Selbstinteresse" (Mühlmann 1940). Rules for war mitigation and a common law of war and peace can, Mühlmann holds, develop only gradually in a situation of hereditary enmity.

Fierce Peoples?

Many peoples traditionally considered to be "fierce" or "ferocious" are, as Turney-High (1949) noticed, militarily rather inept. Even such tribes as the Iroquois, Mohave, Yanomamö, Karankawa, and Plains Indians, who traditionally have had a reputation of extreme warlikeness, may actually ill deserve such a reputation.

There is, for example, considerable evidence that the Iroquoian Confederacy arose as an attempt to establish peace and to live in harmony with the neighboring peoples (e.g., Morgan 1851; Holsti 1913; Turney-High 1949).

Many subdivisions of the Yanomamö were and are, according to Ferguson (1992), not nearly as violent and belligerent as those described and made infamous by Chagnon (1968). Other ethnologists who have conducted field research among the Yanomamö have found Chagnon's reports of violence inapplicable to the people they studied.

Finally, and paradoxically, the Plains Indians' warrior complex, with its emphasis on solism and individual feats of bravery and bravado (as exemplified by counting *coup*—touching the enemy, whether alive or dead—being the ultimate act of bravery), actually limited violence, so that warfare, though incessant, boiled down to a series of small-scale raids of a few "braves" striking *coup* and stealing horses, which were far more important objectives than killing the enemy.

The Inventory of Allegedly Peaceful Societies

"Simple" human societies, according to Knauft (1991; 1994), place great emphasis on generalized reciprocity and far less on balanced competition or negative reciprocity. Concomitantly, collective military action or warfare tends to be rudimentary or absent. This contrasts in aggregate terms with more complex, sedentary, horti- and agricultural societies, among which subsistence and demographic intensification are associated with increasing property ownership and status inequality, and with increasingly competitive politicoeconomic and military rivalry (e.g., Fried 1967).

Accordingly, we should be able to find a number of such "simple" societies without war, or with only rudimentary war, in the literature. Swanton (1943) surveyed the anthropological literature and found that there were about as many societies that were peaceable as warlike. Leavitt (1977) found war absent or rare in 73 percent of hunting and gathering societies (n=22), 41 percent of simple horticultural societies (n=22), and 17 percent of advanced horticultural societies (n=29). Holsti (1913), Hobhouse, Wheeler and Ginsberg (1915), van der Bij (1929), Numelin (1950), Textor (1967), and Bonta (1993), among others, present inventories of a great number of peaceful peoples.

The evidence of a substantial number of peoples without warfare, or with mainly defensive and/or low-level warfare (i.e., seldom exceeding the level of petty feuding or desultory skirmishes) does not support the view of universal human belligerence. It does not support the equally erroneous view of universal peaceability either. Rather, it supports Mühlmann's (1940) and Dentan's (1992) view that peace, as well as war, is the result of illuminated and opportunistic self-interest in the political arena, "an adaptive response (in the Darwinian sense) to particular political ecologies" (Dentan 1992).

Van der Bij (1929) concluded that primitive peoples were peaceful because they were primitive. Steinmetz (1929), on the other hand, concluded that primitive peoples were primitive because they were peaceful. Steinmetz thereby reiterated the statement by Gumplowicz (1892) that peaceful peoples "bleiben auf der Stufe der Affen" [remain on the level of monkeys]. Gumplowicz, by the way, admitted that ethnology offers numerous examples of such peaceful peoples, without giving any explanation of why and how these monkey-like peaceful peoples have been able to survive in so warlike a world as he envisaged.

Peace As the Normal Condition

"The question has been raised whether the traditional view of early society as one of constant warfare is really justified by the facts. There is, in fact, no doubt that to speak of a state of war as normal is in general a gross exaggeration," Hobhouse, Wheeler and Ginsberg (1915) concluded in their extensive survey of some 650 primitive peoples. Similarly, Quincy Wright (1942) stated: "No general golden age of peace existed at any stage of human history nor did any general iron age of war. Neither the Rousseauian nor the Hobbesian concept of natural man is adequate."

In even the most warlike societies, the vast preponderance of time is spent in the pursuit of ordinary, peaceful activities (Gregor and Sponsel 1994).

The unsentimental military analyst Turney-High (1949) proved, in several parts of his work on primitive war, to be a perceptive and keen psychologist. He observed that "primitive war, in spite of the dancing about, honours-counting, scalping, and head-hunting, was remarkably tame.... In all but a few areas the bloodiness of primitive war has been greatly exaggerated.... Cold-blooded slaughter has really never been approved by the bulk of mankind. All have understood the amenities of peace to a greater or less degree. Civilized and savage men understand that war requires regulation and that human death is full of mana, which is a fearsome thing.... Peace, then, seems to be the normal situation in the minds of even warlike peoples."

In discussing the "inevitability belief" (i.e., the belief that war is "natural" and, therefore, inevitable), Ferguson (1989) notes:

[T]he claim for universality [of war] can only be advanced by relying on several dubious procedures: letting one cultural subdivision with war represent a broader cultural grouping which includes some groups without war; letting war at any point in time count, and disregarding what may be much more typical periods of peace; and when these fail, falling back on the untestable assertion that a peaceful people might have had war before the Westerners arrived. Even if we focus on societies where warfare is an undisputed occurrence, periods of active warfare involving a given group usually are relatively brief. The vast majority of humans, living or dead, have spent most of their lives at peace. So one can agree with Hobbes that politically autonomous groups have the potential for war, but this tells us nothing about why real war occurs. Contrary to the Hobbesian image, peace is the normal human condition.

Prudent Feuders

There are a number of instances of tribal communities that do not support individual members in their personal vendettas against outsiders for fear that such revenge actions might escalate intercommunity violence, which would prove detrimental to the collective interests of the whole community. In certain instances, the community may even turn a murderer over to the victim's kin (A. Moore 1978).

Sally Moore (1972) has argued that in situations of homicidal "self-help," nonliterate people consider kin units, such as patriclans, to be corporate entities that share corporate liability. In the classic case, any adult male member of a first group can legitimately avenge a homicidal grievance against a particular individual in a second group by killing any of that group's adult males. When one of their members has become incorrigibly reckless in the matter of actions likely to invite such homicidal retaliation, there are three ways to avoid unnecessary feuds: (1) they may send the culprit into exile; (2) they may renounce the clan's responsibility to avenge him, giving other clans a free license to hunt him down; or (3) his own clan may put him to death (S. Moore 1972; Boehm 1985; 1986).

A clan system of collectivized self-defence and liability 'works' only if clan members are reasonably prudent in committing homicides or in otherwise stimulating members of other clans to kill them. Too much heroic aggressiveness can embroil a clan in so many feuds that it faces serious decimation or cannot earn its subsistence. Warriors living in feuding societies [such as the Pathans (Pashtun) and Montenegrins] are aware of these costs, and mostly they behave accordingly—that is, prudently. They try to be as aggressive as honour demands, but also try not to initiate feuds recklessly or pointlessly. (Boehm 1986)

Peacefulness Does Not Equal Pusillanimity or "Gentleness"

When Gregor (1990) tried to find comparative data to complement his study of the relatively peaceful Xingu communities, he was frustrated by the minimal number of peaceful peoples he could find. He writes:

> Other researchers, who have combed the literature more systematically than myself, have reached the same conclusion. Thus Richard Sipes notes in his study of war and combative sports: 'Relatively peaceful societies are not easy to find. I had to investigate 130 societies to find eleven, of which five were rejected because of insufficient information' (1973: 68). Similarly, Otterbein (1970) found only four peaceful cultures among the fifty in his study of the evolution of war. Turning to advanced, state-level societies the searcher for peace becomes even more disheartened ...
>   The societies that come closest to fitting the model of the truly peaceful culture are small in scale and primarily hunters and foragers. This conclusion is in keeping with research on war by Wright ... and others who have positively associated war with community size and cultural development. Peaceful peoples also tend to be geographically isolated. Otterbein (1970), for example, finds that societies lacking in military organizations, such as the Copper Eskimo, the Dorobo and the Tikopians, live on islands, mountain tops, arctic wastelands and plateaus surrounded by malaria infested jungles. In some cases this isolation is a strategic adaptation to dealing with more aggressive societies that surround them. In most instances, however, peaceful societies appear to achieve their status by evading rather than solving the problems of intertribal relations. (Gregor 1990)

Isolation, splendid or not, seems *prima facie* to be the most prominent condition for peacefulness. So much so, in fact, that Mühlmann (1936; 1940) virtually identified peaceful peoples with *Rückzugsvölker* (literally, evading/retreating peoples).

Why could Gregor find so few peaceful peoples? One of the reasons might be simply because his criteria were wrong. In order to classify a people as "peaceable," some scholars demand not only absolute proof of the absence of *inter*community warring and feuding, but also the absence of every trace of *intra*group violence, aggression, and even conflict. They quite unrealistically require these societies to be "gentle" and pusillanimous in all walks of life.

As Turney-High (1949) already observed: "Such warless people have by no means been friendly and pacific. They have not been ignorant of how to shed human blood, nor have they abhorred it. Neither have they been without social institutions which formalized man-killing.... Field ethnology no more demonstrates that a warless people are per se a kindly one than it shows that a monogamous tribe is sexually chaste."

Bellicosity Does Not Equal Aggression

The conspicuous general absence of intergroup violence in mammals (only a few species apparently have mastered the art) is the major argument against a simple and naive aggression-warfare linkage. All these mammalian species do have aggression in their behavioral repertoire, but very few have war or its nonhuman equivalent (the "lethal male raiding" of the chimpanzees of Gombe, as described by Jane Goodall [1986] and others, is the most convincing example). If war were just another manifestation of aggression, intergroup agonistic behavior should be much more widespread in the animal kingdom than it actually is. Tooby and Cosmides (1988) argued that specific Darwinian algorithms must be involved to account for the coalitional psychology supposed to be operative in chimpanzees and humans.

Whatever function aggression or violence may serve in the life of the individual or the small group, Malinowski (1941) already observed, it does not serve the same function between political units. Wars between bands, tribes, states, or similar political entities are not just magnified quarrels between individuals. Warfare is not just simply aggregated individual aggression.

The profound misunderstanding about aggression and warlikeness, and the fundamental confusion concerning "non-aggressive" and "peaceful" is perhaps best exemplified by Heelas (1989; Cf. also Dentan 1992), who devotes his whole contribution discussing definitions of aggression in his "search for peaceful peoples."

It may be important to note that "peace" as used by Heelas and Dentan, and by many other Anglo-American authors, refers to the absence of physical violence generally (including intra- and inter-group violence), while in most other languages "peace" (except in such metaphors as "peace of mind," etc.) refers preferentially or exclusively to the absence of "war" (as collective, organized, armed, and violent intergroup or interstate conflict).

The only reasonable criterion for peacefulness is the presence or absence of *offensive war* or warlike behaviors (which implies that it is an *inter*group phenomenon), and not the presence or absence of any and all forms of *intra*group violence, or aggression, or conflict. The confusion rests on the, mostly implicit, assumption that war in some unspecified way is the result of the collective outpouring of accumulated "raw aggression." In a previous publication (van der Dennen 1986) I have tried to outline the fallacies involved in this kind of reasoning, especially the fallacy of subreption (the "moves unaccounted for" in equating aggression and war) and the cumulative fallacy (the confounding of levels of analysis).

It was also pointed out in that study that even in an extremely warlike society, such as the Yanomamö, boys fear pain and personal danger, and that elaborate training and indoctrination is required to turn them into "fierce warriors." And even then, men may fake illness and find other excuses to stay home or desert from a raiding party, or to call the whole enterprise off at the last moment (Chagnon 1968; Goldschmidt 1988; 1989; Ferguson 1992; 1994).

According to Kennedy (1971) and numerous other authors (see van der Dennen 1986), aggression is obviously correlated with, and an integral aspect of, war, but the relationships between war and aggression are reciprocal, complex, and mediated by intervening variables. There is no simple cause-and-effect relationship, and as White (1949) and others have long contended, there is probably more evidence to support the proposition that war produces aggression than the reverse. Ember and Ember (1992; 1994) found empirical evidence that among primitive peoples socialization for aggression is more likely to be a consequence than a cause of war. Grudges of "unemployed" warriors after coercive pacification have sometimes been misconstrued as evidence of some kind of innate bellicosity.

The frequency of wars, or even the "war experience," cannot be taken as a valid measure of "warlikeness," if we do not consider whether the warfare is defensive or offensive, and what the motives and the issues at stake are. For example, the Pueblo Indians in New Mexico were frequently engaged in defensive warfare against marauding neighboring tribes. Yet, it makes little sense to call them "warlike" (van der Dennen 1986).

Robarchek and Robarchek (1992), discussing the Waorani in Amazonia (who are probably unique in deliberately and consciously abandoning feuding and warfare), draw attention to the often limited options available in a hostile environment: "In such a situation, where warfare is endemic [and rampant], a people's options are rather limited: they can either flee, fight back, or be overwhelmed. Given the sociocultural environment of the region (and with no safe refuge available), engaging in at least defensive warfare becomes a functional necessity for group survival. Warfare, under these conditions, is contagious; once one group adopts it as a tactic for advancing its ends, others must either take it up or be destroyed."

In such a situation, fear, as Whiffen (1915) long ago, and Mühlmann (1940) and Meyer (1977) more recently, pointed out, seems to be the predominant war motive.

There is, furthermore, a strong androcentric bias in the accounts relating aggression and warfare in primitive societies; "with a sleight-of-hand extension of man into Man ... Woman is either ignored or presented as innately less aggressive than man. The arguments for a biological difference in the sexes in this regard are far from conclusive, but in cases where such a difference is put forward, the general conclusions of humanity's aggressive nature are not revised" (Howell and Willis 1989).

These authors also draw attention to the fact that aggression/violence/warlikeness, though considered "natural" particularly or exclusively in males, is also condemned as "bad," while its perceived opposite, peacefulness, carries with it the negatively valued connotations of being passive and inert—qualities that are associated with females. One might go so far as to state that for many males in primitive communities, as well as in our Western culture, "peaceful" equals "weak" equals "unmasculine/feminine" equals "impotent" equals "emasculated/castrated."

Primitive War As a Postcontact Phenomenon

The effects of contact with "civilized" states and colonialism in the warfare patterns of primitive peoples have, until recently, not sufficiently been acknowledged. Virtually all over the globe such contact has exacerbated warfare within and among nonstate societies to a degree that we are only beginning to sense (e.g. Blick 1988; Ferguson 1992a,b; Ferguson and Whitehead 1992; Sponsel 1994).

"Accepted wisdom even now holds that 'primitive' cultures are typically at war and that the primary military effect of contact with the West is the suppression of ongoing combat. In fact, the initial effect of European colonialism has generally been quite the opposite. Contact has invariably transformed war patterns, very frequently intensified war and not uncommonly generated war among groups who previously had lived in peace. *Many, perhaps most, recorded wars involving tribal peoples can be directly attributed to the circumstances of Western contact*" (Ferguson 1992b; italics added). A consequence of this is, as he explains elsewhere (Ferguson 1990), a systematic exaggeration of images of warlike behavior in supposedly "first contact" accounts.

The Characteristics of Peaceful Peoples

Fabbro (1978) analyzed five peaceable primitive societies, including the Semai, the Siriono, the Mbuti, the !Kung, and the Copper Eskimo. To these "traditional" groups, Fabbro added two literate peaceful communities for reasons of comparison, the Hutterites and the Islanders of Tristan da Cunha. Contemporary peaceful groups, such as the Hutterites and Amish, living in permanent communities based on a common religion, are also called "cenobites."

A peaceful society, according to Fabbro's criteria, is one that is not involved in internal (i.e., intracultural) collective violence; one that exhibits relatively little interpersonal violence; one that provides no special role for warriors; and one that has values and sanctions precluding violence as a means for resolving conflict. Peaceability should not be confused with pacifism, which is only one genre of peaceability (Dentan 1992).

McCauley (1990) presented the results of a study of the Semai and two other peaceful societies, the Buid of the Philippines, and the South American Xingu River conglomeration of tribes. Various combinations of the peaceable communities mentioned above were also present in the analyses of Gregor (1990) and Dentan (1992; 1994). From the combined analyses of this rather small sample, a number of patterns emerge:

- All peaceful societies are essentially small, local, face-to-face, communities with a very low degree of social stratification, and open and egalitarian decision-making.

- The "traditional" societies do not maintain an exclusive monopoly over an area of land. Other groups may come and go, and in times of shortage an incumbent band may share the food and water resources with another less fortunate group. But conflicts within these groups are also partly responsible for personnel changes, fission being used as a dissociative conflict resolution form.
- The traditional societies produce little or no economic surplus. Material inequality between individuals on a long-term basis is, therefore, impossible. As a corollary, leadership remains on the level of personal authority rather than coercive power because there is no surplus to appropriate.
- The differences in child-rearing practices between the traditional and the cenobite societies are open to a number of possible explanations. Cenobites generally are more authoritarian with children than are peaceable "refugees" like the Semai, and they approve the spanking and whipping of children as corporal punishment of last resort (Dentan 1992; 1994).

    Enculturating nonaggression may be a relatively minor factor in the creation of peaceability (e.g., Riches 1987; Dentan 1992; Eibl-Eibesfeldt 1993), though some cross-cultural studies find a positive correlation between child abuse, neglect, or harsh socialization practices and bellicosity (e.g., Levinson and Malone 1980; Ross 1992).
- Many of the peaceful societies develop what Gregor (1990) calls an "antiviolent" value system: cultural norms and ideologies that discourage both intra- and intergroup violence (an important component of which seems to be *Gelassenheit*, at least among cenobites). Nonviolence is supported by stigmatizing quarreling, boasting, stinginess, anger, and violence, and by according prestige for generosity, gentleness, and conflict avoidance. This value system is supported by supernatural beliefs (McCauley 1990).
- Peaceability and nonviolence among primitive peoples and cenobites seems to stem from a psychology of defeat: "Defeat tamed them ... those that survived did so by learning virtues of political accommodation or withdrawal from temporal affairs" (Barkun 1986; see Dentan 1992; 1994). Or, as Bigelow (1969) put it, "their 'peacefulness' was imposed on them by force." "Islets of peaceability" can arise as an adaptive response to defeat by neighboring peoples when there are relatively unpopulated areas (called "refuges" or "enclaves") to flee to.

- Peaceable "refugees" tend to be insulationist and xenophobic. Lacking the oppositional frontier processes that create peaceable "refugees," cenobites need specific mechanisms to maintain the boundaries between their people and the "others" by means of physical isolation. Peaceable peoples like the Semai contrast themselves with the peoples they fear, creating a counterculture. The antiviolent value system is embodied in a contrast between the peacefulness of the in-group and the violence of outsiders. Outsiders are bloody, violent, dangerous, ugly, evil, animal-like, and, in a real sense, less than human. Children are warned against outsiders and especially about behaving like outsiders. Apparently, "hating violence requires violent people to hate" (McCauley 1990).
- The gender-equality characteristic of many egalitarian band-level societies is not a necessary correlate of peacefulness among enclaved peoples, although the two phenomena can co-occur.
- None of the peaceful societies would seem to operate on the premise that its members would automatically refrain from violence even when aggressive models are absent. Even the most peaceful of these societies employ various forms of social conditioning and indoctrination to constrain and deflect the tendencies to resort to violence, as well as community inducements to discourage violence and instructions in the virtues and arts of nonviolent conflict resolution. Tribal cosmology, rituals, legends, and religious and ethical concepts and precepts reinforce the nonviolent norms of the society. And social ostracism is typically inflicted on individuals who violate these norms (S. Brown 1994).

The 52 "peaceful societies" investigated by Melko (1973) are not really societies in the ethnological sense but particular historical periods of particular civilizations, such as the Han and T'ang dynasties in China, without major internal physical conflicts. Yet, some of his findings may be summarized for reasons of comparison.

- No one form of government, no one economic system, no one structure of society, no one system of education seems to be essential to peace.
- Moderate powers seem to have had the advantage over great powers in maintaining peace. They are strong enough to resist attack, but not ambitious enough to become overextended.

Small powers that have been successful in maintaining peace have refrained from interfering in the affairs of their neighbors. Great powers seem to succeed in attaining peace only if they conquer all other great powers within range.

- Peace is the normal internal condition for a society. Conflict involving physical fighting is exceptional. When it occurs, most people involved in it are not fighting most of the time. Most people in most places in most periods of history have not been killed or injured in war.

In the next section, I shall more fully discuss some of the strategies and mechanisms of peacemaking in primitive societies.

A Typology of Peace

Dissociative (separative) peace

Peace by isolation; accomplished by
(1) geographical distance; insurmountable barriers; large no-man's lands;
(2) absence of technical means of telecommunication;
(3) conscious insulation, "splendid isolation," and nonintervention policies

Peace by extermination or annihilation

Peace by flight and migration

Peace by defeat or stalemate peace

Peace by incorporation or subjugation (debellatio)
(1) conquest and annexation of the territory of the vanquished and/or
(2) subjugation of the population resulting in
    (a) slavery
    (b) vassalage
    (c) tribute
    (d) satellite group
    (e) colonization
    (f) assimilation

Peace by war-weariness

Peace by deterrence

Associative (sociative) peace

Peace through union by means of
(1) fusion
(2) alliance
(3) federation and confederacy

Peace by convention
(1) armistices, truces, and cease-fires
(2) peace treaties, covenants, and ceremonies

Means to enforce peace treaties:
(1) intervention by invisible powers (magic, religion)
(2) hostages
(3) cautions and guarantees
(4) military occupation or reprisals

Institutions for safeguarding peace
(1) sanctuaries, asylums, and refuges
(2) neutrality
(3) *treuga Dei*

Institutions and conventions tending to counteract or mitigate war
(1) connubium; exogamy and intermarriage
(2) arbitration and mediation by religious authorities or third parties
(3) permanent international jurisdictions
(4) commercium; trade
(5) diplomacy; messengers, heralds, envoys, couriers
(6) intercommunity rites and feasts; corroboree, etc.
(7) hospitality
(8) war substitutes (e.g., potlatch)
(9) personal union (blood brotherhood and friendship)
(10) formal declaration of war
(11) fixing time and place of battle in advance
(12) postbattle compensation, indemnification, and reparation

Ius in bello:

(1) inviolability of certain persons (women, children, arbitrators)
(2) inviolability of certain places: refuges; neutral areas; tabooed times
(3) use of special, sublethal weapons (e.g., arrows without points or shafts: California), or special tactics (e.g., the custom of counting *coup* in Plains warfare)

(4) expiatory combat; judicial duels; sham battles
(5) chivalry and courtesy in battle
(The typology draws on Holsti 1913; Mühlmann 1940; Turney-High 1949; Numelin 1950; Gilissen 1961; Galtung 1965; 1968; Oliver 1989; Gregor 1990; a.o.)

Negative or dissociative peace in a pure form is based on minimal relationships: "Good fences make good neighbours" (see Galtung 1968). War presupposes contact between political entities. When these entities live apart and separated without any mutual contact, problems of war or peace are nonexistent. Other classic forms of negative peace are peace by deterrence (Gregor 1990); peace by annihilation or "peace of the graveyard"; peace by incorporation or subjugation; peace by defeat or stalemate peace; and peace by war-weariness or exhaustion (Oliver 1989).

Positive (associative) peace depends on the exchange of goods, services, and peoples. One of the effects of exchange is to create loyalties that are divided by both territory and bonds of interest, such as kinship and economics. These competing allegiances attract a natural constituency in favor of maintaining peaceful relations. Moreover, exchange may lead to the creation of a common culture. Parallel institutions in different societies may generate a consensus of values and stimulate interdependence (Galtung 1968; Gregor 1990).

Most of the strategies, institutions, customs, and conventions of positive peace mentioned in the typology are more or less self-evident and well known in our contemporary repertoire of peacekeeping efforts. I shall review here a number of strategies and conventions of positive peace and mitigation of war among primitive peoples that may be less self-evident (not necessarily in the same sequence as mentioned in the typology).

Diplomacy. Many primitive peoples have employed women both as messengers and envoys. Females were not uncommonly sacrosanct, i.e., enjoying personal inviolability in war, and were consequently available for intercommunity diplomatic missions, trade, and peacemaking (Holsti 1913; Numelin 1950). Young men were generally not regarded as reliable diplomats. They were suspected of trying to stir up warfare in the hope of being able to acquire personal prestige by performing deeds of valor.

Connubium. "Exogamous tribes generally—though there are exceptions—live in peace with each other," Numelin (1950) claims, though this seems not to be unequivocally substantiated by the cross-cultural evidence (see Conclusion). Exogamy, or marriage outside the group, is claimed to be an aid in binding groups together. Exogamy, according to Tylor (1889), was an extraordinary factor of peace, for it developed a bond of solidarity between the groups by making them dependent on each other for wives and children. For primitive men the choice was, as Tylor emphasized, "between marrying out and being killed out" (Tylor 1889; see also Melotti 1990).

Also Fox (1967) noted this pacifying effect: "You would not try to exterminate a band whose wives were your daughters and whose daughters were your potential wives; you would become, in one sense at least, one people; you would be dependent on each other for your continuity and survival." Thus, far from being only an economic "exchange of women" in the Lévi-Straussian sense, exogamy is basically an exchange of genes (Melotti 1990).

Kinship and marital bonds may also lead to divided loyalties and conflicts of allegiance, which, in turn, may lead to neutrality and war mitigation; an idea already expressed by Mühlmann (1940). Among the Alaskan Inuit (Eskimo), for example, relatives were neutral when their communities were in conflict. But, building upon the idea of divided loyalties, conflicts may, in effect, be resolved by expanding them (Goldschmidt 1994; cf. Oliver 1989). As the number of parties increases, so does the likelihood of conflicts of allegiance.

The same effect can be obtained not only by bonds of marriage but also by bonds of friendship. If a man in one tribe in the New Hebrides had a friend in one of the groups to be attacked, it was his prerogative to refuse to fight alongside his own tribe, and no question as to his bravery was involved. To avoid hurting or killing one's relative or friend, a man could also fight on the other end of the battlefield in some New Guinea tribes (Pospisil 1994).

Persons, especially women, related by kinship or marriage to both belligerent parties were sometimes allowed to pass with impunity from one camp to another to carry proposals of peace (Holsti 1913; Numelin 1950). A person related to both hostile parties was often spared among the Maori.

Not only more or less permanent exchange of women in exogamy, but also short-term exchange of women is sometimes part of the peacemaking ritual. Among some Papuans, the peacemaking feast that each enemy tribe gives its opponent includes giving their hosts access to their women to enjoy. Also, women are exchanged between enemies as part of the peace negotiations, ideally one woman from one tribe for each man slain in the other (Goldschmidt 1994). Among the Australians, the exchange of women is part of the peacemaking ceremony, as well as of direct dispute settlement: when a party to be attacked does not want to fight, it sends a number of its women over to the attackers. If the latter are willing to settle the matter in dispute without fighting, they have sexual intercourse with the women; if not, they send them back untouched. The Aborigines have no desire to exterminate each other's groups, for, if they did, where would they obtain their wives?

A related phenomenon that may sometimes mitigate war is common worship or religion. Common worship has also led to the custom of forbidding war during religious festivals, a custom analogous to the Western *treuga Dei* (peace of God).

Commercium: Trade as promoter of intertribal relations. Barter exists virtually all over the primitive world. Silent trade probably originated from distrust, fear, or enmity, prohibiting any direct contact with strangers. Territorial boundaries gradually came to be recognized as neutral areas where one might occasionally meet for mutual benefit, if not on friendly terms, at least without hostility. "As distrust declines, the former silent trade becomes less silent and the tribal representatives (mostly women) begin, though at first shy, to meet at regular intervals: The primitive market. The market day necessarily has the character of a rest day or holiday, affording opportunities for social intercourse, sport and amusement, during which hostilities are suspended. The market place can also become a kind of asylum, violation of which is sacrilege" (Numelin 1950).

Intercommunity rituals, feasts, and festivals. Mühlmann (1940) regards the male initiation ceremonies as the evolutionary matrix of the amphictyony because several sovereign clans unite for the occasion. In Australia, hostile tribes met in peace during the performance of certain initiation rites; all hostilities were suspended for the time being. Persons traveling to or from such feasts could pass unmolested through the territory of hostile tribes.

There are instances of peaceful relations being maintained between primitive tribes by means of festivals specially arranged for the invocation of peace. All fighting is placed under a ban or taboo for the time of the festival, and this ban may sometimes have great and lasting consequences (e.g., corroborees, *Mindarie* feast of the Dieri, etc.) (Numelin 1950). On the other hand, instances are not lacking in which the former enemy was invited to a feast in the other's camp or village only to be treacherously attacked there (e.g., Yanomamö: Chagnon 1968).

Postbattle indemnification and compensation. In her study of Melanesian warfare, Camilla Wedgwood (1930) found that peacemaking procedures usually "fall into two distinct parts: the making of compensation for injuries inflicted during the fighting; and the performance of some ceremonial, such as the exchange of gifts or food, which symbolically unites the erstwhile opponents."

McCorkle (1978) comments on the effects of compensation and indemnity payments (blood money) in the Californian region: "It also appears that regional, intertribal adherence to the unwritten law that each injury must be exactly recompensed limited armed aggression, since restraint served to save wealth and goods that would have to be expended at the settlement marking the end of hostilities."

Another kind of compensation (nonmonetary) is related by Whitehead (1990): among some South American peoples, ceremonies of peace were concluded by individuals interchanging as many blows with a club as amounted to complete satisfaction for both parties.

(Third party) mediation. Whitehead (1990) also presents an example of successful third party mediation and peacemaking among some South American tribes. Among the North American Plateau tribes, hostilities were limited to petty feuds and occasional small-scale raids by self-interested volunteers. Headmen and chiefs of villages and bands, however, disapproved of such entrepreneurial raids and went to great lengths to maintain peace, sometimes risking their lives in negotiations with hostile outsiders. For cross-cultural studies of mediation and negotiation, see also Gulliver (1979) and Greenhouse (1985).

Formal declarations of war. A further step toward the mitigation of war is the formal declaration of war (*indictio belli*) and the ultimatum (Mühlmann 1940).

A declaration of war seems to have been the custom among many peoples. The Caribs and many other American tribes declared war by hurling arrows or javelins into the enemy country, or sticking them into the ground at the boundary.

The effect of these war declarations is, as Numelin (1950) states, obviously to give the enemy a fair chance and can thus be considered to be some kind of chivalrous action. Turney-High (1949) offered the following observations: "Many tribes in varying states of culture considered war the unusual, so unusual that it required some formal act of declaration. It is impossible to say that this idea correlates with either the very simple or the complicated cultures. It has been evident in all degrees of cultural development." The Patagonians and Araucanians made a rude image of a man, around which they stuck spears, arrows, and clubs. This they set up as a declaration of war. The Huron sent a black wampum belt to the enemy-to-be. The Natchez declared war by leaving a "hieroglyph" picture in enemy territory to announce their intention of attacking at a certain phase of the moon. "This, to be sure, destroyed the surprise element, which may be why modern nations have lost their manners" (Turney-High 1949).

Fixing time and place of battle in advance. A further step toward the mitigation of war is, in addition to the formal declaration of war, the agreement on the war theater or battlefield and, by implication, the neutrality of other localities (Mühlmann 1940). The most important development of the "law of war" is the transition from the treacherous attack to the pitched battle on an agreed-upon battlefield. All other developments can be more or less logically derived from this primordial achievement: neutrality of certain places; nonbelligerence and truces at certain times; neutrality and inviolability of certain persons, especially noncombatants (women and children); asylums and safe havens; use of sublethal weapons, etc.

Davie (1929) considers the sparing of women and children in war to be the beginning of a common law of war and peace. Efforts to confine armed conflict to the fighting male population have also been observed by Eibl-Eibesfeldt (1986) to be part of the institutionalization of rules of warfare that help to avoid unnecessary bloodshed. Cultural evolution, he submits, here phenocopies ritualizations that in the animal kingdom repeatedly led from damaging fights to tournament-like contests.

Among the New Guinea Kapauku, the women, being tabooed from injury by the enemy, moved around the battle lines collecting arrows for their husbands (Pospisil 1994). This has also been commonly reported of Californian societies (e.g., Kroeber 1925).

The idea of neutral zones and the right of asylum probably arose originally from magical and religious conceptions of spirits dwelling in certain places that are sacred and must be kept free from disturbances, as Westermarck (1907) suggested. The graves of chiefs and ancestors are often sacred and taboo, as are the sanctuaries and temples beside them. Such "holy" places can become asylums where fighting is prohibited. Among many primitive peoples there are taboo or fetish houses where protection and peace is secured for all who enter. Sometimes related tribes could take refuge in one another's territory. Like "holy" places, there are also "holy" days when peace and rest must be observed (Holsti 1913; Mühlmann 1940; Numelin 1950).

Expiatory combat and judicial duels. Hobhouse, Wheeler, and Ginsberg (1915) leave little misunderstanding about expiatory combat as a conflict-limiting procedure. They state: "The expiatory combats and the regulated fights of the Australians are also all of them palpably means of ending a quarrel, or marking a point beyond which it is not to go. They do not seek to punish a wrong but to arrest vengeance for wrong at a point which will save the breaking-out of a devastating fight."

The judicial "duel of champions" has a similar objective of limiting "devastating fights." Instances of duels and single combats to settle intra- and intertribal disputes have been documented for many preliterate societies, as well as ancient Greeks, Hebrews, and Romans (Numelin 1950), among others.

Marian Smith (1951) described sham battles among the North American Plains Indians, in which the braves could display their strength, boldness, and agility in bloodless contests. An important ingredient of mock fighting seems to be the face-saving it offers to the fierce warriors.

Among the Australians of Arnhem Land, one of the types of battling was itself a peacemaking ceremony, the *Makarata*, in which members of an aggrieved clan were allowed to throw spears, in a controlled and usually nonlethal way, at relatives of the individuals who had killed one of them, until their anger had subsided. The ceremony did not end, however, until the injured clansmen had drawn blood from the actual killers by jabbing spears through their thighs.

Chivalry and courtesy in battle. Chivalry and gallantry paid the Maori poorly when they tried it with modern British troops. "They played the game more fairly than fair in the European concept. They were amazed when the British shot the people whom they sent from the palisades for water, for was not water necessary? When British ammunition ran low they waited for them to bring up supplies, for why fight a man on uneven terms?" (Turney-High 1949). Chivalry in combat can probably develop only in "agonal" types of warfare.

Peace treaties, covenants, and declarations. Fighting among primitive peoples is not only often preceded by ceremonial consultations, but also regularly succeeded by a peace treaty, covenant, or declaration. Frazer (1890) collected a number of cases of covenants by sacrifice of a slave or an animal.

Peace had to be formally declared among the Polynesian Mangaian by announcement on the peace drums and a human sacrifice to the war god. These people recognized war and peace as separate states of affairs (or definite social statuses, or domains of reality) and observed the shift from one to the other by specific rites of passage. Dual chieftainship (separate chiefs for peace and war) may have served the same function (i.e., to demarcate the separate states of affairs) among many North American Indians (Numelin 1950).

Elaborate and complex rituals of peacemaking have been described for a great number of tribes from all over the world. Peace can be ratified by means of exchange of gifts and by a variety of other peace ceremonies, such as burying the hatchet, breaking of spears, planting of trees, smoking the peace pipe or calumet, etc.

Blood brotherhood and friendship. The exchange of blood between persons who are establishing friendship is a relatively common ceremony. Drinking or mixing blood establishes peace relations. Blood brotherhood is, in the primitive world, regarded as one of the chief factors in preventing feuds. Friendship ties between Kapauku headmen of confederacies pacified formerly vicious enemies for the time of their lives.

Also, adoption may work as an avenue for preserving peace. The Inca emperor adopted sons of conquered chiefs and thus cemented his empire into a formidable monolith. Similarly, among the Kapauku adoption of young people of influential families was used to bring lasting friendly relations (Pospisil 1994).

War substitutes and institutions of peace. Goldschmidt (1994) examines in some detail three instances of what he calls the "institutions of peace": the White Deerskin Dance (as practiced by the

Hupa, Karok, and Yurok of California), the potlatch (as practiced by the Northwest Coast Kwakiutl and Tlingit), and the kula (as practiced by the Melanesians). These institutions of peace (or war substitutes, in the case of the potlatch) are, Goldschmidt says, socially constructed patterns of behavior in which antagonism and competitiveness are expressed in ways that are neither lethal nor violent. They do not eliminate war; they do, however, tend to reduce the level of military conflict.

Numelin (1950) ascribes a prominent part in the development of peaceful relations to the secret societies flourishing in the primitive world: "The secret societies seem to be so eminently peaceful in character that it is a question whether one of their chief purposes is not to prevent hostilities between local groups and tribes."

However, Numelin's claim seems in general grossly exaggerated. It is more likely that these secret societies performed internal militia and policing tasks, thus being able to control feuding to a certain extent.

Purification Rituals: Ambivalence Toward the Enemy

We have been led to think that disregard for the enemy´s life and feelings are characteristic of warfare, Turney-High (1949) states, but this is not necessarily so, as evidenced by ambivalent feelings toward the enemy and by guilt-expiating rituals, both of which seem to be universal and to betray "bad conscience."

"War and killing push men into some kind of marginality which is at least uncomfortable, for there seems to be a basic fear of blood contamination, an essential dread of human murder. If man did not consider human killing something out of the ordinary, why has there been such common fear of the enemy dead, the idea of contamination of even a prestigeful warrior of the we-group? We have seen that the channeling of frustration into hatred toward the enemy is good for the internal harmony of the we-group, but the enemy is human, too. Humanity is capable of ambivalent attitudes toward its enemies" (Turney-High 1949).

Ritual seems to have a primarily apotropaic function: it reduces fear and anxiety. It has the effect of coordinating preparations for action among several organisms. It also functions as a means of organizing the perception of reality, i.e., chaos is replaced by binary order (Kennedy 1971; P. Smith 1991; Meyer 1993). Ritual (especially prebattle or preparatory ritual) reduces fear. It reinforces the solidarity of the group by dramatizing its status structure. It strengthens group boundaries, justifies its hostile or defensive activities, and expiates its guilt. It supports the warrior values and the warfare process by ceremonially transforming the guilt of killing into self-righteous virtue and strength. The great ritual efforts to induce commitment may be seen, according to Kennedy (1971), as culturally developed means for overcoming the subconscious repugnance to killing as well as for reduction of fear. The warrior value system apparently needs a great deal of social buttressing, from early training in fierceness through indoctrination, divine validation, and many shaming devices to fear-reducing rituals (Kennedy 1971; see also Turney-High 1949; Andreski 1954; 1964; Potegal 1979; Goldschmidt 1988; 1989).

In a chapter of his *The Golden Bough*, aptly entitled "Taboo and the Perils of the Soul," Frazer (1890) was the first to acknowledge the existence of, and to summarize the available evidence of, disculpation ritual, taboos, and purification ceremonies (or lustration)—indicative of some sense of guilt—in the postwar behavior of primitive peoples. The purpose of the seclusion and the expiatory rites that the warriors who have taken the life of a foe have to perform is, he points out, "no other than to shake off, frighten, or appease the angry spirit of the slain man."

In his *Totem und Tabu*, Freud (1913) was so impressed by these examples of disculpation ritual among primitive peoples that he discussed the subject at length, connecting the expiatory ceremonies following the killing of an enemy with the general ambivalence of taboo: "We conclude from all these regulations that other than purely hostile sentiments are expressed in the behavior toward the enemy. We see in them manifestations of repentance, or regard of the enemy, and of bad conscience for having slain him. It seems that the commandment, Thou shalt not kill, which could not be violated without punishment, existed also among these savages long before any legislation was received from the hands of a God."

Much of the postwar ritual activity in primitive societies seems clearly to indicate the expiation of guilt. Various kinds of ritual penance after killing were widespread in primitive (and ancient) societies. Fasting, sexual abstinence, and separation were common, as were ritual responsibilities, such as sacrifices for vows given. Often the returning warrior was considered sacredly polluted and had to undergo additional purification rituals. The Pima, for example, regarded the killing of an enemy to be such a dangerous act that a Pima warrior withdrew from battle the moment he killed his opponent to begin his rites of purification (Kroeber and Fontana 1987). Similarly, a Papago warrior who had killed an enemy was unclean and dangerous, and the ordeal of purification (lasting sixteen days) necessary to readmit him to society was even more severe than the hardships of the warpath. Among many other tribes victorious slayers had to go through lengthy and troublesome purification rites to purge them from, or to immunize them to, the enemy victim's vengeful spirit.

"There has existed," Turney-High (1949) concludes his percep-tive review, "a dread of taking enemy life, a feeling that if the life of a member of the we-group was precious, so was that of a mem-ber of the other-group. Fear of death-contamination has demanded expiation or purification among many folk."

Conclusion

Although all theories of negative and positive peace are intu-itively reasonable, none of them survives the test of the cross-cul-tural data, Gregor (1990) asserts. Exogamy and trade, for example, are actually positively correlated with war frequency (Tefft 1975). Just as interpersonal violence often occurs in close relationships, the most intense conflicts seem to occur between polities that are similar in structure and intensely engaged with one another. Tefft (1975) notes:

> Interchange of membership through intermarriage does not seem to reduce substantially the frequency of war or to further peaceful rela-tions between political communities. In so far as internal war is con-cerned, political communities with numerous kinship ties war more frequently than those with fewer ties. This is not entirely surprising since internal wars are often fought over issues growing out of inter-marriage (i.e., default of bridewealth, adultery, etc.). More significant is the fact that political communities which have important economic ties with one another fight internal wars less frequently than those whose ties are primarily one of kinship. Economic ties create more mutuality of interest and less division than kinship ties at the tribal level. However, neither kinship nor economic ties create strong enough bonds of mutual interest to prevent external war.

This conclusion is, however, contestable. Tefft does not suffi-ciently distinguish types of warfare, nor does he take into account the various cultural, political, or socioeconomic levels among the societies studied, lumping them all together. It may well be that the mechanisms and processes in question are conducive to peace at some level of socioeconomic development, but not on others. Or only when a particular type of warfare prevails, and not when other types prevail.

Divale, Chamberis, and Gangloff (1976) have proposed an alternative explanation of the Tefft (1975) and Tefft and Reinhardt (1974) findings that internal war (i.e., war between groups within the same culture) was correlated with the presence of peacemaking mechanisms, and external war (war between culturally different societies) with their absence. They suggest that internal war is of a regulatory nature, connected to a system of population control. On the other hand, they suggest that external war is a struggle for survival between two or more societies fighting for space in the same ecosystem. External war is part of a process that leads to the development of matrilocal residence, which is a structural adaptation made by a pre–state level society struggling to maintain its niche. If internal war is regulatory, it follows that there should be many mechanisms to regulate it (i.e., peacemaking mechanisms) or to stop it for long periods (i.e., stable peace). If external war represents a struggle for survival between two societies trying to occupy the same niche, it follows that there can be no compromise or mechanism to regulate it.

Dentan (1992; 1994) sketches a political ecological model for the origin, persistence, and demise of peaceable societies. Dentan argues specifically (1) that ideology by itself does not determine peacefulness; (2) that nonviolence is not due to a psychic or cultural inability to be violent; and (3) that static interpretations of dynamic adaptations and situations are unlikely to be helpful.

Some of the important observations and conclusions of the studies briefly discussed above are the following:

- Peaceability is not disability, not a cultural essence unrelated to a people's actual circumstances. Warlike peoples are capable of peacefulness, while peaceable peoples are capable of waging war under appropriate circumstances. Violence in a particular time and place does not necessarily indicate that peaceability in a different time or place is illusory.
- Many peoples who value peace positively still have relatively high rates of intragroup violence, e.g., Gebusi of New Guinea (Knauft 1987) and San ("Bushmen") of Africa (e.g., Thomas 1994). Thus, a cultural emphasis on interdependence and nur-

turance does not by itself account for nonviolence. Social support networks themselves involve costs and conflicts. Besides, the social cohesion that stems from external stress can be pathogenic. In other words, people are not nonviolent unless they feel nonviolence is good or at least that violence is bad; but peace-loving people on occasion may commit acts of violence, and those occasions may come often.

* The discussion of human violence and nonviolence, war and peace, has suffered from ahistorical essentialism that treats particular historical moments as if they represented universal evolutionary trends or deep-rooted manifestations of quasi-national characters (Sponsel 1989). A Darwinian approach, which takes peace and nonviolence as adaptations to particular political ecological circumstances, seems more viable. Under some circumstances, opting for warfare is fatal. Death obviously decreases one's fitness to zero. The choice of flight, on the other hand, has also severe costs and complex social and psychological consequences. The rise and survival of peaceful societies suggests that human peaceability is not an impossible, anti-Darwinian fantasy, but instead an adaptive response to particular political ecologies (Dentan 1992; 1994).

Note: This contribution is a highly condensed version of Chapter 7 of my book *The Origin of War* (1995). Many examples and an extensive review of the literature can be found there.

References

Andreski, S. (1954/1968). *Military organization and society*. Routledge & Kegan Paul, London; University of California Press, Berkeley.

———. (1964). Origins of war. In *The natural history of aggression* (ed. J. D. Carthy and F. J. Ebling), pp. 129–36. Academic Press, New York.

Barkun, M. (1986). *Crucible of the millennium*. Syracuse University Press, Syracuse.

Bigelow, R. (1969). *The dawn warriors: Man's evolution towards peace*. Little, Brown, Boston.

Bij, T.S. van der (1929). *Ontstaan en eerste ontwikkeling van den oorlog*. Wolters, Groningen.

Blick, J. (1988). Genocidal warfare in tribal societies as a result of European-induced culture conflict. *Man*, **23**, 654–70.

Boehm, C. (1985). Execution within the clan as an extreme form of ostracism. *Social Science Information*, **24**, 309–22.

———. (1986). *Blood revenge: The enactment and management of conflict in Montenegro and other tribal societies*. University of Pennsylvania Press, Philadelphia.

Bonta, B. D. (1993). *Peaceful peoples: An annotated bibliography.* Scarecrow Press, Metuchen N.J.

Brown, S. (1994). *The causes and prevention of war,* 2d ed. St. Martin's Press, New York.

Chagnon, N. A. (1968/1977/1983). *Yanomamö: The fierce people,* 2d and 3d expanded eds. Holt, Rinehart & Winston, New York.

Creveld, M. van (1991). *The transformation of war.* Free Press, New York.

Davie, M. R. (1929). *The evolution of war: A study of its role in early societies.* Yale University Press, New Haven.

Dennen, J. M. G. van der (1986). Four fatal fallacies in defense of a myth: The aggression-warfare linkage. In *Essays in human sociobiology, vol. 2* (ed. J. Wind and V. Reynolds), pp. 43–68. VUB Press, Brussels.

———. (1990). Primitive war and the ethnological inventory project. In *Sociobiology and conflict: Evolutionary perspectives on competition, cooperation, violence and warfare* (ed. J. M. G. van der Dennen and V. S. E. Falger), pp. 247–69. Chapman & Hall, London.

———. (1995). *The origin of war: The evolution of a male-coalitional reproductive strategy.* Origin Press, Groningen.

Dentan, R. K. (1968/1979). *The Semai: A nonviolent people of Malaya.* Holt, Rinehart & Winston, New York.

———. (1978). Notes on childhood in a nonviolent context: The Semai case (Malaysia). In *Learning non-aggression: The experience of non-literate societies* (ed. M. F. A. Montagu), pp. 94–143. Oxford University Press, Fair Lawn.

———. (1992). The rise, maintenance, and destruction of peaceable polity: A preliminary essay in political ecology. In *Aggression and peacefulness in humans and other primates* (ed. J. Silverberg and J. P. Gray), pp. 214–70. Oxford University Press, Oxford.

———. (1994). "Surrendered men": Peaceable enclaves in the postenlightenment West. In *The anthropology of peace and nonviolence* (ed. L. E. Sponsel and T. A. Gregor), pp. 69–108. Lynne Rienner, Boulder.

Divale, W. T., Chamberis, F., and Gangloff, D. (1976). War, peace, and marital residence in pre-industrial societies. *Journal of Conflict Resolution,* 20, 57–78.

Durham, W. H. (1976). Resource competition and human aggression. Part 1: A review of primitive war. *Quarterly Review of Biology,* 51, 385–415.

Eibl-Eibesfeldt, I. (1986). *Die Biologie des menschlichen Verhaltens: Grundriß der Humanethologie,* 2d rev. ed. Piper Verlag, Munich.

———. (1993). Aggression and war: Are they part of being human? In *The illustrated history of humankind, vol. 1: The first humans: Human origins and history to 10,000 BC* (ed. G. Burenhult), pp. 26–29. Harper, San Francisco.

Elias, N. (1978). Transformations of aggressiveness. *Theory & Society,* 5, 229–42.

Ember, C. R. and Ember, M. (1992). Resource unpredictability, mistrust, and war: A cross-cultural study. *Journal of Conflict Resolution,* 36, 242–62.

———. (1994). War, socialization, and interpersonal violence: A cross-cultural study. *Journal of Conflict Resolution,* 38, 620–46.

Fabbro, D. (1978). Peaceful societies: An introduction. *Journal of Peace Research,* 15, 67–83.

Ferguson, R. B., ed. (1984). *Warfare, culture and environment.* Academic Press, New York.

Ferguson, R. B. (1986). Promoting peace: Which way to go? Paper presented at Meeting American Anthropological Association, Philadelphia.

————. (1989). Anthropology and war: Theory, politics, ethics. In *The anthropology of war and peace: Perspectives on the nuclear age* (ed. P. R. Turner and D. Pitt), pp. 141–59. Greenwood Press, London.

————. (1990). Explaining war. In *The anthropology of war* (ed. J. Haas), pp. 26–55. Cambridge University Press, Cambridge.

————. (1992a). A savage encounter: Western contact and the Yanomami war complex. In *War in the tribal zone: Expanding states and indigenous warfare* (ed. R. B. Ferguson and N. L. Whitehead), pp. 199–228. School of American Research, Santa Fe.

————. (1992b). Tribal warfare. *Scientific American*, **266**, 1, 90–95.

————. (1994). The general consequences of war: An Amazonian perspective. In *Studying war: Anthropological perspectives* (ed. S. P. Reyna and R. E. Downs), pp. 85–112. Gordon & Breach, Langhorne PA.

Ferguson, R. B. and Whitehead, N. L., eds. (1992). *War in the tribal zone: Expanding states and indigenous warfare*. School of American Research, Santa Fe.

Foster, M. L. (1986). Is war necessary? In *Peace and war: Cross-cultural perspectives* (ed. M. L. Foster and R. A. Rubinstein), pp. 71–78. Transaction Books, New Brunswick.

————. (1988). Expanding the anthropology of peace and conflict. In *The social dynamics of peace and conflict* (ed. R. A. Rubinstein and M. L. Foster), pp. 1–28. Westview Press, Boulder.

Fox, R. (1967). *Kinship and marriage: An anthropological perspective*. Penguin, Harmondsworth.

————. (1991). Aggression: Then and now. In *Man and beast revisited* (ed. M. H. Robinson and L. Tiger), pp. 81–91. Smithsonian Institute Press, Washington D.C.

Frazer, J. G. (1890). *The golden bough: A study of magic and religion*, 12 vols. Macmillan, London.

Freud, S. (1913). *Totem und Tabu*. Heller, Wien.

Fried, M. H. (1967). *The evolution of political society: An essay in political anthropology*. Random House, New York.

Galtung, J. (1965). Institutionalized conflict resolution: A theoretical paradigm. *Journal of Peace Research*, **2**, 348–97.

————. (1968). Peace. *International encyclopedia of the social sciences*, vol. 11, pp. 487–96.

Gilissen, J. (1961). *Essai d'une histoire comparative de l'organisation de la paix*. Editions de la librairie encyclopédique, Bruxelles.

Goldschmidt, W. R. (1988/1989). Inducement to military participation in tribal societies. In *The social dynamics of peace and conflict* (ed. R. A. Rubinstein and M. L. Foster), pp. 47–65. Westview Press, Boulder; also in *The anthropology of war and peace: Perspectives on the nuclear age* (ed. P. R. Turner and D. Pitt), pp. 15–31. Greenwood Press, London.

————. (1994). Peacemaking and the institutions of peace in tribal societies. In *The anthropology of peace and nonviolence* (ed. L. E. Sponsel and T. A. Gregor), pp. 109–32. Lynne Rienner, Boulder.

Goodall, J. (1986). *The chimpanzees of Gombe: Patterns of behaviour*. Harvard University Press, Cambridge, Mass.

Greenhouse, C. J. (1985). Mediation: A comparative approach. *Man*, **20**, 90–114.

182 | *Johan M. G. van der Dennen*

Gregor, T. A. (1990). Uneasy peace: Intertribal relations in Brazil's Upper Xingu. In *The anthropology of war* (ed. J. Haas), pp. 105–24. Cambridge University Press, Cambridge.

———. (1994). Symbols and rituals of peace in Brazil's Upper Xingu. In *The anthropology of peace and nonviolence* (ed. L. E. Sponsel and T. A. Gregor), pp. 241–58. Lynne Rienner, Boulder.

Gregor, T. A. and Sponsel, L. E. (1994). Preface. In *The anthropology of peace and nonviolence* (ed. L. E. Sponsel and T. A. Gregor), pp. xv–xviii. Lynne Rienner, Boulder.

Gulliver, P. H. (1979). *Disputes and negotiations: A cross-cultural perspective*. Academic Press, New York.

Gumplowicz, L. (1892). *Die soziologische Staatsidee*. Wagner, Innsbruck.

Haas, J. (1990). Warfare and the evolution of tribal polities in the prehistoric Southwest. In *The anthropology of war* (ed. J. Haas), pp. 171–89. Cambridge University Press, Cambridge.

Heelas, P. (1989). Identifying peaceful societies. In *Societies at peace: Anthropological perspectives* (ed. S. Howell and R. Willis), pp. 225–43. Routledge, London.

Hobhouse, L. T. (1956). The simplest peoples. Part II: Peace and order among the simplest peoples. *British Journal of Sociology*, **7**, 96–119.

Hobhouse, L. T., Wheeler, G., and Ginsberg, M. (1915). *The material culture and social institutions of the simpler peoples*. London School of Economics, London.

Holsti, R. (1913). The relation of war to the origin of the state. *Annales Academiae Scientiarum Fennicae*, **13**.

Howell, S. and Willis, R. (1989). Introduction. In *Societies at peace: Anthropological perspectives* (ed. S. Howell and R. Willis), pp. 1–30. Routledge, London.

Kennedy, J. (1971). Ritual and intergroup murder: Comments on war, primitive and modern. In *War and the human race* (ed. M. N. Walsh), pp. 40–61. Elsevier, Amsterdam.

Klineberg, O. (1964). *The human dimension in international relations*. Holt, Rinehart & Winston, New York.

Knauft, B. M. (1987). Reconsidering violence in simple human societies: Homicide among the Gebusi in New Guinea. *Current Anthropology*, **28**, 457–500.

———. (1991). Violence and sociality in human evolution. *Current Anthropology*, **32**, 391–409.

———. (1994). Culture and cooperation in human evolution. In *The anthropology of peace and nonviolence* (ed. L. E. Sponsel and T. A. Gregor), pp. 37–68. Lynne Rienner, Boulder.

Kroeber, A. L. (1925). Handbook of the Indians of California. *Bureau American Ethnology Bulletin*, **78**, Washington.

Kroeber, C. B. and Fontana, B. L. (1986/1987). *Massacre on the Gila: An account of the last major battle between American Indians, with reflections on the origin of war*. University of Arizona Press, Tucson.

Leavitt, G. C. (1977). The frequency of warfare: An evolutionary perspective. *Sociological Inquiry*, **47**, 49–58.

Levinson, D. and Malone, M. J. (1980). *Toward explaining human culture: A critique of the findings of worldwide cross-cultural research*. HRAF Press, New Haven.

Malinowski, B. (1941). An anthropological analysis of war. *American Journal of Sociology*, **46**, 521–50.

McCauley, C. R. (1990). Conference overview. In *The anthropology of war* (ed. J. Haas), pp. 1–25. Cambridge University Press, Cambridge.

McCorkle, T. (1978). Intergroup conflict. In *Handbook of North American Indians, vol. 8: California* (ed. W. C. Sturtevant and R. F. Heizer), pp. 694–700. U.S. Government Printing Office, Washington D.C.

Melko, M. (1973). *52 peaceful societies.* CPRI Press, Oakville, Ontario.

Melotti, U. (1990). War and peace in primitive human societies. In *Sociobiology and conflict: Evolutionary perspectives on competition, cooperation, violence and warfare* (ed. J. M. G. van der Dennen and V. S. E. Falger), pp. 241–46. Chapman & Hall, London.

Meyer, P. (1977). *Kriegs- und Militärsoziologie.* Goldmann, Munich.

———. (1993). Human nature and the origins of warfare: Some evolutionary considerations. Paper presented at 16th meeting, International Society Political Psychology, Cambridge, Mass., July.

Moore, A. (1978). *Cultural anthropology.* Harper & Row, New York.

Moore, S. F. (1972). Legal liability and evolutionary interpretation: some aspects of strict liability, self-help and collective responsibility. In *The allocation of responsibility* (ed. M. Gluckman), pp. 51–107. Manchester University Press, Manchester.

Morgan, L. H. (1851). *League of the Ho-de-no-sau-nee or Iroquois.* Sage & Brothers, Rochester.

Mühlmann, W.E. (1936). *Rassen- und Völkerkunde: Lebensprobleme der Rassen, Gesellschaften und Völker.* Vieweg, Braunschweig.

———. (1940). *Krieg und Frieden. Ein Leitfaden der politischen Ethnologie.* C. Winters Universitätsbuchhandlung, Heidelberg.

Numelin, R. (1950). *The beginnings of diplomacy: A sociological study of intertribal and international relations.* Oxford University Press, London.

Oliver, D. L. (1989). *Oceania: The native cultures of Australia and the Pacific Islands,* 2 vols. University of Hawaii Press, Honolulu.

Otterbein, K. F. (1970/1985). *The evolution of war: A cross-cultural study.* HRAF Press, New Haven.

Pospisil, L. (1994). "I am very sorry I cannot kill you any more": War and peace among the Kapauku. In *Studying war: Anthropological perspectives* (ed. S. P. Reyna and R. E. Downs), pp. 113–36. Gordon & Breach, Langhorne, Penn.

Potegal, M. (1979). The reinforcing value of several types of aggressive behaviour: A review. *Aggressive Behaviour,* 5, 353–73.

Richerson, P. J. (1995). "Warfare" (Ch. 19 of his Human Ecology course at the University of California at Davis).

Riches, D. (1987). Violence, peace and war in "early" human society: The case of the Eskimo. In *The sociology of war and peace* (ed. C. Creighton and M. Shaw), pp. 17–36. Macmillan, London.

Robarchek, C. A. (1994). Ghosts and witches: The psychocultural dynamics of Semai peacefulness. In *The anthropology of peace and nonviolence* (ed. L. E. Sponsel and T. A. Gregor), pp. 183–96. Lynne Rienner, Boulder.

Robarchek, C. A. and Dentan, R. K. (1987). Blood drunkenness and the bloodthirsty Semai: Unmaking another anthropological myth. *American Anthropologist,* 89, 356–65.

Robarchek, C. A. and Robarchek, C. J. (1989). The Waorani: From warfare to peacefulness. *The World and I,* 4, 625–35.

———. (1992). Cultures of war and peace: A comparative study of Waorani and Semai. In *Aggression and peacefulness in humans and other primates* (ed. J. Silverberg and J. P. Gray), pp. 189–213. Oxford University Press, Oxford.

Ross, M. H. (1992). Social structure, psychocultural dispositions, and violent conflict: Extensions from a cross-cultural study. In *Aggression and peacefulness in humans and other primates* (ed. J. Silverberg and J. P. Gray), pp. 271–94. Oxford University Press, Oxford.

Sipes, R. G. (1973). War, sports and aggression: An empirical test of two rival theories. *American Anthropologist*, 75, 64–86.

———. (1975). War, combative sports, and aggression: A preliminary causal model of cultural patterning. In *War, its causes and correlates* (ed. M. A. Nettleship, R. D. Givens, and A. Nettleship), pp. 749–64. Mouton, The Hague.

Smith, M. W. (1951). American Indian warfare. *Transactions New York Academy of Sciences*, 2d ser., 13, 348–65.

Smith, P. (1991). Codes and conflict: toward a theory of war as ritual. *Theory & Society*, 20, 103–38.

Sponsel, L. E. (1989). An anthropologist's perspective on peace and quality of life. In *Peace and development* (ed. D. Sanders and J. Matsuoka), pp. 29–48. University of Hawaii School of Social Work, Honolulu.

———. (1994). The mutual relevance of anthropology and peace studies. In *The anthropology of peace and nonviolence* (ed. L. E. Sponsel and T. A. Gregor), pp. 1–36. Lynne Rienner, Boulder.

Steinmetz, S. R. (1929). *Soziologie des Krieges*. J. A. Barth, Leipzig.

Stewart, K. M. (1947). Mohave warfare. *Southwestern Journal of Anthropology*, 3, 257–78.

Swanton, J. R. (1943). *Are wars inevitable?* Smithsonian Institute War Background Studies, 12, Washington D.C.

Tefft, S. K. (1975). Warfare regulation: A cross-cultural test of hypotheses. In *War, its causes and correlates* (ed. M. A. Nettleship, R. D. Givens, and A. Nettleship), pp. 693–712. Mouton, The Hague.

———. (1988). Structural contradictions, war traps and peace. *Journal of Peace Research*, 25, 149–63.

———. (1990). Cognitive perspectives on risk assessment and war traps: An alternative to functional theory. *Journal of Political and Military Sociology*, 18, 57–77.

Tefft, S. K. and Reinhardt, D. (1974). Warfare regulation: A cross-cultural test of hypotheses among tribal peoples. *Behavioural Science Research*, 9, 151–72.

Textor, R. B. (1967). *A cross-cultural summary*. HRAF Press: New Haven.

Thomas, E. M. (1994). Management of violence among the Ju/wasi of Nyae Nyae: The old way and a new way. In *Studying war: Anthropological perspectives* (ed. S. P. Reyna and R. E. Downs), pp. 69–84. Gordon & Breach, Langhorne, Penn.

Tooby, J. and Cosmides, L. (1988). The evolution of war and its cognitive foundations. *Proceedings Institute of Evolutionary Studies*, 88, 1–15.

Turney-High, H. H. (1949/1971). *Primitive war: Its practice and concepts.* University of South Carolina Press, Columbia.

Tylor, E. B. (1889). On a method of investigating the development of institutions, applied to laws of marriage and descent. *Journal of the Anthropological Institute*, 18, 245–72.

Wedgwood C. H. (1930). Some aspects of warfare in Melanesia. *Oceania*, 1, 5–33.

Westermarck, E. A. (1907). *Ursprung und Entwicklung der Moralbegriffe*. Klinkhardt, Leipzig.

Whiffen, T. W. (1915). *The north-west Amazons: Notes on some months spent among cannibal tribes.* Scribner's, New York.

White, L. A. (1949). *The science of culture: A study of man and civilization*. Farrar, Straus & Cudahy, New York.

Whitehead, N. L. (1990). The snake warriors: Sons of the tiger's teeth. A descriptive analysis of Carib warfare, ca. 1500–1820. In *The anthropology of war* (ed. J. Haas), pp. 146–70. Cambridge University Press, Cambridge.

Wright, Q. (1942/1965). *A study of war*. University of Chicago Press, Chicago.

PART III

INDIVIDUAL BEHAVIORAL MECHANISMS

CHAPTER NINE

PREJUDICE AND INFERENTIAL COMMUNICATION: A NEW LOOK AT AN OLD PROBLEM

Siegfried Frey

Hostile attitudes against other people have shaped the way human beings have dealt with each other probably since the dawn of time. In the early days of humanity, when hunters and gatherers roamed the earth in small bands, a habitual attitude of distrust against members from other groups and even a readiness to aggress may well have had a certain survival value, especially so if we consider that the constant threat originating from environmental dangers did much to keep in-group aggression at bay. However, when the human animal began to settle down and form agricultural communities, the handling of such habitual hostility and aggression must have become much more difficult. On the one hand, the development of larger settlements provided the individual with a degree of security from outside dangers that was totally unknown to the hunter and gatherer. But on the other hand, the social friction originating from increased social interaction presented a constant threat to a society whose functioning had become deeply dependent upon the division of labor.

Early societies attempted to deal with this problem in a strictly normative way. Rules of conduct meant to suppress hostile action among community members can be found in the earliest writings. Formalized legal codes, outlawing diverse forms of aggression among citizens, can be traced back to the time the Sumerians created the first city-states in Southern Mesopotamia. Such rules of conduct were usually grounded in commonly shared religious belief systems. However, already at a very early stage of history, political powers joined in efforts to enforce such regulations. The 282 laws given in the Codex Hammurabi, for example, provide vivid testimony to the drastic measures imposed by King Hammurabi of Babylon (1728–1686 B.C.) on his people in an attempt to ensure peaceful interaction.

The history of the past five millennia leaves no doubt that such normative action did little to reduce humankind's potential for aggression. Hostility and violence have, indeed, been such perennial problems that much of our civilizing effort can be seen as *Homo sapiens'* more or less successful attempt to curb the penchant to attack our own kind. The main effect of measures to control the violence of individuals by legal means may, in fact, have been to simply redirect aggression towards those less well protected by the law. This, at least, would explain why human aggression has always assumed its most horrible form during times of war, when the "enemy" was officially deprived of the right to exist. Likewise, the fact that manifest aggression is so often directed toward people of different ethnic or cultural backgrounds may have less to do with a selective hostility to perceived outsiders than with perceiving them as largely exempt from social protection, and thus as comparatively "easy" victims for aggression.

It was the great achievement of the humanistic movement, starting in the Renaissance, to realize that neither religious belief systems nor bureaucratic rule would ever be able to rid the world of an aggressiveness that derived its main thrust from largely irrational habits, such as superstition and prejudice. To strengthen the power of reason thus became the chief goal of all those who believed that humanity did have the potential to develop, by its own strength, a way of life no longer driven by the primitive impulses of prejudice and physical aggression. Along with this, education rightly assumed a prominent place in the humanists' quest for a more tolerant society.

It is worthwhile to note that at least since the publication of Descartes' *Discours de la méthode pour bien conduire sa raison, et chercher la verité dans les sciences* (1637), education did not mean simply the transfer of knowledge from an information-possessing sender to a supposedly ignorant receiver. Far more important to the humanistic approach to higher education was the encouragement of Cartesian doubt, that is, the systematic questioning of the easy answers that look plausible from the superficial point of view. The individual, therefore, carried the responsibility for his/her own education, and thus for the development of all the intellectual faculties inherent in human beings and unique to them. It was this concept of education that, 150 years later, would lead Kant to declare that the ultimate aim of the *Aufklärung* (Enlightenment) was to instigate "the parting of the human being from his self-inflicted tutelage."[1]

Each of us would probably still subscribe to the assumption that education is crucial for the development of human society. The notion of a *self-inflicted* tutelage, however, has almost completely vanished. In fact, in what might well be a response to the sudden appearance of new and extremely powerful mass communication systems, our view of the responsibilities of the parties involved in the educational process has practically been reversed. Today, the recipient of information is hardly ever held responsible for the way the data presented are processed. Instead, we tend to blame the provider of information for what goes on in the recipient's mind.

Misinformation As the Basis for Prejudice

This conceptual shift has its roots in the behaviorist learning theory of the early twentieth century. The notion that behavior is rigidly controlled by external stimuli left little room for the idea of a human being actively taking part in his or her own intellectual and emotional development. Instead, along with the assumption that nurture determines a person's nature, the conviction spread that if we are to understand an individual's behavior or attitudes, we are to look at the stimulus conditions to which that person was exposed.

The first one to apply that view to the understanding of prejudice was the publicist and culture critic Walter Lippmann. In his seminal work, *Public Opinion*, first published in 1922, Lippmann argued that most of our opinions are based on information obtained from others: "Each of us lives and works on a small part of the earth's surface, moves in a small circle, and of these acquaintances knows only a few intimately ... Inevitably our opinions cover a bigger space, a longer reach of time, a greater

1. *Der Ausgang des Menschen aus seiner selbstverschuldeten Unmündigkeit* (Kant 1784, 481).

number of things, than we can directly observe. They have, therefore, to be pieced together out of what others have reported" (Lippmann 1950/1922, 79). To account for the result of what is pieced together, Lippmann coined the term "stereotype." It was meant to signify a simplified and sometimes even highly distorted picture of the world, depending upon the quality of the information provided by the external source. This stereotype, in turn, was considered to form the basis for the individual's *affective response* towards the issues involved, and thus to account for the high emotional charge regularly associated with prejudice.

Published at a time when people had just learned how effectively their opinions and attitudes had been manipulated by the propaganda departments of World War I, Lippmann's model seemed readily to explain the mechanism involved in the development of ethnic hostility. Further evidence that both the target as well as the holder of prejudice can be the victim of a third party came from the totalitarian systems that were just about to develop in Europe and elsewhere. The concept of stereotyping was, however, not meant to explain only the impact of blatant indoctrination. Its main concern was to tap the more subtle modes of influencing people's attitudes, such as those the mass media exert in democratic systems.

Lippmann himself focused his analysis mostly on the print media. It was quickly realized, however, that his conceptual framework was highly relevant also for understanding the impact that the newly emerging radio broadcasting systems might exert on public opinion. As this new technology for electronic information transmission was able to reach a much larger audience than any traditional mass media ever could, more and more people would derive their knowledge from the same source and at the same time. This, of course, raised the specter that people's opinions and attitudes might become even more "stereotyped," that is, increasingly schematic and biased in a very uniform way.

In what is a rare case of almost unanimous acclaim for a new concept, Lippmann's proposition was instantly adopted within nearly all branches of the social sciences. Within a matter of years, his term "stereotype" became practically synonymous with "prejudice" and eventually even almost replaced it in the scientific literature. Part of the appeal of Lippmann's model was, of course, that it offered a rational explanation for what had long looked like a largely irrational phenomenon. The strange fact that intelligent persons can harbor strong emotional attitudes against people they

have never even seen could now be explained as a natural consequence of cognitive information processing. Even the fact that
once a stereotype is established it tends to function like a self-sustaining process seemed to have its basis in the cognitive mechanism. As Lippmann put it, far from being readily dissolved by
contradictory information, "those preconceptions, unless education has made us acutely aware, govern deeply the whole process
of perception" (Lippmann 1950/1922, 90). And it is for this reason
that he would insist that the "subtlest and most pervasive of all
influences are those which create and maintain the repertory of
stereotypes" (Lippmann 1950/1922, 89f.).

The Failure of a Cognition-Based Program for the Prevention of Prejudice

Besides its theoretical merits, Lippmann's model was also attractive
from a more pragmatic point of view. The notion that conscious
information processing constitutes the core factor in the formation
of prejudice held promise to yield effective measures for its containment. In particular, efforts aimed at raising the level of education within the population, giving liberal access to a wide variety of
informational sources, as well as encouraging and facilitating personal encounters across ethnic or cultural borders, seemed potent
factors to guard against the development of prejudice.

If we take a look at the sociopolitical developments that have
occurred since the end of World War II, it appears almost as if a
prejudice-preventing program in the spirit of Lippmann's idea
had actually been put into effect. Like no other epoch in history,
this past half-century has seen enormous efforts to provide opportunities for higher education to more and more people. Political
developments leading to the downfall of once powerful totalitarian systems liberated many parts of the world from government-
installed opinion manipulators. The gradual easing of
bureaucratic travel restrictions that followed political restructur-
ing created vast new opportunities for cross-national encounters,
especially among young people. Special measures such as the system of "busing" in the United States even installed a mandatory
system to make sure that cross-ethnic encounters would begin at
a very early age. As to the exposure to information, the enormous
increase in the number of journals, radio stations, and TV channels
competing day to day for the individual's attention confronted

the public with a variety of different ideas and different value systems, thus providing additional stimulation for the development of independent thinking. At present, the dramatic progress in interactive communications technology with all its breathtaking possibilities for instant information retrieval seems to further contribute to the creation of seemingly ideal conditions for the development of a well-informed, intellectually emancipated citizenry that will not fall victim to gross stereotyping and prejudice.

Until just a few years ago, one could indeed have had the impression that the program actually worked and that prejudice was fighting a losing battle. To approach one's fellow human beings in an open-minded, unprejudiced way was considered the mark of the generation raised after World War II, which benefited particularly from the increased possibilities for higher education. Their involvement in various sociopolitical issues, such as the civil rights movement in the US, did, in fact, do a lot to attenuate ethnic prejudice or at least rid us of its worst forms. There can also be no doubt that new ways of thinking developed that initiated processes that ultimately broke up many of the traditional role models—to the point that even such archaic clichés concerning typical male and female traits are now on the wane. Indeed, for a while at least, it seemed that the only ones who remained trapped in their prejudiced view of the world were the old folks—those over thirty, who, according to the dictum of the 1960s, were not to be trusted anyhow.

As we approach the third millennium, however, the old ghosts of ethnic prejudice are all of a sudden back to haunt us again. In a matter of years, the seemingly bygone issue has gained a startling new actuality, not only in Eastern Europe, where it is currently most visible, but also in highly industrialized Western countries, including Germany. According to the classic model of prejudice formation, someone must have managed to disseminate, in spite of all the precautions taken, highly biased information to unsuspecting people in order to build up these hostile attitudes. It is hard to imagine, however, especially in these times of "political correctness" with its strong tendency to ban if not to literally outlaw words that could explicitly or implicitly discredit groups of people, that the newly virulent hostility is the result of biased information fed to persons who have no means to verify its validity. We must ask ourselves, therefore, whether the prevailing theoretical model is still adequate to explain the situation which confronts us today.

Prejudice Viewed from a Communicational Perspective

Although the philosophy behind stereotyping is thoroughly grounded in behaviorist thinking, Lippmann did not cast it strictly in terms of classical learning theory. Instead, he became the first scholar who tried systematically to view the formation of prejudice from a communicational perspective. A quarter of a century before Claude Shannon (1948) published his epoch-making *Mathematical Theory of Communication*, Lippmann described the process by which stereotypes develop in a way that closely resembles the three-step mechanism Shannon showed to be at work in machine communication. Spelled out in these terms, stereotypes are generated by a process in which the sender's message is first *encoded* into written or spoken language signals, then *transmitted* by an appropriate medium to a receiver, who finally *decodes* the signals by applying the same code used for the encoding of the message. The assumption inherent in this model, shared by Lippmann and many later scholars—that it is the *encoder* who by using the code of language largely controls the cognitions formed by the receiver—had a lasting impact on the way research in this field was conducted. It made the sender rather than the perceiver the center of attention, and it dealt almost exclusively with verbal behavior.

In order to more fully understand the formation of prejudice, we may have to go beyond this limited scope of investigation. As Sperber and Wilson (1986) have pointed out, the idea that communication is achieved by encoding and decoding messages is so entrenched in Western culture that "[f]rom Aristotle through to modern semiotics, all theories of communication were based on a single model ... the code model" (Sperber and Wilson 1986, 2). This might, in fact, explain why the doubts Shannon himself held about the broad applicability of his theory were not appreciated in the literature. The author of the mathematical theory of communication never ventured beyond the engineering context for which his model was designed and even explicitly referred to the existence of features in human communication that "are irrelevant to the engineering problem" (Shannon 1948, 379). However, from the moment Shannon's treatise was published, writers from nearly all branches of the social sciences insisted that it was to be considered a general model of communication, applicable to all kinds of information interchange, including the one taking place in human communication (Weaver 1949; Ruesch and Bateson

1950; Miller 1953; Hockett 1953; Cherry 1957; Hassenstein 1966; Schleidt 1973).[2]

What has long been overlooked is that the conditions given in the engineering environment permitted Shannon to develop an extremely valuable account of information interchange with a theoretical model that had to deal conceptually only with the problems on the side of the sender—that is, with the problems of how to encode the universe of potential messages into signals that can be safely transmitted through a noisy channel. There is an obvious reason why Shannon did not need to bother much about the decoding done by the receiver—and thus, was able to drastically reduce the complexity of the issue in question. Once the specifications for the encoding of messages are set, the engineer is in the enviable position of having the option to define and to construct the receiver's specification in such a way that it will function exactly like an inverse sender. Clearly, as long as the receiver's decoding activity is a perfect mirror image of the sender's encoding activity, the question of what might go on in the receiver's mind never arises. Under these circumstances, a theory able to explain the functioning of the sender covers, of course, also the decoding done by the receiver and thus can account for the entire communicative interchange.

The Pragmatic Dimension of Communication

In human communication things are very different. Clearly, there is no way to wire the receiver according to the specifications given in the sender. For this reason, the sender is not able, except perhaps with extreme measures of indoctrination, to enforce a signal to be interpreted in a specific way. This feature fundamentally changes the entire constellation of the information interchange. While in technical communication systems the

2. The voice most influential in recommending Shannon's model to social scientists belonged to Warren Weaver, then director of the National Sciences Division of the Rockefeller Foundation. When Shannon's theory, a year after its publication in *The Bell System Technical Journal*, was republished in book form, Weaver added a 23-page memorandum in which he expressed his views about the generality of Shannon's model. Within the humanities this exposition was considered so important that social scientists now routinely refer to Shannon's theory as the Shannon-Weaver theory of communication, even though Warren Weaver had nothing to do with the development of Shannon's concept.

sender controls both the production of the signal and the interpretation given by the receiver, in human interaction the sender's power is reduced to the production of signals to which the receiver's perceptual apparatus is sensitive. As to the interpretation of these stimuli, it is the recipient himself who decides what they mean to him.

The functioning of the communicative interchange among humans therefore deeply depends on the receiver's inferential abilities, that is on his or her aptitude for "making sense" of the stimuli generated by the sender. It was the founder of the field of semiotics, Charles Morris, who first emphasized that in human communication the essential feature is not what is provided by the sender but what matters to the receiver: "[S]omething is a sign only because it is interpreted as a sign of something by some interpreter" (Morris 1938/1971, 20). Or, as Wilbur Schramm later expressed it: "There is no meaning in a message except what people put into it" (Schramm 1973, 3). Rather than to restrict communications research to the semantic and syntactic features of a sign system—topics highly relevant to the explanation of the sender's activity—Morris thought it crucial to study the inference process involved in the recipient's cognitive treatment of utterances. He therefore proposed, in his seminal work *Foundations of the Theory of Signs*, the establishment of a new science meant to deal specifically with "the relation of signs to their interpreters" (Morris 1971, 43)—a field of inquiry for which he coined the term "pragmatics."

Published a decade before the appearance of Shannon's treatise, Morris's terminological trichotomy—*syntactics, semantics,* and *pragmatics*—instantly gained, as Apel has remarked, the standing of "something like a magic formula which since then has never disappeared" from the linguistic literature (Apel 1973, 10). As a field of research, however, pragmatics advanced so slowly that by the late 1960s writers still called it "a science in its infancy, barely able to read and write its own name" (Watzlawick et al. 1967, 13). One major drawback certainly was that the study of the cognitive processing involved in the interpretation of utterances goes well beyond the scope of linguistic research. As the current leaders in the field of pragmatics, anthropologist Dan Sperber and linguist Deirdre Wilson maintain: "Pragmatics, the theory of utterance-interpretation, is a branch of cognitive psychology" (Sperber and Wilson 1981, 281).

Psychologists, on the other hand, were for a long time reluctant to invest in the study of the cognitive processes triggered by communicative stimuli. During the first half of the century, the behavioristic dogma would not permit them to think of language as anything different than a stimulus-response-driven learning process. In fact, up to the 1960s this attitude was, as Osgood et al. relate, so prevalent in American psychology that even a term like "meaning," routinely used in linguistics, seemed "to connote, for most psychologists at least, something inherently nonmaterial ... and therefore to be treated like the other 'ghosts' that J. B. Watson dispelled from psychology" (Osgood et al. 1957, 1).

It took an utterly disconcerting experience to break this habit and to initiate what has come to be called the "cognitive turn" in psychology. That unsettling event came when Noam Chomsky published a devastating critique of B. F. Skinner's *Verbal Behavior*, contending that the conceptual limitations inherent in psychological learning theory made it inevitable that major aspects of verbal behavior would remain mysterious (Chomsky 1959). Chomsky's critique abruptly stalled, as we can see now, any further attempt to explain verbal behavior as a direct response to external stimuli. At the same time, however, it provided a major impulse for the development of a cognition-based approach to the study of communication that eventually led to the establishment of what was then a nascent field of inquiry, christened "psycholinguistics" by George A. Miller (Miller 1954).

With its focus on cognitive information processing, it would have seemed natural for this new science to try to provide an explicit account of how human beings interpret utterances, especially so if we consider that psychologists themselves thought of the pragmatic aspect of language as a profoundly psychological issue. F. H. George, for example, in discussing which areas of communications research belonged to which discipline, unequivocally declared: "Pragmatics is psychology" (George 1962, 41). Even Miller, who would later advocate a close analogy between human and technical information processing, expressed, in his classic *Language and Communication*, the view that "the pragmatic rules of language are, in a sense, fundamental to the semantic and syntactic rules. The psychologist's principal interest is in the pragmatic dimension of language, but he cannot afford to ignore the semantic and syntactic dimensions" (Miller 1951, 107).

As it turned out, however, psychologists would not follow up on this issue. They became considerably more interested in studying the cognitions of the sender than those of the receiver. This, in turn, has to do with the fact that psycholinguistic research was inspired, since its very beginnings in the early 1950s, by the concepts developed by the engineers who laid the groundwork for radar technology and computer networks. George A. Miller, in particular, who at M.I.T. was able to learn firsthand about the engineers' stunning success in building communicating automata, quickly convinced his fellow psychologists that this work had culminated in "a theory so general that we can truly say that any device, be it human or electrical or mechanical, must conform to the theory if it is to perform the function of communication" (Miller 1968, 46).

Recent Developments in Communications Theory

In view of the high promise technical communications theory seemed to hold for understanding human communication, it can hardly surprise that Morris's conceptual framework received little attention from psychologists. In fact, it is probably safe to say that the issue of pragmatics was left entirely to linguistics. Within that discipline, however, it didn't fare too well, either. As Levinson, author of the first textbook on the topic, has pointed out, "pragmatics prior to 1957 … was practiced (if in an informal way)," without actually being taught (Levinson 1983, xii). During the next two decades, the time in which the field seemed totally immersed in what has been hailed as Chomsky's revolution in linguistics, discussions centered so much on syntax that pragmatics looked like an almost forgotten issue. When it finally resurfaced in the early 1980s, it did so only as part of a general attempt to go beyond generative grammar. Or, as Levinson put it: "Pragmatics is a remedial discipline born, or re-born, of the starkly limited scope of Chomskyan linguistics" (Levinson 1983, xii). But even then, the field had progressed so little that, as Sperber and Wilson remarked at the time, "… no consensus on basic concepts and theories, or even on overall goals and research tasks, has yet emerged" (Sperber and Wilson 1981, 281).

These same authors, however, were by then already deeply involved in an attempt to conceptually integrate research that had been accumulating in various fields over the years. The result of this endeavor was the publication of *Relevance. Communication and Cognition*, a treatise conceived as an outline for "a new approach to the study of communication, one based on a general view of human cognition" (Sperber and Wilson 1987, 697). The book became not only an instant classic, but also a "cause célèbre in the theory of communication" (Levinson 1989, 456), which stirred up much controversy in the field (cf. *Behavioural and Brain Sciences*, vols. 10 and 13, 1987 and 1990). However, its appearance in 1986 clearly marked the point in time when communications theory, some fifty years after Morris first drew attention to the role of the recipient's inferences, finally managed to emancipate itself from the exclusively sender-focused technical model.

The most important single force behind this development had been the work of the philosopher H. Paul Grice (1975; 1978; 1989). His views first became public when in 1967 he held the famous William James Lectures at Harvard University. Although the full text of these lectures remained unpublished for more than twenty years, their influence was such that by the early 1980s Grice's ideas had already developed into the cornerstone of most of the work being done under the heading of pragmatics. The view Grice put forward in his lectures was that in human information interchange the sender is never completely free to transmit the information he happens to have and is willing to share. Instead, his freedom of choice is restricted by tacit rules of conduct that oblige the sender to communicate only what is "relevant" to the receiver.

In the case of verbal communication these demands are manifest in what Grice called the "categories Quantity, Quality, Relation, and Manner" (Grice 1975, 45). Within each such category fall a number of implicit communicational "maxims" which call upon the sender to make sure his or her communication is, among other things, neither more nor less informative than is required (Quantity), not untrue or unsubstantiated (Quality), not irrelevant to the issue in question (Relation), and not formulated in an ambiguous or impolite manner (Manner). Grice left no doubt that the receiver has by no means a formal right to enforce such categories to be obeyed by the sender. Similar to the case of Kant's *categorial imperative*, to which Grice alludes, it is ultimately up to the sender to decide whether or not to submit to maxims such as these. But if the communication partners are interested in a good (and continuing) relationship, it is usually in the best interest of the exchange to aspire to fulfill them.

As Grice and many others after him have shown, it is very much in accordance with such demands that in any conversation people tend to formulate their utterances in such a way that much more is *implied* than is actually *said*. In doing so, the sender leaves it to the receiver to infer, on the basis of background knowledge allegedly available to him or her, what has been left out at the level of encoding. Such "implicatures," as Grice called the sender's appeal to the receiver's inferential faculties, honor, at least in principle, the fact that the human receiver is no Shannon-type decoding robot, simply reversing the encoding procedure. They rather acknowledge that the recipient is an autonomous information processing device that is not only able, but will even insist, for the sake of the *relevance* of the information forwarded to it, to apply its own inferential capacities to whatever utterances the sender may produce—or even may fail to produce.

The notion that the sender's encoding is routinely comple-mented by the receiver's inferential activity explains a number of phenomena that have long puzzled researchers in the field. One is that the receiver *can* get the message, and often does, even if at the level of encoding an utterance is found to be syntactically defec-tive and/or semantically underrepresented. Clearly, as long as the recipient's inferential system is able to repair syntactic shortcom-ings and to fill in, by drawing from its own background knowl-edge, the information left out at the level of encoding, understanding can be achieved no matter how incompletely the sender's message may be encoded. This same mechanism also enables interlocutors, as Grice has shown, to deal adequately with very peculiar cases of communication, such as ironic and metaphorical statements, which require the receiver to depart totally from the literal meaning of the message in order to under-stand correctly what the sender "really" meant to say.

The explanatory power of Grice's conceptual framework reaches, however, well beyond the question of how understand-ing is achieved on the basis of incomplete or misleading informa-tion. There are at least three more phenomena inherent in human—but not in technical—communication that his model can deal with. We call them "creative understanding," "creative mis-understanding," and "dismissal" (Frey et al. 1996, 35f). Due to the functional independence of sender and receiver, the recipient is, of course, free to relate the sender's utterances in any way he chooses to the background knowledge available to him. One possible out-come is that the information received may actually trigger infer-ence processes that propel the recipient's understanding of the issue far beyond the sender's own level of cognizance. As a con-

sequence of such "creative" understanding, the recipient may ultimately turn out to be not only as well informed as the sender, but,
in fact, much better. By the same token, however, the inferential
treatment may lead to the opposite result, so that the recipient
becomes confused and thus ends up with a worse understanding
of the issue than the one he had before the conversation took
place. And, last but not least, there remains always the option
to dismiss the information provided by the sender, e.g., because
it is distrusted on the basis of the recipient's background
knowledge, or because it is treated as irrelevant by his or her
inferential system.

With the human recipient retaining so many options to process
the informational input in his/her own "pragmatic" way, we must
assume that even if communication is based on a conventional set
of codes, such as the one provided by verbal language, it is the
exception rather than the rule for an exchange to function according to the encoding/decoding logic laid out in Shannon's model.
This, however, would mean that in a discourse among humans it
is no longer the sender of the message who carries the
exclusive responsibility for the receiver's interpretation. Instead,
the responsibility for any conclusion drawn from the speaker's
utterance can, as Sperber and Wilson said, fall as well "wholly
on the hearer, and in many cases is shared in some proportion
by both" (1981, 283).

Nonverbal Communication

What is true for the verbal component of communication applies
even more to the movement activity accompanying the verbal
exchange. Gestures, postures, and facial displays seem such "natural" parts of the discourse that the literature has come to routinely subsume these behaviors under the heading of "nonverbal
communication." These phenomena cannot be handled, however,
from the perspective of the code model. And if they are, descriptions of instances of nonverbal communication tend to be marred,
as Sperber and Wilson have pointed out, "by spurious attributions
of 'meaning'" (Sperber and Wilson 1986, 60). The reason is that,
with the exception of the very small number of "emblematic"
movement patterns like *head nods* or *shrugs* that stand for a verbal
expression, the movement behavior accompanying speech in
human interaction does not derive its meaning from a stipulated

code. Instead, its potential communicative value stems solely from what the viewer happens to read into it. So if we are to appreciate their role in human communication, these behaviors need to be analyzed within a framework of *inferential communication,* as outlined by Sperber and Wilson.

According to the inferential model, communication is achieved not by encoding and decoding messages but "by producing and interpreting evidence" (Sperber and Wilson 1986, 2). "Evidence" in the sense of pragmatics can, however, be anything to which a perceiver attributes meaning. This, in turn, raises the question about the nature of the nonverbal signs that tend to be taken as relevant by the human perceiver. Sperber and Wilson have argued that any nonverbal action that strikes the viewer as "ostensive" can assume the function of a *sign-vehicle* (Morris's term) for carrying the sender's message. The rationale behind this proposition is that even if a nonverbal action has no conventional meaning, the sheer fact that it is being displayed in an "ostensive" fashion is likely to cause the viewer to wonder *why* the action is being displayed. Depending upon whether or not the sender can actually predict how his counterpart is going to answer that question, he may actually be able to substitute a conventional sign by a nonconventional one and still get the message across. In this way, *ostensive-inferential communication* can, at least in principle, render "communication possible even in the absence of a code" (Sperber and Wilson 1986, 25).

It is worthwhile to note, however, that even if the viewer's inference is successfully controlled by ostensive action, pragmatic "evidence" cannot be assigned by the sender. What the sender can produce is a stimulus; its evidence must be *accorded* by the receiver. In fact, no matter how "ostensive" a nonverbal behavior may look, if it fails to strike a responsive chord with the viewer, it cannot assume a communicative function. On the other hand, any inconspicuous, subtle movement to which the perceiver attributes a definite meaning can be of considerable importance to the communicative exchange, even if the interpretation should be mistaken. So in order to be able to more fully assess the way that nonverbal behavior enters into the process by which *understanding, creative understanding,* or *creative misunderstanding* is achieved, it would seem necessary to find out how the vast variety of nonverbal displays generated during a face-to-face interaction are inferentially processed and what kind of pragmatic evidence they assume "in the eye of the beholder."

The Dogmatic Nature of Visual Perception

While research into the way nonverbal signs "relate to their interpreters" may have ramifications for quite a number of issues relating to the *conditio humana*, it seems particularly important with
regard to questions concerning the formation of prejudice. The reason is that nonverbal action can be a powerful factor in the development of the attitudes and opinions we hold about other people.
Both the static, "physiognomic" features of the body as well as the
dynamic gestural and facial activity displayed in human interaction have long been known to affect deeply the process of person
perception—that is, the way in which we form impressions about
somebody's attitudes, intentions, emotions, and personality traits.
The tendency to judge people by their looks is, indeed, so deeply
embedded in human nature that, as Solomon Asch remarked, we
just have to "look at a person and immediately a certain impression
of his character forms itself in us"—an impression so forceful and
compelling that "we can no more prevent its rapid growth than we
can avoid perceiving a given visual object or hearing a melody"
(Asch 1946, 258). The inferential process by which we arrive at
these conclusions works not only with remarkable speed, but
requires so little cognitive effort that it has long been suspected to
represent an evaluation that "is largely automatic, one of the things
we do without knowing very much about the 'principles' in terms
of which we operate" (Tagiuri 1958, ix).

It was nobody less than Hermann von Helmholtz, the physicist
who has been apostrophized as the nineteenth century's "universal
genius" (cf. Krüger 1994), who first pondered about the way in
which nonverbal displays may shape the cognitive and emotional
attitudes people hold about each other. While studying the psychology of visual perception, the author of the renowned *Handbuch
der Physiologischen Optik* was struck by the dogmatic nature of
visual impressions. Whatever interpretation the human perceptual
apparatus may give to what meets the eye, the resulting impression is, Helmholtz concluded, not open to revision; the human eye,
so to speak, cannot doubt. Optical illusions, for example, do not
disappear once we obtain conclusive evidence that our visual
sense has fooled us into misinterpreting reality. The reason,
Helmholtz suggested, is that visual perception is beyond the control of the higher cortical areas responsible for conscious deliberation. So even if what we *see* strikes us as particularly convincing
and trustworthy, this "evidence" at a glance originates, according

to Helmholtz, from a fully automatic, prerational type of stimulus interpretation that "can never once be elevated to the plane of conscious judgments" (Helmholtz 1925, 27). In order to account for this type of inference, Helmholtz proposed the term *unbewußter Schluß* (unconscious inference). It is meant to indicate an involuntary, reflex-like kind of information processing that not only "lack[s] the purifying and scrutinizing work of conscious thinking" (Helmholtz 1925, 27) but is so unamenable to conscious control that "its results are urged on our consciousness, so to speak, as if an external power had constrained us, over which our will has no control" (Helmholtz 1925, 26).

While optical illusions are the most obvious examples of *unconscious inference*, Helmholtz insisted that there are innumerable instances everywhere in our real-life sensory perception where "the tendency to abide by the false conclusions persists in spite of better insight into the matter based on conscious deliberation" (Helmholtz 1925, 28). As to the way we see our physical environment, he offered the reminder: "Every evening apparently before our eyes the sun goes down behind the stationary horizon, although we are well aware that the sun is fixed and the horizon moves" (Helmholtz 1925, 28). But beyond that, the apodictic nature of the visual sense appeared to him to extend deeply into the way we perceive our social environment—and into how we react emotionally to it. Taking theatrical performance as an example, Helmholtz argued that the strong emotional effect a play can exert on us results mainly from our inability to doubt the visual impressions generated by unconscious inference. Mere exposure to an actor's nonverbal action can thus suffice to elicit spurious trait attribution as well as to create a definite emotional attitude toward that person—while at the same time the perceiver remains totally oblivious to the fact that the stimuli arousing his affective response are just "for show":

> An actor who cleverly portrays an old man is for us an old man there on the stage, so long as we let the immediate impression sway us, and do not forcibly recall that the programme states that the person moving about there is the young actor with whom we are acquainted. We consider him as being angry or in pain according as he shows us one or the other mode of countenance and demeanour. He arouses fright or sympathy in us ... and the deep-seated conviction that all this is only show and play does not hinder our emotions at all, provided the actor does not cease to play his part. On the contrary, a fictitious tale of this sort, which we seem to enter into ourselves, grips and tortures us more than a similar true story would do when we read it in a dry documentary report. (Helmholtz 1867/1925, 28)

Expression and Impression

Published some ten years before the opening of Wundt's laboratory in Leipzig established psychology as an academic science, Helmholtz's conception of the role nonverbal stimuli assume within the process of attitude formation was more than a century ahead of its time. As Gilbert (1989) has pointed out, the psychological reflections of the man who gave to physics the formulation of the *law of conservation of energy* fell on such barren ground that it "is probably fair to say that Helmholtz's ideas about the social inference process have exerted no impact whatsoever on social psychology" (Gilbert 1989, 191). It is only in recent years that research under a variety of headings such as "snap judgments" (Schneider et al. 1979), "nonconscious social information processing" (Lewicki 1986), "spontaneous trait inference" (Newman and Uleman 1989), or "unintended thought" (Ulemann and Bargh 1989) has begun to investigate the functioning of the mechanism that steers the process of person perception. From this research it ultimately became apparent that "Helmholtz presaged many current thinkers not only by postulating the existence of such operations, but also by describing their general features" (Gilbert 1989, 189).

One reason why the notion of unconscious inference has been largely ignored among psychologists may be that it did not square well with the hopes and expectations that have instigated previous investigations in the field. Gestures, facial movements, and the appearance of the body have probably been considered the outward expression of a person's inner traits and states ever since the dawn of time. In fact, involuntary snap judgments produced by unconscious inference must already have been, if Helmholtz is correct, primitive man's favorite way of making psychological sense out of what was observed in other people. Accordingly, the issue has been approached again and again from a psychodiagnostic perspective; the crucial question has been how one can tell the secrets of the soul from the way people look and the way people move. And even though work in this field has been anything but a success story, researchers remained, as has been shown elsewhere (Frey1993a; 1998), so much obsessed with the question of finding out what these phenomena tell about the actor that it hardly ever occurred to them to ask what they might mean to the *perceiver*.

That the scope of research has eventually been expanded to the study of the pragmatic processing of visual displays is mostly due to the work of human ethologists. The pioneering studies of

Lorenz (1935), Tinbergen (1936), and others had long shown that the sheer possession of certain visual features can decisively influence an animal's fate by eliciting behaviors from the social environment that either assist or endanger its survival. The selective pressure originating from other animals' perceptive response can, indeed, reach such proportions that it is even possible, in many cases, to trace specific features in an animal's outward appearance to the way these stimuli are being "viewed" by potential mates or predators (Bates 1862; Wallace 1891). According to the ethological point of view, it is therefore of utmost importance to determine the specific stimulus characteristics that control the "impression" a given morphological or behavioral display creates with other animals. In a series of ingenious experiments, using dummies whose appearance had been systematically manipulated, ethologists have indeed been able to demonstrate the existence of perceptual filter mechanisms that respond only to certain features of a complex display. Simply viewing these features can, however, trigger complex behavioral actions that unfold in such an automatic fashion that ethologists have come to refer to these perceptual filters as "innate releaser mechanisms" (Lorenz 1935; Schleidt 1962).

It was Paul Leyhausen (1951; 1967), a psychologist who became a close collaborator of Konrad Lorenz, who first argued that the same type of filter mechanism regulating the way in which animals perceive each other may also be at work in human interaction. In a paper programmatically entitled *Einführung in die Eindruckskunde* (Introduction to Impression Psychology), he even expressed the view that the mechanism by which nonverbal behavioral displays are interpreted by the human perceiver resides, at least in part, in such ancient cerebral structures that a great deal of this information processing may not even take place "in the visual cortex or in other cortical areas but directly in the midbrain" (Leyhausen 1968, 50). So in order to be able to understand the psychological significance of a person's outward appearance, Leyhausen felt it necessary to analyze the *viewer's* inferential treatment of these phenomena and thus to overcome the limits of a research strategy that for its strong psychodiagnostic bias had been conceptually circling, so to speak, for centuries around the sender. As to the psychological implications he expected to result from the pragmatic inferences drawn from "expressive" displays, it is almost as if he were paraphrasing Helmholtz:

> They will directly translate into sentiments and affective states ... without the participation of reflection, comparisons, reasoning and

judgments. In this way we have already assumed an affective attitude toward our fellow humans, which for the very reason that it cannot be rationally substantiated, resists even more all rational critique. As it also develops prior to any judgment based on conscious observation, it exerts a kind of censure and impairs our objectivity toward the observational material our partner (or the observed subject) is delivering. (Leyhausen 1968, 50)

In recent years, the experimental fieldwork of Eibl-Eibesfeldt and his collaborators (Eibl-Eibesfeldt 1980; 1984; Grammer et al. 1988) has done much to substantiate empirically the view that nonverbal displays assume a direct steering function in the regulation of human social interaction. Following the lead of Lorenz's (1943, 274ff.) suggestion that certain morphological features of a child's head and face function as powerful releasers of parental care, these investigators have asked about the role nonverbal displays assume within such crucial human activities as mate selection and social bonding. For the case of flirtatious advances, it has already been shown that even though *prima facie* this behavior can look quite different in different cultures, it nevertheless contains behavioral sequences that show up in strikingly similar fashion across cultures. Beyond that, the powerful role that visual cues are known to play in the perception of works of art, in advertisements and in social rituals gives good reason to assume that the inferential treatment of nonverbal stimuli not only influences the way people interact with each other, but deeply pervades, as Eibl-Eibesfeldt maintains, all levels of culture and society:

> The dummy experiments done in grand scale by industry and art, as well as certain faults in our aesthetic and moral judgments, indicate that we respond to certain releasing stimulus conditions nearly automatically and in predictable, possibly innate, ways, even though conclusive evidence for that is difficult to gain. (Eibl-Eibesfeldt 1980, 601)

Stereotypes at a Glance: TV-Mediated Person Perception

It has often been deplored that the possession of language has made humans vulnerable to indoctrination from their social environment. The rise and fall of the ideologies that have led humanity on its crooked course through history would indeed suggest that the gift of speech bestowed on us has not always been a blessing. It is even conceivable that the very stubbornness and unteachableness of the inferential system Helmholtz found at work in us may have actually helped limit the degree to which humans can be influenced by verbal means.

On the other hand, there can also be no doubt that the invention of verbal language has done much to liberate the mind of *Homo sapiens* from the iron grip of the reflex-like perceptual mechanisms inherited from his animalic ancestors. The question is, therefore, what consequences will arise from the dramatic increase in the amount of visual stimulation that has come with the current wave of technological progress. What looms large is that the proportion between conscious and unconscious inference will shift so much out of balance that eventually, the prejudice-prone forms of spontaneous inference may gain the upper hand to a degree that is unhealthy for the functioning of society.

Lippmann himself already envisioned that the development of cinematic techniques would dramatically influence the way in which stereotypes and prejudice develop. At a time when this technology was still so much in its infancy that it seemed uncertain to him whether the future would bring, "perhaps, the talking picture," he wrote:

> Photographs have the kind of authority over imagination to-day, which the printed word had yesterday, and the spoken word before that. They seem utterly real. They come, we imagine, directly to us without human meddling, and they are the most effortless food for the mind conceivable. Any description in words, or even any inert picture, requires an effort of memory before a picture exists in the mind. But on the screen the whole process of observing, describing, reporting, and then imagining, has been accomplished for you. Without more trouble than is needed to stay awake the result which your imagination is always aiming at is reeled off on the screen. (Lippmann 1950/1922, 92)

Three-quarters of a century later, the "talking picture" has entered practically each and every home, with millions of people munching day by day what Lippmann felt to be the most effortless food for the mind conceivable. Yet, despite his explicit reference to the visual screen's potential to do the thinking "for you," few attempts have been made to find out about the peculiar ways in which nonverbal stimuli may shape public opinion.

It is mostly due to the efforts of political scientists that in recent years research in this field has got under way. Roger Masters and his collaborators from Dartmouth College in particular (Masters 1981; 1989; 1993; Lanzetta et al. 1985; McHugo et al. 1985) have argued that television has profoundly changed the style of voters' decision-making by rendering the nonverbal behavior of even the most remote and illustrious people accessible to the viewer's eye. According to these authors, the close-up images of political leaders brought to the home of citizens as part of the daily newscasts activate autonomous perceptual routines that "tend to elicit emotional responses to individuals and thus favor viewer involvement in the candidates as 'personalities' rather than in the parties they represent or the issues they espouse" (Lanzetta et al. 1985, 85). Other scholars even suggested that the perceivers' pragmatic treatment of TV-mediated nonverbal stimuli may provoke emotional attitudes that are so uniform across viewers that by selecting a certain visual display to be broadcast, television may give rise to the development of stereotypes pervasive enough to influence elections (Kepplinger 1987).

In order to be able to follow up on these issues, an interdisciplinary group of researchers consisting of psychologists, political scientists, engineers, and linguists conceived, under the auspices of the Maison des Sciences de l'Homme in Paris, during the late 1980s, a research program meant to contribute to what was felt to be a much needed reorientation in the study of human communication—one that would shift the focus of research from the sender to the *receiver* and from verbal to *nonverbal* stimuli.[3] By making use of the technological progress that has recently brought new and powerful tools, both for the description of nonverbal behavior (Frey et al. 1981; 1983; Hirsbrunner et al. 1987) and for the telemetric assessment of the vegetative system's responses under field conditions (Spelman et al. 1991; Stephan 1990), this collaborative work was designed to address the following tasks:

- development of a high-resolution coding system for the nonsemantic description of TV-mediated nonverbal behavior;
- design of an integrated, multichannel approach to the assessment of the viewers' affective and cognitive responses to TV-mediated visual displays;
- development of a computer-animated system for the simulation of natural human movement to be used in perception studies modeled after the logic of dummy-based ethological research.

In a cross-cultural field study done jointly with Roger Masters and Robert Kleck from Dartmouth College and Alfred Raveau and

---

3. Details of this interdisciplinary work are given in Frey, Raveau, Kempter, Darnaud, and Argentin (1993) and in Frey (1998).

Gabriel Argentin of the University of Paris, we investigated the affective and cognitive responses of American, French, and German subjects to video clips of 180 political leaders that had been compiled from newscasts of the two major networks in these countries. In an attempt to find out whether the nonverbal behavior displayed by politicians of different nationalities may contribute to the formation of national stereotypes, we had subjects watch a 35-minute stimulus tape that contained, in randomized order, 180 10-second clips displaying the televised "visual quotes" of the nonverbal behavior of 60 American, 60 French, and 60 German political leaders.[4] In order to be able to study viewers' perceptual response at various levels of information processing, we decided to investigate: (a) to which detail of the visual display the subject's eye was attracted; (b) what kind of affective response it triggered in the viewer; and (c) which evaluative, cognitive judgment of the leaders' personality it evoked.[5]

The results of this study provide forceful evidence that the mere exposure to TV-mediated nonverbal behavior patterns exerts a powerful influence on the process of person perception. At the cognitive as well as the affective level, the different stimulus persons evoked pronounced differences in the way viewers responded. Even though the subjects recognized, on the average, only 32 out of the 180 political leaders shown to them, they developed, on the basis of a 10-second video clip, a definite opinion about these leaders' personality traits. An analysis of the judg-

4. This sample contained virtually all political leaders who had been on screen for a period of ten seconds or longer in any of 172 newscasts broadcast over a one-month period (March 1987) by American (NBC, CBS), French (TF1, Antenne2) and German (ARD, ZDF) networks (Masters et al. 1991).
5. Selective attention to the complex stimulus configuration was measured with an oculometric procedure that indicated, at a scanning rate of 50 hertz, at which spot on the screen the subject was focusing. In order to tap the viewers' affective response to the stream of pictures we assessed, at the same scanning rate, the following eight parameters: pupil reaction (widening or contraction of the pupil), galvanic skin response, skin temperature, electrocardiogram, peripheral blood pressure fluctuations, pulse, respiration, and motility. The cognitive judgments aroused by the nonverbal displays were assessed with the aid of a specially developed semantic differential consisting of 16 bipolar scales. The details of the experimental procedure as well as the technical specifications of the system used for the integrated assessment of the subjects' overt and covert responses are described in Frey (1993b) and in Frey et al. (1993). Parameter formation procedures developed for the analysis of the multidimensional time-series-matrices obtained from this study are given in Kempter (1993).

ments obtained for political leaders *unknown* to the viewers yielded significant differences pertaining to the stimulus persons' nationalities. The American politicians, for example, were judged by American subjects as significantly more "intelligent," "competent," and "powerful" than the French and German politicians. The French politicians were seen by these same subjects as being significantly more "compassionate," more "energetic," and more "cheerful" than their American and German counterparts. The nonverbal behavior of the German politicians, in turn, gave rise to significantly higher scores on the dimensions "boring," "ugly," and "cold" (cf. Frey 1998).

Probably even more startling evidence for what Robert Zajonc (1980) has cast into the famous phrase "preferences need no inferences" has come from a follow-up study in which we reduced exposure time from ten seconds to a quarter of a second. Using an experimental procedure developed by Jendraczyk (1991), we had German subjects rate 45 leaders (15 from each country) after being exposed for 250 milliseconds to single shots taken from the video clips. These data indicate that literally in fractions of a second the pictures evoked trait attributions that were markedly different for the stimulus persons shown, and highly consistent across judges. On a subjective level, the pragmatic processing of the nonverbal displays was so pervasive to the viewers that, upon being asked during the debriefing session, only 3 out of 29 judges stated that exposure time had been too short to make a sensible decision. Comparison of the data obtained for the 250-ms condition with those obtained in the condition in which pictures were permanently exposed indeed indicated that the process of spontaneous trait inference was, in fact, completed within 250 milliseconds; the correlations between the mean scores obtained for the leaders' personality profiles under the two experimental conditions were on the average $r=0.89$ (Kempter and Frey in preparation).

Data such as these strongly attest to the notion that stereotypes do develop in the receiver all by themselves, without any need of being mediated by some sender's verbal output, solely on the basis of an automatic type of inference drawing on the visual image. That these stereotypes are charged also with a strong affective component is evident from the psychophysiological responses to the presentation of the video clips. Simply watching the nonverbal displays stirred up a great deal of arousal in the viewers' vegetative system—a phenomenon which points to the possibility that there is, indeed, a somatic basis for what we refer to as our "gut reaction" to other people. To test whether and in which way these vegetative responses were related to the cognitive judgments, we correlated the personality ratings with all of the electrodermal and cardiovascular measures. No covariation was found, with the sole exception that electrodermal arousal correlated moderately positively with the degree to which the subjects experienced a stimulus person as being "powerful" ($r=0.47$). This gives strong indication that when it comes to the processing of nonverbal stimuli, the vegetative system has, so to speak, a mind of its own that tends to apply its own reading.

Even though research into these issues has only begun, it has already become evident that there is much wisdom in the dictum "racism is the sickness of those who see." What has become evident, too, is that research into the formation of stereotypes and prejudice can profit much from modern communications theory—and vice versa. By trying to explain human information interchange with a model designed for technical communication purposes, the human sciences have been missing essential features of the process by which stereotype and prejudice develop. By conceptually relating nonverbal phenomena to psychodiagnostics rather than to the pragmatics of communication, they have failed to see the powerful role these phenomena play in shaping individual and public opinion.

It is mainly for this reason that some fifty years after television moved into our living rooms we are still puzzled by the unbroken tendency of people to flock to the medium by the millions. At a time when the impetus coming from modern interactive communications technology is shifting the information transfer even more from the verbal to the visual, it seems more urgent than ever to find out where this seemingly insatiable interest in the visual originates, what the basis is for the fascination it exerts, what individual needs it meets, and what social functions it fulfills. In order to be able to answer these questions, we shall have to deal with issues that may be difficult to access empirically and laborious to investigate. But they touch, as Lorenz (1939, 102) has said, "the deepest and oldest structures also of *our own soul*—which we sorely need to understand."

Acknowledgments: Research underlying this article was supported by the German National Science Foundation (DFG-grants Fr697/1-1, Fr697/1-2, Fr697/1-3), by the Maison des Sciences de l'Homme, Paris, and by the Rockefeller Center of the Social Sciences, Dartmouth College, Hanover (US). The author is greatly indebted to Dieter Klumpp of the Alcatel SEL Foundation, Stuttgart, and to Jean-Luc Lory of the Maison des Sciences de l'Homme for many discussions of the issues addressed herein. Special thanks are due to Jonny Andersen (Department of Electrical Engineering) and to Francis Spelman (Center for Bioengineering) of the University of Washington, Seattle for their suggestions regarding the design of the biometrical system used in our cross-cultural studies.

References

Apel, K.-O. (1973). Charles W. Morris und das Programm einer pragmatisch integrierten Semiotik. In *Zeichen, Sprache und Verhalten* (ed. C. W. Morris), pp. 9–66. Schwann, Düsseldorf.

Asch, S. (1946). Forming impressions of personality. *Journal of Abnormal and Social Psychology*, **41**, 258–90.

Bates, H. W. (1862). Contributions to an Insect Fauna of the Amazon Valley. *Transactions of the Linnean Society of London*, XXIII, 495–566.

Cherry, C. (1957). *On human communication*. Wiley, New York.

Chomsky, N. (1959). Review of Verbal Behavior, by B. F. Skinner. *Language*, **35**, 26–58.

Descartes, R. (1987/1637). *Discours de la méthode pour bien conduire sa raison, et chercher la verité dans les sciences*. 350th anniversary edition. Fayard, Paris.

Eibl-Eibesfeldt, I. (1980). *Grundriß der vergleichenden Verhaltensforschung*. Piper, Munich.

Frey, S. (1991). Nachwort. In *Goettinger Taschen-Calender vom Jahr 1778* (ed. G. Lichtenberg). Faksimileausgabe 1991. Diederichs, Mainz.

———. (1993a). Lavater, Lichtenberg, and the suggestive power of the human face. In *The faces of physiognomy: Interdisciplinary approaches to Johann Caspar Lavater* (ed. E. Shookman), pp. 64–103. Camden House, Columbia, S. C.

———. (1993b). Medienwirkung nonverbaler Kommunikation im interkulturellen Vergleich. Eine Untersuchung zur visuellen Präsentation politischer Funktionsträger in Nachrichtensendungen aus der Bundesrepublik, Frankreich und den USA. *Schlußbericht an die Deutsche Forschungsgemeinschaft* (Förderungsnummern: Fr697/1-1, Fr697/1-2, Fr697/1-3).

———. (1998). *Die Macht des Bildes. Der Einfluß der nonverbalen Kommunikation auf Kultur und Politik*. Huber, Bern.

Frey, S., Hirsbrunner, H. P., Florin, A., Daw, W., and Crawford, R. (1983). A unified approach to the investigation of nonverbal and verbal behaviour in communication research. In *Current issues in European social psychology* (ed. W. Doise and S. Moscovici), pp. 143–99. Cambridge University Press, Cambridge.

Frey, S., Hirsbrunner, H. P., Pool, J., and Daw, W. (1981). Das Berner System zur Untersuchung nonverbaler Interaktion: I. Die Erhebung des Rohdatenprotokolls. In *Methoden der Analyse von Face-to-Face Situationen* (ed. P. Winkler), pp. 203–36. Metzler, Stuttgart.

Frey, S., Kempter, G., and Frenz, H. G. (1996). Theoretische Grundlagen der multimedialen Kommunikation. *Spektrum der Wissenschaft*, **8**, 32–38.

Frey, S., Raveau, A., Kempter, G., Darnaud, C., and Argentin, G. (1993). Mise en évidence du traitement cognitif et affectif du non-verbal. MSH-informations. *Bulletin de la Fondation Maison des Sciences de L'Homme*, **70**, 4–23.

George, F. H. (1962). *The brain as a computer*. Pergamon, Oxford.

Gilbert, D. (1989). Thinking lightly about others: Automatic components of the social inference process. In *Unintended thought* (ed. J. S. Uleman and J. A. Bargh), pp. 189–211. Guilford, New York.

Grice, H. P. (1975). Logic and conversation. In *Syntax and semantics, vol. 3: Speech acts* (ed. P. Cole and J. L. Morgan), pp. 41–58. Academic Press, New York.

———. (1978). Further notes on logic and conversation. In *Syntax and semantics, vol. 9: Pragmatics* (ed. P. Cole), pp. 113–27. Academic Press, New York.

———. (1989). *Studies in way of words*. Harvard University Press, Boston.

Grammer, K. and Eibl-Eibesfeldt, I. (1993). Emotionspsychologische Aspekte im Kulturenvergleich. In *Kulturenvergleichende Psychologie* (ed. A. Thomas), pp. 138–41. Hogrefe, Göttingen.

Helmholtz, H. (1867). Handbuch der physiologischen Optik. In *Allgemeine Encyklopädie der Physik*, vol. 9 (ed. G. Karsten). Voss, Leipzig.

Helmholtz, H. von (1925). The perception of vision. In *Helmholtz's treatise on physiological optics*, vol. 3 (ed. J. P. C. Southall). The Optical Society of America, New York.

Hassenstein, B. (1966). *Kybernetik und biologische Forschung*. Athenaion, Frankfurt/Main.

Hirsbrunner, H. P., Frey, S., and Crawford, R. (1987). Movement in human interaction: Description, parameter formation and analysis. In *Nonverbal behaviour and communication* (ed. A. W. Siegman and S. Feldstein), pp. 99–140. Lawrence Erlbaum, Hillsdale, N.J.

Hockett, C. F. (1953). Review of the Mathematical Theory of Communication, C. E. Shannon and W. Weaver. *Language*, **29**, 69–93.

Jendraczyk, M. (1991). "Snap Judgments" in der Personenwahrnehmung. Diplomarbeit im Nebenfach Psychologie. Duisburg University.

Kant, I. (1784). Beantwortung der Frage: Was ist Aufklärung? *Berlinische Monatsschrift*, **12**, 481–94.

Kempter, G. (1993). *Psychophysiologische Effekte medienvermittelter Personenwahrnehmung*. Doctoral Dissertation, Gerhard Mercator University Duisburg.

Kempter, G. and Frey, S. (in preparation). *Spontaneous trait inference from nonverbal cues*.

Kepplinger, H. M. (1987). *Darstellungseffekte. Experimentelle Untersuchungen zur Wirkung von Pressefotos und Fernsehfilmen*. Alber, Freiburg.

Krüger, L. (1994). *Universalgenie Helmholtz. Rückblick nach 100 Jahren*. Akademie Verlag, Berlin.

Lanzetta, J. T., Sullivan, D. G., Masters, R. D., and McHugo, G. J. (1985). Viewers' emotional and cognitive responses to televised images of political leaders. In *Mass media and political thought* (ed. S. Kraus and R. Perloff), pp. 86–116. Sage, Beverly Hills, Cal.

Levinson, S. C. (1983). *Pragmatics*. Cambridge University Press, Cambridge.

———. (1989). A review of relevance. *Journal of Linguistics*, **25**, 455–72.

Lewicki, P. (1986). *Nonconscious social information processing*. Academic Press, London.

Leyhausen, P. (1951). Einführung in die Eindruckskunde. *Schola*, **6**, 895–900.

———. (1967). Biologie von Ausdruck und Eindruck. *Psychologische Forschung*, **31**, 113–227.

————. (1968). Einführung in die Eindruckskunde. In *Antriebe tierischen und menschlichen Verhaltens. Gesammelte Abhandlungen* (ed. K. Lorenz and P. Leyhausen), pp. 48–53. Piper, Munich.

Lippmann, W. (1950). *Public opinion*. (Thirteenth Printing). Macmillan, New York.

Lorenz, K. (1935). Der Kumpan in der Umwelt des Vogels. *Journal für Ornithologie*, **83**, 137–213, 289–413.

————. (1939). Vergleichende Verhaltensforschung. *Zoologischer Anzeiger*. Supplement 12, 69–102.

————. (1943). Die angeborenen Formen möglicher Erfahrung. *Zeitschrift für Tierpsychologie*, **5**, 235–409.

Lorenz, K. and Leyhausen, P. (1968). *Antriebe tierischen und menschlichen Verhaltens. Gesammelte Abhandlungen*. Piper, Munich.

Masters, R. D. (1981). Linking ethology and political science: Photographs, political attention, and presidential elections. In *Biopolitics: Ethological and physiological approaches* (ed. M. Watts), pp. 61–80. Jossey-Bass, San Francisco.

————. (1989). *The nature of politics*. Yale University Press, New Haven.

————. (1993). *Beyond relativism. Science and human values*. Dartmouth College, Hanover, N. H.

Masters, R. D., Frey, S., and Bente, G. (1991). Dominance and attention: Images of leaders in German, French, and American TV news. *Polity*, **23**, 374–94.

McHugo, G. J., Lanzetta, J. T., Sullivan, D. G., Masters, R. D., and Englis, B. (1985). Emotional reactions to expressive displays of a political leader. *Journal of Personality and Social Psychology*, **49**, 1513–29.

Miller, G. A. (1951). *Language and communication*. McGraw-Hill, New York.

————. (1953). What is information measurement? *American Psychologist*, **8**, 3–11.

————. (1954). Psycholinguistics. In *Handbook of social psychology*, vol. 2 (ed. G. Lindzey), pp. 693–708. Addison-Wesley, Cambridge, Mass.

————. (1968). *The psychology of communication. Seven essays*. Allen Lane, The Penguin Press, London.

Morris, C. (1938). Foundations of the theory of signs. In *International encyclopedia of unified science*, vol. 1 (ed. O. Neurath), pp. 77–138. University of Chicago Press, Chicago.

————. (1971). *Writings on the general theory of signs*. Mouton, The Hague.

Newman, L. S. and Uleman, J. S. (1989). Spontaneous trait inference. In *Unintended thought* (ed. J. S. Uleman and J. A. Bargh), pp. 155–88. Guilford, New York.

Osgood, C. E., Suci, G. J., and Tannenbaum, P. H. (1957). *The measurement of meaning*. University of Illinois Press, Urbana.

Ruesch, J. and Bateson, G. (1950). *Communication. The social matrix of psychiatry*. Norton, New York.

Schleidt, W. M. (1962). Die historische Entwicklung der Begriffe "Angeborenes auslösendes Schema" und "Angeborener Auslösemechanismus" in der Ethologie. *Zeitschrift für Tierpsychologie*, **19**, 697–722.

————. (1973). Tonic communication: Continual effects of discrete signs in animal communication systems. *Journal of Theoretical Biology*, **42**, 359–86.

Schneider, D. J., Hastorf, A. H., and Ellsworth, Ph. C. (1979). *Person perception*. Addison-Wesley, Reading, Mass.

Schramm, W. (1973). *Men, messages, and media*. Harper & Row, New York.

Shannon, C. (1948). A mathematical theory of communication. *The Bell System Technical Journal*, **27**, 379–423, 623–56.

Spelman, F. A., Astley, C. A., Golanov, E. V., Cupal, J. J., Henkins, A. R., Fonzo, E., Susor, T. G., McMorrow, G., Bowden, D. M., and Smith, O. A. (1991). A system to acquire and record physiological and behavioural data remotely from non-human primates. *IEEE Transactions on Biomedical Engineering*, 38, pp. 1175–85.

Sperber, D. and Wilson, D. (1981). Pragmatics. *Cognition*, 10, 281–86.

———. (1986). *Relevance. Communication and cognition.* Blackwell, Oxford.

———. (1987). Précis of relevance: Communication and cognition. *Behavioural and Brain Sciences*, 10, 697–710.

Stephan, E. (1990). Eine "High-tech-Entwicklung" in der Psychologie. Den Leib-Seele-Zusammenhängen mit Elektronik auf der Spur. *Forschung in Köln. Berichte aus der Universität*, pp. 18–20.

Tagiuri, R. (1958). Introduction. In *Person perception and interpersonal behavior* (ed. R. Tagiuri and L. Petrullo), pp. ix–xvii. Stanford University Press, Stanford.

Tinbergen, N. (1939). Zur Fortpflanzungsethologie von Sepia officinalis L. *Archives Néerlandaises de Zoologie*, 10, 265–89.

Uleman, J. S. and Bargh, J. A., eds. (1989). *Unintended thought.* Guilford, New York.

Wallace, A. R. (1891). Mimicry and other protective resemblances among animals. In *Natural selection and tropical nature* (ed. A. R. Wallace), pp. 34–90. Macmillan, London.

Watzlawick, P., Beavin, J. H., and Jackson, D. D. (1967). *Pragmatics of human communication.* Norton, New York.

Weaver, W. (1949). Recent contributions to the mathematical theory of communication. In *The mathematical theory of communication* (ed. C. E. Shannon and W. Weaver), pp. 95–117. University of Illinois Press, Urbana.

Zajonc, R.B. (1980). Feeling and thinking: Preferences need no inferences. *American Psychologist*, 35, 151–75.

CHAPTER TEN

SEX AND GENDER IN ADVERTISEMENTS

INDOCTRINATION AND EXPLOITATION

Karl Grammer

... One of the most deep seated traits of man, it is felt, is gender; femininity and masculinity are in a sense the prototypes of essential expression—something that can be conveyed fleetingly in any social situation ...

Erving Goffman, 1979

Advertising is thought to be the foundation and economic lifeblood of the mass media, and the primary purpose of the mass media is to sell audiences to advertisers. The $130 billion advertising industry is a powerful educational force—not only in the United States. For example, the average American is exposed to over 1,500 ads a day and will spend 18 months of his or her life watching television commercials. Ads sell a great deal more than products. They sell values, images, and concepts of success and worth, love, sexuality, popularity, and normalcy. Although ads sometimes seem to be trivial, their cumulative effect may be important. This fact is nicely demonstrated by the "Farrah-effect": males who viewed a short clip from the TV series Charlie's Angels developed unrealistic mate choice criteria in respect to female attractiveness when compared to controls (Kenrick and Gutierres 1980).

Advertising is at the roots of indoctrination, and, according to a United Nation Commission report on the status of women, advertising is named the worst offender in perpetuating the image of women as sex symbols and as an inferior class of human being. If we take a closer look at this statement, it becomes clear that it is itself another attempt at indoctrination. For example, the notion that women are shown almost exclusively as sex objects or as housewives pathologically obsessed with cleanliness (Kilbourne 1993) is unsupported by empirical data or analysis of actual advertisements. On this weak basis, the obsession with dieting, eating disorders, sexual violence, and even the existence of child pornography are attributed as effects of advertisement.

For instance, Kilbourne (1993) emphasizes that the "sex object" in advertisements is a mannequin whose only attribute is conven-

Fig. 10.1 *Advertising—the "hallmark" of female sexual exploitation? This is a typical example used to support the exploitation interpretation of sexual imagery in advertising. This particular image has all the features cited in the feminist critique: the woman is portrayed as being off balance; she is bending in a submissive posture and dressed in underwear in a public setting. Actually, there is no obvious relationship between the product, in this case a heater, and the woman.*

tional beauty. "She has no lines or wrinkles, no scars nor blemishes, indeed she has no pores. As a result, in this view, women are constantly exhorted to emulate this ideal, to feel ashamed and guilty if they fail, and to equate desirability and the capacity for being loved with physical perfection" (637). A first look at advertisements makes this argument seem plausible. Fig. 10.1 needs no words of explanation. This feminist view of advertising ascribes mainly negative effects to it and sees it as being responsible for most of the negative developments in our society.

Seen from this perspective, there is a causal relationship between advertisement and cultural learning of gender stereotypes; but in an evolutionary view, culture is not causeless and disembodied—it is generated in rich and intricate ways by information-processing mechanisms situated in human minds. These mechanisms are in turn the product of the evolutionary process of selection and adaptation. Those individuals who were able to process information in an adaptive way simply were more successful at meeting life's challenges, including survival and reproduction. If this is so, then there is a universal human nature, but this universality exists primarily at the level of evolved psychological mechanisms (Cosmides et al. 1992). Viewed in light of such an approach, advertisements are not successful because they promote stereotypes and behavior, but because they exploit the inherent structures of minds by keying into the way minds themselves process information. If there is exploitation, there has to be something which can be exploited. Thus, we have to design a task analysis defining the nature of the adaptive information processing problem that had to be solved in the evolutionary process. Once the problem is understood, we will be able to generate very specific, empirically testable hypotheses about the information processing structure itself and its possible behavioral consequences. This computational theory (Marr 1982) will show us how these structures can be exploited.

Sex Perception

The basis for the discussion of sex and gender is the "parental-investment theory" developed by Trivers (1972). The basic currency in this theory is reproductive success and investment in the offspring. For investment in offspring and for reproductive success we find a sex difference. Women put higher investment in offspring because they are able to rear only a limited number of children in a given time period, while men could father many. Although men might invest considerably in their offspring, the difference between men and women lies in the minimum possible investment. What is a simple act of copulation for a man can lead to a life-long investment for a woman (Symons 1979). Asymmetric investment leads to a number of constraints, necessities, and opportunities in mate-selection criteria and sex-specific behavior strategies. This does not mean that humans consciously assess the costs and benefits of possible strategies for enhancing their reproductive success. Symons (1979) argues that this discrepancy in investment caused, through natural selection, sex differences in the psychological mechanisms that mediate sexual arousal and mate evaluation. Consequently, men and women evolved complex, dimorphic emotional-motivational mechanisms to recognize and to look after their own interests. It is these basic interests that can be exploited (not only by advertisement) in many ways.

The basic constraint for females is that they should avoid sex with males who are not willing to invest, either emotionally in a relationship or in possible offspring. Since females, overall, encounter higher risks in choosing mates, they should exercise caution. Unselective pairing could endanger their reproductive success. This constraint leads to an opportunity: women should choose actively, and they should test the male's behavioral tendencies and resource providing potential carefully. As a result, females will appreciate male dominance, status, prowess, and nurturance in their mate-selection criteria (Buss 1989; Wiedermann and Allgeier 1992; Kenrick et al. 1990). These preferences should become most salient when resources in a society are not evenly distributed, if it is the males who control resources, or more generally if there is significant variability in male ability or willingness to provide resources to mates and offspring.

The basic constraint for males is somewhat different. When in the evolutionary past some males began enhancing their relative reproductive success by investing in offspring, and females began selecting males who would provide, all males came under selective pressure to do so. Males were exposed to intense competition, both for resources and for women. It was a matter of "provide or perish," in the genetic sense. Yet in order to invest safely, males had to be sure that they were investing in their own offspring. Thus sexual jealousy should be a prominent feature of this sex. For men, reproductive success is limited by access to reproductively valuable or fertile women. Thus there will be a male preference for "attractive" females where attractiveness is generated by reproductive value.

Opportunities for males, then, are quite simple: men can enhance their reproductive success by adopting a philandering strategy while expecting either the women to raise the offspring alone in order not to lose the initial investment in gestation and parturition, or that other males will raise the offspring as cuckolds, unaware that it is not their own. The simple result for the construction of the information processing apparatus is that men simply should be interested more in women than vice versa.

Basically, this theory suggests which gender roles should emerge: women should be interested in a man's status, his possible behavior in long-term relationships, and his ability to reach and keep this status in a society of competing men. On the other hand, men should be interested in chaste, fertile women of high reproductive value. Since these mate selection criteria can be encoded into aspects of appearance, they can be exploited in various ways.

Sex: Faces and Bodies

Mate selection starts with visual discrimination of sex. This perception seems to be prototypical. Burton et al. (1993) had to use 16 single measured traits in order to come to a reliable separation of sex in faces. "Gestalt perception" seems to play a prominent role in sex detection. When information about individual identity is removed (Harmon 1973), humans are still able to extract information about gender from a face. When a low-pass filter is applied to a Fourier-transformed photograph of a face, the high frequencies (short distances) are removed from the face and individual identity is lost, but gender is still recognized very quickly in such manipulated faces (Sergent 1986). We find comparable conditions in the recognition of gender from complete human figures. Individuals refer to the proportion of shoulder width to waist in order to discriminate male figures, and the proportion of waist to hip for female figures (Horvath 1979). This process is simulated for a man and a women in Fig. 10.2 by quantifying photographs of faces. Comparable approaches can be made for sex detection in bodies, involving the proportions of shoulder width, waist, and hips just mentioned.

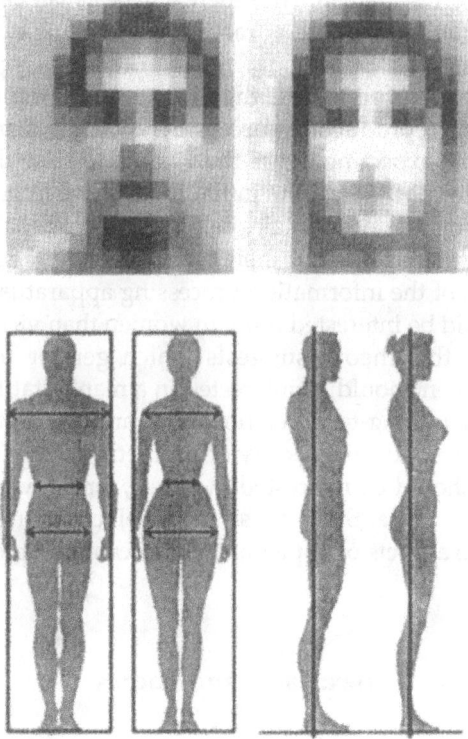

Fig. 10.2 *Human sex-prototypical faces and bodies. Fig. 10.2a shows a male and a female face where the individual information has been removed—the sex of the face can still be recognized in a prototypical way. Fig. 10.2b shows the body contours of males and females. A high shoulder-waist ratio is typical for males, a low waist-hip ratio is typical for females.*

After sex is discriminated in a visual stimulus, the next level of information processing evaluates a person as a possible partner. If evolutionary pressures have acted on our thinking, consensual standards of attractiveness should have evolved over generations that correspond to the regularities of costs and benefits in mate choice. This seems to be true. Henss (1988) found high concordance of attractiveness ratings. Males thus share a common standard. Moreover, we find that youth, health, and lack of skin blemishes are the basic criteria for judgments of female attractiveness (Symons 1979). These criteria would be those that signal reproductive value. In recent years, however, there has been a shift in research on attractiveness from the description of single traits

(Rensch 1963; Cunningham 1986) to a more holistic approach (Langlois and Roggmann 1990; Grammer and Thornhill 1993). This approach is based on the actual way brains process information. One feature of human cognition is the creation of "prototypes." This means that we constantly evaluate stimuli from our social and nonsocial environment and classify these stimuli into categories and concepts, thus reducing the amount of environmental information into "pieces" which can be used or stored very economically. For a first approach let us assume that prototypes are some kind of average representation of stimuli of one class.

There are many hints that our brain processes images of faces this way, solving the problem of storing faces with the help of prototypes. We seem to build facial prototypes and then store particular faces in the form of their deviations from these prototypes. Only the deviations are of interest since the rest is the same for all faces. As soon as prototypes are present, they can be used for learning. We learn very fast and almost irreversibly link personality traits to facial prototypes. This helps us to decode the behavioral tendencies people might have, allowing us to structure our behavior accordingly.

Indeed, studies have repeatedly shown (Galton 1879; Kalkofen 1990; Langlois and Roggman 1990; Müller 1993; Grammer and Thornhill 1993; Perret et al. 1994) that photographically or computer-generated prototypical faces are more attractive than the single faces that have been used to generate them. Fig. 10.3 shows such a face generated out of 16 female faces. While averageness is a trait used to judge female faces, it is not applied to male faces. Male average faces are unattractive for females, who prefer extremes (Grammer and Thornhill 1993).

Transfer of personality traits in the case of the broad chin in men could be responsible for the attractiveness of this feature. If females want dominant males, broad chins may signal a tendency to dominate others. This is indeed the case. Keating et al. (1981) have shown that men with broad chins are perceived in eight cultures as those who are likely to dominate others. Comparable results have been put forward by Mazur et al. (1984). These authors describe careers of West Point cadets—those with broad chins at entrance to West Point rose higher in the military hierarchy than others. In addition, college students with broad chins copulate more often and have more girlfriends (Mazur et al. 1994). Winkler and Kirchengast (1994) have shown that among the San-Bushmen those men with broad chins and a more robust body

Fig. 10.3 *Averageness and beauty: prototypes. This picture shows an attractive prototype generated out of 16 individual faces. The prototype is always more attractive than most of the individual faces.*

build had greater reproductive success. Moreover, a broad chin is coupled with blood testosterone levels, which probably are linked to aggressive tendencies. Another interesting hypothesis begins with the premise that broad chins signal a handicapped immune system (Thornhill and Gangestadt 1993). Testosterone production might be costly, because it suppresses immune function and thereby increases susceptibility to disease during puberty (Fölstad and Karter 1992). Extreme male features that are triggered by testosterone thus advertise honestly that their bearer was sufficiently resistant to parasites to produce them.

Grammer and Thornhill (1993) have shown that facial symmetry is one main factor for ratings of female and male attractiveness (when controlled for averageness). In addition, bodily symmetry correlates with ratings of facial attractiveness (even when the body is not visible) (Thornhill and Gangestadt 1994). The reason for symmetry being attractive has a biological basis. Pathogens are the major environmental perturbations underlying developmental instability; developmental stability may be related to additive genetic variance in disease resistance, which in turn may relate to fitness. One defense against parasites is the production of substantial polymorphism: when a parasite adapts to one genetic allele, alternative alleles may be advantaged. Indeed, attractiveness plays a prominent role in societies where parasites are prominent (Buss and Gangestadt 1993)

Thus symmetry, which cannot be falsified, may be a reliable signal for mate quality. Symmetry seems to be influential in the ratings of attractiveness and thus mate choice. Comparable results can be found for ratings of bodily attractiveness with breast asymmetry (Moeller et al. 1995). Symmetrical breasts are more attractive than asymmetrical breasts.

The signaling value of body features in the case of females seems to be linked to the reproductive stage. Sex differences in body shape depend partly on dimorphism in fat distribution. The fat carried by a woman is responsible for her balance of sex steroids. Thus, the amount of visible fat can predict if a woman is receptive or not, suggesting that body fat came to be distributed in prominent places likes breasts and buttocks in order to strengthen signal value. Indeed, breast size correlates with overall body fat. Furthermore, overall weight is linked to fertility: plump mothers have more children. Whether or not chubby women are appreciated in various cultures seems to depend on environmental stability (Anderson et al. 1992). In unstable environments, where food shortages occur, female body fat is linked to status and to attractiveness. In this regard, prototype theory is not limited to faces—average female body features are also judged attractive. Singh (1992; 1993) describes a single measure that can be linked to bodily attractiveness: the ratio of waist to hip in females. This ratio shows a curvilinear relationship to attractiveness with a maximum of attractiveness at 0.72. Surprisingly, this maximum is related to many health features in females.

Perception of attractiveness seems to exploit human information processing mechanisms. If our brain uses prototypes, averageness might well be coupled with being "prototypical." Thus there might be a better fit between stimulus and the prototypical template. As a result, prototypes could be recognized faster and better, creating more nervous excitation. This could be the reason that averageness is preferred. Our brain could accept more willingly better fitting stimuli. This process has been called "neuroaesthetics" by Müller (1993). Recent research on perception and associated processing has shown that symmetry is one of the main factors causing recognition and reaction to stimuli. Symmetrical stimuli can be learned more easily. Several computer simulations have shown that neural networks, when confronted with stimuli, respond better and more easily to symmetrical ones (Johnstone 1994). Enquist and Arak (1994) have shown that symmetry preferences may arise as byproducts of the need to recognize objects irrespective of their position and orientation in the visual field. Symmetrical stimuli thus would exploit the sensory system of the receiver. Indeed, symmetrical patterns are attractive for humans even in contexts unrelated to signaling.

Sex and Gender: Advertisement and Indoctrination

[W]hen one tries to use the notion that human objectives give off natural objective signs and that some of these expressions can inform us about the essential nature of their producer, matters get complicated ...

Erving Goffman, 1979

Grammer (1993) used the term "triggering signals" for signals connected to age and sex and their prototypical appearance at the stage of optimal reproduction. These signals are necessary if a receiver is to decode meaning, because they carry information on how to understand and interpret a specific signal. Otherwise, interpretation of signals would end in some infinite regression. Compare the case of a smiling child or woman. The child's smile can be interpreted as an expression of friendliness, as can the woman's, but the latter might also be interpreted as a sexual invitation. This discrimination has to be universal, although there is room for learning. Signals that have been decoded with the help of basic triggering signals can be used as new triggering signals and so on. The existence of a fixed rule system for decoding information on the basis of triggering signals opens avenues for exploitation via carefully chosen signals. On this basis, we can generate hypotheses about how advertisements should work and how they exploit basic triggering signals and dimorphic gender roles in accordance with asymmetric investment theory:

- Men in advertisements will be presented as dominant, prosperous, nurturant, and of high social status, as female mate-selection criteria would predict.
- Women in advertisements should be presented as being of high reproductive value (i.e., attractive) and sexually receptive (nude) as male mate-selection criteria would predict.

Basically, two advertisement strategies could be used to exploit men's and women's cognitive adaptations to mate selection and the prototypical triggering signals associated with this complex. The first strategy is sensory exploitation of the opposite sex. This means that advertisements would pair products for one sex with the stimulus of the other sex, thus using the excitation evoked by the stimulus as an attention-getter or reinforcer. The second strategy could be called "comparison with a normative self." In this case, the product for one sex is paired with a same-sex stimulus that would be perfect for the other sex. "Beautiful women use shampoo brand X." The product is presented as making the difference between the consumer and the perfect attractant for the opposite sex. These techniques are honed through exposure to consumer choice, as expressed in sales and marketing research. "Cultural selection" works on the differential success of ads, and the proliferation of the "fittest." The content of ads inevitably reaches a high pitch of effectiveness in eliciting maximum consumer response, within legal constraints.

Methods

[T]he analysis of sexism can start with obviously unjust discriminations against persons of the female sex class, but analysis as such can not stop there. Gender stereotypes run in every direction ...
Erving Goffman, 1966

In order to empirically test these hypotheses, I used an approach suggested by Goffman (1979). In this book he collected ads and classified them according to behavior categories he had derived from evolutionary approaches to behavior. This fascinating approach has several shortcomings, because it does not tell us about the frequencies and uses of advertising strategies. In order to resolve these shortcomings, I used four issues of a glossy monthly magazine published in Austria with a circulation of 700,000. The issues were selected at random: one issue per year from the years 1991 to 1994. This was necessary to avoid dependency in the data because one advertising strategy is repetition. The journal is not directed at one sex or a specific target group. At first, the number and the size of the ads were determined, as well as the advertised product and the target group of the product.

In the next step, the number and the sex of persons who appeared in the advertisements were counted. Visibility was coded separately: only parts of the body visible, face visible, upper body visible, and complete figure visible. Separate codes were used to indicate that a person was presented frontally or from the back. I also determined the amount of visible skin in three categories: no skin (only face, hands, and bare legs are visible up to the knee), partially nude (bare arms, neck line, miniskirt, bathing suits, etc.) and completely nude. Partially nude and completely nude then were combined into the category "sexy ads."

The behavior codes were adopted from Goffmann (1979) and extended by my own codes: gaze behavior, smiles, body postures, and related codes for couples (see results). The analysis covered a total of 357 advertisements amounting to a total of 20.6 square meters. Overall, I analyzed 1,310 pages totaling 66.4 square meters. This means that 31 percent of the journal space was used by ads.

Advertising with Persons and Products

Only 52 percent of the advertisements showed people. In the next step, I looked for differences in the way advertisements for different types of products deploy images of people. The results are shown in Table 10.1.

Table 10.1 Products and People by Sex in 357 Advertisements

Product	Total %	People %	Male Sex	Female Sex
Fashion	9.8	16.0	16.7	15.1
Cars	10.4	8.0	0	4.1
Cigarettes	1.7	3.2	6.7	5.5
Cosmetics	6.7	9.0	13.3	12.3
Electronics	2.2	1.6	3.3	1.4
Entertainment	4.22	2.1	3.3	0
Living	10.6	9.0	0	15.1
Health food	4.8	4.3	3.3	2.7
Alcohol	3.9	4.8	13.3	9.6
Service	14.3	12.2	6.7	4.1
Ideas	5.3	4.3	0	0
Sports	3.1	4.3	3.3	1.4
Travel	9.0	9.0	6.7	12.3
Journals	9.0	9.6	16.7	12.3
Jewelry	5.0	2.7	6.7	4.1
N	100%=357	188	30	73

Table 10.1 gives an overview of product types. Most advertisements were for services (banks, insurance, etc.), followed by cars and living. People are presented in 52 percent of advertisements, being used mainly to sell fashion, service, cars, cosmetics, and living. Most often single men are portrayed (17.4 percent of all ads) followed by single women (15.7 percent), couples (9.5 percent), groups of men (3.1 percent), groups of women (1.7 percent), and families (0.3 percent). Children (0.3 percent) played a minor role in product promotion strategies. For this reason, I will restrict the analysis to males, females, and couples.

Sex in Advertisements

The first question concerns frequency. How often is sexually oriented material presented in advertisement? Seen globally, when compared to all advertisements, such material constitutes only a small fraction: 24 percent of items used material of this kind. If we compare this for both sexes, then only 17.8 percent of all ads showing males used nude or seminudes figures. The situation is completely different for women: 66.1 percent are presented nude or seminude. Comparable figures can hold for couples: here 64 per-

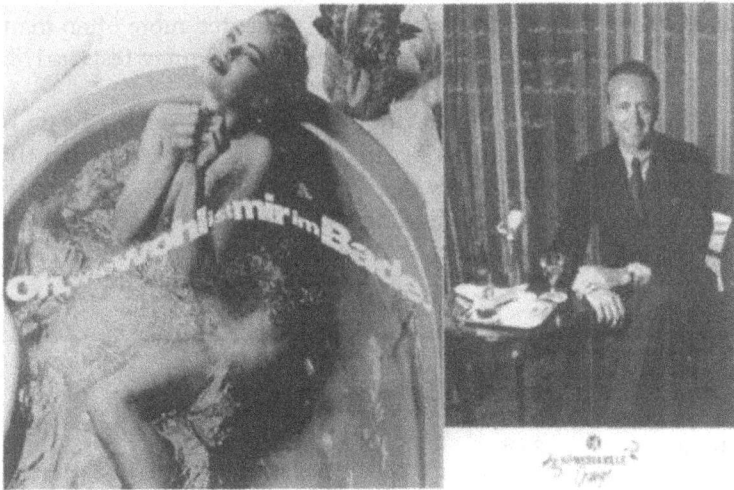

Fig. 10.4 *Female nudity and male competence: examples from our sample. Two typical instances are portrayed. The female's body is twisted and nude, while the male's body is sitting upright and dressed to meet the world.*

cent of items show sexual material. This difference is highly significant (Chi-Square, n= 169, df=3, 38.33, p<0.0001). It is of interest to note that it is the females in couples (64 percent) who are more often presented nude than males (18.8 percent). Figs. 10.4, 10.5, and 10.6 give examples of the presentation of female nudity and male poses.

The second question concerns the use of this material. Is it connected to certain products? Advertisements selling fashion, alcohol, cosmetics, and journals are the clear winners for both sexes, and a striking sex difference becomes visible for advertisements for furniture, etc. (living) where women are shown much more often nude or seminude than men (see Table 10.1).

Behavior: Views and Positions

The next question concerns the photographic presentation of the sexes. Presentation can induce moods and is the main component of "advertising language." The analysis will be done for men and women with regard to the body part viewed and the subject's posture.

Women are more likely to be disembodied, as shown in Table 10.2. Only female body parts are used, never male. Another striking difference is the fact that men's faces are presented more often than women's, and female bodies are presented more often than males'. These differences are significant (Chi-Square test, n=118, df=3, 12.9, p=0.004).

When we compare the postures adopted by subjects in the photographs, sex differences again emerge. Men predominantly assume standing postures (85.7 percent), whereas women are evenly divided between standing and sitting postures (33 percent vs. 34 percent). In addition, women often kneel on all fours (12.2

Table 10.2 Body Views

	Single Males	Males/ Couples	Females/ Couples	Single Females
Body parts	0	0	2.9	3.6
Heads	33.9	14.7	11.8	7.1
Down to waist	21.0	41.2	41.2	12.5
Down to knees	6.5	14.7	14.7	19.6
Whole body	38.7	29.4	29.4	48.2
N	62	34	34	56

percent) or are lying down (19.5 percent). These differences again are significant (Chi-Square test, n=118, df=3, 20.7, p=0.001). Unfortunately, male nudity is too rare to compare it against posture, but this is possible for women. Nude women are usually doing anything but standing (38.8 percent), instead being shown sitting (28.2 percent), kneeling (12.8 percent) or lying down (20.5 percent) (Chi-Square test, n=76, df=3, 13.9, p=0.003).

The sexes are presented from different angles. Whereas women are presented from the front (62.8 percent) and less frequently from the side (27.9 percent), men are presented equally often from front and side (50 percent vs. 47.5 percent). Backs are presented rarely in both sexes (9.3 percent for females and 2.5 percent for males). These percentages do not change for nude figures.

In pairs we find that the man is presented significantly more often either in front of or with his head higher than that of the women (61.8 percent).

The photographic presentation of the sexes thus differs substantially: men are shown sideways in upright positions with an accentuation of the face, whereas women are shown frontally, lying and crouching. If pairs are presented, then the man is higher or more to the front of the picture.

Behavior: Smiles and Submission

The next part of the analysis deals with the behavior of men and women, singly and in couples. I will address two types of behavior: smiles as an indicator of friendliness, and cant positions (see Figs. 10.5 and 10.6) as an indicator of submission. In this posture, the vertical upright body axis is broken into angles. A person assuming such a posture appears submissive. Finally, I look for sex differences according to dominance and submission in couples.

Women smile significantly more often than men (51.2 percent vs. 29.3 percent, Chi-Square-Test, n=84, df=1, 4.177, p=0.04). This difference prevails in pairs. In pairs, men seldom smile alone (10.5 percent), both smile most often together (68.4 percent), and women smile more often than men in 21.1 percent of photographs (Chi-Square-Test, n=34, df=2, 18.95, p<0.0001).

The same sex difference emerges when we look at cant behavior (See Fig. 10.4). Women cant significantly more often than males (37.2 percent vs. 17.1 percent, Chi-Square-Test, n=84, df=1, 4,27, p=0.03). This sex difference is even more pronounced when a

Fig. 10.5 *Couples and traditional gender roles. The presentation of couples follows gender roles which ultimately derive from asymmetric investment. The man is portrayed as more dominant and superior to the woman, who assumes a submissive position leaning back or crouching, or is presented nude.*

female is together with a male: the man stands straight and the women cants in 78.3 percent of all pairs (Chi-Square-Test, n=34, df=2, 20.95, p<0.0001). In both cases nudity does not affect behavior; for instance, smiles are not accompanied more often by nudity.

In summary, this behavioral analysis shows that women are more friendly and show higher rates of submissive signals. This difference becomes more pronounced when men and women appear together.

Target Groups of Advertising

In this part of the analysis I tried to classify the advertisements according to their target group: male, female, or neutral, the last indicating products likely to be purchased by both sexes.

The results are presented in Table 10.3. When there are no persons in an ad, the addressee is either neutral or cannot be identified. This result underlines the assumption that human figures in

Table 10.3: Target Groups of Advertisements

	No. Persons	Males	Couples	Females
Neutral/ unidentified	89.3	45.2	67.6	61.3
Females	2.7	8.2	2.9	32.3
Males	8.0	46.6	29.4	6.5
N	187	73	34	62

advertisements are used to address particular sexes. The first point is that the presentation of men is for products that are intended for male buyers. The same is true for couples. Interestingly enough, women are used predominantly to sell to females. Thus, with the exception of couples, which are used to sell male products, advertising is sex specific. Male figures advertise male products and female figures advertise female products (Chi-Square-Test, n=356, df=6, 114.1, p<0.0001).

When we proceed to nudity in the ads, the results are as we would expect. None of the ads with clothed females is addressed to males, whereas 33.3 percent of the sexy ads are addressed to males. Moreover, none of the ads showing a nude man is addressed to women: they all are addressed to men, whereas again 20 percent of the males are advertising for female products.

Sex, Gender, Advertisements, Exploitation, and Cultural Evolution

Advertising presents us with a natural experiment in cultural evolution. In this process, a product is in competition with other products of the same or different type for a limited resource—the money of the potential customer.

An advertisement, then, is a means for enhancing the "fitness" of its product. Thus we can expect an evolution-like optimization process of advertisement contents. This optimization will be driven by the receivers of the information. As a result, advertisers should use the constructive features of the mind and its tendencies to accept specific decisions and information more easily than others. I have pointed out that these are products of human phylogeny. Thus, the natural experiment of advertising provides an interface between natural and cultural evolution.

The basic results of this study can be found in the fact that the imaging of people in advertisements is sex specific and follows

Fig. 10.6 *Advertising—exploitation of biological "prototypes"? Two pictures that exemplify the use of sexual signals and gender roles as revealed in this chapter in a prototypical fashion. The dominant male does not deign to make direct eye contact with the observer; but the female does, and extends responsiveness to a submissive, canted, and half-nude presentation.*

principles that can be derived from human mate-selection criteria. Men are presented upright and straight, their faces are not looking directly at the viewer, they are sincere in that they smile rarely, and they are almost never presented nude. In this form of presentation men appear honest and dominant but avoid direct eye contact with the customer, which could be interpreted as aggressive (Eibl-Eibesfeldt 1984). Men advertise for men, thus the information in the advertisements should be that the product enhances male fitness in competition with other males for the ultimate outcome of providing access to women.

In sharp contrast, females are presented disembodied or as whole bodies, and their faces are not information carriers. They are presented smiling, canting, and crouching or lying down. In addition, the presentation of female nudity plays a prominent role. Thus, advertisements provide a more submissive and sexual female image.

It is interesting to note that images of men are addressed to other men, and that nude male images are rare. Nicholson (1972) noted that there is no market among women for male nudity: "This market simply does not exist" (12). Male nudity in most cases is addressed to homosexual men. This reflects a basic sex difference. Most women are sex objects for most men. But only a few men are sex objects for women. Women will appear more often as sex objects, because female sexiness can be more easily evoked by physical features. Stauffer and Frost (1976) analyzed reactions to *Playboy* magazine and its female counterpart, *Playgirl* magazine. None of the interviewed men rated the *Playboy* centerfold as being of no interest, whereas 14 percent of the females rejected nude males in *Playgirl*. Comparable sex differences emerge when men and women are asked if opposite sex nudity arouses them sexually. Although newer studies show that men and women respond to sexually explicit material in comparable ways (Heiman 1975), they do so from different motivations. Money and Erhardt (1972) propose that men respond to a picture of a nude female in a sex-object way, imaging themselves copulating with her. In contrast, women seem to identify with a photograph of a nude woman, imaging themselves being in her place.

This exemplifies two biologically based principles. Females should not be interested in male nudity. Symons (1979) brings this to the point: looking at female nudity, and especially new and different stimuli, is a part of the motivational process that maximizes male reproductive success. On the other hand, there seems to be no reason, in terms of biological benefits, for women to wish to look at male nudity. Sexual selection will not promote such a motivation. If male nudity aroused females, then men would try to use this tendency for their own objectives. This finally would lead to random pairings, and females would endanger their reproductive success.

Thus female nudity is the ideal means for the exploitation of the male perceptual apparatus. But we see that this is rarely the case. Female nudity is seldom used for typical male products; instead nude women advertise for female products. This result allows us to identify the advertisement strategies used in the magazine studied in this chapter. The exploitative principle by which advertisements are used is identification with a normative self. The message is: "If you want to be like me, use this product." This clearly contradicts the feminist assumption that images of women are used in advertisements in order to exploit male perception. Indoctrination through identification is the main strategy.

This brings us to gender roles in advertisements. Evolutionary approaches predict that what we perceive as culturally determined, traditional gender roles will be based on the tendencies of an "adapted mind." If couples are presented, they are pictured as being happy, portraying a dominant male and a sexy female. Body size is associated with perceived dominance for males (Wilson 1968). The message is clear for the male: "You will attract submissive sexy females when you buy this product"; and for the female: "You will attract a dominant successful male who provides emotional stability." Seen this way, advertisements use "biological primitives" that have evolved over thousands of generations and that continue to structure our thinking.

Although this analysis has many methodological shortcomings, it shows that media content can be analyzed with ethological methods, testing hypotheses generated from evolutionary theory. In addition, the analysis shows that in a field where it is often assumed that cultural processes alone are at work, evolutionary theories can help discover and elucidate some fascinating and significant phenomena. One such discovery is that indoctrination through advertising exploits the human perceptual apparatus and the species' adherence to norms selected by natural mate-selection criteria.

References

Anderson, J. L., Crawford, C. B., Nadeau, J., and Lindberg, T. (1992). Was the Duchess of Windsor right? A cross-cultural review of the socio-ecology of ideals of female body shape. *Ethology and Sociobiology*, **13**, 197–227.

Burton, A. M., Bruce, V., and Dench, N. (1993). What's the difference between men and women—Evidence from facial measurement. *Perception*, **22**, 153–76.

Buss, D. M. (1989). Sex differences in human mate preferences: Evolutionary hypotheses tested in 37 cultures. *Behavioral and Brain Sciences*, **12**, 1–49.

Cosmides, L., Tooby, J., and Barkow, J. H. (1992). Evolutionary psychology and conceptual integration. In *The adapted mind* (ed. L. Cosmides, J. Tooby, J. H. Barkow), pp. 3–18. Oxford University Press, New York.

Cunningham, M. R. (1986). Measuring the physical in physical attractiveness: Quasi experiments on the sociobiology of female beauty. *Journal of Personality and Social Psychology*, **50**, 925–35.

Eibl-Eibesfeldt, I. (1984). *Die Biologie des menschlichen Verhaltens*. Piper, Munich.

Enquist M. and Arak A. (1994). Symmetry, beauty and evolution. *Nature*, **372**, 169–70.

Fölstad I. and Karter, A. J. (1992). Parasites, bright males and the immunocompetence handicap. *The American Naturalist*, **139**, 603–22.

Galton, F. (1879). Composite portraits, made by combining those of many different persons in a single resultant figure. *Journal of the Anthropological Institute*, **8**, 132–44.

Gangestad, S. W. and Buss, D. M. (1993). Pathogen prevalence and human mate preferences. *Ethology and Sociobiology*, **14**, 89–96.

Goffman, E. (1979). *Gender advertisements*. McMillan, London.

Grammer, K. (1993). *Signale der Liebe*. Hoffman und Campe, Hamburg.

Grammer K. and Thornhill, R. (1993). Human (Homo sapiens) facial attractiveness and sexual selection: The role of symmetry and averageness. *Journal of Comparative Psychology*, **108**, 233–42.

Harmon, L. D. (1973). The recognition of faces. *Scientific American*, **227**, 71–82.

Heiman, J. R. (1975). The physiology of erotica. *Psychology Today*, **8**, 90–94.

Henss, R. (1988). "… wer ist der/die Schönste im ganzen Land?" Zur Beurteilerübereinstimmung bei der Einschätzung der physischen Attraktivität. *Annales—Forschungsmagazin der Universität des Saarlandes*, **1**, 54–8.

Horvath, T. (1979). Correlates of physical beauty in men and women. *Social Behavior and Personality*, **7**, 145–51.

Johnstone, R. A. (1994). Female preference for symmetrical males as a by-product of selection for mate recognition. *Nature*, **372**, 172–5.

Kalkofen, H., Müller, A., and Strack, M. (1990). Kant's facial aesthetics and Galton's composite portraiture—are prototypes more beautiful? In *Proceedings of the 11th International Congress on Empirical Aesthetics* (ed. L. Halasz), pp. 151–4. International Association for Empirical Aesthetics, Budapest.

Keating, C. F., Mazur, A., and Segall, M. H. (1981). A cross cultural exploration of physiognomic traits of dominance and happiness. *Ethology and Sociobiology*, **2**, 41–48.

Kenrick, D. T. and Gutierres, S. E. (1980). Contrast effects and judgements of physical attractiveness: When beauty becomes a social problem. *Journal of Personality and Social Psychology*, **38**, 131–40.

Kenrick D. T., Sadalia, E. K., Groth, G., and Trost, M. R. (1990). Evolution, traits, and the stages of human courtship: Qualifying the parental investment model. *Journal of Personality*, **58**, 97–116.

Kilbourne, J. (1993). Killing us softly: Gender roles in advertising. *Adolescent Medicine*, **4**, 635–49.

Langlois, J. H. and Roggman, L. A. (1990). Attractive faces are only average. *Psychological Science*, **1**, 115–21.

Marr, D. (1982). *Vision*. Freeman, New York.

Mazur, A., Mazur, J., and Keating, C. F. (1984). Military rank attainment of a West Point class effects of cadet's physical features. *American Journal of Sociology*, **90**, 125–50.

Mazur, A., Halpern, C., and Udry, J. R. (1994). Dominant looking male teenagers copulate earlier. *Ethology and Sociobiology*, **15**, 73.

Moeller, A. P., Soler, M., and Thornhill, R. (1994). Breast symmetry, sexual selection, and human reproductive success. *Ethology and Sociobiology*, **16**, 207–21.

Money, J. and Erhardt, A. A. (1972). *Man and woman. Boy and girl.* Johns Hopkins University Press, Baltimore.

Müller, A. (1993). Visuelle Prototypen und die physikalischen Dimensionen von Attraktivität. In *Physische Attraktivität* (ed. R. Niketta und M. Hassebrauck). Hogrefe, Göttingen.

Nicholson, J. (1972). The packaging of rape: A feminist indictment. In *The pin-up: A modest history* (ed. M. Gabor), pp. 9–12. Bell Publications Co., New York.

Perrett, D. I., May, K. A., and Yoshikawa S. (1994). Facial shape and judgements of female attractiveness. *Nature, 368*, 239–42.

Rensch, B. (1963). Versuche über menschliche Auslösermerkmale beider Geschlechter. *Zeitschrift für Morphologische Anthropologie, 53*, 139–64.

Sergent, J. (1986). Microgenesis of face perception. In *Aspects of face processing* (ed. H. D. Ellis, A. A. Jeeves, and J. Shepherd). Martinus Nijhoff, Dordrecht.

Singh, D. (1992). The nature and significance of female physical attractiveness. Manuscript. 1–45.

———. (1993). Adaptive significance of female physical attractiveness—role of waist-to-hip ratio. *Journal of Personality and Social Psychology, 65*, 293–307.

Stauffer, J. and Frost, R. (1976). Male and female interest in sexually oriented magazines. *Journal of Communication, 26*, 25–30.

Symons, D. (1979). *The evolution of human sexuality*. Oxford University Press, New York.

Thornhill, R. and Gangestad, S. W. (1993). Human facial beauty. Averageness, symmetry, and parasite resistance. *Human Nature, 4*, 237–69.

———. (1994). Human fluctuating asymmetry and sexual behavior. *Psychological Science, 5*, 297–302.

Trivers, R. L. (1972). Parental investment and sexual selection. In *Sexual selection and the descent of man, 1871–1971* (ed. B. Cambell), pp. 136–79. Aldine, Chicago.

Wiederman, M. W. and Allgeier, E. R. (1992). Gender differences in mate selection criteria—sociobiological or socioeconomic explanation. *Ethology and Sociobiology, 13*, 115–24.

Wilson, P. R. (1968). Perceptual distortion of height as a function of ascribed academic status. *Journal of Social Psychology, 74*, 97–102.

Winkler, E. M. and Kirchengast, S. (1994). Body dimensions and differential fertility in !Kung San males from Namibia. *American Journal of Human Biology, 6*, 203–13.

CHAPTER ELEVEN

THE ROLE OF SEX AND EMOTIONAL RESPONSE IN INDOCTRINABILITY

EXPERIMENTAL EVIDENCE ON THE "RALLY 'ROUND THE FLAG" EFFECT

James N. Schubert

Ragsdale (1984) identified two key research questions about presidential speeches in the United States that appear relevant to all political leaders. The first question dealt with the circumstances under which major speeches or public addresses are made, while the second involved the impact of such speeches upon public attitudes. Although proceeding to address the first question in the article that followed, Ragsdale noted the virtual absence of behavioral research on the second question:

> As an independent variable, speechmaking demonstrates the extent to which the public behaviour of presidents shapes public attitudes about presidents.... Yet no research has analysed how presidents' own actions may affect their public fortunes. (Ragsdale 1984, 972)

Although the past decade has included some attention to the textual content of political speech in the form of rhetorical and discourse analysis, little progress has been made in understanding the impact of presidential speeches as multimedia events. Ragsdale references Edelman's insightful (1971) work on symbolic politics to underscore the potential importance of broadcast speeches and argues that they may establish "a direct and seemingly intimate relationship between presidents and their audience ... (enabling) presidents to create or modify public opinion at key points during their terms" (971). Relevant to this point is experimental research by Masters, Sullivan and other Dartmouth researchers published over the past decade (Masters et al. 1986; 1987; Sullivan and Masters 1988; Sullivan et al. 1991), demonstrating that televised images of leaders do affect public responses to them. However, the causal connection between presidential speeches and changes in public opinion remains to be explored.

One context in which presidential speeches may be important is in generating public support for decisions to commit military forces abroad in potential combat situations. This "rally 'round the flag" effect (Mueller 1973) reveals a predictable surge in popular support when presidents announce the commitment of military forces. Nationally televised speeches have become a primary vehicle for the communication of such decisions to the public. Indeed, expert commentary on the rally effect accompanied President Clinton's prime-time television speech announcing the Haitian intervention in September 1994, with one network including the insights of John Mueller. Because such presidential speeches may contribute to a rally effect, they present a theoretically interesting and practically significant setting for studying the effects of political speeches upon public opinion.

A remarkably persistent and widely replicated empirical finding in the literature on public opinion and political attitudes involves the difference between males and females in support for the use of military force. Males are more supportive, and the correlation is commonly in the moderate-to-strong range. Conover and Sapiro (1993) comment, "These gender differences are some of the largest and most consistent in the study of political psychology (1095)." Reanalyzing survey data from four national surveys designed by the Chicago Council on Foreign Relations to focus on sex effects, Fite, Genest, and Wilcox (1990) report "... persistent and significant gender differences on foreign policy goals and policy attitudes that persist after the introduction of a variety of demographic controls" (502). Inspired by the discovery of a gender gap in support for President Reagan in the early 1980s, Smith (1984) drew on Gallup, Harris, NORC, NORC-GSS, Roper, and SRC data (as published by Cantril 1947; Mueller 1973; Converse 1980; Cantril and Strunk 1951; Gallup 1972; and Erskine 1970) to examine the relationship between sex and attitudes toward violence in both foreign and domestic policy situations. Smith summarized, "Looking at 285 data points we found that men were more supportive of the violent or forceful option in over 87 percent of the readings." In surveys of U.S. undergraduate students conducted in 1985 and 1987, Gwartney-Gibbs and Denise H. Lach (1989) analyzed the effects of a variety of demographic, psychological, and family background factors upon attitudes (optimism-pessimism) toward nuclear war. They report that "Sex is the only correlate of the [attitudinal] Index that is highly significant and stable over time, with females significantly and substantially more pessimistic in both years" (168). In experimental research designed explicitly to contrast the relative effects of sex and sex role orientation upon attitudes toward the use of military force, Jensen (1987) found that sex retained significant effects, even with sex role orientation controlled. Commenting specifically upon the rally effect, Mueller (1993) noted that males rally more than females and that this effect holds for the Korean, Vietnam, and Persian Gulf wars.

Explanations of observed sex differences in attitudes toward the use of military force are problematic. Some authors ascribe the observed patterns to undefined "biologistic" factors, while others speculate on how the differences may reflect underlying socialization effects or cultural patterns in the social construction of gender. A useful summary of these efforts at explanation is provided by Fite, Genest, and Wilcox (1990) who distinguish four hypotheses within the existing literature. One emphasizes ideology, proposing that the differences may, in part, reflect the more liberal political attitudes held by females and the questionable presumption that liberals are more pacifistic than conservatives. A second explanation draws upon women's "disproportionate share of the lower economic and social strata," their associated tendency to vote left or Democratic in the U.S., leading to a "butter over guns" or "bread not bombs" approach to foreign policy issues. Third is a hypothesis associated with feminist theory, "that the potential for motherhood leads women to different attitudes about war and peace" (496) with emphasis on caring and nurturing (see Gilligan 1982; Ruddick 1989). Fourth, differential socialization into sex role orientations is proposed as an explanation for these differences between males and females. In Mueller's words, "The situation in which men are inclined to favor the use of physical force and women to shy away from it presumably is based on society's preferred sex roles in which men are expected to be firm and aggressive, women quiet and demure (1973, 146)." In general, the evidence is that sex differences retain significant effects upon attitudes toward the use of military force when ideology, political party identification, socioeconomic status, feminism, and sex role orientation are taken into account (Conover and Sapiro 1993). It is interesting in the latter case that in Jensen's (1987) experimental research, although sex role orientation had anticipated effects, males scoring high on femininity were more supportive of military force than females scoring high on masculinity.

Although the hypothesis that a "potential for motherhood" is associated with a more "caring and nurturing" approach to public policy issues and predisposes less supportive attitudes toward the use of military force, none of the studies sufficiently operationalizes the "potential for motherhood" concept to present a reasonable test of the hypothesis. Having actually given birth was used by Fite et al. and by Conover and Saprio as a surrogate variable and was found to have no effect in discriminating among females attitudes. Two problems of research design are (1) that the hypothesis cannot be tested by simply contrasting males and females, and (2) it is not plausible that females would differ substantially in political attitudes based upon their actual reproductive status at any given point in time—especially if one considers female reproductive interest to be defined in terms of inclusive fitness (Hamilton 1964). However, if the important aspect of potential for motherhood lies in its association with the value placed on "caring and nurturing" values, then female attitudes should vary depending upon the nature of the values at stake in a military conflict situation. Specifically, it may be hypothesized that females will rely more substantially upon humanitarian considerations than traditionally conceived "vital national interests" in evaluating the use of military force and, secondly, that females will be more supportive of commitments of military force in situations that substantially present humanitarian, as opposed to geopolitical interests.

Research Design

This study's concern with the impact of the speeches of actual political leaders and with public responses to political decisions that imply very realistic threats to the health and survival of human beings required utilization of naturalistic materials—that is, actual speeches by actual leaders. The concern with the medium of exposure to presidential speeches, as well as the concern over sex differences in the bases of evaluations of political decisions, required utilization of an experimental research design to allow simultaneous manipulation of media and of situational values. An experiment was designed in which the medium of exposure to speeches was varied across four treatment conditions: visual plus vocal (videotape), vocal only (audiotape), verbal only (transcript of speech text), and the control group condition of no direct exposure (newspaper summary of the speech event). The experiment was conducted on 17 November 1994 on a sample of 61 undergraduate college students, randomly assigned to one of the four treatment groups.

Hypotheses. On the basis of existing theory and research, as reviewed above, three main hypotheses were tested in this study. One hypothesis was that video exposure would be more effective than other treatments in producing a "rally" response. Noting that the four treatment conditions—news summary, text, voice, and video—present an ordinal scale of the personalization of the presidential communication, a subordinate hypothesis was that the more personalized the exposure, the greater the rally effect.

A second principal hypothesis was that males would show a stronger rally response to presidential speeches than females. A third hypothesis was that females would be more likely to rally when situations contained humanitarian concerns, as opposed to national interest values. An additional derivative hypothesis involved the potential interaction of sex and exposure medium, specifically that, as a consequence of socialization, males would be more responsive to the more personalized, audiovisual media than females and, in particular, would be more affected by the video treatment condition.

Speeches. Situational values were varied within each treatment group by presenting one speech announcing a traditional national interest conflict situation and a second presenting a situation involving essentially humanitarian issues. President Bush's 8 August 1990 nationally televised speech announcing the commitment of U.S. forces in the Persian Gulf in response to Iraq's invasion of Kuwait was selected for the "vital national interest" stimulus material, while President Clinton's nationally televised speech announcing the commitment of U.S. military forces in Haiti on 15 September 1994 was selected for the humanitarian situation material. The Persian Gulf crisis presents a classic instance of realpolitik, both from the perspective of Iraq's opportunistic invasion, as well as from the U.S. and its coalition's response. The intervention in Haiti, conversely, had little manifest geopolitical, "vital national interest" content. It was an effort to deal with the combined effects of abject poverty and extraordinarily repressive government upon a people living in relative proximity to the United States and its territories. Certainly, it was an effort to deal with the tide of Haitian refugees arriving in Florida, but even that value went beyond the economic burden on the U.S. to include the plight of the Haitians drowning in large numbers on the high seas in efforts to flee their country. Of course, it also reinforced plans to stem the nearby tide of Cuban refugees. However, regardless of any second order national interests served by Clinton's decision, the prospective intervention by U.S. combat forces served far more humanitarian values than the available alternative methods for addressing the situation—such as sinking the refugee boats, returning the refugees to the Haitian government, or containing the refugees at Guantanamo or in Panama—and did so at potentially substantial monetary as well as political cost. Finally, with respect to the domestic political situation, Clinton and his advisors surely were aware that the "rally effect" is a short-lived phenomenon and not likely to last from mid-September until the time of the then pending national election in November.

The presentation of speeches by Bush and Clinton introduced a confounding element of partisanship in the experimental situation. This problem would potentially emerge in any use of naturalistic materials, however realism was considered necessary for stimulus materials to be sufficiently provocative. To test hypotheses where situational values were *not* at stake, responses to the two situations were pooled, thereby nullifying the effects of prior positive or negative attitudes toward the presidents. To test hypotheses where situational values *were* at stake, responses to a "pretest" survey of attitudes toward Bush and Clinton were introduced in analyses as control variables. Change in attitudes in response to speeches was thereby analyzed in terms of change from pretest attitudes, regardless of how positive or negative they initially may have been. Although a variety of differences between the political climates surrounding these speeches might be pointed out, it may be recalled that at the time of the experiment, both presidents had received widespread negative public evaluations of their overall performance: Bush by losing the 1992 election and Clinton by his party's resounding defeat in the 1994 elections.

Sample. The sample of undergraduate students was drawn from two classes of students in upper division political science courses, and the experiment was conducted for one class in the morning and the other in the afternoon of the same day. Enrollment across the two classes included a roughly equal total number of males and females, and the experiment resulted with 29 female subjects and 31 males. Random assignment yielded four treatment groups ranging from 13 to 17 in size with relatively equal numbers of males and females in each. Although more subjects were anticipated in the experimental design, statistical power analysis reveals a marginally sufficient number of subjects across the four groups to enable a rigorous test of hypotheses under the expectation of strong treatment effects.

Data. All the subjects from each class responded to a preliminary questionnaire before being exposed to one of the speeches. Background questions queried respondents' citizenship, sex, college major, college year, and military service of self or kin. Questions of political attitudes and behavior included voting history, party identification, interest in politics, ideology, feminism, and political sophistication.[1] To assess prior attitudes toward the presidents, subjects were asked whether they approved of each president's job performance in foreign policy. Additional questions addressed specific attitudes toward Bush's commitment of forces in the Gulf in 1990 and Clinton's commitment of forces in Haiti in 1994. Finally, subjects were also asked whether they remembered viewing either speech at the time that it was delivered.

Immediately after exposure to a speech, subjects were presented with a questionnaire designed to assess their evaluation of the speech. A key initial question was whether they felt more or less supportive (than before) after exposure to the speech. To enable a direct pretest/posttest contrast of attitudes, one item repeated the pretest question regarding approval of the president's decision to commit forces, using almost identical language. To assess the issue dimensions underlying subjects' evaluations of the speeches, additional items were included querying the persuasiveness of arguments involving national interest and humanitarian issues in the speeches.

Conduct of the Experiment. Videotapes of the speeches were used from CNN and CSPAN sources. The speeches were of simi-

---

1. A minimal test of political sophistication was provided by the task of differentiating the relative conservatism of Bush and Clinton: "... do you think that Clinton is more conservative than Bush, that Bush is more conservative than Clinton, or that they are about the same?"

lar length—ten and fourteen minutes respectively for Bush and Clinton—and both were delivered in the same setting: from the White House Oval Office with a window in the background. The physical framing of the video recording is remarkably similar for the two speeches with the only notable difference being the introduction of flags by Clinton.[2] Audiotapes were made from the audio track of the videotapes. Official transcripts were used for the speech text materials, and next-day accounts from the Washington Post were employed for the news summary treatment condition. Presentation order of the speeches was varied across treatment groups for the morning class and varied again within groups in reversed order for the afternoon class. The management of each group session, including the administration of questionnaires, was provided by a pair of graduate students, who were assigned to different treatment groups for the two classes.

The experiment began with a brief statement of purpose by the author and a request for voluntary consent. Subjects were then assigned to treatment groups and taken to separate rooms for each condition. Following administration of the pretest questionnaire, a speech was presented and then evaluated, followed by presentation of the second speech. The entire process occurred within the time span of one hour.

Results

Pretest Data. Although subjects were randomly assigned to treatment groups, with so few subjects the possibility of differences between groups occurring by chance in potentially important characteristics remains. Table 11.1 reports the significance of between-group differences on relevant variables. For background characteristics, the groups had very similar composition.[3] The four groups were also quite similar in reported acts of political participation, political knowledge, and political sophistication. On the last variable, 75 percent of the subjects correctly reported the ide-

2. Indeed, it appears plausible that Clinton's advisors studied and replicated the structure of the Bush speech, not only in visual structure, but in the textual content as well.

3. The only significant difference was in recent military service for the subject or immediate family members, and here, where 20 percent of the subjects responded affirmatively in three of the groups, the news summary group reported no such service experience.

ological relation between Bush and Clinton—only four subjects identified Clinton as more conservative than Bush. In political attitudes, there were marginally significant differences between groups in party identification. Although quite similar in Republican identification (including the "leaning toward" category, the four totals were 53 percent, 54 percent, 62 percent, and 53 percent with Republican identification), the groups did show some difference in Democratic identification that varied from a low of 19 percent to a high of 36 percent. Differences in ideology were not significant. Overall, these data reveal that random assignment of subjects resulted in four groups that were remarkably similar in background, political participation and political attitudes.

The four groups were also quite similar in their perceptions of Bush and Clinton as foreign policy leaders and of their decisions to use force, respectively in the Persian Gulf and Haiti. Overall, 53 percent of the subjects approved of Bush's foreign policy performance, in contrast to 30 percent approval for Clinton. Bush's commitment to

Table 11.1: Between-Group Differences on the Pretest Questionnaire

Variable	Chi Square	p<
Background Characteristics		
Sex	1.310	0.726
College Major	1.730	0.630
Class Standing	6.890	0.648
Armed Forces: Kin	8.417	0.038
Armed Forces: Friends	0.860	0.836
Political Participation		
Voted '92?	5.196	0.519
Voted for in '92	7.858	0.548
Voted '94?	5.607	0.469
Political Interest		
TV News Viewing	9.529	0.390
Newspaper Reading	7.842	0.550
Political Sophistication	5.921	0.748
Political Attitudes		
Party Identification	19.868	0.070
Ideology	15.787	0.201
Feminism	11.603	0.478
Prior Attitudes Toward Bush and Clinton		
Bush Foreign Policy	3.584	0.937
Clinton Foreign Policy	11.147	0.266
Bush Gulf Decision	12.043	0.211
Clinton Haiti Decision	15.860	0.195

Table 11.2: Media, Sex, and the Rally Effect

Experimental Group

	News Summary	Speech Text	Audiotape	Videotape
No Rally	80.00	84.62	81.25	64.71
Rally@	20.00	15.38	18.75	35.29
Total	100%	100%	100%	1.000
N=	15	13	16	17

Sex differences

	Female	**Male**
No Rally	79.31	75.00
Rally@	20.69	25.00
Total	100%	100%
N=	29	32

use force in the Gulf was approved by 65 percent, while only 26 percent approved of Clinton's decision. Clearly, there was opportunity for substantial improvement to be caused by the exposure to Clinton's speech, but constrained opportunity for increased approval for Bush. In sum, these data show no significant differences between the treatment groups in attitudes toward Bush or Clinton as foreign policymakers, nor in their decisions to commit armed forces abroad, prior to the experimental exposure to the presidential speeches.

Media Effect. A principal concern in this study is with the effects of televised speeches upon the "rally 'round the flag" effect. A "rally" response to a speech was defined by an answer of "much more supportive" or "more supportive" to the question: "After (*viewing*) President _____'s speech, are you more supportive or less supportive of the President's decision to commit United States military forces in _____?" Subjects might rally in response to both speeches, only one, or neither. In Table 11.2, subjects are regarded as showing the rally response only if they rallied for both speeches, thereby revealing support for the commitment of military forces regardless of president and situation. There is marked similarity in responses across the three nonvideo conditions, and the results show that 17 percent more of the subjects in the group exposed to the videotapes rallied than in the other groups, a difference that was significant at the 0.05 level.[4]

---

4. The Chi-Square value (4.06) was calculated based on the number of behavioral observations represented in each cell (i.e., n=122).

Sex Effect. No significant main effect is found for sex. As predicted, males rallied more than females, but the difference is quite small. Therefore, these data provide no support for the general proposition that females are more pacifistic in their response to the use of military force than males.

Sex-Media Interaction. It was proposed, however, that males are more sensitive than females to personalized appeals for patriotic response from their leaders, as presented in the face-to-face setting of televised speeches. Fig. 11.1 presents data on the interaction of exposure medium and sex upon the rally effect. It is particularly interesting to observe that males and females in the nonvideo groups displayed virtually identical patterns of rally behavior. Rather, what discriminates males and females is the effect of the television exposure. Twenty-two percent more of the males rallied under the video condition, compared to 10 percent more of the females. Thus, although both males and females showed greater responsiveness to the televised speeches, males were twice as responsive as females. An interesting pattern appears for males, but not females, when the single rally subjects are separated from the no-rally subjects. As illustrated in Fig. 11.2, the more personalized the exposure medium (from news summary to text only to audio to video), the greater the rally response for males. Considering the single rally category to represent a degree of cognitive

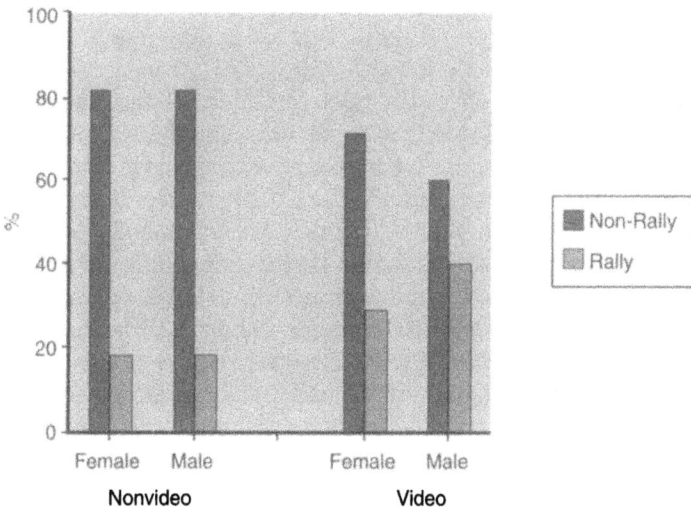

Fig. 11.1 *The Interaction of Sex and Media in the Rally Effect*

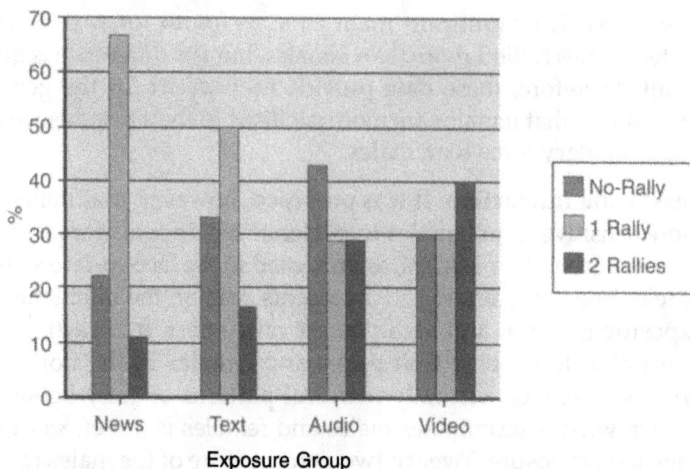

Note: 1 rally is for Bush or Clinton, 2 rallies are for both.

Fig. 11.2 *Medium of Exposure and Male Rally Behavior*

discrimination, males were far more discriminating in their responses when exposed to textual than audiovisual materials. There was no trace of this pattern for females.

Situation Effects. Table 11.3 presents data on the rally effect broken down by the situation/president manipulation. First, it may be observed that subjects were substantially more influenced by Clinton's speech than Bush's and that this pattern holds for both the video and nonvideo conditions. This result may reflect the more negative prior attitudes towards Clinton's Haitian decision. Perhaps because of this effect, the video condition produced a stronger rally response for Clinton than for Bush, although subjects showed a stronger rally response for television in both cases. With so few subjects in the tables and modest-sized effects, the differences do not reach critical levels for significance in either tabulation.

With respect to the interaction of situation and sex, the results were very much as expected for Bush's Gulf Crisis speech. Males rallied far more strongly than females, and the difference is significant. Female subjects were generally not responsive to the Bush speech, while over half the males felt more supportive afterwards. The more intriguing finding emerges in the responses to Clinton's speech. Here, females rallied far more strongly than males—indeed, two-thirds of the females reported feeling more supportive after exposure to the speech, while only 40 percent of the males did. This result may be interpreted against a baseline in

Table 11.3: Media, Sex, and the Rally Effect by Situation

	Haitian Intervention		**Gulf Crisis**	
Television Exposure				
	Nonvideo	**Video**	**Nonvideo**	**Video**
No Rally	52.27	35.29	61.36	52.94
Rally@	47.73	64.71	38.64	47.06
Total	100%	100%	100%	100%
N=	44	17	44	17
Chi Square	1.42		0.360	
p<	0.234		0.549	
Sex differences				
	Female	**Male**	**Female**	**Male**
No Rally	34.48	59.38	72.41	46.88
Rally@	65.52	40.63	27.59	53.13
Total	100%	100%	100%	100%
N=	29	32	29	32
Chi Square	3.78		4.100	
p<	0.052		0.043	

which only 27 percent of the females and 25 percent of the males reported approving or strongly approving of the Haitian intervention prior to exposure to the speech. Both the Bush and Clinton speeches caused rally effects; however, males rallied primarily for Bush's Gulf decision while females rallied for Clinton's Haitian decision. The sex differences are substantial in each situation at 25 percent, and the results are statistically significant. The findings with respect to females and the Clinton Haitian decision clearly and directly contradict the pattern of findings published to date on the "rally 'round the flag" effect and on sex differences in support for the use of military force.

The interactions of sex, media, and situation in the rally effect are illustrated in Fig. 11.3. First, it may be observed that females were virtually unmoved by the video exposure to Bush's speech. Second, although females were very much moved by the Clinton speech in general, they were most responsive to the video exposure. All but one in the latter group rallied to Clinton. Males, in contrast, rallied more under the video condition in both situations, but only somewhat more so for Clinton than for Bush. Overall, these data show that females were far more discriminating in their rally behavior than males and particularly so in their responsiveness to the television medium.

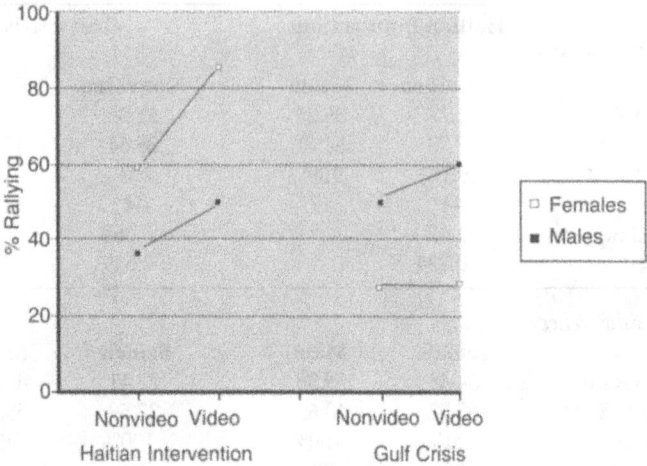

Fig. 11.3 *Sex, Media, and Situation in the Rally Effect*

Effects of Prior Attitudes. To examine the effects of prior attitudes toward the presidents and their decisions to use military force, ordinary least squares analyses were performed with sex and video condition treated as dummy variables. The evaluative questionnaire used in the experiment was designed to allow a direct pretest and posttest contrast of attitudes. These questions were virtually identical with the exception of the introductory clause— pretest ("To the best of your recollection, how did you feel ...") and posttest ("Based upon the President's speech and the situation at the time of the President's decision, how do you feel ...")—providing for the observation of change in absolute evaluation of the decisions on a five-step Likert scale. It should be noted here that the opportunity for measured improvement was essentially constrained to those subjects who were initially neutral or opposed to the decisions on the pretest questionnaire.

The results presented in Table 11.4 reveal that pretest attitudes had equivalent effects upon posttest attitudes for both speeches, although significant only in Clinton's case. The partial effects for sex—that is, with pretest attitudes held constant—are at the margin of significance and consistent with the observed effects associated with the "supportive response" questions analyzed above. Male approval for the Gulf decision increased after exposure to the Bush speech, and female approval for the Haitian intervention increased after the Clinton speech.

Table 11.4: The Effects of Intervening Variables: OLS Analysis

Variables	Haitian Intervention		Gulf Crisis	
	Regression Coefficient	p<	Regression Coefficient	p<
Constant	1.376		3.772	
Sex	0.275	0.073	–0.452	0.061
Video/Nonvideo	–0.281	0.097	–0.045	0.839
Prior Decision Attitude	0.329	0.000	–0.205	0.159
R square	0.289		0.067	
F	7.704		1.346	
p<	0.000		0.269	

Sex and Situational Values. Preliminary to examining the relationship between sex and reliance upon national interest versus humanitarian values, the data for all subjects were analyzed to explore whether the subjects correctly interpreted the Gulf Crisis as primarily involving national interests and the Haitian intervention as primarily involving humanitarian concerns. Subjects rated each speech with respect to the persuasiveness of vital national interest arguments and humanitarian issues on a five-step scale that ranged from "extremely persuasive" to "not persuasive at all." The mean ratings on these scales were significantly different for each situation (Gulf T=1.841, p<.07; Haiti T=4.446, p<.000). For the Haitian speech, respondents rated humanitarian concerns as more persuasive than national interest arguments, while for Bush's Gulf speech the emphasis is reversed. These data demonstrate that the subjects correctly perceived the values at stake in these two situations.

Fig. 11.4 presents data on the relationship between sex and situational values in subjects' evaluations of the two speeches. First, it may be observed that both males and females found national interest arguments more persuasive in the Gulf speech and humanitarian issues more persuasive in the Haiti speech. Second, females were significantly more likely than males to find the humanitarian issues persuasive for the Haitian intervention. Third, males were marginally (in a one-tailed test) more likely to find vital national interest arguments more persuasive in the Gulf situation. In short, these data lend clear-cut support to an explanation of sex differences in rally behavior for the Gulf and Haitian decisions based upon the quality of issues and values at stake in

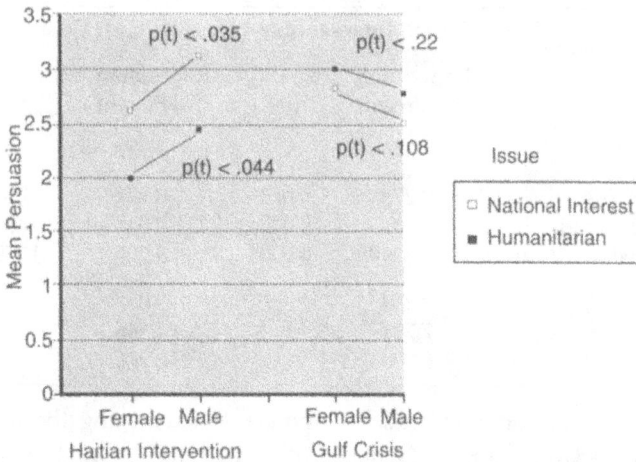

Fig. 11.4 *Sex and Persuasion by Issue and Situation*

these situations. Females appear to have rallied for the Clinton decision because it addressed humanitarian issues, while males appear to have rallied for the Bush decision because it addressed so-called vital national interests.

Discussion

The principal purpose of this study was to explore the impact of televised political speeches upon public attitudes. There is a wealth of anecdotal and qualitative evidence supporting the hypothesis that they do have effects, but there is little direct empirical evidence. The "rally 'round the flag" effect was chosen as a potentially provocative context for exploring the impact of U.S. presidential speeches. A first and critical research question was whether the rally effect could even be replicated in experimental research using presidential speeches as stimuli. In this respect, the experiment was quite successful.

A second research question was whether television played an important role in enhancing the impact of political speeches. In this study, television clearly did make a difference. Subjects exposed to television were more likely to rally than those who were not, and males appeared sensitive to the more personalized audiovisual media of communication. In the future, prime-time nationally televised addresses may be the principal form in which leaders in the United States seek public support for their decisions committing military forces. This study finds such speeches to be effective in changing attitudes, well after the fact.

A third research question involved the well-replicated and widely accepted difference between males and females in foreign policy attitudes toward support for the use of military force in foreign situations. On the one hand, the experiment was expected to replicate this well-established pattern in human behavior. On the other, thinking theoretically about the explanation for sex differences led to an additional hypothesis that, despite lower overall support for the use of force than males, females would be more supportive of the use of force in situations involving humanitarian rather than national interest values. On this basis, we expected that the difference between males and females would diminish for conflicts that raised moral and humanitarian issues. The finding that females were far more likely than males to rally for the Haitian intervention was a much stronger effect than initially expected. It was reinforced by both the result that females were very much influenced in this behavior by the televised version of the speech and the additional finding that they found Clinton's humanitarian arguments most persuasive. All of these results (as illustrated in Table 11.5) were observed in a context in which, prior to exposure to the speech, females were just as negative as males, both in their evaluation of Clinton's foreign policy performance and of his commitment of troops to Haiti. This finding is very much at odds with the existing literature and requires some explication.

To explain a result so much at variance with the existing literature, it may be observed that this literature was built during the Cold War era in which almost all actual and seriously considered situations for the use of military force involved traditional justifications of national interest and geopolitical imperatives. Although slightly following this era, the Gulf War surely fits the historic pattern for the use of military force. Prior research may have missed the sex effect observed here because it was contextually bounded within an era when foreign military involvements were overwhelmingly guided by narrow conceptions of national interest. Since the Gulf War, the commitment of U.S. combat forces, first in Somalia and then in Haiti (and arguably in Bosnia in 1995), has responded to fundamentally humanitarian concerns through interventions in domestic crises and conflicts. To the extent that

Table 11.5: Media and the Persuasiveness of National Interest and Humanitarian Arguments

Analysis Variance

	Haitian Intervention National Interests		Haitian Intervention Humanitarian Issues		Gulf Crisis National Interests		Gulf Crisis Humanitarian Issues	
	F	p<	F	p<	F	p<	F	p<
Exposure Medium	2.590	0.063	3.480	0.002	0.272	0.845	0.304	0.823
Sex	0.259	0.613	0.861	0.236	0.002	0.963	0.076	0.783
Sex by Exposure Medium	2.984	0.040	0.192	0.810	1.187	0.324	0.786	0.507
Feminism	7.215	0.010			9.665	0.003		
Ideology	5.026	0.030						
Prior Attitude	6.094	0.017			3.339	0.073	2.918	0.094
Party ID			2.488	0.047				
R Square	0.546		0.347		0.314		0.141	

Least Squares Adjusted Means @

	Haitian Intervention National Interests Mean	Haitian Intervention Humanitarian Issues Mean	Gulf Crisis National Interests Mean	Gulf Crisis Humanitarian Issues Mean
Exposure Medium:				
News	3.120	2.920	2.686	2.704
Text	3.030	2.373	2.795	2.926
Audio	2.960	1.835	2.679	3.050
Video	2.450	1.954	2.554	2.851
Sex:				
Female	2.890	2.141	2.965	2.921
Male	2.940	2.400	2.817	2.845

@Mean Values are for a scale ranging from 1 = "extremely persuasive" to 5 = "not persuasive at all"

caring and nurturing propensities are ever manifest in foreign policy decisions, surely they were in these cases. In the post–Cold War era, these were New World Order conflict situations. To all appearances, there will be many more such situations confronting the major powers of the world in the future. If this finding holds up in replication studies, it will reveal a supportive constituency for a reinvigorated role for moral considerations in foreign policy. Such a role would, of course, be very much at odds with the traditional practice of realpolitik.

A second problem raised by this finding is to explain why females may be more supportive of military force when humanitarian issues are involved or why they may display more "caring and nurturing" values. One theoretical basis for an explanation is found in the concept of reproductive interest for males and females and in the different behavioral strategies they adopt to secure those interests (Trivers 1974). If female interest lies in the survival and reproduction of offspring and kin, then it would not be well served by military involvements remote from the homeland that include substantial risk of harm to group members for the sake of abstract constructions of national interest. Certainly in this case, although there was some risk involved in the Haitian intervention, it was minuscule in contrast to the risk posed by Iraq to U.S. forces. In this respect, sex differences in attitudes may be influenced by different thresholds of acceptable risk.

A second basis of explanation is that because female reproductive strategies necessarily involve substantial investment in a limited set of offspring and kin, females are disposed toward a more generalized "caring and nurturing" approach to social relations than males—extending beyond immediate family to broader social groupings. Thus, females may be more responsive to themes of human suffering associated with starvation and oppression than males. During the debriefing session following the experiment, one female subject in the video group commented explicitly that she showed support for the Haitian decision because it was an opportunity to do good and to do so at little risk.

This argument is very clearly not that females are disposed toward more pacifistic attitudes, but that they may respond more or less hawkishly to different issues and values. There is growing evidence in other bodies of literature challenging the proposition that females are not aggressive or competitive in their social behavior (Bjorkquist 1994). Rather, such behavior may take different forms and occur under different conditions among females than males.

Strategies for males to secure reproductive interest are far more flexible and variable than those available to females, and male reproductive strategy (Low 1992; Manson and Wrangham 1991) may find expression in collective behavior that is remarkably consistent (Schubert 1993) with the theoretical model of political realism (Morgenthau 1948), otherwise known as realpolitik, and the mechanisms of balance-of-power politics, as formalized by Kaplan (1968). Organized, collective violence among human males to secure so called "vital national interests," involving resource capabilities, coalition formation, alliance maintenance, and adjustments of intergroup equivalencies have a well-established, widely accepted, and fairly well understood tradition within the traditionally male realm of formal politics in human affairs. Morgenthau (1948) paraphrased this essential feature of political behavior by arguing that "... statesmen think and act in terms of interest defined as power." Morgenthau was certainly describing a world of male behavior in this observation, and a theoretical consideration of sexual differentiation in reproductive strategies suggests that the generalization may be conditional for males. Females may be disposed toward a different conception of "interest" and a different evaluation of the conditions under which the use of collective violence to secure national interests is justified.

Conclusion

This chapter presents a first trial of an experimental design to study the effects of speeches by political leaders seeking to generate public support for decisions to commit military forces to potential combat situations abroad. The results of this initial run of the experiment may be regarded as preliminary and tentative, depending upon replication in subsequent trials with the research design. These results are provocative, in that they (1) indicate the important effects of leaders' speeches on public attitudes toward the use of force, (2) indicate the special effectiveness of the television medium in affecting public attitudes, and (3) qualify conventional wisdom that males are more supportive of the use of force than females.

Perhaps the most important result is the finding that it is possible to generate a simulation of the rally effect by exposing people to actual political speeches under the controlled conditions of experimental research design. The rally effect is especially interesting as a case in which people form attitudes in the relatively short term—often with little prior knowledge and in response to novel stimuli—in response to a patriotic appeal from their political leader. Under such conditions, the rally effect presents an instance of political indoctrination that bears directly upon the prevalence and incidence of the use of military force in human intergroup relations.

The importance of sex differences in attitudes toward the use of force is not just a matter of academic and theoretical concern. If female political behavior differs from male political behavior, the relatively recent arrival of females in the traditionally exclusive male domain of formal government and politics may produce fundamental changes in the nature and conduct of politics in the future as the representation of females increases. This research focuses upon a critical point of difference in which the available evidence suggests that the differential behavior of males and females is not just a function of socialization and culture and might be a function of different reproductive strategies. If supported and elaborated through subsequent research, this phenomenon would have intriguing theoretical and practical implications.

References

Bjorkqvist, K. (1994). Sex differences in physical, verbal, and indirect aggression: A review of recent research. *Sex Roles*, **30** (3/4), 177–88.

Cantril, H. (1947). *Gauging public opinion*. Princeton University Press, Princeton.

Cantril, H. and Strunk, M. (1951). *Public opinion, 1935–1946*. Princeton University Press, Princeton.

Conover, P. J. and Sapiro, V. (1993). Gender, feminist consciousness, and war. *American Journal of Political Science*, **37**, 1079–99.

Converse, P. E. (1980). *American social attitudes data sourcebook, 1947-1978*. Harvard University Press, Cambridge, Mass.

Edelman, M. (1971). *Politics as symbolic action: Mass arousal and quiescence*. Academic Press, New York.

Erskine, H. (1970). The polls: Is war a mistake. *Public Opinion Quarterly*, **34**, 134–50.

Fite, D., Genest, M., and Wilcox, C. (1990). Gender differences in foreign policy attitudes. *American Politics Quarterly*, **18**(4), 492–513.

Gallup, G. (1972). *The Gallup poll: Public opinion, 1935–1971*. 3 vols. Random House, New York.

Gilligan, C. (1982). *In a different voice*. Harvard University Press, Cambridge, Mass.

Gwartney-Gibbs, P. A. and Lach, D. H. (1989). Sex differences in attitudes toward nuclear war. *Journal of Public Relations*, 162–73.

Hamilton, W. D. (1964). The genetical theory of social behaviour. *Journal of Theoretical Biology*, **7**, 1–32.

Jensen, M. P. (1987). Gender, sex roles, and attitudes toward war and nuclear weapons. *Sex Roles*, **17**, 253–67.

Kaplan, M. A., ed. (1968). *New approaches to international relations*. St. Martin's, New York.

Manson, J. H. and Wrangham, R. W. (1991). Intergroup aggression in chimpanzees and humans. *Current Anthropology*, **32**, 369–90.

Masters, R. D., Sullivan, D., Feola, A., and McHugo, G. (1987). Television coverage of candidates' display behavior during the 1984 democratic primaries in the United States. *International Political Science Review*, **8**, 121–30.

Masters, R. D., Sullivan, D., Lanzetta, J., and Englis, B. (1986). The facial displays of leaders: Toward an ethology of human politics. *Journal of Social and Biological Structures*, **9**, 319–43.

Mueller, J. E. (1973). *War, presidents and public opinion*. Wiley, New York.

———. (1993). American public opinion and the Gulf War. In *The political psychology of the Gulf War: Leaders, publics, and the process of conflict* (ed. Stanley A. Renshon). University of Pittsburgh Press, Pittsburgh.

Morgenthau, H. J. (1948). *Politics among nations*. Knopf, New York.

Ragsdale, L. (1984). The politics of presidential speechmaking, 1949–1980. *American Political Science Review*, **78**, 971–84.

Ruddick, S. (1989). *Maternal thinking: Towards a politics of peace*. Beacon Press, Boston.

Schubert, J. (1993). Realpolitik as a male primate strategy. Paper presented at the annual meeting of the International Studies Association, Mexico, 25 March 1993.

Smith, T. W. (1984). The polls: Gender and attitudes toward violence. *Public Opinion Quarterly*, **48**, 384–96.

Sullivan, D. and Masters, R. D. (1988). Happy warriors: Leaders' facial displays, viewers emotions, and political support. *American Journal of Political Science*, **32**, 345–68.

Sullivan, D., Masters, R. D., Lanzetta, J., Englis, B., and McHugo, G. (1991). Facial displays and political leadership: Some experimental findings. In *Primate politics* (ed. G. Schubert and R. D. Masters), pp. 221–47. Southern Illinois University Press, Carbondale and Edwardsville.

Trivers, R. L. (1974). Parent offspring conflict. *American Zoologist*, **14**, 249–64.

Note: The research upon which this paper is based was performed in cooperation with a graduate seminar in political psychology at Northern Illinois University. Participants in that seminar made a substantial contribution to the research, including Greg Belcher, Jonathan Conrad, Peter Holaves, Matthew Johnson, Susan Johnson, Debra Krankovitch, Andrew McCarter, Brent Meyers, Dianne Piper-Rybak, Patrick Stewart and Steve Wellington.

CHAPTER TWELVE

IDEOLOGY AND PHYSIOLOGICAL REGULATION

Michael T. McGuire, Alfonso Troisi, Michael J. Raleigh, and Roger D. Masters

Overview

It was Karl Marx who declared, "Religion is the opiate of the masses." It was the late James Danielli (1980) who suggested that Marx's assertion was more accurate than Marx could have known. Danielli suggested that many religious observances have the effect of releasing enkephalins and endorphins, endogenous neurotransmitters that reduce pain and promote feelings of integration, control, and well-being. Hence, Danielli argued, religious beliefs and practices can be viewed as the self-administration of an "opiate," a way of achieving a desirable, rewarding physiological state.

Conventionally, it is assumed that the "goal" in goal-seeking behavior is the consummatory behavior (e.g., eating, sexual satisfaction). Consummatory behavior entails proprioceptions of motor behaviors and physiological states that are directly associated with consummatory actions. In complex social animals like primates, including *Homo sapiens*, goal-seeking is often dissociated from narrowly programmed, largely instinctive, behavior sequences that characterize consummatory behavior among many nonprimate species. In this chapter we will focus on one example of such behavior: available data suggest that for many individuals an important behavioral goal is to engage in information-related events that lead to hormonal and neurochemical homeostasis.

Homeostatic states equate with desired (often pleasurable) feelings, and they increase the probability that one will again engage in behavior that leads to such states. Nonhomeostatic states result in the opposite outcomes. Among monkeys, apes, and human beings, changes in neurotransmitter function and hormonal concentrations can be triggered by information. Thus, the effects of information on brain and body metabolism may be important in explaining homeostatic and nonhomeostatic states. Information can be conveniently divided into external (nonsocial environmental cues), social (the behavior of others), physiological (the proprioception of bodily states, including emotions), and cognitive information (an individual's thoughts or beliefs).

Findings from the neurosciences make it possible to reformulate Danielli's insight in both broader and more specific terms. The effects of social interactions, cognition, and emotions on physiological activity can now be understood in terms of regulation-disregulation theory (RDT). In addition, experimental models suggest that the physiological effects of information may result in enduring alterations in neural function. Within these frameworks, we hypothesize that the probability that an ideology will be endorsed enthusiastically correlates with the degree to which embracing it increases the likelihood of attaining physiological homeostasis.

This chapter is divided into three parts. The first part reviews RDT, selected experimental models, and supporting data. The second part focuses on the behavioral and social functions of ideologies that interact with physiological states. The concluding section uses points from the first two parts to develop predictions about the conditions under which ideologies will be accepted or rejected.

Webster's dictionary defines ideology as a body of doctrine, myth, and/or symbol of a social movement, institution, class, or large group that influences behavior. Examples include beliefs in religion, rule of law, nationalism, and political doctrines. For the purposes of this chapter, the preceding definition lacks the required specificity. Thus, for this discussion, an ideology: (1) contains or implies an explanatory theory of human experience and the external world; (2) sets out a program, in general terms, of social and political organization; (3) underscores that the program entails some type of struggle; (4) seeks not only to persuade but also to recruit loyal adherents (although this may be denied), demanding commitment; and (5) addresses a wide public, but may confer some special role of leadership on its founders or intellectuals.

We recognize that our focus is narrow. Many interesting and well-documented features, functions, and consequences of ideologies, behavior, and physiology will not be considered (e.g., Masters 1978; Knight et al. 1995). Our narrow focus is consistent with the view that ideologies are transmitted from person to person and from generation to generation by cultural mechanisms that operate differently from genetic transmission systems (Richerson and Boyd, this volume; Dawkins 1976). However, our emphasis does imply that an analysis of ideology without consideration of ideology-physiology interactions will be incomplete.

Regulation-Disregulation Theory and Experimental Models of the Physiological Effects of Information

RDT has its origins in attempts to explain the influence of external information on changes in central nervous system (CNS) neurotransmitter activity among nonhuman primates (McGuire and Troisi 1987a). It has since been expanded to include humans and the effects of internal information (e.g., thoughts) on neurotransmitter function and hormonal states. The idea that information originating outside of an individual can influence one's physiology is not original. The concept extends back well beyond antiquity, although its experimental demonstration had to await the work of Walter Cannon during the early twentieth century. The term regulation refers to physiological homeostasis, a state in which multiple, often opposing physiological forces are balanced. As used here, homeostasis is associated with efficient physiological and psychological functioning; feelings of well-being, control, commitment, group membership; and interest and participation in valued events in the world. The term disregulation references a state of physiological nonhomeostasis, which is often associated with unpleasant feelings, such as boredom, fear, anxiety, depression, loneliness, and ennui, as well as a reduced interest and participation in events in the world.

External social information, internal information, and seeking out social environments with specific characteristics have different physiological effects. These differences will be reviewed in order.

External social information. One key point of RDT is that, in the absence of specific types of external information, selected CNS physiological systems "drift" from regulated to disregulated states. This type of drift is analogous to what occurs with the glucose system: central and peripheral glucose concentrations decrease (drift) from optimal levels to suboptimal levels unless there is frequent glucose replenishment; and decreases in glucose levels are associated with unpleasant feelings, a reduced ability to concentrate, and the search for food. Applying this concept to humans, infants require holding, touching, and talking to in order to attain and maintain homeostasis (Hofer 1984). Deprived of such information, infants are irritable and fail to thrive. If social or informational deprivation is extreme and extended, infants will die (Spitz 1945). The information deprivation studies conducted during the 1960s on normal, healthy, young adult subjects led to such a high frequency of physiological and psychological disturbances that the studies had to be discontinued (Schultz 1965). Similar findings have been reported for well-controlled studies of prisoners placed in solitary confinement. Compared to prisoners of the same age and sex who are free to engage in social interactions, those in solitary confinement show significant increases in the frequency of psychosis, depression, and attempted suicide (Volkart et al. 1983). Psychosis and depression are among the more dramatic indices of CNS physiological disregulation.

The presence of specific types of external information can have either regulating or disregulating effects. For example, the approach of a frightening dog leads to a rapid increase in the circulating levels of epinephrine and norepinephrine, as well as psychological and anatomical preparations for flight or fight. Information about the loss of a significant other can initiate feelings of depression that are coupled with alterations in the CNS neurotransmitters norepinephrine and serotonin. Ambiguous stimuli presented to nonhuman primates lead to dramatic electrical changes in the amygdala (a CNS region that processes emotional stimuli; Lloyd and Kling 1991), as well as an increase in resting cortisol concentrations (McGuire et al. 1986). Winning a competitive, non–physical contact sporting event (e.g., tennis) among two males is followed by an elevation of the hormone testosterone in the winner while no changes in testosterone levels are observed in the loser (Mazur and Lamb 1980). A review of the many primate physiological systems that undergo alterations in response to external information and different types of social interactions can be found elsewhere (McGuire 1988).

Recent positron emission tomography (PET) studies indicate that different parts of the brain are involved in processing different types of external information. For example, recognizing others' emotions involves the right anterior cingulate and the bilateral inferior frontal gyri (George et al. 1993), while listening to others talk about emotions involves both superior temporal gyri (Wise et al. 1991).

More complex interactions between others' behavior and physiological states are perhaps best illustrated by studies of the neurotransmitter serotonin in adult male vervet monkeys (*Cercopithecus aethiops sabaeus*). In this species, high social status in adult males is associated with peripheral serotonin levels almost twice as high as those of low social status males (Raleigh et al. 1984). Differences in CNS serotonin sensitivity (as measured by behavioral responsivity to changes in CNS serotonin levels) are equally impressive (Raleigh et al. 1985). If a high-status animal becomes low-status, its peripheral serotonin and CNS serotonin sensitivity measures change to those characteristic of low-status males. Conversely, if low-status males become high-status, the opposite changes occur (Raleigh et al. 1984).

The behavior that initiates serotonin changes is thought to be the frequency with which an adult male receives submissive displays from other adult males in his social group. High-status animals receive submissive displays from low-status animals throughout the day; and should the number of displays decrease, as happens, for example, when high-status animals are temporarily removed from their groups, measures of serotonin begin to decline (McGuire et al. 1983a, b; Raleigh et al. 1984). In this model, low status is viewed as a disregulated state, while high status is viewed as a regulated state. Serotonin changes do not occur rapidly in response to external information, as is often the case with the neurotransmitter norepinephrine or the hormone cortisol. Days to weeks are required, and the absence of submissive displays by subordinate males needs to be repetitive for such changes to occur.

Among vervet monkeys, high levels of serotonin are associated with increased frequencies of prosocial behavior (e.g., grooming), tolerance toward other animals, and decreased frequency of initiated aggression, while low levels of serotonin are associated with the opposite behavior profile (McGuire et al. 1983). Among humans, low levels of serotonin are frequently linked with feelings of depression and aggressive behavior, while high levels of serotonin are associated with feelings of relaxation and satisfaction (reviewed in Masters and McGuire 1994).

Similar findings from studies of other primate species have also been reported (e.g., Sapolsky 1990; Reite and Field 1985). These observations are consistent with predictions from RDT and underscore two basic features of the theory: selected physiological systems interact with the type and frequency of external information, and, in the absence of such information, these physiological systems change to disregulated states.

Internal information. In many persons, meditation results in reduced cortisol and other stress-related hormone concentrations, as well as in a lowering of blood pressure (a chemically mediated event). Sexual fantasies and anticipation of victory in competitive events increase CNS serotonin activity and reduce CNS dopamine and norepinephrine activity (reviewed in McGuire and Troisi 1987b). PET studies show that dysphoric thoughts (i.e., unpleasant thoughts) alter CNS glucose utilization profiles, particularly in the inferior and orbital frontal regions of the brain (Pardo et al. 1994); memory activates hippocampus function (Squire et al. 1992); and attention activates the right prefrontal and superior parietal cortex (Pardo et al. 1991). Studies of cerebral blood flow demonstrate that induced, temporary sadness and happiness in healthy women lead to significant changes in regional blood flow in the limbic system, as well as other brain regions. These transient emotional states affect different brain regions in divergent directions and are not merely opposite activities in identical brain regions (George et al. 1995). An implication of these findings is that, within limits, one can work oneself into a state of physiological and psychological arousal, or into a calm and aggravated state, through the effects of repeated thoughts on physiological activity in different parts of the brain.

Seeking out specific social environments. Vervet monkeys, chimpanzees, humans, and other primates are far from passive recipients of information. High-status vervet monkeys seek out low-status monkeys and initiate dominance displays to which subordinate animals respond with submissive displays (McGuire et al. 1983a). Further, the observation that animals compete for high social status, not low social status, suggests that high status is associated with a more regulated and desirable physiological state compared to low status. Analogous events are likely to occur among humans, although they have been less well studied. Specific friends are sought out when one is bored or depressed, and persons who are mean or unresponsive are avoided. Specific environments, such as rock concerts or a quiet walk in the mountains, are attractive in part because of their predictable effects on one's emotions (see Schore 1994). That external information can significantly influence CNS physiology is the most parsimonious conclusion from findings showing that different types of enduring CNS glucose utilization patterns (as measured by PET) result from behavior modification therapy—a form of therapy involving information exchange, not drugs, or physical contact (Baxter et al. 1992).

Much of human behavior may also represent attempts to self-regulate one's physiological state. Further, such attempts to self-regulate one's internal milieu may be tied to preferences for specific ideologies. Persons explore ideologies for many reasons; one likely reason is that they anticipate that an ideology will be associated with a desired state of feeling.

Another set of findings ties some of the preceding points to personality. Among human males, peripheral measures of serotonin differ as a function of social status (Madsen and McGuire 1984; Madsen 1985; 1986). Individuals who perceive themselves and are perceived by others as possessing high social status exhibit higher levels of peripheral serotonin compared to those who perceive themselves and are perceived by others as possessing low social status. Among college students, high levels of blood serotonin are associated with either competent social leaders or competitive, socially manipulative, and somewhat amoral (sometimes called Machiavellian) personalities. There are, however, some exceptions: a small percentage of persons with high levels of peripheral serotonin are deferential, submissive, and yielding to others (Madsen 1985; 1986). Persons with deferential personalities would be predicted to be more disregulated than Machiavellians. Related studies show that the behavioral features of personality types can be understood if different ratios among the three classical monoamine neurotransmitters—serotonin, dopamine, and norepinephrine—are taken into account (Cloninger 1986). Thus, in the case of serotonin, there appears to be at least a three-way interaction between serotonin measures, personality, and social status.

For the purposes of this chapter, individual differences in personality and serotonin are important because they permit predictions about interactions between personality type and the acceptance or rejection of ideologies. For example, other things being equal, persons with Machiavellian personalities are more likely to use (in contrast to embrace) ideologies for self-interested purposes. By contrast, deferential persons are more likely to embrace an ideology if it is strongly asserted by another and if it increases physiological regulation. Said differently, the CNS physiological systems of deferential individuals will be easier for others to manipulate than will the physiological systems of Machiavellians. It follows that the same ideology can have different effects on individuals with different personalities. The exception—which proves the rule—would be a small cohesive group (or "cell") of believers who minimize contact with the outside society, similar to cults, communes, and sectarian groups.

To summarize thus far, ways in which information alters CNS physiological states have been reviewed. These include the absence of social information; positive and negative external information; and thoughts. In addition, we have argued that individuals seek out specific persons and/or environments because they are associated with predictable physiological states. In this context, ideologies are both internal and external sources of information: internal when one thinks about them, and external when others respond either positively or negatively to one's own ideology. It follows that the attractiveness of an ideology will be in part a consequence of the physiological sequelae of embracing or rejecting that ideology: should one embrace a socially unpopular ideology, as currently would be the case for communism in most parts of the United States, disregulating effects would be predicted because of others' negative responses.

Finally, there is a difference between moment-to-moment CNS physiological adjustments and longer-term CNS physiological change. Individuals embrace ideologies for extended periods of time; in most instances, ideologies are not hastily embraced or rejected. This point suggests that either longer-term, or repeated same-type, short-term physiological changes are essential for explaining ideology-physiology interactions. If only intermittent short-term changes in neurochemical or hormonal states were involved (moment-to-moment minor physiological adjustments), strong bidirectional physiology-ideology relationships would not be expected.

Ideologies—Functions That Affect Physiological Systems

Given the preceding discussion, we are now in the position to review the functions of ideologies that are predicted to influence physiological states.

Ideologies organize and prioritize thoughts. Whatever their type (e.g., religious, political, social), ideologies organize and prioritize thoughts and concepts, and thereby reduce ambiguity and uncertainty about events both within and outside one's control. Meanings are given to symbols, myths, doctrines, and behavioral scenarios. Specific ideas and acts are valued while others are not. Causal explanations may be present (e.g., God put humans on earth to carry out His plans). Experimental primate work suggests that a reduction in uncertainty and ambiguity correlates with diminished amygdala electrical activity (as measured by implanted electrodes) and cortisol release. In humans, similar physiological changes are likely to be reinforcing and rewarding, thereby contributing to the perpetuation of belief in an ideology.

Ideologies are associated with improved self-esteem, one's sense that one has purpose and direction, and one's sense that one has a place in the world. Embracing an ideology, especially one that is respected in one's social group (e.g., rule of law), provides direction, purpose, and place. Such thoughts, as well as the responses of others (e.g., one is a member of an "ideological" group), have physiological effects. Self-reports of persons who undergo religious conversions are consistent with this point.

Ideologies facilitate the identification of in-group and out-group members and are associated with in- and out-group identifications. Revealing one's ideology to others who share the same ideology signals that one is committed to specific interpretations of events, that one will behave in predictable ways, and that specific responses can be expected in social interactions. Revealing one's ideology to others who fail to share the same ideology has the opposite effects, e.g., advocating racism to persons who abhor racism. Others' responses to in-group and out-group membership affect one's physiology.

Ideologies are associated with specific in-group reciprocation rules. This function is implied in the preceding paragraph, but its importance justifies a separate discussion. Explicit and implicit reciprocation or helping rules differ across groups and are in part influenced by rules associated with ideologies. Reciprocation rules deal with such points as when one can request help, the conditions under which one is expected to help, the degree of helping that should be provided in different circumstances, the time frame within which helping should be reciprocated, and the types and amount of reciprocation that are appropriate. A key feature of such rules is that they increase the predictability of in-group interactions, and hence the probability that individuals can predictably engage in behaviors that have desired physiological outcomes.

Ideologies are associated with rituals. Rituals, such as praying, singing, chanting, and marching, contribute to a sense of solidarity and belongingness and alter physiological states, both through enacting rituals and via others' responses.

Ideologies are associated with desirable emotional states. Membership in a group can have its physiological rewards. For example, many religious groups in the United States use television as a means not only of communicating their ideologies, but also for implying that those who embrace their ideologies will achieve desired emotional states and social acceptance, e.g., by showing groups of individuals holding hands, singing, and smiling.

Ideologies create status structures. "High priests," acolytes, and followers characterize literally all ideologies. An implication of this point is that group membership is at least as important as social status: e.g., persons will often accept positions of low status if this is required for group membership. The regulating effects of group membership may in part offset the disregulating effects of low social status.

To summarize this section, different social behavior and cognitive functions of ideologies influence physiological states in different ways. One way is through the organization and prioritization of one's thoughts. Organization and prioritization not only reduce uncertainty and its disregulatory effects, but also, through the thoughts associated with an ideology, alter physiological systems. A second way is through the social interaction effects of shared ideologies and the impact of others' responses on one's physiological state. That these effects are nontrivial is suggested by a variety of findings. For example, there is a positive correlation between religious commitment (participation in ceremonies and social support) and measures of both physical and mental health (Larson et al. 1992). A third way is by knowing with whom to interact in order to achieve a desired physiological state.

Application of the Hypothesis and Predictions

Under what conditions are ideologies likely to be embraced or rejected? The preceding discussion leads to several compatible predictions (a number of which have already been stated or implied), each of which includes some feature of the original hypothesis: the probability that an ideology will be embraced will positively correlate with the degree to which embracing an ideology results in physiological regulation.

Prediction #1. Ideologies that organize and prioritize thoughts in ways that induce physiological homeostasis are more likely to be embraced than ideologies that fail to do so. Religious conversions may be explained by this hypothesis. This prediction also invites inquiries into the details of the content, meaning, and structure of ideologies and their differential physiological effects. For example, those ideologies that explain and give meaning to the unknown (e.g., life after death) may flourish while those that fail to give such meaning on the basis of the absence of evidence may be attractive to only a few.

Prediction #2. Ideologies that are associated with identifiable indices of in-group membership have a greater probability of being embraced than those that are not so associated. This prediction covers a broader range of possibilities than prediction #1; for example, motivations to be a group member may take priority over the content and meaning of an ideology. Religious and political conversions as well as commitments to specific ideologies associated with nationalism and war may be explained by this hypothesis. The prediction may also explain why most members of a culture embrace the prevailing cultural ideology.

Prediction #3. Persons who are socially isolated or ostracized (states which are associated with physiological disregulation) will be more likely to embrace an ideology than persons who are socially integrated. The reported high percentage of religious conversion among the homeless is a possible illustration of this point. Most early Christians were members of ostracized groups.

Prediction #4. Ideologies will be gradually rejected if they do not accommodate to changing social customs and values. Others will be less likely to respond positively to persons who embrace ideologies that are in conflict with current cultural values, hence the reduced attractiveness of such ideologies. The declining number of persons committed to once powerful ideologies in the United States (e.g., labor unions, the Catholic Church, communism) may be explained in this way.

Prediction #5. Persons with deferential personalities will be more likely to embrace a new ideology compared to persons with Machiavellian personalities. An extension of this prediction is that specific ideologies may be sought out because they fit one's physiological profile, e.g., personality.

Prediction #6. Ideologies will flourish when face-to-face groups and local communities are uprooted by rapid socioeconomic, technological, and/or cultural change. Among other things, such changes disturb established routines and reduce the effectiveness of familiar behavior patterns in bringing about or maintaining homeostasis. The recent rise of religious fundamentalism as a response to Westernization in the Third World is a possible example.

Conclusion

We have outlined ideological-physiological relationships with an emphasis on the direct and indirect effects of information on physiological regulation and disregulation. This presentation remains speculative and does not provide a comprehensive analysis of ideologies and their multiple personal and social functions. Yet, the points developed above may offer insights into the causes of variance in preference for ideologies (individual differences) as well as why some interesting and potentially important ideologies are rejected.

Acknowledgments: Douglas Madsen, Marsden McGuire, and Peter Richerson provided helpful comments in early drafts of this chapter. We thank them. Much of the authors' research would not have been possible without support from the Giles and Elise Mead Foundation.

References

Baxter, L. R., Schwartz, J. M., Bergman, K. S., Szuba, M. P., Guze, B. H., Mazziotta, J. C., Alazraki, A., Selin, C. E., Ferng, H-K, Munford, P., and Phelps, M. E. (1992). Caudate glucose metabolic rate compulsive disorder. *Archives General Psychiatry,* **49**, 681–9.

Cloninger, C. R. (1986). A unified biosocial theory of personality and its role in the development of anxiety states. *Psychiatric Developments*, 3, 167–226.

Danielli, J. F. (1980). Altruism and the internal reward or the opium of the people. *Journal of Social and Biological Structures*, 3, 87–94.

Dawkins, R. (1976). *The selfish gene*. Oxford University Press, Oxford.

George, M. S., Ketter, T. A., Gill, D. S., Haxby, J. V., Ungerleider, L. G., Herscovitch, P., and Post, R. M. (1993). Brain regions involved in recognizing facial emotion or identity: An oxygen-15 PET study. *Journal of Neuropsychiatry*, 5, 384–94.

George, M. S., Ketter, T. A., Parekh, B. A., Horowitz, B., Herscovitch, P., and Post, R. M. (1995). Brain activity during transient sadness and happiness in healthy women. *American Journal of Psychiatry*, 152, 341–51.

Hofer, M. A. (1984). Relationships as regulators: A psychobiologic perspective on bereavement. *Psychosomatic Medicine*, 46, 183–97.

Knight, C., Power, C., and Watts, I. (1995). The human symbolic revolution: A Darwinian account. *Cambridge Archaeological Journal*, 5, 75–114.

Larsen, D. B., Sherrill, K. A., Lyons, J. S., Craigie Jr., F. C., Thielman, S. B., Greenwold, M. A., and Larson, S. S. (1992). Association between dimensions of religious commitment and mental health reported in the *American Journal of Psychiatry* and *Archives of General Psychiatry: 1978–1989. American Journal of Psychiatry*, 149, 557–9.

Lloyd, R. L. and Kling, A. S. (1991). Delta activity from amygdala in squirrel monkeys (*Saimiri sciureus*): Influence of social and environmental context. *Behavioral Neurosciences*, 105, 223–9.

Madsen, D. (1985). A biochemical property relating to power seeking in humans. *American Political Science Review*, 79, 448–57.

———. (1986). Power seekers are biochemically different: Further biochemical evidence. *American Political Science Review*, 80, 261–9.

Madsen, D. and McGuire, M. T. (1984). Whole blood serotonin and the Type A behaviour pattern. *Psychosomatic Medicine*, 46, 546–8.

Masters, R. (1979). On the ubiquity of ideology in modern societies. *Revue Européenne des Sciences Sociales et Cahiers Vilfredo Pareto*, 17, 159–72.

Masters, R. D. and McGuire, M. T., eds. (1994). *The neurotransmitter revolution*. Southern Illinois University Press. Carbondale, Ill.

Mazur, A. and Lamb, T. A. (1980). Testosterone, status, and mood in human males. *Hormones and Behavior*, 14, 236–46.

McGuire, M. T., Raleigh, M. J., and Johnson, C. (1983a). Social dominance in adult male vervet monkeys: General considerations. *Social Science Information*, 22, 89–122.

———. (1983b). Social dominance in adult male vervet monkeys: Biochemical relationships. *Social Science Information*, 22, 311–28.

McGuire, M. T. (1988). On the possibility of ethological explanations of psychiatric disorders. *Acta Psychiatrica Scandinavia*, 77 (Suppl), 7–22.

McGuire, M. T. and Troisi, A. (1987a). Physiological regulation-disregulation and psychiatric disorders. *Ethology and Sociobiology*, 8, 9–12.

———. (1987b). Unrealistic wishes and physiological change. *Psychotherapy, Psychosomatics*, 47, 82–94.

McGuire, M. T., Brammer, G. L., and Raleigh, M. J. (1986). Resting cortisol levels and the emergence of dominance status among male vervet monkeys. *Hormones and Behavior*, 20, 106–17.

Pardo, J. V., Fox, P. T., and Raichle, M. E. (1991). Localization of a human system for sustained attention by positron emission tomography. *Nature*, **349**, 61–64.

Pardo, J. V., Pardo, P. J., and Raichle, M. D. (1993). Neural correlates of self-induced dysphoria. *American Journal of Psychiatry*, **150**, 713–9.

Raleigh, M. J., McGuire, M. T., Brammer, G. L., and Yuwiler, A. (1984). Social and environmental influences on blood serotonin concentrations in monkeys. *Archives of General Psychiatry*, **41**, 405–10.

Raleigh, M. J., Brammer, G. L., McGuire, M. T., and Yuwiler, A. (1985). Dominant social status facilitates the behavioral effects of serotonergic agonists. *Brain Research*, **348**, 274–82.

Reite, M. and Field, T., eds. (1985). *The psychobiology of attachment and separation.* Academic Press, New York.

Sapolsky, R. M. (1990). Adrenocortical function, social rank and personality among wild baboons. *Biological Psychiatry*, **28**, 862–78.

Schore, A. N. (1994). *Affect regulation and the origin of the self: The neurobiology of emotional development.* Lawrence Erlbaum, Hillsdale, N.J.

Schultz, D. P. (1965). *Sensory restriction.* Academic Press, New York.

Spitz, R. (1945). *Hospitalism. The psychoanalytic study of the child,* vol 1., pp. 53–74. International Universities Press, New York.

Squire, L. R., Ojemann, J. G., Miezin, F. M., Petersen, S. E., Videen, T. O., and Raichle, M. E. (1992). Activation of the hippocampus in normal humans: A functional anatomical study of memory. *Proceedings National Academy of Science, USA*, **89**, 1837–41.

Volkart, R., Dittrich, A., Rothenfluh, T., and Paul, W. (1983). Eine kontrollierte Untersuchung über psychopathologische Effekte der Einzelhaft. In *Revue Suisse de Psychologie Pure et Appliquée* (ed. H. Huber), pp.1–24. Verlag, Bern.

Wise, R., Chollet, F., Hadar, U., Friston, K., Hoffner, E., and Frackowiak, R. (1991). Distribution of cortical neural networks involved in word comprehension and word retrieval. *Brain*, **114**, 1803–17.

PART IV

❦

SYMBOLISM

CHAPTER THIRTEEN

ART AND INDOCTRINATION

FROM THE *BIBLIA PAUPERUM* TO THE THIRD REICH

Christa Sütterlin

Introduction

We live in a time when monuments are once again thrown from their pedestals, books are burned and their authors pursued, and archaeological masterpieces are returned to looted collections and museums. The question of the political impact of art has been reanimated in a time when the artistic freedom to express opinion is still defended.

What is the problem? Evidently, the fact that a structure such as an artistic object—which is, at least in part, a spatial rather than a verbal medium—may convey messages of explosive density still surprises the public. How is it possible that certain messages have passed unperceived through the filters of private and official censorship and, like illicit ideas, have achieved belated recognition? Are works of art well-packed secrets or well-coded information that any official should look at with special care? What is the exceptional impact of art that exceeds other forms of communications?

The role of art as a tool of indoctrination has interested political scientists and practitioners alike for many years (e.g., Welch 1993; Lenin 1929). The behavioral approach to art, with which this chapter is concerned, views it as an extraordinary means of communication and seeks to understand it in part by studying its roots in human phylogeny (e.g., Eibl-Eibesfeldt and Sütterlin 1992). There is a large literature on related topics of ethnographic variation and sociocultural origins of art (Layton 1991; Dissanayake 1992). But the question of interest here is why art is such an excellent mediator of indoctrination. How does it happen that *values* are transmitted and perceived through visual or auditory stimuli, and that these stimuli turn into symbols upon touching the human mind?

Let me answer first as an art historian, from my initial training, and then provide a second answer from the perspective of human ethology, the biological study of human behavior.

Predefined Semantic Units in Art History

From descriptive to iconographic: primordial symbolism in painting

The *representational* power of art can be simply described. The *Biblia Pauperum* at the end of the thirteenth century may be called the most striking example of a collective instruction renouncing the verbal form throughout the history of Christendom. The visual impact of what could not be understood by reading—the events of the Old and New Testament in pictures—was certainly considerable. Special emphasis could be laid on certain scenes such as the birth of Mary and the birth of Christ, on mystic performances like the healing of the lame, or on the passion of Christ, and scenes of minor eminence could be simply omitted. In fact, a very significant assortment of episodes could be presented according to the preference of the artist. If the literary tradition of the salvation story was already a condensation of events, the figural representation went even further. Examples of these selected themes and subjects survived in the iconography of official art and have been admired in frescoes and altarpieces up to the present day. We all know that particular scenes, such as the Madonna with the child, suffering Christ on the crucifix, the resurrection from the tomb, the betrayal of Judas, etc., were selectively emphasized from the Holy Cycle and repeatedly presented. Some, like the "pietà" (the mourning godmother with the corpse of Christ), were even worshipped in their own right, as special devotional paintings (*Andachtsbilder*).

Fig. 13.1. *Virgin Mary with Jesus Child. Sculpture by Tilman Riemenschneider, end of fifteenth century. The theme is one of the most popular of the illustrated Holy Cycle, referring to the early mother-child relationship as a central experience in human life.*

The instruments and possibilities of art—*emphasis, omission, selection,* and *reduction*—are already obvious in this early cycle of representative art that was meant to be purely descriptive. But the sheer illustration of aspects considered important was always a legitimate means of representation and was regarded as artistic freedom.

The message is more subtle when the Virgin Mary, for instance, is depicted with an apple, indicating her spiritual character as the new Eve—the personification of conquered sin symbolized in the figure of the Old Testament. And when Jesus is depicted as *Christus Rex Triumphans* in the apotheosis of Monreale (Sicily), nobody would misunderstand the dominant position the Son has reached over the world and even God his Father! Clues to a figure's dominance lie in posture and gesture. Mastery is denoted by a front-on stance to the viewer, by an expressionless face, and by arm and head orientations expressing revelation.

Art by its nature and constraints tends to symbolic representation since it is forced to present parts and pieces standing for wholes, to present an abstract rather than extended description, a "here for a there." It is tuned to conceptualize the world it is hinting at.

Fig. 13.2. *Christus Rex Triumphans. Mosaic in the Dome of Monreale, Sicily, twelfth century. Monumental frontal presentation adds to the authority of Christ portrayed as head of the official religion.*

But there is still a more subtle way to manipulate audiences by artistic means. This becomes clear if we reflect on the fascination of architecture and music, media which offer relatively little scope for representational portrayal of concrete events or subjects. How does it happen that we respond so sensitively to purely structural elements and proportions of a building or to a simple arrangement of tones? What further possibilities does art offer to human communication that other forms of indoctrination cannot match?

Structural semantics and the meaning of architectural form

It was the Swiss art historian Heinrich Wölfflin who in the 1950s introduced terms like "the linear" (*das Lineare*) and "the pictorial" (*das Malerische*) into art interpretation to describe different emotional effects caused by simple *style*. As a consequence, these terms were applied to architectural styles as well. The "linear style," defined by its accentuation of straight lines and flat surfaces, implied a purely rational and distancing impression, whereas the "pictorial style" with its curved lines, irregular surfaces and interplay of light and shadow, was defined to appeal more to

Fig. 13.3. *Hotel de Rohan-Strasbourg in Paris. Urban Palais built by Pierre Alexis Delamair, eighteenth century. The cool, flat, and rigid design of the façade is an example of what Wölfflin described as "linear style."*

Fig. 13.4. *St. Nikolaus in Prague by Christoph Dientzenhofer. The baroque conception of the façade mirrors the dynamics of contrasts, i.e., of light and shades, curves and straight lines defined by Wöllflin as "pictorial style."*

the sensual pleasure of seeing, to our sense of mystery, and to emotional agreement.

This distinct characterization and attribution of meaning to nonrepresentational art (*ungegenständliche Kunst*) by purely formal and proportional qualities is an interesting phenomenon to which we shall return. Wölfflin's typology of artistic expression was shaped by criteria rooted mostly in a formal aesthetic and did not apply to historical conditions at all. This vision of an ageless, apolitical, and independent development of styles was criticized for its insensitivity to historical development, as well as on methodological grounds.

There is, furthermore, a long-lasting tradition in art history of conceptualizing architecture as "meaningful" (*Bedeutungsarchitektur*, M. Warnke 1983, 7). As a result, terms such as "talking architecture" (*architecture parlante*), "citation architecture," etc., became customary. As a reaction to its abuse, this terminology was rejected and largely abandoned after World War I, and the return to an architecture restrained by its purely functionalistic purpose was inaugurated by the famous Bauhaus movement, dating from 1919, whose influence increased during the 1930s and 1940s. Interestingly enough, the movement elaborated a strict program that required *non*meaningful architecture. The date of foundation is remarkable as well, as a reaction to the highly ideological use of possibilities inherent in architectural design in a time of rising nationalism. It actually sounded like a prohibition of meaning.

In fact, the existence of functional distinctions, like official and private architecture, station architecture, the architecture of hospitals, hotels, and banking houses, is an obvious fact and constitutes on a more neutral level a whole spectrum of representative typology that implies differential semantic properties as well. A building for the fire brigade certainly asks for a different architectural iconography than a city hall!

One of the most pronounced and unmistakable examples of architectural typology, of course is the church. There a further representational level became evident from the beginning: the idea of the *house of God*, of the *body* or even the *state of God* (*Gottesstaat*) was a leading one in Christian iconology. Nobody really dared to contest this concept since the words of Abbot Suger, the patron of St. Denis (Paris), who declared the twelve columns of the nave to symbolize the Twelve Apostles and the twelve columns of the side aisles the Twelve Prophets, who all together supported the upper part of the church, being the symbol of the state of God (Bandmann 1981, 64). The ground plan of a Greek or Latin cross was supposed to represent the sacrifice of Christ on which basis the earthly state of God could arise. These were all well known and even part of the official iconological program. Other related topics referred to the church being the body of all confessing Christians or to the new Jerusalem, and all single parts of the building—the façade, towers, and dome— were of course seen and constructed to correspond to this embracing allegory. Even the light effects in the Gothic cathedral took part in this *mise en scène* of a divine presence on earth (Lützeler 1969, 107), whereas the Romanic cathedral seemed to insist more on the allegory of the fortress: God being the unity, support, and protection of all the faithful.

Fig. 13.5. *The plan of Cluny Cathedral in Burgundy, France (destroyed in the nineteenth century). Cluny, begun in the eleventh century, became the biggest church in Europe and epitomized the power and organization of the "state of God."*

In later times, however, additional levels of meaning seemed to be superimposed on an exclusively Christian significance. The fact that fascination with Christian monuments survived the times of Early Christian faith and also drew the admiration of people of different confessions made it seem likely that the architectural language involved aspects of a more complex symbolism. Already Hans Sedlmayr, who introduced and defended the notion of the church as "celestial Jerusalem" (*Himmlisches Jerusalem*), revised and enlarged his concept (1959) in his propositional essay, "The Gothic Cathedral As King's Cathedral" (1948). E. Baldwin Smith, more pointedly, talked of the dome as of an "imperial symbol" (1950).

The issue centered on the monumental qualities of architecture, that is, on the evidence that the actual scale and magnificence of buildings often exceeded their immediate purposes; as if art were not always defined by a special "more than," which constitutes its artistic legitimacy! The *political* aspects of monumental style in art and architecture became conscious—again not without historical reasons—and invaded the purely referential theological symbolism of the Christian monuments with a new social criticism. This criticism, often exaggerated, included in part a new model of thinking: the openness for a dimension so far neglected in the semantic spectrum of visual symbols. This definitely more human, more social dimension could not avoid considering art symbolism in terms of *communication*.

Fig. 13.6. *Teotihuacan, Mexico; the so-called "Sun Pyramid." In all times the rulers of totalitarian systems glorified their regency with exuberant monuments erected "in the honor of a highest god," but actually substantiating the status of their own leadership.*

After all, no science, even of a strictly historical self-definition, could seriously contend that monumental buildings erected in the name of a highest God were restricted to the Christian Occident. Often these monuments were openly dedicated to the power of a king, pharaoh, or other great figure, but symbolized as well the status of its profane governor (Eibl-Eibesfeldt and Sütterlin 1992; Salter 1995).

Finally, the influence of famous patrons such as Pope Julius II was decisive for most ambitious projects, as with the reconstruction of old St. Peter in Rome. Whether the cathedral should be based on a Greek or a Latin cross, if it should be embodied by a central or longitudinal plan, were decisions made by humans: Bramante, Raphael, Michelangelo, finally Maderno, and above all, Julius II (Hauser, 1967). The effect is, as we all know, one of the most representative monuments of Christianity.

There were, of course, attempts to explain the monumental style of official or clerical buildings in terms of economics. For instance, Trigger (1990) argues that to invest other peoples' labor in nonfunctional production was a means by which the upper classes controlled the lower classes through the awe engendered by conspicuous consumption (after Veblen 1931). This would mean that monumental style is found only in complex class-based societies. Wilson (1988) added to these considerations the concept of "material evidence" of power to which the spectator might relate.

Fig. 13.7. *The plan of St. Peter in Rome embodies the dominant and embracing role of the main church of all faithful Christians.*

Returning to the Christian example of monumental style in churches, nothing seems more plausible than to construct a community that was more than national, but European, including many different cultures—Roman, German, French, Scandinavian, and Slavic. Symbols of identification had to be found that could unify the members into a new family, the family of faithful Christians. That is another theme to which we shall return.

It should now be clear that the relationship between artistic representation and the human mind always exceeded purely functionalistic or descriptive values. Whether we are able to attribute a pictorial and architectural line as conveying "coldness," "warmth," "friendliness," "distance," or "dominance," or a structural dynamic property as "royal," "imperial," "capitalist," or "socialist" depends perhaps on our favorite vocabulary. In general, the fact that we tend to *read* and *interpret* inanimate nature as we interpret human gestures, behaviors and faces is worth further attention. What are the roots (or dispositions) of this tendency in humans to anthropomorphize the nonhuman environment? This question is deeply linked to perception and communication.

Ethological Aspects of Human Visual Communication

Konrad Lorenz, in his essay on "innate forms of experience" (*die angeborenen Formen möglicher Erfahrung*), described our disposition for what he called "innate knowledge" (*angeborenes Erkennen*), which allows for recognition without prior individual experience of the object. Our understanding of our environment was shaped during a long hominid and mammalian evolutionary history, leading to reliable, species-typical patterns of interpretation (*Deutungsschemata*) in the service of survival.

Human perception is evidently biased to selectively attend to certain characteristics of our environment. In order to react in an adaptive way to conditions and situations in the external world, we needed, and still need, to recognize immediately and reliably their significance for our survival. That is, we needed a built-in pattern-recognition and -evaluation program. That some such program was part of our innate perceptual apparatus was strongly assumed by Lorenz from his ethological work and verified by studies that became classic examples of experimental psychology. Neuropsychologists had finally proved the specific sensitivity of our senses to particular shapes and conditions and

how they interact with their environment by selectively reinforcing and suppressing information (Hubel and Wiesel 1959). This
was also the scientific basis for Gestalt psychology. Our sense of
order and regularity, our bias in noticing contrast, clear lines, and
the constancy of size and color—all those features that
so characterize our perception are means of organizing our perceptual environment in the service of objective identification
and recognition.

Furthermore, the famous study of the "visual cliff" by Gibson
and Walk, or the study by Ball and Tronick of the avoidance and
defense responses of small children in viewing simulated
approaching obstacles, provided evidence that patterns of recognition and evaluation are present at an early stage in humans. The
same is true for our capacity for face recognition and decoding
of expression.

Species-specific biases seem to be at work in our affiliative reaction to the "baby schema" and preferences for the body contours
and proportions of the opposite sex. The predilection for a "green"
environment, for flowers and plants (*phytophilia*), for a view
encompassing open water (e.g., Mealey and Theis 1995) indicates
a preference for natural environments that is perhaps part of
our phylogeny.

These perceptual prejudices are so strongly linked to emotional
needs that we tend to take them as interpretational patterns for
perceiving and understanding our world. The generalization of
these innate "prototypes" or archetypes was an early concept of
Lorenz and discussed under the heading of *Physiognomisieren*
("physiognomize" or "anthropomorphize") and *Semantisieren*
("semantize"). These prototypes work as referential and emotional bases for interpretation and therefore are also sensitive to a
communicative and aesthetic attitude towards animate and inanimate nature.

That we tend, for instance, to project our bias for faces and proportional body contours onto artificial structures such as façades
and other tectonic masses corresponds to our need for recognizing
shapes and figures that we know and that we like. This adds to
the familiarization of a neutral or even strange and hostile environment. We like to judge a house as "friendly," "inviting," or
"rejecting," etc., making use of our communicative and inter-
personal-evaluative patterns of understanding to make sense of
the artificial environment. Interpretational patterns like judging a
camel's face as being "arrogant" because of its nose shape, and

young dogs and cats as appealing because they bear certain features of the human "baby schema" are further examples of aesthetic prejudices inappropriately projected onto nonhuman objects. But Lorenz was right to feel the weight of consequences this semantic susceptibility would have for the emotional impact of artificial structures on the human mind.

To summarize these points, we can say that our "perception" (in this larger sense) does the same thing as art does on a higher level: it chooses highly selectively from given information; it underlines and exaggerates some aspects and suppresses others. It is evidently how we generally deal with information and how we communicate. The way we encode messages is also the way we understand them. Art simply reflects these mechanisms and makes them more conscious. In fact, it even brings them to a higher level of accomplishment. It makes art an appropriate instrument for communication, also in the sense of transmitting specific values. As soon as there are certain established codes of perception, people can use them for any purpose.

In this context, art can create an artificial structure or reality that exceeds natural stimulus values. It can exploit human perceptual biases, the desire for better forms and patterns of evaluation for simple aesthetic pleasure, as well as the need for emotional (nonaesthetic) ties.

From Communication to Indoctrination

As we understand from the common roots of perception and art, a germ of manipulation or even indoctrination is naturally present in *any* perceptional manifestation like art. The particular way something is performed or represented affects the way it is perceived and evaluated. Art can make use of these inherent messages for culture-specific purposes.

Which psychological mechanisms tie individuals to large, anonymous groups, such as modern mass society? The same question applies to people's allegiance to political ideas. Now, people have claims and needs connected to their identification with ethnic and political groups. Indeed, if individuals are to be bonded to a cultural or national identity, an emotional tie must be formed based on the primary affective bond of family. Rational insight alone is not sufficient to establish this new relationship. As Eibl-Eibesfeldt has pointed out, indoctrination can only direct our evolved emotional dispositions for bonding or rejecting, loving and hating. It cannot establish such emotions, since they are already part of our nature. Nobody can be taught how to love or to hate, but we can be taught *whom* or *what* to love or to hate, and how much. Art can contribute to this cultural elaboration of political goals by transferring perceptual prejudices onto prejudices defined by the social system.

Emotional and perceptional "clues" are apt to bind our attention in a way that triggers our response to the message enclosed. Art, by its immediate access to our affective life, is able to create emotional engagement and hence readiness to act.

On a more evident and simple level, art can thematicize social change as a basic conflict, such as the transition of loyalty from the familial to the communal. An example is the portrayal of internal dilemma as shown in pictures of a son leaving his family for war, for the sake of what he perceives to be his larger family. We see a crying mother, supported by her husband's arm, and a son who steps out of the parents' house, where he grew up, giving expression to his proud conviction to serve a higher social destiny. Yet he is torn by leaving his original family to which he owes his existence, upbringing, and education. In such a case, art can offer advice on his conflict and how it might be resolved. The advice is transmitted via our identification with the subject. Art may also describe on a more allegorical level the conflict of loyalties, for example, as in the Old Testament scene of Abraham sacrificing his son Isaac.

In general, pictorial representations illustrate on a more sensual and vivid level—compared to what any verbal description can give—the dilemma caused by the change or extension of original commitment. We shall return to the implications and power of representation later.

Art has the capacity of communicating subjects and themes in a more immediate and realistic way by means of *illusion*. The more subtle and indirect way to transmit values is, however, to create *symbols of identification*, as discussed above with regard to churches.

Let's have a look at other ideological standard themes or "stereotypes" used repeatedly by a multitude of ideologies for propaganda.

Clues and clichés used by art

Large scale. The most common way to visualize social or political supremacy is to impress by sheer size. In general, official buildings like city halls, houses of parliament, and palaces tower above

Fig. 13.8. *Persepolis, Iran. Audience hall of Darius I (521–485 B.C.), where he and his son Xerxes received their vassals of the empire.*

Fig. 13.9. *Chambord Castle, Loire (France). The castle was built from 1519 to 1547 under François I and was one of the most ambitious and renowned buildings in the splendid competition of nearly three hundred castles that arose in the Loire region during that era. Magnificence is combined with the trustworthiness of the fortress.*

neighboring buildings. They can dominate a city's skyline. The most common example is the town church. In some medieval towns, status competition within the community led to quite extravagant family towers that in some ways anticipated the skyscrapers of modern cities.

The use of monumental proportions can have ambivalent connotations. On the one hand, the "architecture of magnificence" (*Prachtarchitektur*) can intimidate, but it can also inspire pride in group identity, depending on whether one self-identifies as an outsider or insider.

Order and regularity: the straight line. Structures of high regularity and consistency inspire the idea of *reliability of the political system*. Order is stringent and unambiguous: there are a hundred ways to fail or misunderstand a given order, but only one way to fit into it. The dominant straight line is the basis of any redundant order in larger (constructive or graphic) systems. Artists such as Kandinsky and Hundertwasser called the straight line the most rigid product of human mental abstraction, since it is not provided in nature. Therefore, buildings stressing the straight line symbolize principles of clarity, authority, human will power, and the triumph over chaos and chance.

The strong foundation. Here the idea of nation is symbolized in the image of a strong house or building that inspires confidence in the foundation, safety or wealth of its physical power and the *protection* guaranteed by its firm (architectural) body. In politics, the term

Fig. 13.10. *Leningrad, House of the Soviets. By N. A. Trockij (1935–40). The highly regular structure of buildings for national administration imply the reliability of the political system. The straight line as the supporting element inspires clarity and unambiguity.*

"House of Europe" has become a contemporary metaphor for the European Community, involving the idea of unity in diversity.

The reassuring language of monumental architectural structures (grand entrances, columns, spaces, etc.) is adhered to by the common features of modern banking houses and cultural palaces that broadcast solidity and trustworthiness. The same principle applies in traditional cultures to clan houses, which advertise group prestige and invulnerability. Symbolic protection is afforded by sumptuous decorations containing aversive and dominant symbolism, invoking the blessing and support of the ancestors.

Togetherness (*Einigkeit, Brüderlichkeit*). The idea of a community that shares convictions, perspectives, and goals includes not only deeply rooted conceptions of archaic group cohesion, but also the belief that cooperation empowers the group. The model of an efficient group that draws its superiority from ethnic diversity and mutual complementarity was and is characteristic of many political systems. Numerous examples of sculptures, paintings, and songs propagate this idea. "Strength through unity" and "United we stand, divided we fall" are clichés representing this theme, repeated in many states and many political systems, including nineteenth-century United States and fascist Italy. Fig. 13.12 gives an example from the Soviet Union stressing ethnic harmony.

Fig. 13.11. *Bordeaux, France. Main façade of the Grand Theatre. By Victor Louis (1773–80). Cultural buildings or banking houses often "quote" the magnificence of official architecture to underline their importance and draw the public.*

Fig. 13.12. *Stephan Karpov: "The friendship of nations" (1923/24). In many examples of indoctrinating art, the solidarity of different ethnic groups is promoted as a worthy achievement.*

Future (*Vorwärts!*). Another stereotype with universal appeal is the concept of the future. The promise of prosperous, unlimited prospects for everyone is a topic found not only in songs, but in the plastic and graphic arts. The heroic dimension of the slogan "Future!" appeals mainly to the youth. Consider the Hitler Youth marching song: "Vorwärts, vorwärts, schmettern die hellen Fanfaren, vorwärts, vorwärts, Jugend kennt keine Gefahren!" ("Forward, forward, raise the light fanfare, forward, forward, Youth knows no danger!"). The opening lines of this youth song latch onto a cliché found in the repertoire of many other indoctrinating songs of the era.

Freedom. Like the future, the topic of freedom is vastly exploited in propagandistic texts and art. In slogans such as "Brüder zur Freiheit, zur Sonne" (Brothers, up to freedom, up to sunlight), revolutionary dynamism feeds on the idea of the liberation process rather than on the philosophical value of freedom. It involves the image of the gloomy state of slavery, from which the new political movement will lead to light and freedom. In fact, promises of freedom are prescriptions for self-deceit, since in general unification processes through new political systems require rigid methods and restrictions on the individual level. In single cases they may well liberate

Fig. 13.13. *Poster from Ivos Katje (Lithuania), entitled: "We are approaching a big future." The promise of the "future" was a strong appeal in every new political system. The prospect of hope and glory is especially attractive to the youth.*

from the dominance of other systems, but certainly not from the prosocial dominance that is necessary in any social system.

Health (*Der schöne gesunde Körper*). Propaganda, whether political or commercial, often associates its virtues with physical integrity and attractiveness. The belief in a mystical accord between the true and the beautiful, of the "right thing" making people healthy and happy is deeply rooted in our concept of adaptedness and fitness. It is plausible to suppose that a bad system cannot produce people who are strong and sound; the system they live in could not be wrong or detrimental. Rather, a sound system is regarded as the source and origin of any kind of well-being.

Equality (*Gleichheit*) ("We are all equal"). Egalitarianism entails primarily the ideal of equal rights and chances for everyone—an old humanitarian model that deserves our respect. It also deserves our skepticism, since the goal has never been accomplished outside of hunter-gatherer societies. Egalitarian processes are allowed to present themselves in the vestment of physical uniformity, indicating both the price and reward of membership in any large group. Take as an example the painting by Gerhard Keil titled *Turner* (Athletes, circa 1940) (Fig. 13.16) portraying extremes of standardization and synchronization in the shape of four young

Fig. 13.14. *The famous painting of Eugene Delacroix: "Liberty is guiding the people" refers to the revolution in July 1830 in Paris, where the tyranny of the absolutist monarch Charles X was overthrown and replaced by the popular Louis-Philippe of Orléans, called the "civil king." Here the allegory of "liberty" is represented by a bare-bosomed woman who leads the people to victory.*

men. The image was looked on favorably by the Nazi regime, perhaps because the message is clear: giving up individual interests and autonomy in favor of a larger community is a virtue repaid by the advantages of belonging to a larger group— equality, security, and even the relinquishing of responsibility. Photographs of the orderly ranks of identically outfitted Nazi Party members during the infamous Reich Party Day in Nuremberg (*Reichsparteitag*) reveal the power and perfect staging of the *new order* in which the individual partakes of—and to a degree dissolves into—an overwhelming process of depersonalization.

Repetition—the illusion of eternity. Repetition as verbal style parallels spatial order in the temporal realm. In language, it maintains an aspect of regularity and reliability. In verbal performances, such as speeches, the degree of repetition of certain words and phrases indicates the degree of dogmatism. It also invokes the illusion of continuity of process by rhythmic assonances. The latter tend to induce a blurring of mind and trance-like emotional

Fig. 13.15. *Arno Breker: Die Wehrmacht (Armed Forces) (1938). The sculpture of a perfect athlete was placed in the internal court of the new Reichskanzlei in Berlin. The strong and balanced body was more than a cliché— it was an ideal in the era of National Socialism in Germany. In art, it was mostly portrayed as representing the beneficence of the political system. Physical integrity and beauty itself became the symbol of a well-functioning national organism.*

Fig. 13.16. *Gerhard Keil: Turner (Athletes, 1940). Uniformity and synchronization are the main elements of the painting, which inaugurates the dynamic functioning of the new state.*

states that are associated with rhythmical music. Consider the following Nazi marching song:

> Wir schreiten ernst, wir schreiten still
> Es weiß das Herz, wohin es will
> Der Weg ist hart, der Weg ist weit
> Wir schreiten in die Ewigkeit
>
> (We march earnestly, we march quietly
> The heart, it knows where to go
> The way is hard, the way is far
> We march into eternity)

We have looked briefly at only some of the many clichés used to indoctrinate. They all work by communicating ideas through our sensual and emotional perceptions. In contrast to these largely nonverbal techniques, many clichés rely on verbal allusion in poems, texts, and songs. Such ideas include honor and the symbolism of light and darkness, of height and depth.

Conclusion: The Issue of Art

What are the special advantages of art as a means of communication and hence of indoctrination? Which qualities does it possess that verbal means lack? I mentioned the *representational* power of art, literally the capacity to simulate a situation as being sensually and spatially *present*. The illusion of physical presence is an urgent and seductive one and certainly more effective than any verbal description.

The power of representation refers to the temporal dimension as well. "Future" is a strong ideological appeal, all the more when the ideal state being praised is represented in the here and now as already present and by implication as achievable. The image is an implicit promise.

Art can furthermore present a combination of persons, objects, and events that normally would not occur in the special constellation and time under real conditions. The effect of an intentional setting and spatial montage is a unique one for plastic and pictorial art. Themes of *togetherness, fraternity*, and *unity* can be demonstrated in an incomparably persuasive way.

References

Arnheim, R. (1980). *Die Dynamik der architektonischen Form*. Dumont, Cologne.

Baldwin Smith, E. (1950). *The dome*. University of Princeton Press, Princeton.

———. (1956). *Architectural symbolism of Imperial Rome and the Middle Ages*. University of Princeton Press, Princeton.

Bandmann, G. (1981). *Mittelalterliche Architektur als Bedeutungsträger*, 7th ed. Mann, Berlin.

Caudle, F. M. (1989). Advertising art: Cognitive mechanisms and research issues. In *Cognitive and affective responses to advertising* (ed. P. Cafferata and A. Tybot), pp. 161-217. Lexington Books, Toronto.

Dissanayake, E. (1992). *Homo Aestheticus: where art comes from and why*. Free Press, New York.

Eibl-Eibesfeldt, I. (1988). *Human ethology*. Aldine de Gruter, New York.'

————. (1994). Kultur im Dienste der Wertevermittlung. In *Kulturethologie* (ed. M. Liedtke), pp. 168–80. Realis, Munich.

Eibl-Eibesfeldt, I. and Sütterlin, C. (1992). *Im Banne der Angst. Zur Natur- und Kunstgeschichte menschlicher Abwehrsymbolik*. Piper, Munich.

Hauser, A. (1967). *Sozialgeschichte der Kunst und Literatur*. Beck, Munich.

Hubel, D. and Wiesel, T. N. (1959). Receptive Fields of Single Neurons in the Cat's Striate Cortex. *Journal of Physiology*, **148**, 548–91.

Layton, R. (1991). *The anthropology of art*, 2d ed. Cambridge University Press, Cambridge.

Leiss, W., Kline, S., and Jhally, S. (1990). *Social communication in advertising*, 2d ed. Nelson, Canada.

Lenin, V. I. (1929). *Agitation und Propaganda*. Verlag für Literatur und Politik [original in Russian], Berlin.

Lorenz, K. (1943). Die angeborenen Formen möglicher Erfahrung. *Zeitschrift für Tierpsychologie*, **5**, 235–400.

Lützeler, H. (1969). *Europäische Baukunst im Überblick. Architektur und Gesellschaft*. Herder, Freiburg.

Mealey, L. and Theis, P. (1995). The relationship between mood and preferences among natural landscapes: An evolutionary perspective. *Ethology and Sociobiology*, **16**, 247–56.

Noever, P. (1994). *Die Tyrannei des Schönen. Architektur der Stalin-Zeit*. Katalog zur Ausstellung im Museum für Angewandte Kunst, Vienna.

Pochat, G. (1983). *Der Symbolbegriff in der Ästhetik und Kunstwissenschaft*. Dumont, Cologne.

Salter, F. K. (1995). *Emotions in command. A naturalistic study of institutional dominance*. Oxford University Press, Oxford.

Tabor, J., ed. (1994). *Kunst und Diktatur. Architektur, Bildhauerei, Malerei, in Österreich, Deutschland, Italien und der Sowietunion 1922-1956*, 2 vols. Grasl, Vienna.

Trigger, B. (1990). Monumental architecture: A thermodynamic explanation of symbolic behaviour. *World Archaeology*, **22** (2), 119–32.

Veblen, T. B. (1931/1899). *The theory of the leisure class*. Viking, New York.

von Moos, S. (1984). Der Palast als Festung. In *Politische Architektur in Europa* (ed. M. Warnke), pp. 106–56. Dumont, Cologne.

Warnke, M. (1984). *Politische Architektur in Europa*. Dumont, Cologne.

Welch, D. (1995). *The Third Reich: Politics and propaganda*. Routledge, London and New York.

Wölfflin, H. (1963). *Kunstgeschichtliche Grundbegriffe*. Schwabe, Basel.

CHAPTER FOURTEEN

PROBING IMAGES OF POLITICIANS AND INTERNATIONAL AFFAIRS

CREATING PICTURES AND STORIES OF THE MIND

Robert D. Deutsch

To involve the audience we must start with something they know and like—a character that is familiar and appealing. It can be a situation everyone has experienced, an emotional response universally shared, a facet of personality easily recognized. But there must be something that is known and understood if we are to achieve audience involvement. Once the audience has become involved with a character, almost anything is possible. The character must be as comfortable as an old shoe, yet exciting. He can be heroic or bigger than life, but basically the audience first has to understand him as a person if they are to feel his emotions.

Walt Disney, talking about creating Mickey Mouse

Introduction

When trying to understand how mass indoctrination works, two separate but related processes must be examined: the design of the pictures and words served up in the media, and how the audience transforms those portrayals into personally meaningful sentiments.

In interpreting the world, people reduce complexity to sensibility. Regardless of the time and the degree of contact we have with a person or circumstance, certain things about those presentations stand out. Meaning is extracted selectively from only a small portion of what is actually observable. We take those things that stand out and make them fit with what we already know and expect. (Mind you, we do not think our way through this; we just do it). Using this abbreviated list of attributes having personal meaning, we assume consistency with what might yet come, fill in any blanks, and concoct an image with an emotional bottom line: positive or negative. Through this reduction process we are taking something from the outside and making it our own; the image becomes part of our-*selves*.

What we remember from a montage of pictures and words and how we make it fit with what we already think and feel is an unconscious but directed selection process. The path from objectively observable presentation to subjectively created image is a route through our own self-image. This process applies whether the raw materials for the creation of images are seen on TV, on the "big" screen, on newsstands, in our photo albums, or in our offices, playgrounds, and homes. However, there is a vast difference between the world we experience directly (in an unmediated way) and the world created by those "behind the message."

Images created by the media are *already* in a compressed and exaggerated form: a space shuttle liftoff, soldiers in battle, the Statue of Liberty, starving babies, the first atomic bomb explosion, the landscape as motherland, a beer commercial, the O.J. Simpson trial. Image makers intend to interrupt our ongoing routine, make us orient to that interruption and react according to their design. They seek to limit the variability in audience response by engineering the reduction process. They *deliberately* evoke emotions based upon primitive expectations of belonging and the need to feel secure and powerful. If they are successful, they have created a sense of an enhanced order wherein we believe and feel what they intended.

Media consultants are not alone in their effort to have us buy in to what they are selling. TV, a visual fantasy of fact, constrains how images are created and helps all sides along. Time and network competition both demand a strategy of persuasion that ensnares our image creation process. In this chapter I define the design principles behind these communication traps.

In contemporary society with its preponderance of mediated experiences, images have pervaded our vernacular. More than ever before, images dominate our consciousness. The word "image" is everywhere (as are "spin-doctors"). Corporate images, product images, celebrity images, and images of political leaders and international crises are now part of our milieu. Attempts at image creation streak across our field of vision like spaceships in a video game: Ronald Reagan on horseback, Reagan and Gorbachev holding a baby in Red Square, Michael Jackson moonwalking for Pepsi, Saddam Hussein chatting with hostages, the strut of Mick Jagger, the fall of the Berlin Wall, the rise of Madonna, the rubble produced by the San Francisco earthquake, Rocky, the Challenger explosion, *Lifestyles of the Rich and Famous*. Nowadays, even self-image has become a market commodity. People are now buying more things at greater expense to enhance their self-image.

To be sure, we are dealing here with something that is powerful and indigenous. Images do matter. The images we have of ourselves shade how we interpret the world and influence our choice of actions. We cast those close to us in roles that coincide with our image of them, *and we hold them to it*. Corporate and product images attempt to influence what we buy. The images we have of a politician or celebrity can determine if they get our support.

Attempts at image creation are now an invasive part of our environment: some pollute and some enhance human experience. By concentrating in this chapter on how political images emerge, I am seeking to get a grasp on the enormity of the generic image process, a process that addresses no less than the question of how mediated experience can be taken to represent "real life." In other words, I am dealing here with what is authentic and what is not.

Central to my discussion will be a description of how a person's "self"—an emotionally invested story that uniquely defines an "I am"—can be seized upon by attempts at image making, particularly political image making. In much the same manner and degree that political images can obscure deficiencies in intent, self-images can serve to defend against negative or confused feelings, as well as objectively suspect motives and behaviors. In the concluding section, implications will be drawn for the analysis of public presentations and public opinion.

My underlying purpose in this look at images is twofold:

(1) To show that, contrary to conventional wisdom, people do not create images because of information overload or superficial attention. *Images are fundamental to the way human beings operate; they are a prime knowledge system and a basic mode of presence to ourselves and others.* Images of "self" and "other" are necessary and pervasive in everyday life. Without images, the "other" would be

absolute and unfathomable (a stranger); the "self" would be fragmented and vulnerable.

To say images operate in the domain of politics is in one sense simply to say, THAT'S WHAT WE DO, ANYWAY! What makes politicians such a special case is that they are inherently attention-getting and our contact with them is mostly indirect (via the media). As "leaders" they take advantage of certain predispositions in our evolved social responsiveness. With television now functioning as the political soapbox, a politician's relative inaccessibility shunts us aside into the role of passive audience. This provides us *more leeway* in creating images. Also pivotal is the fact that slick editing styles and the managed self-presentation of politicians perfect the otherwise spontaneous and loose process that normally characterizes our firsthand relations with others. These factors give a *running jump* to a process that has actually been in place since humans first appeared.

Pundits complain that content is absent from political debate. Images ride herd over substance. Political media consultants, having replaced the power of the party, are berated for their expedience in manipulating symbols to evoke emotions, not thought. The press is ridiculed for showing only what is attention-getting and dramatic. Yet these explanations do not seem wholly adequate. The medium is new, the players are different, but the mechanism they activate is age-old and ageless. *As image gatherers we are all aboriginal hunters: archetypal and artful.*

(2) It will also be demonstrated that the image we have of "others" and the image we have of "self" is recursively and irremediably linked. The choice of a leader or the choice of a product represents a mapping of the chooser's "self" onto the selection process. This process involves an inescapable intertwining of a subjective sense of personal identity and a recasting of a politician's traits or a product's qualities into symbols that are either congruent with or discrepant from the chooser's self-image. People create images in their own image and respond to images that reflect aspects of their own selves. Detailing just how this process works will be one of my main tasks.

The subtlety of political propaganda and indoctrination, as blatant as they often appear in content, is that they implicitly address the efficacy of "self." Propagandists, whatever they purvey out loud, are also whispering in the ears of their audience and suggesting:

You should have this [be it an idea or object]. You need this. It is the best. It is the best deal. You are clever if you pick this one. People will think better of you when they see the quality of your choices and the wisdom they represent. Your life will have obvious, tangible evidence of success. You will be less lonely. Choose, because you really need this to be a better person, and your choice will prove that you are.

Political Popularity and the Developmental Context of Self-image

Recall the lines Marlene Dietrich sang in the movie, *Blue Angel*:

> Falling in love again, Never wanted to,
> What am I to do, Can't help it.

We all know that love can be sublime or lethal, and is accounted for by no rational list of sought-after qualities. Love just *is*. It's as if something in our minds were saying to us, "Listen, Buster, sit back and be quiet, I'm in charge here."

The relationships we have with those in our face-to-face world is one thing, our bond with politicians, whom we see only on television, quite another. Or is it? Does Dietrich's motivational disclaimer, "Can't help it," in any way capture the basis of our attachment (or lack thereof) to certain politicians and their ideologies? Despite their handlers' advice to "act naturally," some politicians come off in the media as insulated, stultified, or unreal. But there are exceptions: with television as our major source of information, there are politicians whose managed presentations clearly evoke an immediate connection between themselves and "the people." What is the nature of this media-based bonding?

Crucial is the fact that images constantly fly in the face of formal logic. There are reasons why "reasoned judgement" and "substance" need not affect how we create political images; audience inattention and the complexity of issues are not among them. Political images can seem so contorted when viewed from the standpoint of objective analysis because they are created with reference to our own self-image—something that is itself based on purely emotional experience developed early in childhood at a time before we even acquired language.

As an infant grows, a "self" comes into being out of an interaction with significant "others"—usually, the mother and father. The "self" is initially unstructured and open to the environment. Psychological boundaries between the infant and those around him or her are blurred. The infant has no language or sophisticated abstraction capabilities. Where once the infant was part of an undifferentiated whole with these significant others, he or she slowly and gradually begins to separate and develop an autonomous self. This is done in phases.

At first, a *rigid* identification takes precedence between "self" and "other." Feelings based on sameness predominate. The unity with the mother, if satisfactory, gives the infant a basic ration of the experience of omnipotence. As of yet, the infant has no well-bounded and definitive "self." This is a period of absolute dependence. *The "other" is defined as like me.*

Next, the infant gradually establishes a *congruent* identification with the "other." The predominant theme is "I am me, you are you, and in certain ways we are *similar*." Differences based upon self- reference are now forming and are affirmed, but likenesses are still emphasized. This is a period of relative dependence.

During this time, if the mother is experienced as reliable and exhibits a capacity to react empathetically, the infant will develop a high degree of confidence in her. This allows the infant to tolerate certain insults to his or her desire for sameness. The infant's bias towards a rigid identification begins to loosen. Small independencies will be attempted and encouraged. Mother will be expected to "be there" when needed, but this is not all the time. The infant also expects that mother will not abandon him or her when the infant shows vulnerability. Trust develops, allowing the awareness, "you" and "I" are different. *The "other" is defined as liking me.*

From this basic trust, a *tangential* identification is slowly accomplished. Out of similarity, the child comes to understand his own uniqueness ("I am me, you are you, and in certain ways we are *different*"). A sense of independence and a true autonomous "self" emerges. The child is able to disallow the illusion of the unit, mother-me, even though this is initially uncomfortable. For the young child, this perceived difference implies the recognition that "the other is more than me." However, if previous stages have progressed satisfactorily, *in being more than me, the "other" is defined as the one who creates the context for me to be more.*

A positive image is created by the politician (or product) who recapitulates and satisfies the yearnings that correspond to these three levels of self-development. *The image creation process is a reflection of what we do developmentally in our own lives to separate from the "other" and develop a "self."*

For indoctrination to be effective, it must entrain this three-tiered process of audience interpretation. Moreover, I suggest that human consciousness parses all it surveys according to these three dimensions. If so, Eibl-Eibesfeldt's description and photograph of a Yanomamo warrior greeting (Fig. 14.1) depicts more than a ritual salutation. In establishing a likeness between the visiting and host tribe, and having a child offer flowers while a warrior displays his power, the nature of subjectivity itself is enacted.

Fig. 14.1 *A Yanomamo warrior greeting (photo by Eibl-Eibesfeldt)*

A politician gains ascendancy in the public mind by designing his behavior not so he is liked, as much as by offering himself up so the public feels *he likes them*. Specifically, the successful politician:

1. creates an "atmosphere" of *familiarity* (can be identified with, seen as "like me");
2. establishes a sentiment of *appeasement* (I know he is not me, but I feel understood, valued, cared for and liked; I trust him);
3. provides a sense of *power* (he is more than me, and will provide the context for me to be more; he gives me hope and optimism).

Familiarity in Politics

Familiarity is the instantaneous recognition of something already known. People are attracted to the familiar. The familiar is what stands out. We might orient to the novel and unexpected, but for it to have lasting meaning it must be brought in line with what is familiar. Familiarity provides a continuity and coherence to current experience. Within the experience of the familiar, a direct connection is made between "then" and "now." Our response to what is familiar is a gut reaction—we "can't help it."

Familiarity as felt by an audience means many things: privacy, a foreknowledge as to what to expect, a feeling that "I don't have to start over again." One can habituate to the familiar, take things at face value, assume business as usual. In such an assumed routine context you can let down your guard. And just such a relaxation process allows for the image creation process to proceed apace. Once the politician creates a sense of familiarity, the potential for further manipulation is already in the air.

We know from American presidential campaigns dating back to Andrew Jackson how pervasive symbols of familiarity can be. Candidates are presented as "a man of the people," "a common man," "a man against big government." Pictures are flashed: a log cabin; the American flag; the candidate with rolled-up shirt sleeves, on street corners, with show business celebrities (something we all share).

We see campaigning politicians visiting a farm, milking cows, pressing the flesh, kissing babies, going fishing, riding on horseback, wearing a hardhat while with construction workers, invoking the names of the Founding Fathers. Places and events from our nation's history and everyday scenes are mythologized and roll across the television screen in such a way that an illusion of participating in a "familiar" past is experientially possible. The idea that we are one big, happy family feels cozy. It is comforting.

Appeasement in Politics

Along with a sense of familiarity, the individual seeking the attainment or maintenance of power must establish a sentiment of appeasement. No matter how successful in establishing a sense of familiarity, we inevitably come up against the implicit recognition that the leader is "not me, we are different." To temper this essential difference, the leader must provide the audience with the feeling that they are understood, cared about and valued as separate individuals. Just as in the developmental stage of "congruent identification" where the infant is beginning to form a separate, autonomous "self," trust is the most important issue. The audience must feel that if they displayed their vulnerability, the person vying for leadership would not "bite" them.

Familiarity is bound up with *belonging*. In appeasing, the leader must demonstrate, at least symbolically, that "the people" as *separate* from her have value and are "good" in and of themselves— that their "goodness" is not inextricably bound up with hers. Appeasement allows us to affirm our positive image of self, thus satisfying our need for a sense of control. Ronald Reagan, for example, was exceptionally good at this. Rarely did he ever take credit for any achievement. Whatever we accomplish, he would say, is due solely to the hard work and moral stature of the American people. And we all can recall his many State of the Union messages, where the common man as hero was ever present.

Power in Politics

Lastly, a leader must project a sense of power, of being *more* than any one of us: the one who keeps the lid on all the chaotic and catastrophic possibilities of life and who knows something about the *future*. As social beings, the craving we have for a leader is deep-seated. The presence of a leader makes us feel less alone, part of something bigger than we are—something invincible, powerful, and enduring. And paradoxically, believing that the leader "knows the way," "knows the labyrinth," enables us to feel more independent, autonomous, and confident to manage "our own little world"—*we* feel empowered.

The leader must become the apotheosis of "everyman"—the mythic hero, but still maintain a common touch. If he seems too powerful (e.g., Alexander Haig), or too intelligent (e.g., Paul Simon with bow tie and thick, black glasses), or too businesslike (e.g., Michael Dukakis), or *too* anything, then that becomes an idiosyncracy that cannot be made part of the audience's self-referring story.

The leader's life, too, must come to represent *a ritual joust with evil*; where his destiny, his mission, and his duty is to take up "the cause," to sacrifice, and to overcome. He must appear ready for this: optimistic, confident, committed, but not immune to danger (excitement is provided for by the combination of risk and hope). He must not be invulnerable, but invincible. A popular embodiment of this type of personage is Luke Skywalker in *Star Wars*.

Reagan's demeanor of courage and good humor while being wheeled into the operating room after being shot be John Hinckley is, of course, part of his mythic image. In his famous 30-minute campaign advertisement, where Reagan recounts the attempted assassination and states that "God must have been sitting on my shoulder" and "the time I have left now belongs to God," add to his mythic role (as in *Star Wars*, "the force" was with him). His ability to paint his adversaries (big government, the Soviet Union), at least early in his administration, as distinct and identifiable evil demons is also part of his mythic appeal, as was his certainty in himself and an unswerving belief in his cause.

The leader's power provides us with a feeling that with his or her help we can be more than we are now. In this way, power is linked back to familiarity in terms of *hope*. During development, aspects of a child's self are distorted or left incomplete (even the best of parents cannot meet all of a child's needs). A sense of power leads one to feel able to make up for these gaps; one can complete uncompleted tasks that represent parental failure.

The amalgamation of familiarity, appeasement, and power provides a behavioral definition of "looking presidential." With these three steps accomplished, the probability that the audience will feel "I like him" is maximized. We are primed to orient to such a performance. We feel it (without logical processing) and respond to it as inherently compelling. We bond to such a presentation without any conscious and objective analysis. It is simply taking advantage of what is "bred in the bone," ingrained in the way we develop a self.

When a politician's behavior successfully embodies the dimensions that reflect how the "self" develops, a positive and global emotional response by the audience can be achieved. This response is immediate, spontaneous, effortless, inescapable, irrevocable, holistic, difficult to verbalize, yet irremediably activated without much thought.

Images that probe into the depths of the "self" are so affect laden, they can, and often do, persist even if a completely logical or empirical invalidation of their original basis can be supplied. In this case, too, the affective dimension of images can become completely separated from content: a woman quoted in *Time* says, "I liked the way President Reagan handled that crisis ... I forgot which one." Likewise, people can say, "Sony makes the best products," without really knowing what they are basing that judgment on. Rational consideration serves us less when creating images than in justifying them afterward. Hence, the possibility for indoctrination.

Self-Image and the Image of the Leader

Although someone actually far removed from "my-self" (the "self" as originally created in the developmental context), a political leader, by virtue of being an inherent archetype of the significant "other" (the parent), is placed in intimate juxtaposition alongside a person's self-image. This match or mismatch leads to the political leader's image.

Memories evoked by the resemblance between the two experiences of being parented and being led are at once clear in tone (affect) and confused in content (words). When you can imagine yourself under the protection of "the leader," a transformation takes place. You feel like you are dreaming, but dreaming the way you do when you dream you are dreaming. You remember everything—not as you lived it, but as you wished it had happened. The past is transformed into a fantasized reality—a fantasy you want to be real. You delight in the similarity between the two experiences. You "see" the leader as a vision and the vision as a reality.

Self-images and the images we have of political leaders are a mirror-imaging process. Like standing in front of the Vietnam

Memorial and seeing our reflection meld with those names etched in granite, our own silhouette of self-definition becomes an overlay on the presentation of the leader.

The raw material people latch onto to create an image of a world leader may consist of the following:

- A prop (Churchill's cigar or cane)
- Iconic representations of physiognomy (e.g., height, style of hair, the shape of a smile, facial composition)
- Characteristic vocal expressions (e.g., Reagan's "Make my day"; "Khrushchev's "We will bury you")
- Nonverbal behavior (e.g., manner of gesticulation, gait; Khrushchev pounding the podium with his shoe)
- Some inner dynamic (e.g., confidence)
- A piece of behavior (Gorbachev, in D.C., getting out of his limousine to shake hands with "the people")

Forms of "raw data" stand out and cling to the individual like a statically charged sock from the clothes dryer, because they are compatible self-reference points—in some manner, they "fit" with a person's self-definition and the characteristic way he or she defines "others." A self-referring story is composed. Connections are made between the pieces of an image's "raw data" and the "self." An image is born—direct, immediate, complete (appears full-blown)—admitting no ambiguity or relativity. Images are naive, credulous, self-contained, and self-referenced. They exist without formal logic or rationality. Peeks, glimpses, reflections, and "sparks" (gleaned from "raw data") all mix together and find their way into the whirlpool of "self," then dissolve into self-reflecting images. If they do not, they are essentially rejected and remain external and unincorporated.

This mirror-imaging process mainly emphasizes analogy and metaphor. Analogy and metaphor are devices perfectly suited to image creation: they allow for *loose* associations. An example of a sequence of analogies is given by Umberto Eco in his book, *Foucault's Pendulum*, (1989, 618):

> Potato crosses with apple because both are vegetable and round in shape. From apple to snake, by Biblical association. From snake to donut, by formal likeness. From donut to life preserver, from life preserver to bathing suit. Then from bathing to sea, sea to ship, ship to shit, shit to toilet paper, toilet to cologne, cologne to alcohol, alcohol to drugs, drugs to syringe, syringe to hole, hole to ground, ground to potato.

Analogy in image creation is comprised not only of connections made by these kinds of iconographic or conceptual similarities, but also by *emotion*. Analogizing in the service of image creation needs to have very little in terms of a consensual iconographic base. For example, in 1988, while interviewing people about their image of Gorbachev, a typical reasoning pattern included, "He is very personable ... not a 'hawk'."

On further questioning as to the connection between "personable" and "not a hawk," an interviewee provided the following kind of reasoning:

- "Both attributes—"personable" and "not a hawk"—are positive." [Note that their "equality" is based exclusively on their emotional valence.]
- "Gorbachev does not seem like a bad guy. He has a pleasant face, a nice smile, and does not wear those bland, forbidding suits that past Soviet leaders have worn. He dresses like us." [familiarity]
- "What I like, too, is that he is accessible: he gives a lot of interviews to the American press and gets out of his limousine to greet the American people when visiting our country." [familiarity]
- "He is powerful, but does not seem mean or competitive. I feel relaxed when watching him; I don't think he will threaten my future." [power and appeasement]
- "Most of all, I feel he's interested in other people. He's a good listener, and in my experience, you don't usually listen to someone you don't like." [familiarity and appeasement]

When this interviewee was further asked about personal experiences with powerful individuals (individuals known face-to-face), the reply included the following statements:

- "Powerful people are usually not very nice. I mean they're very competitive. They want you ... demand from you, that you always be your best. But they also do not want you to be as good as them. They give you a lot of mixed messages. If they ever thought you were as good as them, they would reject you." [familiarity and power]
- "Powerful people never listen, they just make arbitrary demands. Powerful people talk in monologues. It doesn't matter what you say or do. It's as if you don't exist." [familiarity and power]

- "Powerful people think their way is the only way. They don't give you any room to do something your own way, and they don't let you sometimes fail in order to learn." [familiarity and power]
- "Powerful people think they are perfect, that they know it all. That's why I like Gorbachev's birthmark. With that on his face, he knows he's not perfect; and I know he knows." [familiarity, appeasement, and power]

When these statements about powerful people were recounted by the interviewer, and when the interviewee was asked about people (not by name) or roles associated with these interpretations of power, the interviewee said (with a chuckle and while looking down), "I guess I'm really talking about MY PARENTS! But I'm not like them. I think of myself as a tough person, but I listen to others."

This statement represents the "self" coming full circle in terms of the image creation process. For the "self," power provides for a sense of hope (future). With hope, a person can feel "I can be more than what I am now." In this way, power is linked back to familiarity in terms of a hoped-for familiarity. Gorbachev, for this interviewee, symbolizes a counterpoint to parental behavior that was deeply felt as threatening. Gorbachev's behavior also serves to reaffirm the interviewee's need to perceive self as different from parent(s). A strong positive image obtains.

As this example shows, images jump back and forth between the context in which the "self" developed and the domain of politics. Attributes from the two that have no apparent relationship blend together. They are quickly wrested from their original frame of reference and given a common plane, most often defined by only the most global and disjointed of similarities. The image of a politician is created in a house of mirrors, all reflecting our subjective and emotionally based image of "self" and the context in which it emerged.

How Are Images Formed and Why Are They Potent?

A direct mental representation. The simplest and least potent form of an image is a direct mental representation that is pictorially linked to its external referent. A picture of a tree by an amateur photographer is seen as just that: a picture of a particular tree.

Here our response is perceptually based, limited by the thing itself, by its original sphere of denotation and by external (objective) conventions that inform its structure. My mental representation of a painting, a photograph, or an imagined person or thing can be fairly straightforward and consensual. It also can be seen as a lot more. The difference lies in how precisely the display taps into the structure of "self." If the "self" is accessed, images form that derive their meaning much more from the person's functional and subjective frame of reference. The deeper the "self" is involved (innervating the "tacit"), the more personalized and illogical is the image.

Potent images are always needful and totally self-indulgent. The only relevant issue is "How do I feel?" When we view a great photograph, we usually do not comment on how beautiful it is. Instead, we immediately reflect back on ourselves. We talk about how it makes us feel or what it reminds us of. Great photographs are true images—they are iconographic of the self; the "self" is the only convention that applies.

A conventional rendition. Apart from simple mental representations (re-presentations of the thing itself), the word "image" is sometimes used when speaking of a conventional or traditional rendition of a subject. The Republican elephant and the Democratic donkey are examples. Another example of this type of conventionality is the way some Americans, especially those born after World War II, think of Sir Winston Churchill. They might know that he was a political leader in Great Britain during World War II, and that he was "tough." But no real feeling is associated with these interpretations. Nevertheless, as their first association to hearing the word "Churchill," these individuals picture in their mind a facsimile of Churchill's face with a large cigar in his mouth or with his hand gesture in the form of a "V" (for victory) sign.

Emotion without specific representation. Ascending in potency, the next class of images that appear are those that have powerful feelings attached to them, but have no specific iconographic representation, except by default. For example, sometime between the initiation of union strikes in Poland in 1981 and the non-Communist takeover of power in 1989, the image many Americans had of Lech Walesa simply entailed an affective association. For many, midway between 1981 and 1989, no concrete and specific memories remained of Walesa or the events surrounding the formation of the Solidarity trade union. If shown a picture of Walesa, most of these individuals would recognize it; but they themselves have no characteristic pose in mind. However, the image these people have of Walesa is relatively potent and lasting: a common man, a simple carpenter, a man of the people who stood up against "all that" (the Communist government of Poland). Despite its imprecision in visual representation, this is a powerful image because it is a metaphor of what all of us face everyday in our lives, except it is on a grander scale.

On a mundane level, we are all trying to control and make sense of the forces that impinge on us as individuals, especially the ones that seem not to make any sense at all or the ones we have little control over. The emotionally based image of Walesa presents both the subject "Walesa" and the way in which the subject is presented. Walesa is no longer "the thing" itself; it is *about* something ... and that something is me. I identify with it.

Self-empowerment (standing up against the Communist government in Poland), the idea that one can make up for some past slight (being jailed by the Communists), or some distortion in self-definition (being labeled a criminal), and the hope that things can be set straight (as when the Communists are forced out of power) are all seen reflected on the image of Lech Walesa. The feeling that I can make up for the past, I can be more than how the "other"— either a Communist-led Poland or parent—defines me, is what underlies the potency of Walesa's image. This image allows me to say to myself, "More things are possible than meet the eye." Imagine, I can actually change my "familiarity" in a way that enhances my "self."

This same dynamic underlies the popularity of the movie, *Field of Dreams*. Like Superman bending a twisted crowbar back into shape, the Kevin Costner character, by listening to a voice that tells him to level a corn field and build a baseball diamond in its place, can both prove false the criminal allegation against his father's old hero, "Shoeless" Joe Jackson, and "right the old wrong" he himself did to his now deceased father. Moreover, building the baseball field becomes a concrete act of self-definition. The Costner character tells his wife

> I can't think of one good reason why I should build this field, but I'm 36 years old, I have a wife, a child, a mortgage, and I'm scared to death I'm turning into my father. By the time my father was as old as I am now, he was ancient. He must have had dreams, but he never did anything about them. For all I know, he may have heard voices too, but he sure didn't listen to them. The man never did one spontaneous thing

in all the years I knew him. I'm afraid of that happening to me. Something tells me that this may be my last chance to do something about it. I want to build that field.

Although many who saw this film might not remember this exact scene, the emotion that it evokes remains and becomes part of the nonspecific visual image we have of this movie.

Images that represent "standing up against all that" inherently have potential potency. Power and control are dominant themes in human experience. There is little of consequence in human thought that does not contain ways of dealing with power and security.

Emotion with specific representation. A photograph such as the one we saw in newspapers on 6 June 1989 of a Chinese student standing defiantly in the path of approaching tanks during the protests in Tiananmen Square can instantly become a true image. In fact, it did. This and the exploding Challenger space shuttle are the two pictures that appeared in all decade-end pictorial reviews of the 1980s. Articles in *Life, Time,* and *Newsweek,* as well as network programs by NBC and ABC, all included these two picture/images as lead items. Why?

A long-distance picture, shot from the rear of a Chinese student facing an oncoming Army tank in Tiananmen Square. The tank symbolizing the thick-skinned, insensitive "other" who is unfathomably different from me, impenetrable. Unequal power. Impossible odds. Yet the enemy (the "bad" version of me) is confronted. Power and control will not be conceded by the weaker of the two. But the picture is not as simple as that. Many other reflections of the self-structure appear. Two sides of a unity meet in opposition. Both acting on orders: the soldier probably just obeying his commanding officer; the exposed student doing what he must to affirm some subterranean self-definition dictated by the supreme tyrant, the tacit self.

Another example is Christa McAuliffe—woman, mother, wife, teacher, everyperson-as-astronaut (literally, the one who can leave this world and return). We saw her walk out of that preparatory hangar with a commanding stride, head held high. One giant step for each individual. We watched in anxious anticipation. Proud. The next moment, with our heads tilted upward, eyes squinting, face smiling, all we saw were trails of white smoke. The end!

How simple and powerful this image. Death is always the raw material for strong images. Apart from that, the death of Christa

McAuliffe is a portrayal, set against a background of blue sky, of a basic fact of existence we are all trying to ignore: we are constantly at the mercy of events and forces out of our control, even out of our awareness. This is something the tacit self knows all too well.

This idea is perhaps best represented by a character named Mel in Ann Beattie's book, *Picturing Will*. This is from Mel's journal:

> Do everything right, all the time, and your child will prosper. It's as simple as that, except for fate, luck, heredity, chance, the astrological sign under which the child was born, his order of birth, his first encounter with evil, the girl who jilts him in spite of his excellent qualities, the war that is being fought when he is a young man, the drugs he may try once or too many times, the friends he makes, how he scores on tests, how well he endures kidding about his shortcomings, how ambitious he becomes, how far he falls behind, circumstantial evidence, ironic perspective, danger when it is least expected, difficulty in triumphing over circumstance, people with hidden agendas, and animals with rabies.

Photographs that instantaneously become true images extend beyond themselves to envelop the viewer in a kind of self-referring reverie. Pictures like this, by reproducing directly and immediately an unposed experience, provide a shorthand of sensation that register the sheer and brutal fact of existence. This becomes a metaphor by dint of making novel a submerged but felt familiarity, as if seeing it for the first time. The more that photographs like these embody contradictions—the startling and commonplace, corporeal and ghostly, sensual and morbid, beautiful and horrific—the more they open up explorations of the self, and hence the more potent an image they become. These contradictions keep you off balance; you can shift focus and rearrange the pieces. Then in a moment of surprise, the pieces cohere and some self-insight is revealed.

Professional photography of the highest caliber can be said to almost force the viewer, through composition, lighting, camera angle and distance—no matter what the content—to examine a fragment of time as never before. At some level of consciousness, the viewer feels that the photograph possesses a secret; it has in it an implicit narrative about the "self."

The image such a photograph can evoke is almost accidental, a moment of transcendence that manifests itself while the focus is on the mundane.

So we have here a general strategy for tapping into the structure of "self":

1. present a depiction of the self's "tacit knowledge" in such a way that it is felt as familiar and interesting, but not rejected as being too threatening to current self stories;
2. allow the viewer to explore its familiarity but at a different level of experience (in a nonfamiliar way);
3. so that the viewer looks at the familiar as if novel;
4. this informs the viewer's "familiar" in a way that seizes (and possibly extends) his or her definition of "self."

There are many other examples of pictures that have become powerful images because they reflect structures of tacit knowledge that the "self" embodies. Consider the following:

- The young, naked Vietnamese girl running away from a napalm attack (symbolizing the same thing as the Chinese tank, only this time survival is depicted in the form of flight, not fight)
- JFK looking out of the Oval Office window with his back to the camera (his back to the camera, the shadows cast and the low camera angle signifying the loneliness of responsibility and the absoluteness of the "leader")
- The mushroom cloud of a nuclear explosion (symbolic of death, mortality, the "end")
- The fall of the Berlin Wall (Germany as a divided "self" now reintegrated and self-empowered to make up for the past, set free to re-create the original familiarity of wholeness)

It should be noted here, parenthetically, that a verbal description of a metaphorical image simply does not have the power of the image it describes. Words are linear, abstract, cognitive. The power of an image has meaning only in terms of feelings that arise from a different "world" compared to words. The non-substitutability of words for an image is part of its potency.

Survival situations that depict a person's response to eternal contingencies of self-continuity, and that do so with a specificity and frankness that are artfully rendered, are ones predisposed to image creation. These situations, which are the frame for political "photo opportunities," are mythic in nature.

Myth explains the working of the world (it reveals the world as predictable). In the ritual enactment of myth, participants are involved in something transcendent while in the temporal plane.

Myth inspires us to overcome obstacles and loss. Self-empowerment is the goal; good and evil, the main characters. Outcomes are
thought of in terms of destiny. Myth is the objectification of proto-
typic self-other interactions that lie deep in the human spirit. Myth
is a boiling down of the universality of experience as regards the
self-other transaction. The image of death is the origin of myth
(e.g., the Neanderthal funeral caves).

Many of the symbols that are politically significant are overtly
nonpolitical. These symbols are rooted in the human condition of
selfhood and its relation to the power of the "other." Symbols of
life crises or transitions are the ones that are most politically significant: death, initiation of the young (e.g., education), unpredictable misfortune (e.g., the extent and rapidity of governmental
response to hurricane and earthquake devastation), and international relations (e.g., war).

Similarly, from the perspective of the present discussion, the
volatility of issues like abortion and taxes is understandable. Taxes
represent the power of the "other" to arbitrarily take what "I"
think is rightfully mine; taxes diminish me, they are an assault on
the "self." Abortion, by definition, symbolizes dominion over oneself, the tension between my responsibility to myself versus my
responsibility to others, and questions about the meaning of life
(why am I here? who am I?). These issues of identity, self-control,
the balancing act between being separate and belonging are part
and parcel of the structure of "self."

Why are symbols of life crises or transitions so universally
manipulated in politics? The answer is simple: they deal with
problems that are not amenable to scientific solutions. Rather they
pose questions that are complex, often ambiguous, and are too
spiritual in nature for rational explanations to suffice. Hence, they
are just the topics for which images, borne out of their tie to emotionally based self-structures, are naturally employed.

Very loose analogies based on only the "logic" of emotions can
incite images that are as ungraspable as smoke and frayed at the
edges, but rock solid and determinate as far as public opinion. Yet,
as we have seen, images are neither arbitrary nor solely the product of fantasy. Images are infused with luminosity: they possess an
interior radiance that transfixes the imagination by virtue of their
relationship to "self." Once formed, all that matters is immediate
re-cognition (self-congruency), not analysis. Images, by their very
nature, acquire the power of natural fact.

The emotional responsivity involved in the general quality of behavior that underlies approach-avoidance (friend/foe) is a fundamental part of face-to-face social behavior. World leaders, of course, are usually seen only on television. But on television, what do we see? We see *behavior*, close up. We see bodies in motion in what looks like three-dimensional space. Behavior on television not only looks real, it is hyperreal, a fantasy of fact. It is exaggerated, condensed, and simplified. We can easily project our-selves into it. This prettied-up behavior, combined with the peculiar psychological attraction a leader can engender, makes the images that citizens create of president, prime minister, and king all the more primitive and self-referenced.

No matter how a person's self-designed world is put together, it would still be a fragile thing, if not for images. In fact, that world—that "twig hut"—can be blown away with one big huff and a puff. Images of world leaders, products, and other performance figures serve as a technological device, a prosthetic to prop up the "self," to buttress us and provide a resiliency against such a catastrophic insight. Images help us adapt to our vulnerability in the face of adversity. The provision of hope, a feeling of certainty, a defense against loss are the lifeblood of an image. We wear images like a corset. We use them to "hold it all together" so we can walk, chin out and proud—so we can say to ourselves, "I'm all right. I can do it. I'll do it my way. I'll be the mythmaker."

PART V

❦

GROUP PROCESSES

CHAPTER FIFTEEN

REINVENT YOURSELF

LABILE PSYCHOSOCIAL IDENTITY AND THE LIFESTYLE MARKETPLACE

Hiram Caton

> Our premise—the flexibility of human nature—had already been turned to point to a social philosophy of cultural change.
>
> Margaret Mead

> You can fool all the people all the time if the advertising is right and the budget is large enough.
>
> Joseph E. Levine

Introduction

"Indoctrination" is strongly toned by negative affect because Cold War propaganda associated it with the suppression of freedom by totalitarian governments. The propaganda image, common to popular belief and academic studies, depicts indoctrination as a violation of the sanctity of the person, a soul-snatching technique that "dumbs down" individuals and masses to puppets on a string. The indoctrinated person is a victim of false consciousness, alienated to his or her own true "Inner." This view has also been extended to soul-snatching by religious cults.

The opposition propaganda reverses this image. Western Leftists claimed that this depiction is based on a small sample of prisoners of war and political refugees who were tortured and brutalized—in much the same way that police in capitalist countries terrorize their underclasses. But socialist countries did not and could not process hundreds of millions of workers through brainwashing camps. What the bourgeois stigmatized as brainwashing was the spontaneous enthusiasm of the masses for socialism and their solidarity with freedom fighters everywhere. The capitalist slander of socialism distracts attention from the relentless capitalist propaganda and indoctrination in the schools, through the mass media and film, and through advertising. The entire system is wired to brainwash the public to obey bosses, to support capitalist oppression abroad, to keep the underclass powerless.

Now that the Cold War is over, these mock fights may be safely discarded. The prevailing Western concept is flawed in supposing that indoctrination is a new phenomenon deriving from totalitarian government. It is also flawed in not recognizing that indoctrination is nearly always perceived by the indoctrinated as a very positive thing. So positive, indeed, that status is often graded in proportion to thoroughness of indoctrination. This is because indoctrination into a common mind and character is the only means yet discovered to mold individuals into cohesive, coordinated groups capable of carrying out complex operations. It occurs in elite schools, in elite segments of the professions, in molding corporate culture, in trade unions, in pietistic religious communities, in elite military and police units, and so on.

If the belief that indoctrination is a recent development misrecognizes about three millennia of relevant evidence, it does reflect a heightened belief, from around 1900, among commercial and governing elites in the manipulability of the masses, and the ambition of those elites to "improve" society. This ambition was not regime specific: the reformers of Margaret Mead's generation were as committed to it as were fascists and socialists. The literature on Chinese and cult indoctrination, reviewed by Salter in this volume, is a valuable inventory of indoctrination techniques. But they are as old as the pyramids. And in these two cases, they are mere technique detached from productive life. Mao unleashed the Cultural Revolution as a last-ditch effort to salvage his ebbing power from the grasp of party and army elites. In doing so he precipitated civil war, nearly destroyed the governing infrastructure, and set the economy back a decade. Today the Cultural Revolution and Mao's companions in evangelical vandalism are execrated in China. Cults are religious confidence games operated by men (mostly) whose egos crave adulation. In some cases, the narcissist syndrome may be implicated.

My claim that indoctrination is a positive thing refers in the first instance to the positive affect that the acquisition of a strong group identity has on people. It instills pride, energy, commitment, a sense of power and well-being, and operational competence. These rewards create a craving for indoctrination—the tougher, the better, since the capacity to endure hardship and pain are signs of strength. The value of these attributes to mission performance is confirmed by most organizational heads and by organization theorists. Their importance for the evolution of culture cannot be overestimated. Cold War thinking would have it that these traits are wholesome and admirable in ourselves and allies, but odious and fanatical in opponents.

Setting prejudices aside, there remains a serious obstacle to dispassionate study of indoctrination and propaganda. I mean the ineluctable impression of the childishness of it all. The beliefs and attitudes expressed are childish; the emotions approach the infantile; the rituals and games used to give indoctrination effect seem to come straight from the playground. These observations prompt patronizing and exploitative attitudes among practitioners. Thus, an architect of "consent engineering" (advertising), Edward Bernays, believed that the public forms its opinions on the basis of little information and that its reasoning is based wholly on association of images or suggestion (Combs and Nimmo 1993). Once formed, opinions and tastes are "logic-proof," Bernays believed. He advised politicians to substitute pseudoarguments for rational persuasion and to create pseudoevents to dramatize their objectives. "Democracy" is a phrase to lull the herd into believing in its power while the reality is the invisible manipulation of public life by elites. This line of thought could be illustrated indefinitely from observations by practitioners and scholars alike. Lies, hoax, fraud, puffery, twaddle, imposture, madness—these terms constantly recur in the literature. But this unending stream of pulp fiction really is what the public wants (Preston 1975; Schudson 1986). They like melodious babbling. It is soothing to hear "Coke: It's the real thing," and "You can trust your car to the man in the star."

Imitative Learning and Internal Models

There is a saying that to understand the child you must become as a child. One way to implement this advice is to relinquish the ivory tower and reflect on one's childish enthusiasms for sports operas, *The Simpsons*, and sentimental causes. Another way is to spend some hours playing with children and notice what you do. Unless you are a reluctant playmate, you will automatically "dumb down" to mimic the moods and thoughts of the kids.

Adults can communicate with children partly for the same reason that children and adults communicate with animals and animals communicate across species. The common language is the nonsemantic signifiers of basic intentions, such as approach and avoidance, threat, nurture, play, and so on. Beyond that, the more relevant reason, for my purposes, is the elucidation by child development and animal behavior studies of the centrality of imitation to learning. Imitation is the learning process through which the infant acquires its sense of self; the learning process basic to child and adolescent cognitive development; and the primary learning process for the acquisition of roles and of group identity. These studies, which build on the investigations of Jean Piaget, are largely ethological in method and conceptual orientation (Parker, Mitchell and Boccia 1994). They help understand why indoctrination and propaganda achieve such effects as they do, while throwing light on the irrational elements of life.

The lability of the self's psychosocial identity derives from the fact that "self" is not a homogeneous medium but is relational, and in a double sense. First, the infant acquires the capacity to experience self only in relation to "alter." This is a fact of developmental history, but it is also a permanent fixture of all subsequent psychosocial organization. The reason is that ego recognizes self thanks to social mirroring, that is, having one's behavior sent back to oneself (imitated) by alter (Meltzoff 1990; Gopnick and Meltzoff 1994; Watson 1994). One test of this thesis, relevant to mention in this context, is what happens psychosocially when self is deprived of alter, as in solitary confinement. The results are analogous to sensory deprivation—disorientation, hallucinations, and other disturbances known in the prison idiom as "stir crazy." No prison punishment is dreaded more than the ultimate—ostracism.

The second sense in which self is relational is in respect to itself. This relation is called "self-practice." Infants express it in automanipulations of the body and in imitating (mirroring) behaviors expressed by alter. These early behaviors lie in the developmental path to the acquisition of hand-eye coordination, acoustical-visual coordination, and ego-alter emotional and behavioral synchrony. The infants' self-practice develops into a "theory of mind." The theory includes an "internal working model" (IWM) by which it compares actual behavior with intended behavior, e.g., in learning to walk or to play automanipulation games with alter. The IWM operates a feedback loop enabling the infant to observe its own behavior, compare it with the IWM image of self, edit out the flaws, and replay to achieve the desired effect. Goals are for the most part presented by alter as actions that the infant is meant to imitate, e.g., saying bye-bye. Alter may wave her hand, or she may wave baby's hand to show what is wanted. Leaving aside discussion of age thresholds when the infant's cognitive capacities accelerate by leaps, the process is one in which the infant acquires competence to produce a desired effect by modeling in imagination the action to be performed, then rehearsing it (Donald et al. 1993; Freedman and Gorman 1993; Mehler and Dupoux 1994; Parker and Milbrath 1994). This is true of physical control as well as of social interaction. Here are the main points to be distilled from this analysis:

1. Imitative learning occurs through an iterated series of trials, or performed actions, whose goal is the competent performance of a model behavior. The goals and models are acquired by the infant-child through interactions with alter that call up the infant's native psychophysical potential. The spontaneous babbling that is a precursor to language acquisition is an illustration.

2. The activity of imitative learning is play. It is play in the sense of improvisation (trying oneself out to see what happens), in the sense of amusement (infants have a lively sense of humor), and in the sense of "just kidding" (feigning, shamming, hoaxing). Shamming mood states and social interactions is the self-practice that the infant and child rehearse in acquiring social competence. By that I mean the capacity to recognize alter's nonverbal signals of mood state and to reproduce those signals for alter. By the age of three, the child has acquired dexterity in recognizing and producing these elements of communicative competence and is likely to delight in fast-moving Muppets theater. Adults also enjoy Muppets, even though the actors and the props are transparent frauds. The unreality actually enhances the fantasy game.

3. Hoaxing and self-hoaxing are indispensable to building the child's social competence (Groos 1899; Piaget 1951; Fagan 1984;

Parker and Milbrath 1994; Watson 1994). Unlike communication between computers, human communication requires that interactants express their mood states. Thus, greeting exchanges are the ritual opening of communicative mood synchrony. To be socially competent, according to the studies I summarize, means to have the capacity to call up mood states, or signs of them, as occasion requires. (Autism, shock, and mental illness impair this capacity.) The child, in shamming a mood—to terrify alter, for example—is often captured by the sham and breaks the play by becoming really terrified. It may then be said that the child hoaxes itself.

4. The social play of children consists of uninhibited mingling of mood and character imitation (shamming, let's pretend) and actually intended signals. This is why play is so volatile and often results in blows and tears. But children are learning behavioral scripts (characters and roles) whose performance and onset/offset come increasingly under their control. To put it another way, by learning to "role play," they are becoming proficient in mature lying. Children who are very adept in such games become actors, confidence artists, entertainers, moralists, politicians, writers, etc.

5. The child of ten years has memorized many behavioral scripts and can perform them tolerably well as occasion requires. Scripts standardize personal performance for defiance and submission, conscience and transgression, bullying and comforting, exaltation and sadness, reverence and blasphemy. Some of these scripts are detachable, generic roles that can be played in all seasons. Others are specific to personal and social identity.

6. The extensive shamming of games insinuates the standing awareness that identities can be faked. The child uses this competence to lie his or her way out of trouble. But awareness of "serious" psychosocial identity lability occurs during the developmental changes associated with puberty. Adolescents discover stirrings not previously experienced. Sexuality becomes a vast mystery to be explored, anxiously or with passion. There is a growth spurt of physical prowess and associated feeling of power. Constellations of potential new social identities loom in peer bonding. Adolescents learn new social roles, become conscious of competition for status, and play evasion games with teachers and parents. Each has acquired many selves and an awareness of the potential for acquiring more.

Human delight in darting from one self to another leaves its mark everywhere. Consider the soccer tribe. They stream into the grounds wearing the team's colors and waving their banner. Some will don costumes and body decoration that mimics the club's totem. For several hours they go into a frenzy of cheering their side and execrating the opponents. For a moment, the contest is the most important thing in the world. Yet the childish hatred and tribal solidarity are entirely theatrical, that is, a self-hoax. The ritual is respectable so long as it controlled and is confined to the soccer grounds. But it is a rehearsal for war frenzy.

Self-Amplification and Group Identity

It is a fundamental property of culture that the expression of self through roles is enhanced by material signs, such as costumes, body decoration, civic architecture, tombs (Groos 1899; Piaget 1951). They serve both to define the many selves available in a culture and to enlarge the presence of an individual acting a particular role. Many animals are able to enlarge themselves for courtship, sexual competition, and defense. The piloerection of the domestic cat makes it appear twice its actual size. It is a bluff. Similarly, warrior costumes make men appear larger and more ferocious according to animal attributes designed into the costume. Donning the costume is a technique for pumping up the emotions to match the appearance (Eibl-Eibesfeldt 1989). Again, it is a bluff, and it confers no advantage against opponents trained to disregard it.

Techniques for amplifying selves took a prodigious leap with the discovery of photography, radio, and high-speed printing (van Ginneken 1992; Stephenson 1967). Everyone could now be famous for five minutes. Technology created celebrity and public opinion and now, in the age of television and the Internet, has created what Kevin Kelly calls "the hive mind" and what I call "continuous universal imposture" (Kelly 1995). When the natural variation occurring in large populations is combined with a galaxy of representational technologies, there is no end to the variety of selves that may be mimicked, packaged, and marketed. Cosmetic surgery to mask aging, political transvestitism ("sexual equality"), the steroid-built body (to trump the transvestite imposture), telephone and cyberspace sex, and morphed extraterrestrials, all belong to this self-replicating set of virtual realities (Kelly 1995; Rushkoff 1994; Peters 1992). The "hive mind" is in a permanent state of continuously changing piloerections and puffery.

I will illustrate self-amplification by discussing the most highly publicized American political hoax of the 1970s, the abduction of media heiress Patty Hearst, then a nineteen-year-old student at the University of California. She was abducted from her apartment by three members of the Symbionese Liberation Army (SLA), a self-styled revolutionary group. This squad of about eleven middle-class university students, influenced by the heroics of Latin American urban guerrillas, had dedicated themselves to saving the United States from fascism. Within days of her capture in February 1974, the first in a series of audiotapes was received by the media and by Patty's family. It declared the SLA's revolutionary intention and hinted that Patty was a hostage to be exchanged for two "brothers" held in San Quentin prison. In the next tape Patty assured her parents that she was safe and well. She told her father of the SLA's demand that he must supply every Californian on welfare with a week's groceries. This bizarre if colorful demand was met, at a cost of $2.4 million to Mr. Hearst, amidst much confusion. In subsequent tapes Hearst endorsed the SLA's social analysis and denounced her capitalist parents. Headlines called it "brainwashing." Not long after, she participated as an armed accomplice in bank robberies. She remained at large with two other members of the SLA for seventeen months. On her arrest, she was charged with federal offenses. The defense called psychiatric experts on brainwashing to argue in lengthy pretrial hearings for the charges to be dropped, on the grounds that she acted under duress and did not meet the legal definition of a reasonable person. The prosecution's experts testified to the opposite effect. Their point was that Hearst had not availed herself of many opportunities to flee her captors. Neither prosecution nor defense took any notice of the fact that Hearst and her companions in revolution were sky-high from the massive media coverage, which, by reflecting back to them their urban guerrilla identities, validated them. Hearst was tried, convicted, and sentenced to prison. (Her sentence was commuted by President Carter in January 1979.) Meanwhile, the Los Angeles police located the SLA's "safe" house. When the rebels refused to surrender, about 120 local and federal lawmen poured thousands of rounds of small arms fire into the dwelling, killing all six occupants.

On its face, the SLA adventure is just another crime file. The group's potential for harm was no more than other criminal groups of comparable size. Yet the SLA launched itself out of the base-line average into celebrity orbit by adroit public relations.

Abductions are not especially newsworthy (they happen every day), but the abduction of an heiress grabs headlines because socialites weigh more in the public mind than ordinary mortals. The SLA turned a common felony into a propaganda bonanza by making it the launch platform for publicizing their revolutionary aims. That these aims were entirely sham was irrelevant. Here again a statistically average event is rescued from tedium by the SLA's publicity savvy. Self-styled revolutionary groups were at that time graffiti on the social map of crazies. The SLA agenda was indistinguishable from other liberation babbling. But the agenda attracted wide attention thanks to the media drama. The zany threat to overthrow the government acquired serious purport, even at the FBI, simply by becoming an endlessly repeated news item.

But the publicity moon shot was to transform the debutante Miss Patty Hearst into the militant "Tania." This activated the hive's anxiety about Communist soul-snatching. The initial evidence of her conversion, the tapes, was inconclusive. But nine weeks after the abduction, a bank security video photographed her as an armed accomplice in a robbery. The video did not indicate that she was guarded by other SLA members. "Tania" was Tania.

Hearst's conversion involved two transformations commonly associated with brainwashing: altered sociopolitical identity and altered psychosocial identity.

Rejecting capitalism meant switching loyalty to America's Cold War rival. To J. Edgar Hoover and middle America, such a thing has been treason since the first "Red Scare" (1917). Lawyers remonstrated that such attitudes, given force by government agencies or vigilantes, nullified constitutional guarantees of personal freedom. Despite or because of such sanctions, many Americans opted for one or another radical personae. The personal meaning of such an identity change varies with the actions it entails. In Hearst's case, the change appeared to be deep. She rejected friends and associations, and abandoned social and financial security for the risky life of bandit-heroes. It was this that so amazed the middle-America hive, whose weekly lottery tickets testify to its dreams of wealth and status. Patty had these, but threw them away for a life of crime and sleaze! Yet ostentatious dumbing down was then the moral fashion on campuses, especially at Berkeley. By adopting the manners, speech, and dress of the downtrodden, affluent youth symbolically defied aspirations imposed by their parents. Defiance signals anger, and anger needs reasons to argue. The stigma attached to the parent generation was hypocrisy (Rothchild and Wolf 1976). This is a "can't-lose" accusation since everyone over forty has made some morally serious compromises. In this case, the hypocrisy consisted of preaching social equality while practicing accumulation and ego gratification. This translated into a cluster of condemnations of the political system for having abandoned the American dream at home and for supporting fascist despotisms abroad.

Tania's persona included denunciation of her parents and their class values. Rejection of parents and the symbols of parental authority are hallmarks of indoctrination. Bolsheviks, Nazis, Maoists, and numerous cults have used it as a litmus for the transfer of loyalty to the indoctrinating group. The Unification Church, for example, requires acolytes to acknowledge Rev. and Mrs. Moon as their natural parents and moral preceptors; the ostensible natural parents are labeled as impostors sent by the Devil. While the child's repudiation is a grievous blow for parents, it is not a psychosocial marvel. The normal developmental path from adolescence to adulthood includes displacing parental authority by peer affiliation. The tumultuous teenager is a stock type, even in Asian cultures where familial loyalty is paramount. Thus, despite Japan's familial regimentation, identification with left-wing protest formed university sociopolitical identity in the postwar era. In America's urban slums, a high proportion of parents then and now lose control of their offspring to the street culture. To be sure, coming of age usually does not involve denouncing parents in the national media. Yet that ritual was fashionable at the time (in the rollicking phrase from Columbia University: "Up against the wall, motherf**ker!"). In Hearst's case, the bonding that mediated parental denunciation was infatuation with the SLA bandit "Cujo" (Willi Wolfe, the son of a prominent liberal doctor). Patty eventually made up with her parents, as happens with ex-cult members.

Another feature of the SLA's modus operandi was the mixed sex group: half were women. The action groups of the Bolsheviks, IRA, and PLO were all male, because in those cultural groups violence is men's business. Mao's Cultural Revolution shock troops, by contrast, were mixed-sex teenagers; their job, however, was shaming, not shooting. The SLA drew its models from Latin American urban guerrillas, but they might just as well have borrowed from the mainstream symbol factory. In the 1960s, Hollywood invented the androgyne "Rambird." Her career commenced as the pretty pistol-packin' private eye or cop in television series and as the voluptuous man-eaters of James Bond films (Stephenson 1967). SLA women were out to prove themselves as men. To hang back from action was to betray the revolution. Although Patty's upbringing did not include tomboyism or martial arts, risking it with the comrades excited her.

Despite its rump size (about a dozen) and political isolation, the SLA hoaxed law enforcement agencies to take it seriously as a security threat. Three levels of agencies laid siege to the safe house with a quantum of force far beyond what was required to subdue a few unpracticed gunpersons. The cops played to the hilt the role assigned to them by the SLA's script. So did the SLA, for the bandits died the glorious death of revolutionary heroes.

The SLA drama illustrates how indoctrination works in bourgeois societies. The difference between the SLA's actions as private choices and public affairs was the media projection. Without that stage, the choices would have been private fantasy games of no public import. By jumping into the evening news, the SLA commandeered the hive's nervous system. The SLA's guerrilla theater expropriated prime time to market a hot cultural consumer item, the rebellious lifestyle. The abduction, food distribution, and success in defeating the police search for Patty achieved instant brand-name recognition for the SLA. They won some support in the street culture and in radical chic circles, but there was also strong criticism of their amateur tactics. The choice of hostage was a double stroke that placed law enforcement agencies in a supplicant posture while inflicting retributive justice on the exploiting class. Wealth is a token of prestige in market societies. The ransom (the $2.4 million food distribution) humiliated the exploiters while displaying the SLA's taste for serious money. Just as the hive cheers Robin Hood's daring exactions against the Sheriff of Nottingham, so the SLA wrote its script to attract applause for a gratifying transfer of wealth. The Robin Hood legend is a folk instruction about social identity (Knight 1994). It turns the tables on the Sheriff and the authority structure he represents by depicting the bandit as the hero. (In some versions of the legend, the bandit shoots the sheriff and inherits his job.) This was Patty Hearst's experience, as it was the experience of many youths of her generation hungry for an authentic lifestyle, that is, a life in which something was at stake (Hearst 1982). Her Robin Hood was Willie Wolfe, a Berkeley student of her social class who had been converted through his experience working among imprisoned blacks. She said that he was "the gentlest, most beautiful man I've ever known. He taught me the truth as he learned it from the beautiful brothers in California's concentration camps [i.e., prisons]. We loved each other so much, and his love for the people was so deep ... neither Cujo or I had ever loved an individual the way we loved each other ... probably because our relationship wasn't based on fucked-up bourgeois values, attitudes and goals" (Bryan 1975, 126) In telling her story, she acknowledges that the SLA caper was a "romantic dream," but a dream worth dreaming. On release from prison, she merged back into high society.

In ruling that Patty Hearst was responsible for her actions, the court applied standard legal tests for determining that an accused knowingly and freely willed the unlawful act. The tests have ancient roots in common law. They are also deeply embedded in Western cultural traditions, religious and secular, that construct personhood as capable of bearing attributes of impartiality, rational choice, dignity, and the capacity to distinguish right from wrong. That persona, known in common law as the "reasonable person" (formerly "reasonable man") is a legal artifact that tolerably approximates the personae of professional, ethical, vocational, and religious traditions. But the multiplication of selves in the era of continuous and universal imposture strains the concept. Indeed, judicial impartiality itself is under fire as an imposture of patriarchal or racist societies. Lawyers, for their part, undermine or magnify expert testimony as suits their needs, and scientific objectivity is said to be faked infallibility masking prestige competition and material interests. Judges, priests, and savants are perennial models of integrity of self. Today they are, culturally speaking, a bore, since they exclude the thrill of transgression and the excitement of possessing a wardrobe of selves to match each mood or aspiration (Rushkoff 1994). They are also dysfunctional in the nanosecond changes of the modern environment (Peters 1992). Whole industries are dedicated to manufacturing selves. I want to discuss one of them, the motivators.

New Lives for Old: The Motivators

Did you know that you need never again forget a name or a face? That you can break the bad habit that has withstood your New Year's resolutions? That nothing but procrastination stands between you and financial success? That poor self-esteem can be replaced by a positive, winning self-image? That you can acquire wealth to your heart's desire, and at the same time improve all those personal relationships so important in your life? That your potential personal power is unlimited? That all this can be yours effortlessly, right now?

If you did not know these things, you have not met the motivators, a new breed of faith healers. Their annual gross in the United States is $2–5 billion, depending on how you count. The faith they market is belief in your unlimited potential to succeed. At anything. Starting now.

The superstars of the success industry are the Forum Foundation, the Covey Leadership Center, Edward de Bono, Tony Robbins, M. Scott Peck. The founding fathers of the business are Dale Carnegie (*How to Win Friends and Influence People*) and Norman Vincent Peal (*The Power of Positive Thinking*). The influence of these two East Coast religious Brahmans is still visible in some industry sectors, particularly the Covey Center, but the presiding influence is the human potential movement. This movement emerged from therapeutic practice (EST and Esalen) in California in the 1950s, and was marketed to businesses as "sensitivity training" and "T-groups." The pitch to clients was that "team-building" would improve the bottom line by improving the organization's communication, cohesion, self-awareness, and sensitivity to humanistic values (Beer 1980; Milner 1988). Although the prestigious firms that contracted for these services could not often associate them with favorable movements in the bottom line, they nevertheless were part of the trend that slowly replaced the command structure of yesterday with the consensual structures of today.

The industrial T-group package was a toned-down version of the original T-group, which was offered in the therapeutic setting of psychiatric treatment and psychological counseling. In California, the home of humanistic psychology, psychological exotica of a kind never seen in Kansas flourished (Conway and Siegelman 1978; Ferguson 1982). The new psychologists agreed with Freud that hang-ups are expressions of unresolved inner conflicts, but they innovated in two crucial respects. They abandoned Freud's pessimism that ego structure could never be reconciled with the libido. They championed the opposite view that the ego flourished best when sexual desire was openly expressed. To this end, they espoused reform of traditional notions of marriage and family (abolition of the nuclear family was meant, though for practical reasons it was not always said). They also championed group therapy against private therapy. Group therapy mobilizes the psychological force of group esteem and censure and social mirroring of selves in the group as hammers to knock away socially acquired selves that block the full expression of potential. T-groups set up a collective demand (guided by the counselor) that all members of the group come clean with their repressed anger, anxieties, lusts, fantasies. These were confession sessions that became famous as orgies of love and hate (Plumb 1993). But I wish to stress the paradox of group therapy. The objective is to liberate the "True Inner" of each self from socially acquired helplessness (e.g., moral scruples). Yet this can be achieved only through social mirroring. The paradox is resolved in the present analysis by the observation that T-groups are indoctrination vehicles in which participants learn to substitute a set of selves acquired through socialization for another set endorsed by the group (Dawes 1994; Plumb 1993; Ferguson 1982). The unique individuals emerging from sensitivity training are remarkably alike in their tastes, values, and lifestyles. They express ideal personhood as conceived by humanistic psychologists. They are "open," "sensitive," "concerned," "unconventional," "deep." They also have a lifelong counseling dependency. But they do not regard the need to return to the group as a dependency. It is more like their church (Plumb 1993; Samways 1994).

The modus operandi of motivators varies. A few focus on loosening up thinking. Others cover wider territory but draw the line at sex. My investigation suggests, however, that motivation seminars (usually of about two days' duration) are formatted to the basic T-group structure devised by Kurt Lewin (Lewin 1952). It is the "Unfreeze-Move-Refreeze" sequence. Unfreezing thaws aspects of the public persona shared by most people. For example, it is taboo for a stranger to touch, and touch intimately, another, especially in a public gathering. But motivators easily induce this behavior by giving the group limbering up exercises, which includes massaging the shoulders, then the waist, of the person next to them. The Move phase instills the new self-image of unlimited power. The highlight of this phase is "miracles and special effects" (MSE), which are a sort of audience-participation magic show. Miracles in vogue are fire walking, walking on glass, feats of memory, feats of strength performed under hypnosis, banishing fears and phobias, breaking habits, telling off the boss. This phase is highly emotional. It happens thus. The motivator first constructs a group consensus around a group mind. This is easily done. They make themselves into cheerleaders for the success ideal. This commonly expressed achievement goal now becomes a norm for group behavior. Then each individual is put in the "hot seat." They are required to declare before the group what their personal desires are and why they think that they are not achieving them. This personal information is adroitly steered into a confession extracted by the force of group expectation (implicit norm: you can't let down your mates). The scene swings wildly between hilarity and tears. Failure is not permitted (Dawes 1994). Anyone who falls from the ladder has his or her dignity rehabilitated.

The Refreeze segment confirms the new self of unlimited power. This is where the motivator moves into action with his or her scam. If motivators really were the success messiahs that they claim to be, most of those who exit from the seminar would soon be millionaires, not to mention the gratifying weight loss they would achieve. This promise is prominent in promotional material. But if this were true, word of mouth advertising would long since have stampeded hundreds of millions to the seminars. Motivators must instead leave their clients with a surrogate for success that they can clutch like a rosary in the absence of significant change in their personal lives. This surrogate is belief in the unlimited power of the motivator and the groups he or she creates. The psychology is about the same as for secret societies and elite cadres. I call it the belief in "Elect Presence." Secret societies believe that they are the operational unit in the divine plan for humanity. You can't get much more powerful than that. Acceptance of this belief imbues life with meaning and purpose. Instead of the divine plan, motivators talk of the "energy field" or the "new consciousness" in which clients now are oriented. The motivator asks them if they wish to be among the select few in whom unlimited power for good has been unleashed. That power changes their lives, and each going their separate ways will contribute to making the world a better place (Plumb 1993; Ferguson 1982; Hassan 1988). It's an offer one can't refuse, especially when everyone else enthusiastically grasps it. Some motivators reinforce the salvation message by giving each person a secret code, like a personal mantra, that identifies him or her in the army of rising consciousness. All this is credible because the intense, novel emotions of the seminar, collectively experienced, together with the MSE, have made an ineffaceable impression. Something powerful has reached into their lives (comparable to falling in love) and it requires a suitably lofty interpretation. The logic of the teaching leads ineluctably to the conclusion that the motivator is the messiah.

In the absence of controlled studies, there is no way of telling whether personal development courses are a net benefit to clients. The testimonials that motivators splash across full-page ads are the last word in puffery. Here are a few.

> It's hard to put into words how enthusiastic we feel about David Ryan's course. It was one of the greatest experiences of our lives ... we were filled with vitality and enriched with ideas beyond measure with the techniques David taught us.

> Totally awesome!—much more than I ever expected. I came with enthusiasm to learn more. I left with such a high I can't find words to describe the feeling. Unlimited destiny is what I now have the power to bring into my life.

> I am elated ... information has become knowledge, procrastination has yielded to action, fear to courage, lethargy to energy, frustration to enthusiasm, confusion to clarity.

Parading childlike enthusiasm is a standard promo gimmick. Toyota ads feature the jump for joy and the hymned slogan "Oh, what a feeling!" Creative people in advertising explain it by saying that emotions are infectious. The ethological model of communication substitutes for "infection" the concept of mood synchrony. You cannot communicate with the child without provisionally adopting its mood. On the other hand, the adult can gain control of mood by drawing the child into an activity that captures its attention. This the Toyota ad does. David Ryan's testimonials faithfully reflect his success in imparting enthusiasm to clients. The mood becomes self-sustaining when 150 people gush about David Ryan's wisdom. It's like the soccer ground.

Growing up involves developing emotional control. The inner journey launched by motivators—to get in touch with yourself, to change the programming of the unconscious—is a regression to childhood emotional lability and to spontaneity of feeling. It can be deeply satisfying to expose private thoughts, to weep and rejoice openly and in synchrony with others. Theater achieves this catharsis by a controlled, feigned exhibition of deeply felt emotions. In motivation seminars, however, clients become actors in a therapeutic vehicle that humanistic psychology calls "psychodrama." At the end of the drama they are elated, ecstatic, on a high. Elevated mood states are not an auspicious climate for making important decisions, since absorption in a rapturous vision depresses the discursive examination of facts relevant to the decision. Motivators encourage decision-making in a state of rapture (they call it "being clear"!) because they fuse the success goal with bold self-change and a permanent high. This linkage is the psychology of innumerable ads. Buy a Toyota and Oh, what a feeling.

In the absence of a controlled study, the results of decision-making under the influence of rapture is known only anecdotally. Here is a typical, bad outcome.

A successful executive programs himself for the instruction to be "clear" about his objectives and consistent in carrying them out. The emotional upheaval of his session in the "hot seat" made it "clear" to him that he is being "held back" by his wife. Accepting the logic of "clarity," he peremptorily tells her after the seminar that he will file for divorce. She is incredulous, but he shatters her affection with personal abuse. At work he decides that from now on he will act like an executive. He does some plain talking to the CEO and fellow vice presidents. Within weeks the boss terminates his employment. He interprets the failure as a sign that the "cosmic energy" (the IWM of the motivator) wants him to start his own business. He pours his savings into a venture that fails within six months. The family is destitute. He scratches together the money to attend another motivation seminar (Samways 1994).

A comparison between motivator and cult indoctrination psychology would reveal many similarities. One is the Unfreeze-Move-Refreeze indoctrination template. Another is the conviction of Elect Presence. Steven Hassan, who became a cult "deprogrammer" after his exit from the Unification Church, said that his decision to commit to the "Moonies" occurred under the influence of the "incredible elation" of feeling that he had been chosen by God. "I thought my every action had monumental historical significance" (Hassan 1988, 22).

The persona that chose Hassan was the IWM of alter that the Moonies skillfully install in recruits. There is no doubt that the IWM of alter can do the sort of thing that Hassan experienced. Motivators, by contrast, come from the opposite side of the structure of consciousness. They manipulate ego's IWM of the aspirational self. In consumer societies this IWM is strongly formed by the ubiquitous advertising for products and services that help you become whatever self you choose to be (Peters 1992; Schudson 1986; Wolf 1991). Without this toad-to-prince fairy tale, motivators' potential client pool would be rather smaller than it is. Motivators promote the belief that they are the fairy whose magic wand will effect this transformation. The wand is the belief that life outcomes are determined by motivation and associated mind control. Talent, chance, health states, and so on are not independent of the will. The irony is that the IWM conscience installed in clients' minds during seminars is the imago of the motivator. Whether they succeed or not, they need to come back to him. The "unlimited power" they acquire is dependency on the motivator-therapist.

References

Beer, M. (1980). *Organizational change and development: A systems view.* Goodyear, Santa Monica.

Bryan, J. (1975). *This soldier still at war.* Harcourt, Brace, Jovanovich, New York.

Combs, J. E. and Nimmo, D. (1993). *The new propaganda: The dictatorship of palaver in contemporary politics.* Longman, New York.

Conway, F. and Siegelman, J. (1978). *Snapping: America's epidemic of sudden personality change.* Lippincott, Philadelphia.

Dawes, R. M. (1994). *House of cards: Psychology and psychotherapy built on myth.* Free Press, New York.

Donald, M. et al. (1993). Précis of origins of the modern mind: Three stages in the evolution of culture and cognition. *Behavioral and Brain Sciences,* 16, 737–91.

Eibl-Eibesfeldt, I. (1989). *Human ethology.* Aldine, New York.

Fagan, R. (1984). Play and behavioral flexibility. In *Play in animals and humans* (ed. Peter K. Smith), pp. 159–74. Blackwell, New York.

Ferguson, M. (1982). *The Aquarian conspiracy: Personal and social transformation in the 1980's.* Paladin, London.

Freedman, D. G. and Gorman, J. (1993). Attachment and transmission of culture—an evolutionary perspective. *Journal of Social and Evolutionary Systems,* 16, 297–329.

Gopnick, A. and Meltzoff, A. N. (1994). Minds, bodies and persons: Young children's understanding of the self and others as reflected in imitation and theory of mind research. In *Self-awareness in animals and humans: Developmental perspectives* (ed. Sue Taylor Parker, Robert W. Mitchell, and Maria L. Boccia), pp. 166–86. Cambridge University Press, New York.

Groos, K. (1899). *Die Spiele der Menschen.* Gustav Fischer, Jena.

Hassan, S. (1988). *Combatting cult mind control.* Park Street Press, Rochester, Vt.

Hearst, P. (1982) *Every secret thing.* Methuen, London.

Kelly, K. (1995). *Out of control: The new biology of machines.* Fourth Estate, London.

Knight, S. (1994). *Robin Hood: A complete study of the English outlaw.* Blackwell, Oxford.

Lewin, K. (1952). Group decision and social change. In *Readings in social psychology* (ed. G. E. Swanson, T. M. Newcomb, and E. L. Harley), pp. 459–73. Holt, New York.

Mehler, J. and Dupoux, E. (1994). *What infants know: The new cognitive science of early development.* Blackwell, Oxford.

Meltzoff, A. N. (1988). Imitation, objects, tools, and the rudiments of language in human ontogeny. *Human Evolution*, 3, 45–64.

Milner, J. B. (1988). *Organizational behavior: Performance and productivity*. Random House, New York.

Parker, S. T., Mitchell, R. W., and Boccia, M. L. (1994). Expanding dimensions of the self: Through the looking glass and beyond. In *Self-awareness in animals and humans: Developmental perspectives* (ed. S. T. Parker, R. W. Mitchell, and M. L. Boccia), pp. 3–19. Cambridge University Press, New York.

Peters, T. (1992). *Liberation management: Necessary disorganisation for the nanosecond minutes*. Macmillan, London.

Piaget, J. (1951). *Play, dreams, and imitation in childhood*. Norton, New York.

Plumb, L. D. (1993). *A critique of the human potential movement*. Garland, New York.

Preston, I. L. (1975). *The great American blow-up: Puffery in advertising and selling*. University of Wisconsin Press, Madison.

Rothchild, J. and Wolf, S. (1976) *The children of the counterculture*. Doubleday, New York.

Rushkoff, D. (1994). *Media virus! Hidden agendas in popular culture*. Random House, New York.

Samways, L. (1994). *Dangerous persuaders: An expose of gurus, personal development courses and cults, and how they operate in Australia*. Penguin, Ringwood, Vic.

Schudson, M. (1986). *Advertising, the uneasy persuasion*. Basic Books, New York.

Stephenson, W. (1967) *The play theory of mass communication*. University of Chicago Press, Chicago.

van Ginneken, J. (1992). *Crowds, psychology and politics 1871-1899*. Cambridge University Press, Cambridge.

Watson, J. S. (1994). Detection of self: The perfect algorithm in self-awareness. In *Self-awareness in animals and humans: Developmental perspectives* (ed. S. T. Parker, R. W. Mitchell, and M. L. Boccia), pp. 131–65. Cambridge University Press, New York.

Wolf, N. (1991). *The beauty myth: How images of beauty are used against women*. Viking, New York.

CHAPTER SIXTEEN

INDOCTRINATION AND GROUP EVOLUTIONARY STRATEGIES

THE CASE OF JUDAISM

Kevin MacDonald

It must not be forgotten that although a high standard of morality gives but a slight or no advantage to each individual man and his children of the same tribe, yet an increase in the number of well-endowed men and advancement in the standard of morality will certainly give an immense advantage to one tribe over another. A tribe including many members who, possessing in a high degree the spirit of patriotism, fidelity, obedience, courage, and sympathy, who were always ready to aid one another, and to sacrifice themselves for the common good, would be victorious over most other tribes; and this would be natural selection.

Charles Darwin, *The Descent of Man and Selection in Relation to Sex*

Indoctrination is a phenomenon that occurs within groups and, as a result, raises fundamental evolutionary questions regarding the relationship between the individual and the group. It has long been apparent to evolutionists that highly cohesive, altruistic groups would outcompete concatenations of individualists. The purpose of this chapter will be to develop the idea of a group evolutionary strategy and to support the contention that indoctrinability is an adaptation that facilitates the development of such groups. With few exceptions, the data relevant to these theoretical interests will be drawn from historical and contemporary Jewish communities (see also MacDonald 1994).

For purposes of this chapter, a group is defined as a discrete set of individuals that is identifiably separate from other individuals (who themselves may or may not be members of groups). Groups become interesting to an evolutionist when there are active attempts to segregate the group from the surrounding peoples, a situation that results in what Erikson (1966) termed "cultural pseudospeciation" (see discussion by Eibl-Eibesfeldt 1979, 122). Creating a group evolutionary strategy results in the possibility of cultural group selection resulting from between-group competition in which the groups are defined by culturally produced ingroup markings (Richerson and Boyd 1995). Theoretically, group strategies are underdetermined and unnecessary. A group evolutionary strategy may be conceived as an "experiment in living" rather than the outcome of natural selection acting on human populations or the result of ecological contingencies acting on universal human genetic propensities.

In the case of Jews, in traditional societies there was a wide range of actively sought marks of separateness from surrounding peoples (MacDonald 1994). Factors facilitating separation of Jews and Gentiles have included religious practice and beliefs; distinctive languages, such as Yiddish, Hebrew, and Ladino; mannerisms (e.g., gestures); physical appearance (hair styles) and clothing; customs (especially the dietary laws); occupations that were dominated by the group; and living in physically separated areas that were administered by Jews according to Jewish civil and criminal law. All of these practices can be found at early stages of the diaspora, and in the ancient world there were a large number of prohibitions that directly limited social contacts between Jews and Gentiles, such as the ban on drinking wine touched by Gentiles or the undesirability of bantering with Gentiles on the day of a pagan festival in the Greco-Roman world of antiquity. Perhaps the most basic badges of group membership and separateness, appearing in the Pentateuch, are circumcision and the practice of the Sabbath.

Given this actively sought separation, there is the possibility that there will be genetic differences between Jewish and Gentile populations that are maintained over long stretches of historical time. There is considerable evidence for gene frequency differences between Jewish populations and populations they have lived among for centuries (e.g., Carmelli and Cavalli-Sforza 1979; Kobylianski et al. 1982; see MacDonald 1994 for a review). Moreover, there is little doubt that over long stretches of historical time there was little genetic admixture, due to the functioning of the segregative mechanisms described previously but also due to negative attitudes regarding intermarriage and proselytism (see MacDonald 1994).

A dispersed group that actively maintains genetic and cultural segregation from surrounding societies must develop methods to ensure social cohesion and prevent defection. Fundamental to Jewish group integrity over historical time have been social controls and ideologies that depend ultimately on human abilities to monitor and enforce group goals, to create ideological structures that rationalize group aims both to group members and to outsiders, and to indoctrinate group members to identify with the group and its aims.

Social controls on group members are central to group evolutionary strategies. Social controls can range from subtle effects of group pressure on modes of dressing to laws or social practices that result in large penalties to violators (Campbell 1979; Salter 1995). Recently Robert Boyd and Peter Richerson (1992) have shown that punishment can result in the stability of altruism or any other group attribute (and see Eibl-Eibesfeldt 1982). In the case of human groups, punishment that effectively promotes altruism and inhibits nonconformity to group goals can be effectively carried out as the result of culturally invented social controls on the behavior of group members. Thus, while it may well be that group-level evolution is relatively uncommon among animals due to their limited abilities to prevent cheating, human groups are able to regulate themselves via social controls so that theoretical possibilities regarding invasion by selfish types from surrounding human groups or from within can be eliminated or substantially reduced.

Facilitating altruism by punishing nonaltruists can be viewed as a special case of the general principle that social controls can act to promote group interests that are in opposition to individual self-interest. Group strategies must typically defend themselves against "cheaters" who benefit from group membership but fail to conform to group goals. Human societies are able to institute a wide range of social controls that effectively channel individual behavior, punish potential cheaters and defectors, and coerce individuals to be altruistic.

Besides social controls, group strategies also are typically characterized by elaborate ideological structures that rationalize group goals and behavior within the group and to out-group members.

By far the most important form of such ideology in human history is what we term religion, and in the following it will be apparent that indoctrination into Judaism as a group evolutionary strategy involved the inculcation of religious beliefs that rationalized behavior essential to the group strategy.

Indoctrination into the Group Ethic of Judaism

Judaism has been able to retain a high level of group cohesion and within-group altruism over a long period of historical time, at least partly because of social controls acting within the group that served to penalize nonaltruists and noncooperators, while cooperative altruists were ensured a high level of social prestige (MacDonald 1994). Nevertheless, social controls do not appear to be the whole story. If only social controls were involved, Judaism or any similar group evolutionary strategy would be a sort of police state in which the only motivations for socially prescribed behavior would be fear of the negative consequences of noncompliance.

However, it is difficult to imagine that such a group would long endure, and, in any case, a salient feature of historical Judaism has been the indoctrination of individuals into psychological acceptance of group aims. One area of psychological research relevant to conceptualizing the role of indoctrination in group evolutionary strategies such as traditional Judaism is that of research on individualism/collectivism (see Triandis 1990; 1991 for reviews). Collectivist cultures (and Triandis 1990, 57 explicitly includes Judaism in this category) place a high emphasis on the goals and needs of the in-group rather than on individual rights and interests. In-group norms and the duty to cooperate and submerge individual goals to the needs of the group are paramount. Collectivist cultures develop an "unquestioned attachment" to the in-group, including "the perception that in-group norms are universally valid (a form of ethnocentrism), automatic obedience to in-group authorities, and willingness to fight and die for the in-group. These characteristics are usually associated with distrust of and unwillingness to cooperate with out-groups" (55).

Socialization in collectivist cultures stresses group harmony, conformity, obedient submission to hierarchical authority, and honoring parents and elders. There is also a major stress on in-group loyalty as well as trust and cooperation within the in-group. Each of the in-group members is viewed as responsible for every other member. However, relations with out-group members tend to be "distant, distrustful, and even hostile" (Triandis 1991, 80). In collectivist cultures morality is conceptualized as that which benefits the in-group, and aggression towards and exploitation of outgroups are acceptable (Triandis 1990, 90).

As with all collectivist cultures (Triandis 1990; 1991), Judaism depends on inculcating a powerful sense of group identification. Triandis (1989, 96) proposes that identification with an in-group is increased under the following circumstances: membership is rewarding to the individual; in-groups are separated by signs of distinctiveness; there is a sense of common fate; socialization emphasizes in-group membership; in-group membership is small; the in-group has distinctive norms and values. In addition, evolutionists (see Johnson 1986; Eibl-Eibesfeldt 1972) have emphasized that socialization for in-group membership often includes an emphasis on the triggering of kin recognition mechanisms (such as references to the kinship nature of the group; e.g., "fatherland"; "the Jewish people") and phenotypic similarity (such as similar dress and mannerisms). Operant and classical conditioning are often used, as when individuals are publicly rewarded for group allegiance and altruism.

All of these mechanisms have undoubtedly been present within historical Jewish communities. I have noted the prevalence of external signs of separateness from Gentiles among Jews in traditional societies, including language, clothing, and mannerisms. In the present context, these signs serve to enhance the phenotypic similarity of the in-group and mark off a distinctive set of in-group norms and values. Moreover, the goal of education in traditional societies was to promote the consciousness of separateness from out-groups and a sense of common fate among widely dispersed Jewish groups stretching forward and backward in historical time.

These trends can be seen clearly in historical Jewish communities as well as among contemporary Hasidic and Orthodox Jewish groups. Kamen (1985) notes that the Hasidim are concerned about contamination from the secular culture and work very hard to minimize their children's contact with or even awareness of the wider culture. Similar to all Jewish societies prior to the Enlightenment, there are a great many markers of in-group status, including speaking a Jewish language (in this case, Yiddish), distinctive modes of dress, and distinctive Jewish names (Kamen 1985, 43). A young Hasidic man commented that "I call my clothing a personal weapon because if I am tempted to do something which by law is not right, one look at myself, my hat, my coat, my tstitsis reminds me who I am. Nobody is there to see except me, and believe me that's enough" (in Kamen 1985, 88–89). The last part of the quote is particularly significant: this individual is clearly following the law not because of fear of negative sanctions by the community, but because he completely accepts the psychological desirability of doing so.

Education is of course extremely important, but a major goal in the Hasidic community is group enculturation rather than imparting subject matter (Mayer 1979). Television and other means of integrating with the wider culture are forbidden so that the child is simply not exposed to these influences. In addition, there are numerous holidays that are utilized in the school curriculum as a means of discussing particular events important in Jewish history or religious practice.

Critical to Jewish indoctrination have been practices whereby, from a very early age, individuals are placed in situations where group activities involve positive experiences of great emotional intensity. These experiences are perhaps analogous to the phenomenon of "love-bombing" as an aspect of indoctrination in religious cults (see Salter's chapter in this volume), except that this type of indoctrination begins at an early age and continues throughout life. In the traditional shtetl communities of Eastern Europe, beginning at birth children were socialized not simply as an individual or as a family member but as a member of the entire community. The child's birth was celebrated by the entire community, and there were special roles for children in a variety of religious events. Thus at the Passover celebration, the youngest child asks the Passover questions, "quivering with excitement" (Zborowski and Herzog 1952, 387). The elaborate ceremony functions to make the child very aware of the intimate connection of the child to the family and the family to the wider group of Jews extending backward in historical time. Another holiday, Lag ba Omer, is given over entirely to the pleasures of children, and a prominent part of Hanukkah is when children go around to relatives to receive money. The boy's bar mitzvah is fundamentally a ceremony marking the child's new relationship to the group (Zborowski and Herzog 1952, 351).

Positive group experiences continue into adulthood. Among the Hasidim studied by Kamen (1985), group meetings and positively valanced social events are common. There are weekly meetings of the males (the tish) at which the children participate in group singing. After the singing, there is a discourse on the Torah, followed by singing and dancing. Group dancing by males is particularly striking and also occurs at weddings and other social events. The men join arms and dance together in an atmosphere of great joy and excitement—a clear indication of the powerful, positive affective forces joining together members of the group. At these social events children are introduced in a very positive manner to group membership.

Synagogue services were also a positive group experience in traditional Jewish society. Zborowski and Herzog (1952, 54) note the swaying and communal chanting as a prominent aspect of synagogue services in the traditional European shtetl communities:

> The whole room is a swaying mass of black and white, filled with a tangle of murmur and low chantings, above which the vibrant voice of the cantor rises and falls, implores and exults, elaborating the traditional melodies with repetitions and modulations that are his own. The congregation prays as one, while within that unity each man as an individual speaks directly to God.

In addition to positive experiences that foster extremely positive attitudes toward the group, there are also negative sanctions on failure to conform to group goals. Conformity to group attitudes and behavior is an important aspect of social control in traditional Jewish communities. "A sense of correct behavior, Hasidishe behavior, takes precedence over individual deviations. Indulgence in contrary behavior is not tolerated by the group; the majority acts quickly to reprimand any member whose demeanor reflects negatively on his comrades" (Kamen 1985, 82–83).

Mayer (1979, 136ff, 141–2) also describes elaborate mechanisms of social control within the Orthodox community that spring into action to oppose any sign of nonconformity, such as a yarmulke that is too small or too brightly colored or a hemline that is too high. Zborowski and Herzog (1952, 226–7), writing of traditional European shtetl societies, also document elaborate mechanisms that ensure conformity within the community. People are greatly concerned about the good opinions of others. Everyone knows everything there is to know about everyone else, and withdrawal and secrecy are seen as intolerable.

Indoctrination also involves negatively valanced procedures akin to hazing as emphasized in Salter's chapter in this volume. After bar mitzvah and for approximately seven years until marriage, the boys spend 16 hours per day with their peer group, including communal breakfast, communal ritual baths, communal studying and prayer. At this age, studying itself is done with a great deal of emotion. Accounts indicate considerable sleep deprivation and a great deal of pressure to perform well within the peer group. The boys/men of this age are expected to relate primarily to the peer group, and if a child spends too much time at home, his behavior reflects poorly on himself and his family.

Efforts to socialize children and adults to the group are also apparent in much less traditional Jewish groups. Judaism in contemporary American society is best viewed as a civil religion (Woocher 1986), and, perhaps because of the lessening prevalence of many of the traditional segregating mechanisms that have facilitated group cohesion over the centuries, the civil religion goes to great lengths to prevent group defection, especially by attempting to strengthen Jewish education. Those who do defect are simply written off, and group continuity and integrity are maintained by a central core of highly committed individuals. Because of the assimilatory pressures from the surrounding society, great importance is placed on "the recognition of Jewish education as the most vital element in the preservation of the Jewish people" (Woocher 1986, 34; see also Elazar 1980, 211).

Jewish identification is actively facilitated by encouraging trips to Israel by high school and college students, and, indeed, Elazar terms Israel "the central focus of American Jewish educational effort" (291). Woocher (1986, 150) notes that the trips to Israel are often overlaid with "mythic" overtones from Jewish history (e.g., visits to Holocaust memorials), and have as their goal increased commitment to a Jewish identification on the part of the visitors. The retreats function as a sort of religious experience that attempts to effect attitude change by removing participants from their normal lives; by emphasizing group-oriented activities and a sense of community, nostalgia and "specialness"; and by renewing commitment to group identification and group goals (151–2).

Social Identity Consequences of Indoctrination

As a prelude to developing an evolutionary theory of indoctrinability, I will first consider the expected consequences of the indoctrination practices described above in terms of social identity theory (see Hogg and Abrams 1987 for a review). Social identity theory proposes that individuals engage in a process whereby they place themselves and others in social categories. Clearly a major effect of the indoctrination procedures described above is to highlight the salience of in-group membership to those being indoctrinated. From the standpoint of social identity theory, there are several important consequences of this process.

The social categorization process results in discontinuities such that individuals exaggerate the similarities of individuals within each category (the accentuation effect). Thus, there is a psychological basis for supposing that, given the highly salient cultural separatism characteristic of Judaism, both Jews and Gentiles would sort others into the category "Jew" or "Gentile" and would exaggerate the similarity of members within each category. By this mechanism, people reconceptualize continuous distributions as sharply discontinuous; the effect is particularly strong if the dimension is of importance to the categorizer. In the case of intergroup conflict, the dimensions are in fact likely to be imbued with great subjective importance.

Moreover, the individual also places himself or herself into one of the categories (an in-group), with the result that similarities between self and in-group are exaggerated and dissimilarities with out-group members are exaggerated. An important result of this self-categorization process is that individuals adopt behavior and beliefs congruent with the stereotype of the in-group.

Social identity research indicates that the stereotypic behavior and attitudes of the in-group are positively valued, while out-group behavior and attitudes are negatively valued. Thus, the homogenization of the behavior of in-groups and out-groups has strong affective overtones, and individuals develop favorable attitudes toward in-group members and unfavorable attitudes toward out-group members. In-group and out-group members are both expected to develop highly negative attitudes regarding the behavior of members of the other group and generally to fail to attend to individual variation among members of the other group. The in-group develops a positive distinctness, a positive social identity, and increased self-esteem as a result of this process. Within the group there is a great deal of cohesiveness, positive affective regard, and camaraderie, while relationships outside the group can be hostile and distrustful.

Social identity theorists propose that the primary affective mechanism involved in social identity processes is self-esteem and that, indeed, the need to achieve a positive self-evaluation via this social categorization process functions as a theoretical primitive. Individuals maximize the differences between in-group and out-group in a manner that accentuates the positive characteristics of the in-group. They do so precisely because of this (theoretically) primitive need to categorize themselves as a member of a group with characteristics that reflect well on the group as a whole and therefore on themselves individually. For example, Gitelman (1990, 8), describing Jewish identity processes in the former Soviet Union, noted that Jews developed a great curiosity about Jewish history "not merely from a thirst for historical knowledge, but from a need to locate oneself within a group, its achievements, and its fate. It is as if the individual's own status, at least in his own eyes, will be defined by the accomplishments of others who carry the same label. 'If Einstein was a Jew, and I am a Jew, it does not quite follow that I am an Einstein, but....'"

Further, people easily adopt negative stereotypes about out-groups, and these stereotypes possess a great deal of inertia (i.e., they are slow to change and are resistant to countervailing examples). Resistance to change is especially robust if the category is one that is important to the positive evaluation of the in-group or the negative evaluation of the out-group. It would be expected that people would be more likely to change their categorization of the hair color of out-group members on the basis of counterexamples of a stereotype than they would change their categorization of out-group members as stupid or lazy or dishonest.

The results of these categorization processes are group behavior that involves discrimination against the out-group and in favor of the in-group; beliefs in the superiority of the in-group and inferiority of the out-group; and positive affective preference for the in-group and negative affect directed toward the out-group. Although groups may be originally dichotomized on only one dimension (e.g., Jew/Gentile), there is a tendency to expand the number of dimensions on which the individuals in the groups are categorized and to do so in an evaluative manner.

Thus a Jew would be expected not only to sharply distinguish between Jews and Gentiles, but to come to view Gentiles as characterized by a number of negative traits (e.g., stupidity, drunkenness), while Jews would be viewed as characterized by corresponding positive traits (e.g., intelligence, sobriety).

> A series of contrasts is set up in the mind of the shtetl child, who grows up to regard certain behavior as characteristic of Jews, and its opposite

as characteristic of Gentiles. Among Jews he expects to find emphasis on intellect, a sense of moderation, cherishing of spiritual values, cultivation of rational, goal-directed activities, a "beautiful" family life. Among Gentiles he looks for the opposite of each item: emphasis on the body, excess, blind instinct, sexual license, and ruthless force. The first list is ticketed in his mind as Jewish, the second as goyish. (Zborowski and Herzog 1952, 152)

As expected, Zborowski and Herzog (1952, 152) find that this world view was then confirmed by examples of Gentile behavior that conformed to the stereotype, as when Gentiles suddenly rose up and engaged in a murderous pogrom against the Jews. There was also a clear sense that the attributes of the in-group are superior qualities, and those of the out-group are inferior. Jews valued highly the attributes on which they rated themselves highly and viewed the characteristics of Gentiles in a negative manner. There was a general air of superiority to Gentiles. Jews returning from Sabbath services "pity the barefoot goyim, deprived of the Covenant, the Law, and the joy of Sabbath ...' We thought they were very unfortunate. They had no enjoyment ... no Sabbath ... no holidays ... no fun ...' 'They'd drink a lot and you couldn't blame them, their lives were so miserable.'"

The negative attitudes were fully reciprocated. Zborowski and Herzog note that both Jews and Gentiles referred to the other with imagery of specific animals, implying that the other was subhuman. When a member of the other group dies, the word used is the word for the death of an animal. Each would say of one's own group that they "eat," while members of the other group "gobble." "The peasant will say, 'That's not a man, it's a Jew.' And the Jew will say, 'That's not a man, it's a goy'" (1952, 157).

There was thus a powerful tendency toward reciprocity of negative attitudes and stereotypes. Stories about the other group would recount instances of deception (157), and everyday transactions would be carried on with a subtext of mutual suspicion. "There is beyond this surface dealing, however, an underlying sense of difference and danger. Secretly each [Jewish merchant and Gentile peasant] feels superior to the other, the Jew in intellect and spirit, the 'goy' in physical force—his own and that of his group. By the same token each feels at a disadvantage opposite the other, the peasant uneasy at the intellectuality he attributes to the Jew, the Jew oppressed by the physical power he attributes to the goy" (Zborowski and Herzog 1952, 67). While the documentation is not always as explicit as that provided in the case of Poland, there is a convincingly large body of evidence across numerous societies indicating that reciprocal hostility between Jew and Gentile tends to arise for most or perhaps all combinations of Judaism and Gentile socioreligious tradition (for Sephardic and Romaniote Jews, see Shaw 1991; for Sephardic Jews in Spain prior to the expulsion, see Neuman 1969/1942; for contemporary fundamentalist Judaism, see Heilman 1992).

An Evolutionary Interpretation of Social Identity Processes and Collectivism

The empirical results of social identity research are highly compatible with an evolutionary basis for group behavior. Vine (1987) notes that the evidence supports the universality of the tendency to view one's own group as superior. Moreover, social identity processes occur very early in life, prior to explicit knowledge about the out-group (Hogg and Abrams 1987). An evolutionary interpretation of these findings is also supported by results indicating that social identity processes occur among advanced animal species such as chimpanzees. Van der Dennen (1991, 237) proposes, on the basis of his review of the literature on human and animal conflict, that advanced species have "extra-strong group delimitations" based on affective mechanisms. Among humans, one affective mechanism may well be the self-esteem mechanism central to social identity theory. Another positive emotion revealed by research on religious cults is the profound sense of relief that individuals experience when they join these highly collectivist, authoritarian groups (see Galanter 1989a). However, successful socialization into a highly cohesive group would also be expected to lead to feelings of guilt at the possibility of failure to conform to group goals. These latter mechanisms, although not considered by social identity theorists, would result in strong positive feelings associated with group membership and feelings of guilt and distress at the prospect of defecting from the group.

The powerful affective components involved in social identity processes are difficult to explain except as an aspect of the evolved machinery of the human mind. I have noted the powerful tendency to seek self-esteem via social identity processes as a theoretical primitive in the system. As Hogg and Abrams (1987, 73) note, this result cannot be explained in terms of purely cognitive processes, and a learning theory seems hopelessly ad hoc and gratuitous. The tendencies for humans to place themselves in social categories and for these categories to assume immense affective and evaluative overtones involving the emotions of self-esteem, relief, distress, and guilt are the best candidates for the biological underpinnings of participation in highly cohesive collectivist groups.

Also, the fact that social identity processes and tendencies toward collectivism increase during times of resource competition and threat to the group (see Hogg and Abrams 1987; Triandis 1990; 1991) suggests that these processes involve facultative mechanisms that emerged as a result of selection at the level of the group. As emphasized by evolutionists such as Alexander (1979) and Johnson (1995), external threat tends to reduce internal divisions and maximize perceptions of common interest among group members. This perspective is compatible with Wilson and Sober's (1994) proposal of group-selected psychological mechanisms that facilitate group goals on a facultative basis, i.e., in response to specific contingencies. Under conditions of external threat, there is an increase in cooperative and even altruistic behavior. I propose that external threat is a situation that elicits an evolved facultative tendency to identify more strongly with the group and to submerge individual interests to group interests. (As Wilson and Sober 1994 emphasize, such mechanisms do not imply conflict between individual and group goals: individuals engaging in altruistic or other types of group-oriented behavior may continue to monitor their individual self-interest. The point is that the group becomes the unit of selection.)

This perspective implies that the awareness of anti-Semitism would tend to foster a sense of group identity and social cohesion in the face of threat—the "common fate" or "shared enemy" syndrome studied by psychologists (Berkowitz 1982; Hogg and Abrams 1987). Feldman (1993, 43) finds robust tendencies toward heightened Jewish identification and rejection of Gentile culture consequent to anti-Semitism at the very beginnings of Judaism in the ancient world and throughout Jewish history. Historically, anti-Semitism and the perception of anti-Semitism have been potent tools for rallying group commitment and for legitimizing the continuity of Judaism (e.g., Hertzberg 1995; Schorsch 1972, 121, 207–8; Woocher 1986, 46).

A permanent sense of imminent threat appears to be common among Jews, and, as indicated above, such a threat would be expected to enhance commitment to the group. Writing on the clinical profile of Jewish families, Herz and Rosen (1982) note that for Jewish families a "sense of persecution (or its imminence) is part of a cultural heritage and is usually assumed with pride. Suffering is even a form of sharing with one's fellow Jews. It binds Jews with their heritage—with the suffering of Jews throughout history." This comment indicates once again the importance of a sense of common fate and historical continuity to Jewish identification. Zborowski and Herzog (1952, 153) note that the homes of wealthy Jews in traditional Eastern European shtetl communities often had secret passages for use in times of anti-Semitic pogroms, and that their existence was "part of the imagery of the children who played around them, just as the half-effaced memory was part of every Jew's mental equipment."

This evolved response to external threat is often manipulated by authorities attempting to inculcate a stronger sense of group identification. Thus Heller (1988, 135) notes that a prominent feature of Soviet propaganda throughout its history was the inculcation of the belief that the Soviet Union was a "besieged fortress." "In a besieged fortress it is essential to fear and to hate the external enemy, who has surrounded the stronghold, is undermining the walls and threatening your 'home' and your life."

The inculcation of a siege mentality also appears to be an aspect of contemporary Judaism. Within this world-view, the Gentile world is conceptualized as fundamentally hostile, with Jewish life always on the verge of ceasing to exist entirely. "Like many other generations of Jews who have felt similarly, the leaders of the polity who fear that the end may be near have transformed this concern into a survivalist weapon" (Woocher 1986, 73). Thus, for example, Woocher notes that there has been a major effort since the 1960s to have American Jews visit Israel in an effort to strengthen Jewish identification, with a prominent aspect of the visit being a trip to a border outpost "where the ongoing threat to Israel's security is palpable" (150).

Indeed, Jewish religious consciousness centers to a remarkable extent around the memory of persecution, including the holidays of Passover, Hanukkah, Purim, and Yom Kippur. Lipset and Raab (1995, 108) note that Jews learn about the Middle Ages as a period of persecution in Christian Europe, culminating in the expulsions and the Inquisitions. There is also a strong awareness of the persecutions in Eastern Europe, including especially the Czarist persecutions. And recently, the Holocaust has assumed a pre-eminent role in Jewish self-conceptualization (Hertzberg 1995; Wolffsohn 1993, 77ff).

Given the importance of external threat in cementing group ties, complete acceptance by the Gentile community may be viewed negatively, or at least with ambivalence, by those interested in maintaining group cohesion. One hears quite often of Jewish leaders in contemporary America expressing concern about being "loved to death," since complete acceptance may lead to intermarriage and a loss of Jewish identity (see, e.g., Eliot A. Cohen 1992, 141; Lipset and Raab 1995, 75). Perhaps as a result, American Jews tend to overestimate the actual amount of anti-Semitism. For example, Lipset and Raab (1995, 75) describe survey results from 1985 indicating that one-third of a sample of affiliated Jews in the San Francisco area stated that a Jew could not be elected to Congress at a time when three of the four congressional representatives from the area were "well-identified" Jews, as were the two state senators and the mayor of San Francisco. Survey results from 1990 indicated eight out of 10 American Jews had serious concerns about anti-Semitism, and significant percentages believed anti-Semitism was growing even though there was no evidence for this, while at the same time 90 percent of Gentiles viewed anti-Semitism as residual and vanishing (Hertzberg 1995, 337).

Also compatible with the proposal that individuals are more prone to submerge themselves in cohesive groups during times of external threat, there is evidence that the collectivist tendencies of Jewish communities became even more pronounced during periods of group conflict. For example, as was typical of traditional Jewish communities, there was an extreme level of conformity and thought control among Jews in the Ottoman Empire in the early modern period (Shaw 1991, 137ff). The community regulated precisely every aspect of life, including the shape and length of beards, all aspects of dress in public and private, the amount of charity required of members, the numbers of people at social gatherings, the appearance of graves and gravestones, the precise behavior on Sabbath, the precise form of conversations, the order of precedence at all social gatherings, etc. The rules were enforced "with a kind of police surveillance," and failure to abide by the rules could result in imprisonment in community prisons, or, at the extreme, in excommunication. Although these practices occurred during a period of economic prosperity, these hyperconformist tendencies became even more extreme during a subsequent period of persecution and economic decline.

While the above presents a static picture of the mechanisms related to group commitment, there may also be selection within the Jewish community over historical time for traits related to social identity and collectivism. As conceptualized by Triandis, individualism/collectivism is an individual-differences dimension, and it would appear that there are quite a few cases of individuals who are extreme on such a dimension to the point where defecting from the group is not an option. Especially striking has been the phenomenon of individuals who undergo martyrdom or commit suicide rather than abandon the group. We see examples periodically in modern times (such as the Jonestown massacre), and there are many historical examples, ranging from Christian martyrs in ancient times to a great many instances of Jewish martyrs over a 2,000–year period.

Recently there has developed a fairly large literature on religious cults with characteristics that illustrate the importance of social identity processes and that clearly place them on the extreme collectivist end of the individualism/collectivism dimension. These charismatic groups are highly cohesive, collectivist, and authoritarian (e.g., Galanter 1989a,b; Levine 1989; Deutsch 1989). Within the group there is a great deal of harmony and positive regard for group members combined with negative perceptions of outsiders. Psychological well-being increases when the person joins the group, and individuals who disaffiliate experience psychological distress.

This affective motivation may be increased by personal feelings of threat prior to joining the cult. Many individuals who join cults are not satisfied with their lives and feel personally threatened (Clark et al. 1981)—a finding that I interpret as resulting from the triggering of collectivist mechanisms in a facultative manner as a response to external threat or simply from feelings of "not doing well" in life. Indeed, Galanter found that the individuals who experienced the greatest relief upon joining cults were those who were most distressed prior to joining, and case study material indicates that many of these individuals were experiencing economic, social, and/or psychological stresses (e.g., change of residence, being fired from a job, illness of relatives [1989a, 92]). Sirkin and Grellong (1988) found similar associations in their sample of cult members from Jewish families.

Jewish martyrdom and the extreme intensity of Jewish group commitment have long been apparent to historians. Johnson (1987, 3) calls the Jews "the most tenacious people in history," but even this judgment seems inadequate. Jewish groups have persisted for centuries even though they have been isolated from other Jewish groups and subjected to persecutions, and even under circumstances where they were forced to engage in crypsis for many generations (see MacDonald 1994, Ch. 8).

The suggestion is that among Jews there is a significant critical mass for whom deserting the group is not an option no matter what the consequences to the individual. Consider, for example, the behavior of groups of Ashkenazi Jews in response to demands made to convert during the disturbances surrounding the First Crusade in Germany in 1096. Jewish behavior in this instance was truly remarkable. When given the choice of conversion or death, a contemporary Jewish chronicler noted that Jews "stretched forth their necks, so that their heads might be cut off in the Name of their Creator.... Indeed fathers also fell with their children, for they were slaughtered together. They slaughtered brethren, relatives, wives, and children. Bridegrooms [slaughtered] their intended and merciful mothers their only children" (in Chazan 1987, 245).

It is unlikely that such people have an algorithm that calculates individual fitness payoffs by balancing the tendency to desert the group with anticipated benefits of continued group membership. The obvious interpretation of such a phenomenon is that these people feel obligated to remain in the group no matter what, i.e., that there are no conceivable circumstances that would cause them to abandon the group, go their own way, and become assimilated to the out-group. As indicated above, selection at the level of the group need not imply that organisms do not attend to the individual costs of group membership. Nevertheless, the suggestion here is that many fully committed members of highly cohesive groups do not in fact have an algorithm that assesses the individual costs and benefits of group membership. Via indoctrination and/or selection processes for genes that predispose individuals to such behavior, it appears to be possible to produce extreme self-sacrifice in human groups.

While I do not suppose that such an extreme level of self-sacrifice is a panhuman psychological adaptation, it may well be the case that a significant proportion of Jews are extremely attracted to group membership to the point that they do not calculate the individual payoffs involved. The proposed model is that over historical time average group standing on the trait of collectivism has increased among Jews because individuals low on this trait (in this case, individuals who do not conform to expected standards of group behavior) are more likely to defect voluntarily from the group or be forcibly excluded.

It has often been observed among historians of Judaism that the most committed members of the group have determined the direction of the group (e.g., Sacks 1993, ix-x), and such individuals are likely to receive a disproportionate amount of the rewards of group membership. Moreover, Jordan (1989, 138) notes that Jews who defected during the Middle Ages (and sometimes persecuted their former coreligionists) tended to be people who were "unable to sustain the demands of [the] elders for conformity." (The Sephardic philosopher Baruch Spinoza is a famous example of a nonconformist who was expelled from the Jewish community.) This trend may well have accelerated since the Enlightenment because the costs of defection became lower. Israel (1985, 254) notes that after the Enlightenment, defections from Judaism due ultimately to negative attitudes regarding the restrictive Jewish community life were common enough to have a negative demographic effect on the Jewish community.

Moreover, in traditional societies there was discrimination within the Jewish community such that the families of individuals who had apostatized or engaged in other major breaches of approved behavior had lessened prospects for marriage. Writing of thirteenth-century Spain, Neuman (1969/1942) notes that measures were taken to protect converts to Christianity from abuse by their former coreligionists. The interesting thing is that conversion was "a blot on the family. The disgrace of one convert in a family was enough cause to warrant the disruption of the wedding engagement of an innocent relative. His former brethren regarded him as a renegade and ostracized him" (Neuman 1969, II 190).

This type of social control in which individuals were punished on account of their relatives' contravention of group norms was common throughout Jewish history. Goitein (1978, 33, 45), writing of medieval Islamic times, notes that the responsibility of the extended family was recognized by public opinion, although it was not a formal part of Jewish law. Hundert (1992; see also Katz 1961) notes that in traditional Ashkenazi society the son of a convert was ostracized and ridiculed because of his father's apostasy, indicating that conversion had negative effects on the entire family even beyond the immediate generation. And Deshen (1986) describes a nineteenth-century Moroccan case in which a man was allowed to break an engagement with a woman whose aunt had given birth out of wedlock. The decision was based on a precedent in which a man was allowed to break an engagement with a woman whose sister had converted to Islam. To the extent that there is heritable variation for such nonconformity (and all personality traits are heritable [e.g., Digman 1990]), such practices imply that there will be strong selection pressures concentrating genes for group loyalty and social conformity within the Jewish gene pool.

There has probably always been cultural selection such that people who have difficulty submerging their interests to those of the group have been disproportionately likely to defect from Judaism. Such individuals would have chaffed at the myriad regulations that governed every aspect of life in traditional Jewish society. In Triandis's (1990, 55, see Ch. 8) terms, these individuals are "idiocentric" people living in a collectivist culture, i.e., they are people who are less group oriented and less willing to put group interests above their own.

It is therefore likely that there has been within-group selection for genes predisposing people to collectivism to the point that they are simply incapable of acting selfishly based on estimates of individual payoffs of group membership. This hypothesis is supported by the finding that Jews have been overrepresented among non-Jewish religious cults (Marciano 1981; Schwartz 1978). Galanter (1989a, 23) finds that 21 percent of the Divine Light commune, organized by Maharaj Ji, were Jewish despite the fact that Jews represented only 2 percent of the U.S. population. Moreover, 8 percent of Galanter's sample of members of the Unification Church of Reverend Sun Myung Moon were Jewish (131). This confirms the hypothesis that Jews have a stronger tendency toward collectivism in general (see also MacDonald 1994, Ch. 8). In addition, a large percentage of Jews are involved in specifically Jewish groups (including, I would suppose, the haredim, Orthodox Jews, and Conservative Jews in the contemporary world) characterized by many of the features (cohesion, collectivism, and authoritarianism) ascribed to religious cults. The milieu selecting for such characteristics was traditional diaspora Judaism, which was Orthodox.

It is interesting in this regard that highly committed Jews appear to seek out relatively small synagogues of relative ethnic homogeneity where there is a deep sense of group identification. The main purpose of these smaller synagogues seems to be to satisfy the need for close feelings of group identification—what Mayer (1979, 110) terms a "we-feeling" of shared intimacy in a group. Mayer describes a trend whereby those trained in Orthodox yeshivas seek out Hasidic synagogues as adults because of their greater feelings of group intimacy.

Further, Sirkin and Grellong (1988) found that cult members from Jewish families had a higher number of highly religious relatives than contrast Jewish families. This occurred despite the fact that the contrast Jewish families were actually more religiously observant than the families of cult members. These findings offer further confirmation of the hypothesis that cult membership is influenced by genetic variation: Jewish cult members come disproportionately from relatively unobservant families who nevertheless have a strong familial predisposition toward membership in highly collectivist groups. The relative lack of religious observance among these cult-involved families may have resulted from their greater tendency toward intellectual, cultural, and political activities that were seen as incompatible with traditional religious observance. However, these cultural activities failed to provide the psychological sense of intense group involvement desired by the children, with the result that they were prone to join religious cults.

Conclusion

A clear message of the foregoing is that indoctrinability is a critical human adaptation that enables the formation of highly cohesive groups. Group strategies are very powerful in competition with individual strategies within a society, as has been the case with Judaism. The power of the Jewish group strategy has derived from the following: (1) Judaism has been characterized by cultural and eugenic practices that produced a highly talented and educated elite that was able to improve the fortunes of the entire group; (2) universal Jewish education resulted in an average resource acquisition ability that was above that of the rest of the society; and (3) there were high levels of within-group altruism and cooperation (see MacDonald 1994).

Given the presence of a powerful group strategy within a society, there is the expectation that dynamic processes will develop between the strategizing group and the rest of the population. In particular, as a group strategy such as Judaism comes to be increasingly salient and powerful within a society, out-group members are expected to be increasingly likely to join highly cohesive groups in an effort to further their own interests. The theory and data discussed in this chapter, therefore, not only provide a perspective on evolutionary strategies such as Judaism, but also provide a tool for understanding the development of antithetical group strategies, as represented historically by anti-Semitic movements (MacDonald, 1998). External threat results in a higher sense of group cohesion among Jews, but the same processes occurring among Gentiles imply that they would be increasingly likely to join cohesive, relatively altruistic groups when they perceive themselves as engaged in resource competition and threatened by a highly cohesive group. From the perspective of Gentiles, the social identity processes summarized above imply that the presence of a cohesive, distinctive out-group (i.e., the Jews) would result in a heightened salience of in-group (i.e., Gentile) identification and corresponding devaluation of the out-group. In situations of external threat, group members close ranks and there is an increase in cohesiveness, solidarity, and the acceptance of collectivist rather than individualist social norms. Negative stereotypes regarding the out-group are developed, and there are cognitive biases such that negative information about the out-group is preferentially attended to and points of disagreement highlighted.

My suggestion is that in the long run highly successful group strategies spawn mirror images of themselves as nongroup members increasingly perceive a need to organize against the group strategy. The result is a fascinating historical dynamic in which the individualistic tendencies of prototypical Western societies have been punctuated in critical historical eras by the development of highly collectivist Western societies with powerful overtones of anti-Semitism (late Roman and medieval Western Christianity, Nazism). However, these issues lead well beyond the present chapter (see MacDonald, 1998).

References

Alexander, R. (1979). *Darwinism and human affairs.* University of Washington Press, Seattle.

Baron, S. W. (1952). *A social and religious history of the Jews,* vol. II: *Christian era: The first five centuries,* 2d ed. The Jewish Publication Society of America, Philadelphia.

Berkowitz, L. (1982). Aversive conditions as stimuli to aggression. In *Advances in experimental social psychology*, vol. 15 (ed. L. Berkowitz), pp. 249–88. Academic Press, New York.

Boyd, R. and Richerson, P. J. (1992). Punishment allows the evolution of cooperation (or anything else) in sizable groups. *Ethology and Sociobiology*, **13**, 171–95.

Campbell, D. T. (1983). Legal and primary-group social controls. In *Law, biology and culture. The evolution of law* (ed. M. Gruter and P. Bohannan), pp. 159–71. Ross-Erikson, Santa Barbara, Cal.

Carmelli, D. and Cavalli-Sforza, L. L. (1979). The genetic origin of the Jews: A multivariate approach. *Human Biology*, **51**, 41–61.

Chazan, R. (1987). *European Jewry and the First Crusade*. University of California Press, Berkeley.

Clark, J. G., Langone, M. D., Schecter, R. E., and Daly, R. C. (1981). *Destructive cult conversion: Theory, research, and treatment*. American Family Foundation, Weston, Mass.

Cohen, E. A. (1992). A letter from Eliot A. Cohen. In *In search of anti-Semitism* (ed. W. Buckley), pp. 140–1. Continuum, New York.

Deshen, S. (1986). The Jewish family in traditional Morocco. In *The Jewish family: Myths and reality* (ed. S. M. Cohen and P. E. Hyman), pp. 29–41. Holmes & Meier, New York.

Deutsch, A. (1989). Psychological perspectives on cult leadership. In *Cults and new religious movements: A report of the American Psychiatric Association* (ed. M. Galanter), pp. 147–63. American Psychiatric Association, Washington.

Digman, J. M. (1990). Personality structure: Emergence of the five-factor model. *Annual Review of Psychology*, **41**, 417–40.

Eibl-Eibesfeldt, I. (1972). *Love and hate: The natural history of behavior patterns* (trans. G. Strachan). Holt, Rinehart and Winston, New York (Original German edition 1970, R. Piper, Munich).

———. (1979). *The biology of peace and war: men, animals, and aggression* (trans. E. Mosbacher). Thames and Hudson, London.

———. (1982). Warfare, man's indoctrinability and group selection. *Ethology (Zeitschrift für Tierpsychologie)*, **60**, 177–98.

Elazar, D. J. (1980). *Community and polity: Organizational dynamics of American Jewry* (first published in 1976). The Jewish Publication Society of America, Philadelphia.

Erikson, E. H. (1966). Ontogeny of ritualization in man. *Philosophical Transactions of the Royal Society of London*, **B 251**, 337–49.

Feldman, L. H. (1993). *Jew and Gentile in the ancient world: Attitudes and interactions from Alexander to Justinian*. Princeton University Press, Princeton.

Galanter, M. (1989a). *Cults: Faith, healing, and coercion*. Oxford University Press, New York.

———. (1989b). Cults and new religious movements. In *Cults and new religious movements: A report of the American Psychiatric Association* (ed. M. Galanter), pp. 25–40. American Psychiatric Association, Washington.

Gitelman, Z. (1991). The evolution of Jewish culture and identity in the Soviet Union. In *Jewish culture and identity in the Soviet Union* (ed. Y. Ro'i and A. Beker), pp. 3–24. New York University Press, New York.

Goitein, S. D. (1971). *A Mediterranean society*, vol. II: *The community*. The University of California Press, Berkeley.

————. (1978). *A mediterranean society*, vol. III: *The family*. The University of California Press, Berkeley.

Hartung, J. (1995). Love thy neighbor: The evolution of in-group morality. *Skeptic*, **3** (November), 86–99.

Heller, M. (1988). *Cogs in the wheel: The formation of Soviet Man* (trans. D. Floyd). Collins Harvill, London.

Hertzberg, A. (1995). How Jews use antisemitism. In *Antisemitism in America today: Outspoken experts explore the myths* (ed. J. A. Chanes), pp. 337–47. New York: Birch Lane Press.

Herz, F. M. and Rosen, E. J. (1982). Jewish families. In *Ethnicity and family therapy* (ed. M. McGoldrick, J. K. Pearce, and J. Giordano), pp. 364–92. The Guilford Press, New York.

Hogg, M. A. and Abrams, D. (1987). *Social identifications*. Routledge, New York.

Hundert, G. D. (1992). *The Jews in a Polish private town: The case of Opatow in the eighteenth century*. Johns Hopkins University Press, Baltimore.

Israel, J. I. (1985). *European Jewry in the age of mercantilism*. The Clarendon Press, Oxford.

Johnson, G. (1986). Kin selection, socialization, and patriotism: An integrating theory. *Politics and the Life Sciences*, **4**, 127–54.

————. (1995). The evolutionary origins of government and politics. In *Human nature and politics* (ed. A. Somit and J. Losco), pp. 243–305. JAI Press, Greenwich, CT.

Johnson, P. (1987). *A history of the Jews*. Perennial Library (Harper & Row), New York.

Jordan, W. C. (1989). *The French monarchy and the Jews: From Philip Augustus to the last Capetians*. University of Pennsylvania Press, Philadelphia.

Josephus, F. (1989). *The works of Josephus, complete and unabridged* (trans. W. Whiston). Hendrickson Publishers, Peabody, Mass.

Kamen, R. M. (1985). *Growing up Hasidic: Education and socialization in the Hasidic community*. AMS Press, New York.

Katz, J. (1961). *Tradition and crisis: Jewish society at the end of the Middle Ages*. The Free Press of Glencoe, New York.

Kobylianski, E., Micle, S., Goldschmidt-Nathan, M., Arensburg, B., and Nathan, H. (1982). Jewish populations of the world: Genetic likeness and differences. *Annals of Human Biology*, **9**, 1–34.

Levine, S. V. (1989). Life in the cults. In *Cults and new religious movements: A report of the American Psychiatric Association* (ed. M. Galanter), pp. 95–107. American Psychiatric Association, Washington.

Lipset, S. M. and Raab, E. (1995). *Jews and the New American Scene*. Harvard University Press, Cambridge.

MacDonald, K. (1994). *A people that shall dwell alone: Judaism as a group evolutionary strategy*. Praeger, Westport, Conn.

————. (1998). *Separation and its discontents: Toward an evolutionary theory of antiSemitism*. Praeger, Westport, Conn.

Marciano, T. D. (1981). Families and cults. *Marriage and Family Review*, **4**, 101–18.

Mayer, E. (1979). *From suburb to shtetl: The Jews of Boro Park*. Temple University Press, Philadelphia.

Neuman, A. A. (1969). *The Jews in Spain: Their political and cultural life during the Middle Ages*, vols. I and II. Octagon Books, New York (originally published in 1942).

Rabinowitz, L. (1938). *The social life of the Jews of northern France in the XII–XIV Centuries as reflected in the rabbinical literature of the period.* Edward Goldston Ltd, London.

Richerson, P. J. and Boyd, R. (1995). The evolution of human ultra-sociality. Paper presented at the Ringberg Symposium on Ideology, Warfare, and Indoctrinability. Ringberg Castle, Germany.

Sacks, J. (1993). *One people? Tradition, modernity, and Jewish unity.* The Littman Library of Jewish Civilization, London.

Salter, F. (1995). *Emotions in command. A naturalistic study of institutional dominance.* Oxford University Press, Oxford.

Sanders, E. P. (1992). *Judaism: Practice and belief. 63 BCE-66 CE.* SCM Press, London.

Schwartz, L. L. (1978). Cults and the vulnerability of Jewish youth. *Jewish Education*, **46**, 23–26.

Shaw, S. J. (1991). *The Jews of the Ottoman Empire and the Turkish Republic.* New York University Press, New York.

Simon, L. (1960). *Ahad Ha-Am (Asher Ginzberg): A biography.* Jewish Publication Society of America, Philadelphia.

Sirkin, M. I. and Grellong, B. A. (1988). Cult and non-cult Jewish families: Factors influencing conversion. *Cultic Studies Journal*, **5**, 2–22.

Triandis, H. C. (1990). Cross-cultural studies of individualism and collectivism. Nebraska Symposium on Motivation 1989. *Cross-Cultural Perspectives*, **37**, 41–133. University of Nebraska Press, Lincoln, Neb.

———. (1991). Cross-cultural differences in assertiveness/competition vs. group loyalty/cohesiveness. In *Cooperation and prosocial behaviour* (ed. R. A. Hinde and J. Groebel), pp. 78–88. Cambridge University Press, Cambridge, UK.

van der Dennen, J. M. G. (1991). Studies of conflict. In *The sociobiological imagination* (ed. M. Maxwell), pp. 223–41. The State University of New York Press, Albany.

Vine, I. (1987). Inclusive fitness and the self-system. The roles of human nature and sociocultural processes in intergroup discrimination. In *The sociobiology of ethnocentrism* (ed. V. Reynolds, V. Falger, and I. Vine), pp. 60–80. The University of Georgia Press, Athens.

Wilson, D. S. and Sober, E. (1994). Re-introducing group selection to the human behavioral sciences. *Behavioral and Brain Sciences*, **17**, 585–654.

Wolffsohn, M. (1993). *Eternal guilt? Forty years of German-Jewish-Israeli relations* (trans. D. Bokovoy). Columbia University Press, New York.

Woocher, J. S. (1986). *Sacred survival: The civil religion of American Jews.* Indiana University Press, Bloomington.

Zborowski, M. and Herzog, E. (1952). *Life is with people: The Jewish little-town of Eastern Europe.* International Universities Press, New York.

CHAPTER SEVENTEEN

GENETIC SIMILARITY THEORY, ETHNOCENTRISM, AND GROUP SELECTION

J. Philippe Rushton

Introduction

Genetic similarity theory, an extension of the kin-selection theory of altruism, postulates that people detect genetic similarity in others ("nonkin" as well as "kin") in order to provide mutually supportive environments, such as marriage, friendship, and social groups. In line with prediction, studies using blood antigens and heritabilities reveal that sexually interacting couples and same-sex friendships are based partly on genetic similarity (Rushton 1989a; 1995). As such, a new theory of attraction and friendship is constituted, and the conditions for the evolution of human altruism are enhanced. Genetically biased preferences are not limited to social partners but extend to adopting other cultural practices maximally compatible with genotypes. Ethnocentrism and patriotism may be fitness-enhancing mechanisms that enable group selection to occur.

Choosing social partners is among the most important decisions individuals make affecting their social environment. The tendency is to choose similarity. For example, spouses tend to resemble each other in such characteristics as age, ethnic background, socioeconomic status, physical attractiveness, religion, social attitudes, level of education, family size and structure, intelligence, and personality. The median assortative mating coefficient for standardized intelligence tests averages about 0.35. Correlations tend to be higher for opinions, attitudes, and values (0.40 to 0.70) and lower for personality traits, personal habits, and physical features (0.02 to 0.30).

Most explanations of the role of similarity in human relationships focus on immediate, environmental effects, for example, their reinforcement value. Recent analyses, however, suggest that genetic influences may also be involved. According to "genetic similarity theory," genetic likeness exerts subtle effects on a variety of relationships and has implications for the study of social behavior in small groups and even in large ones, both national and international. The main purpose of genetic similarity-seeking is to enhance altruism.

The Paradox of Altruism

As recognized by Darwin (1871), altruism represents a paradox for theories of evolution: How could altruism evolve through "survival of the fittest" when, on the face of it, altruistic behavior diminishes personal fitness? If the most altruistic members of a group sacrifice themselves for others, they run the risk of leaving fewer offspring to pass on the very genes that govern the altruistic behavior. Hence, altruism would be selected against, and selfishness would be selected for.

The resolution of the paradox of altruism is one of the triumphs that led to the new synthesis called sociobiology. By a process known as kin selection, individuals can optimize their inclusive fitness rather than only their individual fitness by increasing the production of successful offspring by both themselves and their genetic relatives (Hamilton 1964). According to this view, the unit of analysis for evolutionary selection is not the individual organism but its genes. Genes are what survive and are passed on, and some of the same genes will be found not only in direct offspring but in siblings, cousins, and nephews and nieces, as well as more distant kin. If an animal sacrifices its life for its siblings' offspring, it ensures the survival of common genes because, by common descent, it shares 50 percent of its distinct genes with each sibling and 25 percent with each sibling's offspring.

From an evolutionary perspective, altruism is a means of help-ing genes to propagate. By being most altruistic to those with whom we share genes, we help copies of our own genes to repli-cate. This makes "altruism" ultimately "selfish" in purpose. Pro-mulgated in the context of animal behavior, this idea became known as "kin selection" and provided a conceptual break-through by redefining the unit of analysis away from the individ-ual organism to his or her genes, for it is these that survive and are passed on. Another way sociobiologists have suggested that altru-ism could evolve is through reciprocity. Here there is no need for genetic relatedness; performing an altruistic act need only lead to an altruistic act in return.

Detecting Genetic Similarity

In order to pursue a strategy of directing altruism toward kin, the organism must be able to recognize degrees of relatedness. There is clearly no such thing as "genetic extrasensory perception." For individuals to direct altruism selectively to genetically similar individuals, they must respond to phenotypic cues. This is typi-cally accomplished by detecting similarities between self and oth-ers in physical and behavioral cues. Four processes have been suggested by which animals recognize relatives: (1) innate feature detectors, (2) matching on appearance, (3) familiarity, and (4) loca-tion. They are not mutually exclusive. If there are evolutionary advantages to be gained from the ability to detect genetic similar-ity, all the mechanisms may be operative.

Innate feature detectors. Individuals may have "recognition alle-les" that control the development of innate mechanisms allowing them to detect genetic similarity in strangers. Dawkins (1976) sug-gested a thought experiment to illustrate how this could come about, known as the "green beard effect." In this, a gene has two effects: it causes individuals who have it (1) to grow a green beard and (2) to behave altruistically toward green-bearded individuals. The green beard serves as a recognition cue for the altruism gene. Altruism could therefore occur without the need for individuals to be directly related.

Matching on appearance. The individual may be genetically guided to learn its own phenotype, or those of its close kin, and then to match new, unfamiliar individuals to the template it has learned—for example, Dawkins' (1982) "armpit effect." Individuals that smell (or look or behave) like oneself or one's close kin could be distinguished from those that smell (or look or behave) differently. This mechanism would depend on the existence of a strong correlation between genotype and phenotype.

Familiarity or association. Preferences may also depend on learning through social interaction. This may be the most common means of kin recognition in nature. Individuals that are reared together are more likely to be kin than nonkin.

Location. The fourth kin recognition mechanism depends on a high correlation between an individual's location and kinship. The rule states: "If it's in your nest, it's yours." Where an individual is and whom the individual encounters can also be based on similar genes, for example, if parents exert discriminatory influence on where and with whom their offspring interact.

Kin Recognition in Animals

There is dramatic experimental evidence that many animal species recognize genetic similarity. For example, bees block the nest to prevent intruders from entering. In one study, bees bred for 14 different degrees of genealogical relationship were introduced near nests (Greenberg 1979). There was a strong linear relationship ($r=0.93$) between the ability to pass the guard bee and the degree of genetic relatedness.

Mammals are also able to detect degrees of genetic relatedness (reviewed in Fletcher and Michener 1987). For example, squirrels produce litters that contain both sisters and half-sisters. Despite the fact that they shared the same womb and inhabit the same nest, full sisters fight less often than half-sisters, come to each other's aid more, and are less prone to chase one another out of their home territory. Recent experiments with squirrels demonstrate how rearing (together or apart) and relatedness (littermates or non-littermates) affect juveniles' social interactions. Play-bout frequencies were ordered (high to low): littermates reared together > non-littermates reared together > littermates reared apart > non-littermates reared apart. Statistical analysis revealed that both rearing and relatedness contributed to this ordering (Holmes 1995).

Similarity Recognition in Humans

In earlier papers, my colleagues and I extended the kin-selection theory of altruism to the human case by proposing that, if a gene can ensure its own survival by acting so as to bring about the reproduction of family members with whom it shares copies, then it can do so by benefiting any organism in which copies of itself are to be found (Rushton, Russell and Wells 1984; Rushton 1989a). Rather than merely protecting kin at the expense of strangers, organisms might identify genetically similar others so as to exhibit altruism toward these "strangers" as well as toward "kin." Kin recognition would be just one form of genetic similarity detection.

Humans are capable of learning to distinguish kin from nonkin at an early age. Infants can distinguish their mothers from other women by voice alone at 24 hours of age, know the smell of their mother's breast before they are 6 days of age, and recognize a photograph of their mother when they are 2 weeks old. Mothers are also able to identify their infants by smell alone after a single exposure at 6 hours of age, and to recognize their infant's cry within 48 hours of birth.

Human kin preferences follow lines of genetic similarity. For example, among the Ye'Kwana Indians of South America, the words "brother" and "sister" cover four different categories ranging from individuals who share 50 percent of their distinctive genes (identical by descent) to individuals who share only 12.5 percent of their genes. Hames (1979) has shown that the amount of time the Ye'Kwana spend interacting with their biological relatives increases with their degree of relatedness, even though their kinship terminology does not reflect this correspondence.

Anthropological data also show that in societies where certainty of paternity is relatively low, males direct material resources to their sisters' offspring (to whom their relatedness is certain) rather than to their wives' offspring (Kurland 1979). Paternity uncertainty exerts other predictable consequences. Grandparents spend 35 to 42 percent more time with their daughters' children than with their sons' children (Smith 1981). Following bereavement, grandparents grieve more for their daughters' children than for their sons' children (Littlefield and Rushton 1986). Family members feel only 87 percent as close to the fathers' side of the family as they do to the mothers' side (Russell and Wells 1987). Finally, mothers of newborn children and her relatives spend more time commenting on resemblances between the baby and the putative father than they do about the resemblance between the baby and the mother (Daly and Wilson 1982).

When the level of genetic similarity within a family is low, the consequences can be serious. Children who are unrelated to a parent are at risk: a disproportionate number of battered babies are stepchildren. Children of preschool age are 40 times more likely to be assaulted if they are stepchildren than if they are biological children (Daly and Wilson 1988). Unrelated people living together are more likely to kill each other than are related people living together. Converging evidence shows that adoptions are more likely to be successful when the parents perceive the child as similar to them.

Mate Choice

A well-known phenomenon that is readily explained by genetic similarity theory is positive assortative mating, that is, the tendency of spouses to be nonrandomly paired in the direction of resembling each other (described in the introduction). This tendency even extends to socially undesirable characteristics, including aggressiveness, criminality, alcoholism, and psychiatric disorders such as schizophrenia and the affective disorders. Although alternative reasons can be proposed for this finding, such as unsuccessful competition for the most attractive and healthiest mates, it does suggest that the tendency to seek a similar partner may override considerations such as mate quality and individual fitness.

A study of cross-racial marriages in Hawaii found more similarity in personality test scores among males and females who married across ethnic groups than among those marrying within them (Ahern, Cole, Johnson, and Wong 1981). The researchers posit that, given the general tendency toward homogamy, couples marrying heterogamously with respect to ethnicity tend to "make up" for this dissimilarity by choosing spouses more similar to themselves in other respects than do persons marrying within their own ethnic group.

Assortative mating is found in taxa ranging from insects to birds to primates, and it can be observed in the laboratory as well as in nature (Fletcher and Michener 1987). Assortative mating also occurs in plants (Willson and Burley 1983). To have evolved independently in such a wide variety of species, assortative mating must confer substantial advantage. Advantages thought to accrue in human mates include (1) increased marital stability, (2) increased relatedness to offspring, (3) increased within-family altruism and (4) greater fecundity.

The upper limit on the fitness-enhancing effect of assortative mating for similarity occurs with incest. Too much genetic similarity between mates increases the chances that harmful recessive genes may combine. The negative effects of "inbreeding depression" have been demonstrated in many species, including humans. As a result, the "incest taboo" has been hypothesized to have an evolutionary basis, possibly mediated through negative imprinting on intimate associates at an early age (van den Berghe 1983). Optimal fitness, then, may consist in selecting a mate who is genetically similar but not actually a relative. Van den Berghe (1983) speculates that the ideal percentage of relatedness is 12.5 percent identical by descent, or the same as that between first cousins.

Other animal species also avoid inbreeding. For example, several experiments have been carried out with Japanese quail, birds that, although promiscuous, proved particularly sophisticated. They preferred first cousins to third cousins, and both of these relatives to either unrelated birds or siblings, thus avoiding the dangers of too much or too little inbreeding (Bateson 1983).

I tested the hypothesis that human mating followed lines of genetic similarity by examining blood antigen analyses from nearly 1,000 cases of disputed paternity (Rushton 1988). Seven polymorphic marker systems (ABO, Rhesus (Rh), MNSs, Kell, Duffy (Fy), Kidd (Jk), and HLA) at 10 loci across six chromosomes were examined in a sample limited to people of North European appearance (judged by photographs kept for legal identifications). These blood groups are sufficient to correctly identify more than 95 percent of cases in paternity disputes. They also reliably distinguish between fraternal twins. My results showed that genetic similarity within pairs related to (1) whether the pair was sexually interacting or randomly generated from the same sample, and (2) whether the pair produced a child. Sexually interacting couples shared about 50 percent of measured genetic markers, part way between mothers and their offspring, who shared 73 percent, and randomly paired individuals from the same sample, who shared 43 percent. Couples who produced a child together were 52 percent similar on this metric, whereas those who did not were only 44 percent similar ($p < 0.05$).

In other tests of the genetic similarity theory of assortative mating, studies show that mate choice is greater on the more heritable of a set of homogeneous items. This prediction follows from theory because more heritable items better reflect the underlying genotype. Examples of differing heritabilities used to establish the theory include: for physical characters, 80 percent for mid-finger length versus 50 percent for upper arm circumference; for intelligence, 80 percent for the general factor versus less than 50 percent for specific abilities; for personality, 41 percent for having a preference for reading versus 20 percent for having many different hobbies; and for attitudes, 51 percent for agreement with the death penalty versus 25 percent for agreement with Bible truth. Thus, Russell, Wells, and Rushton (1985) found spouses were more similar on the more heritable of 36 anthropometric variables, 5 perceptual judgment variables, and 11 personality variables. Rushton and Russell (1985) found heritabilities predicted similarity between spouses for 54 personality traits, 15 cognitive tests, and 13 anthropometric variables. Rushton and Nicholson (1988) found that spouses were most similar on the more heritable of 15 IQ subtests from the Hawaii Family Study of Cognition and 11 subtests from the Wechsler Adult Intelligence Scale.

Intrafamilial Relationships

One consequence of genetic similarity between spouses is an increase of within-family altruism. Several studies have shown that not only the occurrence of relationships but also their degree of happiness and stability can be predicted by the degree of matching on personal attributes (reviewed in Rushton 1989a).

A related prediction can be made about parental care of offspring that differ in similarity. Sibling differences within families have often been overlooked as a topic of research. Positive assortative mating makes some children genetically more similar to one parent or sibling than to another. For example, if a father gives his child 50 percent of his genes, 10 percent of which he shares with the mother because of parental similarity, and the mother gives the child 50 percent of her genes, 20 percent of which she shares with the father because of parental similarity, then the child will be 60 percent similar to the mother and 70 percent similar to the father.

Genetic similarity theory predicts that parents and siblings will tend to favor those who are most similar. Littlefield and Rushton (1986) tested this hypothesis in a study of bereavement following the death of a child. Respondents picked which side of the family the child "took after" more, their own or their spouse's. Spouses agreed with each other 74 percent of the time on this question. Both mothers and fathers grieved more intensely for children perceived as resembling their side of the family.

Other evidence of within-family preferences comes from a review by Segal (1988) of feelings of closeness, cooperation, and altruism in twin pairs. Compared with fraternal twins, identical twins worked harder for their co-twins on tasks, maintained greater physical proximity, expressed more affection, and suffered greater loss following bereavement. Subsequently, Segal, Wilson, Bouchard, and Gitlin (1995) found that degree of genetic relatedness predicted degree of bereavement and that the loss of a co-twin resulted in the same level of grief as the loss of a child or a spouse.

A Genetic Basis for Friendship

Friendships also form on the basis of similarity, whether as perceived by the friends or for a variety of objectively measured characteristics, including activities, attitudes, needs, personality, and anthropometric variables. Moreover, in the experimental literature on who likes whom and why, one of the most influential variables is perceived similarity. Apparent similarity of personality, attitudes, or any of a wide range of beliefs has been found to generate liking in subjects of varying ages and from many different cultures.

The tendency to choose similar others as friends is genetically influenced. In a study of delinquency among 530 adolescent twins by Rowe and Osgood (1984), path analysis revealed not only that antisocial behavior was about 50 percent heritable, but that the correlation of 0.56 between the delinquency of an individual and the delinquency of his friends was mediated genetically. Adolescents genetically disposed to delinquency were genetically inclined to seek each other out for friendship. In a study of 396 adolescent and young adult siblings from both adoptive and non-adoptive homes, Daniels and Plomin (1985) found that genetic influences were implicated in choice of friends: biological siblings were more similar to each other in the types of friends they had than were adoptive siblings.

In a study to examine similarity among male friendship pairs, I used the same blood markers and differential heritabilities as in my study of sexual partners. The best friends were 54 percent similar to each other using 10 loci from 7 polymorphic blood systems (ABO, Rhesus (Rh), MNSs, P, Duffy (Fy), Kidd (Jk), and HLA). An equal number of randomly chosen pairs from the same overall sample were significantly less similar. Stratification effects were unlikely because within-pair differences in age, education, and occupation did not correlate with the blood similarity scores. Similarity between friends was strongest on the more heritable of 36 conservatism items and 81 personality items.

Independent corroboration that attitudes with high heritability are stronger than those with low heritability has come from a series of studies by Tesser (1993). Each subject responded "Agree" or "Disagree" to attitudes with known heritabilities. Attitudes higher in heritability were responded to more quickly, were more resistant to change when attempts were made at social influence, and were more predictive of liking of others who shared similar attitudes. For example, similarity on more heritable attitudes correlated higher with attraction to a stranger imagined as a potential friend, a romantic partner, and a spouse than did similarity on less heritable items.

Epigenetic Rules in Social Development

Both the evolutionary and social sciences err in not making more explicit that social learning is dependent upon the innate capacities and biases of the learner. For example, most models of cultural transmission within the family (i.e., vertical, from parent to child, and horizontal, from sibling to sibling) imply that siblings will resemble each other, over and above shared genes, as a result of a common family environment. An epigenetic model, in contrast, in which genes incline individuals to acquire patterns of behavior best fitting their particular genotype, leads to the expectation that siblings will differ from each other. While it may seem intuitively correct to assume that common family environment shapes individual development, consideration of data reveals quite a different set of relationships.

Social development is guided by epigenetic rules that incline individuals to particular learning experiences. As in the studies of friendship formation among delinquents described in the last section, behavior genetic designs provide powerful tests of alternative hypotheses about the genetic and social influences on family resemblances. Comparing 573 pairs of adult monozygotic and dizygotic twins who had been reared together, Rushton, Fulker, Neale, Nias, and Eysenck (1986) examined the cultural and genetic inheritance of individual differences in altruism and aggression. We found not only a strong association of genetic factors with the characteristics in question but also a negligible influence of the twins' shared environment. Rather, the distinct experiences of the individual accounted for almost all the environmental influence.

The discovery that common family environment plays a very limited role in social development (even for traits that parents are expected to indoctrinate, such as altruism) runs counter to prevailing theories of personality development that assume that the important environmental variance is between families, not within. Yet the observation that the environmental factors that influence development are those that are specific to each sibling, rather than common, is robust, having been replicated using other research designs (like adoption studies) and other social characteristics. Regardless of whether one considers the transmission of socially undesirable traits, such as crime, obesity, and schizophrenia, or more normative personality characteristics, such as vocational interests and value systems, the evidence reveals that whereas genetic influences have an important role to play, the common family environment alone has little apparent effect.

A compelling test of models of transmission has been made in the context of social attitudes. Since attitudes are more flexible than personality, purely cultural models of transmission might be considered especially likely, with at least some vertical transmission occurring from parent to child. Yet in one compilation of results, Eaves, Eysenck, and Martin (1989) showed that social scientists have typically misconceived the role of cultural inheritance in attitude formation. Individuals acquire little from their social environment that is incompatible with their genotype.

So far the discussion has been limited to individual social development. However, the potential of epigenetic rules to bias behavior and affect society goes well beyond ontogeny. Via cognitive phenotypes and group action, altruistic inclinations may be amplified into charities and hospitals, creative and educative dispositions into academies of learning, and martial tempers into institutes of war. Such macrocultural innovations can be expected to influence the genetic composition of future generations.

Ethnocentrism

The implications of the finding that people moderate their behavior as a function of genetic similarity and epigenetic biases are far-reaching. They suggest a biological basis for ethnocentrism. Despite enormous variance within populations, it can be expected that two individuals within an ethnic group will, on average, be more similar to each other genetically than two individuals from different ethnic groups. According to genetic similarity theory, people can be expected to favor their own group over others.

Ethnic conflict and rivalry, of course, is one of the great themes of historical and contemporary society. Local ethnic favoritism is also displayed by group members who prefer to congregate in the same area and to associate with each other in clubs and organizations. Understanding modern Africa, for example, is impossible without understanding tribalism there. Many studies have found that people are more likely to help members of their own race or country than they are to help members of other races or foreigners, and that antagonism between classes and nations may be greater when a racial element is involved.

Traditionally, political scientists and historians have seldom considered intergroup conflict from an evolutionary standpoint. That fear and mistrust of strangers may have biological origins, however, is supported by evidence that animals often show fear of and hostility toward strangers, even when no injury has ever been received. Analogies may be drawn between the way monkeys and apes repel intruding strangers of the same species and the way children attack another child who is perceived as being an outsider.

Many of those who have considered nationalist and patriotic sentiment from a sociobiological perspective, however, have emphasized its apparent irrationality. Johnson (1986) formulated a theory of patriotism in which indoctrination through socialization and conditioning engage kin-recognition systems so that people behave altruistically toward in-group members as though they were genetically more similar than they actually are. In Johnson's analysis, for example, patriotism may often be an ideology indoctrinated by the ruling class to induce the ruled to behave contrary to their own genetic interests, while increasing the fitness of the elite. He noted that patriotism is built by referring to the homeland as the "motherland" or "fatherland," and that bonds between people are strengthened by referring to them as "brothers" and "sisters."

According to genetic similarity theory, patriotism is more than just "indoctrinated" altruism working to the individual's genetic detriment. It is a strategy by which genes typically replicate copies of themselves more effectively. The developmental processes that Johnson (1986) and others have outlined undoubtedly occur, as do other forms of manipulated altruism. However, if these were sufficient to explain the human propensity to feel strong moral obligation toward society, patriotism would remain an anomaly for evolutionary biology. From the standpoint of optimization, one might ask whether ethical systems would survive very long if they consistently led to reductions in the inclusive fitness of those believing in them.

If epigenetic rules do incline people toward constructing and learning ideologies which increase their fitness, then patriotic nationalism, religious zealotry, class conflict, and other forms of ideological commitment can be seen as genetically influenced cultural choices that individuals make that, in turn, influence the replication of their genes. Religious, political, and other ideological battles may become as heated as they do partly because of implications for fitness; some genotypes may thrive more in one ideological culture than in another. According to this view, Karl Marx did not take the argument far enough: ideology serves more than economic interest; it also serves genetic fitness.

Two sets of falsifiable propositions follow from this interpretation. First, individual differences in ideological preference are partly heritable. Second, ideological belief increases genetic fitness. There is evidence to support both propositions. With respect to the heritability of differences in ideological preference, it has generally been assumed that political attitudes are mostly determined by the environment; however, as mentioned, both twin and adoption studies reveal significant heritabilities for social and political attitudes as well as for stylistic tendencies (Eaves, Eysenck, and Martin 1989). Of course, no behavioral geneticist believes that genes are 100 percent responsible for complex social behavior. The battle is between those who believe 100 percent in environmental determinism and those who think that both genes and environments affect behavior.

Examples of ideologies that increase genetic fitness include religious beliefs that regulate dietary habits, sexual practices, marital customs, infant care, and childrearing (Reynolds and Tanner 1983). Amerindian tribes that believed it important to cook maize with alkali had higher population densities and more complex social organizations than tribes that did not, partly because cooking with alkali releases the most nutritious parts of the cereal, enabling more people to grow to reproductive maturity (Katz, Hodiger, and Valleroy 1974). The Amerindians did not know the biochemical reasons for the benefits of alkali cooking, but their cultural beliefs had evolved for good reason, enabling them to replicate their genes more effectively than would otherwise have been the case.

By the way of objection, it could be argued that although some religious ideologies confer direct benefits on the extended family, ideologies like patriotism decrease fitness (hence, most analyses of patriotism rest on indoctrination and social manipulation). Genetic similarity theory may provide a firmer basis for an evolutionary understanding of patriotism, for benefited genes do not have to be only those residing in kin. Members of ethnic groups, for example, often share the same ideologies, and many political differences are genetic in origin. One possible test of genetic similarity theory in this context is to calculate degrees of genetic similarity among ideologues in order to examine whether ideological "conservatives" are more homogeneous than the same ideology's "liberals." Preserving the "purity" of an ideology might be an attempt to preserve the "purity" of the gene pool.

Because ethnic conflict has defied explanation by the standard social science disciplines, genetic similarity theory may represent an advance in understanding. Eibl-Eibesfeldt (1989b) agreed with me that if attraction toward similarity has a genetic component then it provides a basis for xenophobia as an innate trait in human beings. He reiterated that ethnocentrism is a phenomenon manifested in all cultures so far studied and presented his view that generalized altruism began with maternal caretaking, a turning point in the evolution of vertebrate social behavior, which up to that time had been based on dominance and submission. The mother-child bond established the possibility of gradients in familiarity-trust/strangeness-suspicion.

Van den Berghe (1989) also endorsed the genetic similarity perspective, stating that ethnicity had a "primordial dimension." In his 1981 book, *The Ethnic Phenomenon*, he had suggested that ethnocentrism was a case of extended nepotism, with even relatively open and assimilative ethnic groups policing their ethnic boundaries against invasion by strangers by using badges as markers of group membership. These were likely to be cultural rather than physical, he argued, such as linguistic accent or clothing style. Now, it seemed to him (van den Berghe 1989), identifying fellow ethnics using shared traits of high heritability provided a more reliable method than cultural, flexible ones, although these other membership badges could also be used.

Adopting a gene-based evolutionary perspective for ethnic conflict may prove illuminating, especially in the light of the conspicuous failures of environmentalist theories. With the breakup of the Soviet bloc, many Western analysts have been surprised at the outbreak of the fierce ethnic antagonisms long thought over. Lynn (1989, 534) put it directly:

> Racial and ethnic conflict is occurring throughout the world—between Blacks and Whites in the United States, South Africa, and Britain; Basques and Spaniards in Spain; and Irish and British in Northern Ireland. These conflicts have defied explanations by the disciplines of sociology, psychology, and economics ... genetic similarity theory represents a major advance in the understanding of these conflicts.

Lynn (1989) raised the question of why people remain as irrationally attached as they do to languages, even almost dead ones such as Gaelic and Welsh. One function of language barriers, he suggested, was to promote inbreeding among fellow ethnics. The close mapping recently found to occur between linguistic and genetic trees is compatible with Lynn's hypothesis. Cavalli-Sforza, Menozzi, and Piazza (1994) combined 120 allele frequencies from 42 populations into a phylogenetic tree based on genetic distances and related it to a taxonomy of 17 linguistic phyla. Despite the apparent volatility of language and its capacity to be imposed by conquerors at will, considerable parallelism between genetic and linguistic evolution was found.

The theoretical stance taken so far predicts that the ease of producing patriotic sentiment and internal harmony varies with the genetic homogeneity of the national group. As van den Berghe (1981, 27) put it: "Ethnicity can be manipulated but not manufactured." Since ethnic aspirations are rarely justified in terms of naked genetic self-interest, any analysis will necessarily have to be conducted at a deeper level than surface ideology. Political interests are typically couched in the highest of ethical terms, no matter how utilitarian, transparent, or heinous these appear to opponents.

Genetic similarity is only one of many possible influences operating on political alliances. Obviously, causation is complex, and it is not intended to reduce relationships between ethnic groups to a single cause. Fellow ethnics will not always stick together, nor is conflict inevitable between groups any more than it is between genetically distinct individuals. As indicated, people can be manipulated into working for "other groups." People also work for other motives, such as economic success as well as reproductive success. However, as van den Berghe (1981) pointed out, from an evolutionary perspective, the ultimate measure of human success is not production, but reproduction.

While cultural evolution and organic evolution are undoubtedly different, they are linked reciprocally in complicated ways and seem to share certain properties. Both appear to "strive" to replicate their units, if necessary at the expense of the other system's units (alleles in the case of organic evolution; "memes" or "culturgens" in the case of cultural evolution). Their seat of battle is the individual human mind, which only dimly perceives the consequences of its choices, based as they are on many competing elements. Thus, ideologies can arise which have the paradoxical effect of dramatically decreasing fitness. A classic example of such a lethal culturgen is found among the Shakers, a religious sect which considers sex to be so sinful that it imposes celibacy upon even its married members. This ideology has nonetheless been quite successful in replicating itself through several generation, new adherents being recruited, largely via adoptions. The members' genes, of course, fail to replicate.

Selection of Groups

Humans have obviously been selected to live in groups. Typically, they hold a territory in common that they fill with symbols of their group and that they are willing to defend (Eibl-Eibesfeldt 1989a). The line of argument presented so far may have implications for determining whether group selection occurs among humans. Although the idea of group selection, defined as "selection that operates on two or more members of a lineage group as a unit" (E. O. Wilson 1975, 585) was popular with Darwin, Spencer, and others, in recent decades it has often been thought not to play a major role in evolution. Hamilton's (1964) theory of inclusive fitness, for example, has been typically regarded as an extension of individual selection, not group selection (Dawkins 1976; 1982).

Group selection was brought to center stage by Wynne-Edwards (1962) in the context of altruism. He suggested that whole groups of animals collectively refrained from overbreeding when the density of population became too great, even to the point of killing their offspring. Such self-restraint, he argued, protected the animals' resource base and gave them an advantage over groups that did not practice restraint and became extinct as a result of their profligacy. This extreme form of the group selection claim was immediately disputed, and a great deal of argument and data was marshaled against the idea (Williams 1966). There did not seem to exist a mechanism (other than favoring kin) by which altruistic individuals could leave more genes than selfish individuals who cheated.

A compromise was offered by E. O. Wilson (1975), who suggested that although genes are the units of replication, their selection could take place through competition at both the individual and the group levels; for some purposes these can be viewed as opposite ends of a continuum of nested, ever enlarging sets of socially interacting individuals. Kin selection is thus seen as intermediate between individual and group selection. Group selection may have been prematurely rejected due to a failure to see that with genes as "replicators," it is irrelevant whether it is individuals, social groups, or still higher-level entities that are the "vehicles" of selection (for an extended discussion see D. S. Wilson and Sober 1994).

Among humans, genetic similarity theory makes group selection especially likely because altruism is conferred beyond immediate kin. Through language, law, religious imagery, and patriotic nationalism, all replete with kin terminology, ideological commitment extends altruistic behavior enormously. Groups made up of people genetically disposed toward honesty, trust, temperance, willingness to share, loyalty, and self-sacrifice will have a distinct genetic advantage over groups that do not have this makeup. In addition, if strong socialization pressures, including "mutual monitoring" and "moralistic aggression," are used to shape values within the group, a mechanism is provided for controlling, and even removing, the genes of cheaters.

As indicated, social learning is genetically biased. Social psychological studies of cultural transmission show that people pick up trends more readily from role models who are similar. It is likely that different ethnic groups learn from different trendsetters and that the variance among groups is increased, thereby increasing the efficacy of group selection. Those groups adopting an optimum degree of ethnocentric ideology may have replicated their genes more successfully than those that did not. Evolution under biocultrally driven group selection, including migration, war, and genocide, may account for a substantial amount of change in human gene frequencies. E. O. Wilson (1975, 573–74) put it forcefully:

> If any social predatory mammal attains a certain level of intelligence, as the early hominids, being large primates, were especially predisposed to do, one band would have the capacity to consciously ponder the significance of adjacent social groups and to deal with them in an intelligent organized fashion. A band might then dispose of a neighboring band, appropriate its territory, and increase its own genetic representation in the metapopulation, retaining the tribal memory of this successful episode, repeating it, increasing the geographic range of its occurrence, and quickly spreading its influence still further in the metapopulation. Such primitive cultural capacity would be permitted by the possession of certain genes.... The only combination of genes able to confer superior fitness in contention with genocidal aggressors would be those that produce either a more effective technique of aggression or else the capacity to preempt genocide by some form of pacific maneuvering. Either probably entails mental and cultural advance. In addition to being autocatalytic, such evolution has the interesting property of requiring a selection episode only very occasionally in order to proceed as swiftly as individual-level selection. By current theory, genocide or genosorption strongly favoring the aggressor need take place only once every few generations to direct evolution. This alone could push truly altruistic genes to a high frequency within the bands.

References

Ahern, F. M., Cole, R. E., Johnson, R. C., and Wong, B. (1981). Personality attributes of males and females marrying within vs. across racial/ethnic groups. *Behaviour Genetics*, 11, 181–94.

Cavalli-Sforza, L. L., Menozzi, P., and Piazza, A. (1994). *The history and geography of human genes*. Princeton University Press, Princeton.

Daly, M. and Wilson, M. (1982). Whom are newborn babies said to resemble? *Ethology and Sociobiology*, **3**, 69–78.

———. (1988). *Homicide*. Aldine de Gruyter, New York.

Daniels, D. and Plomin, R. (1985). Differential experience of siblings in the same family. *Developmental Psychology*, **21**, 747–60.

Darwin, C. (1871). *The descent of man*. Murray, London.

Dawkins, R. (1976). *The selfish gene*. Oxford University Press, Oxford.

———. (1982). *The extended phenotype*. Freeman, San Francisco, Cal.

Eaves, L. J., Eysenck, H. J., and Martin, N. G. (1989). *Genes, culture and personality*. Academic, London.

Eibl-Eibesfeldt, I. (1989a). *Human ethology*. Aldine de Gruyter, New York.

———. (1989b). Familiality, xenophobia, and group selection. *Behavioural and Brain Sciences*, **12**, 503–59.

Fletcher, D. J. C. and Michener, C. D. (1987). *Kin recognition in animals*. Wiley, New York.

Greenberg, L. (1979). Genetic component of bee odor in kin recognition. *Science*, **206**, 1095–97.

Hames, R. B. (1979). Relatedness and interaction among Ye'Kwana: A preliminary analysis. In *Evolutionary biology and human social behavior* (ed. N. A. Chagnon and W. Irons), pp. 238–49. Duxbury, North Scituate, Mass.

Hamilton, W. D. (1964). The genetical evolution of social behaviour: I and II. *Journal of Theoretical Biology*, **7**, 1–52.

Holmes, W. G. (1995). The ontogeny of littermate preferences in juvenile golden-mantled ground squirrels: Effects of rearing and relatedness. *Animal Behaviour*, **50**, 309–22.

Johnson, G. R. (1986). Kin selection, socialization, and patriotism: An integrating theory (with commentaries and response). *Politics and the Life Sciences*, **4**, 127–54.

Katz, S. H., Hodiger, M. L., and Valleroy, L. A. (1974). Traditional maize processing techniques in the new world. *Science*, **223**, 1049–51.

Kurland, J. A. (1979). Paternity, mother's brother, and human sociality. In *Evolutionary biology and human social behavior* (ed. N. A. Chagnon and W. Irons), pp. 145–80. Duxbury, North Scituate, Mass.

Littlefield, C. H. and Rushton, J. P. (1986). When a child dies: The sociobiology of bereavement. *Journal of Personality and Social Psychology*, **51**, 797–802.

Lynn, R. (1989). Balanced polymorphism for ethnocentric and nonethnocentric alleles. *Behavioural and Brain Sciences*, **12**, 535.

Reynolds, V. and Tanner, R. E. S. (1983). *The biology of religion*. Longman, New York.

Rowe, D. C. and Osgood, D. W. (1984). Heredity and sociological theories of delinquency: A reconsideration. *American Sociological Review*, **49**, 526–40.

Rushton, J. P. (1988). Genetic similarity, mate choice, and fecundity in humans. *Ethology and Sociobiology*, **9**, 329–33.

———. (1989a). Genetic similarity, human altruism, and group selection (with commentaries and author's response). *Behavioral and Brain Sciences*, **12**, 503–59.

———. (1989b). Genetic similarity in male friendships. *Ethology and Sociobiology*, **10**, 361–73.

———. (1995). *Race, evolution, and behaviour*. Transaction Publishers, New Brunswick, N.J.

Rushton, J. P., Fulker, D. W., Neale, M. C., Nias, D. K. B., and Eysenck, H. J. (1986). Altruism and aggression: The heritability of individual differences. *Journal of Personality and Social Psychology*, **50**, 1192–8.

Rushton, J. P., and Nicholson, I. R. (1988). Genetic similarity theory, intelligence, and human mate choice. *Ethology and Sociobiology*, 9, 45–57.

Rushton, J. P., Russell, R. J. H., and Wells, P. A. (1984). Genetic similarity theory: Beyond kin selection. *Behaviour Genetics*, 14, 179–93.

Russell, R. J. H. and Wells, P. A. (1987). Estimating paternity confidence. *Ethology and Sociobiology*, 8, 215–20.

Russell, R. J. H., Wells, P. A., and Rushton, J. P. (1985). Evidence for genetic similarity detection in human marriage. *Ethology and Sociobiology*, 6, 183–87.

Segal, N. L. (1988). Cooperation, competition, and altruism in human twinships: A sociobiological approach. In *Sociobiological perspectives on human development* (ed. K. B. MacDonald), pp. 168–206. Springer-Verlag, New York.

Segal, N. L., Wilson, S. M., Bouchard, T. J., Jr., and Gitlin, D. G. (1995). Comparative grief experiences of bereaved twins and other bereaved relatives. *Personality and Individual Differences*, 18, 511–24.

Smith, M. (1981). Kin investment in grandchildren. Unpublished doctoral thesis, York University, Toronto, Ontario, Canada.

Tesser, A. (1993). The importance of heritability in psychological research: The case of attitudes. *Psychological Review*, 93, 129–42.

van den Berghe, P. L. (1981). *The ethnic phenomenon*. Elsevier, New York.

———. (1983). Human inbreeding avoidance: Culture in nature (with commentaries and author's response). *Behavioural and Brain Sciences*, 6, 91–123.

———. (1989). Heritable phenotypes and ethnicity. *Behavioural and Brain Sciences*, 12, 544–45.

Williams, G. C. (1966). *Adaptation and natural selection*. Princeton University Press.

Willson, M. F. and Burley, N. (1983). *Mate choice in plants*. Princeton University Press.

Wilson, D. S. and Sober, E. (1994). Reintroducing group selection to the human behavioural sciences. *Behavioural and Brain Sciences*, 17, 585–654.

Wilson, E. O. (1975). *Sociobiology: The new synthesis*. Harvard University Press, Cambridge, Mass.

Wynne-Edwards, V. C. (1962). *Animal dispersion in relation to social behaviour*. Oliver and Boyd, Edinburgh.

CHAPTER EIGHTEEN

ETHNOCENTRISM VS. PRAGMATISM IN THE CONDUCT OF HUMAN AFFAIRS

Irwin Silverman and Danielle Case

Introduction

The concept of inclusive fitness (Hamilton 1964) maintains that behavioral dispositions are selected, not only for their adaptive value for the survival of the organism and its offspring, but for the survival of counterparts of the individual's genotype in other individuals of common descent. Thus it is presumed that natural selection favors preferential treatment of others in proportion to their genetic relatedness. This has afforded an apt explanation of intrafamilial nepotism and, in this context, is sometimes referred to as kin selection. It has been suggested also by a number of writers (e.g., Alexander 1979, 161; Dawkins 1976, 101; Hamilton 1975, 141–4; Symons 1979, 7) that the concept of common descent can be extended beyond direct kin, and may thereby account for the phenomenon of ethnocentrism in intra- and intergroup relations. Van den Berghe (1981) characterized ethnocentrism, so conceived, as "ethnic nepotism." Based on the same model, Rushton and his colleagues (Rushton et al. 1984; 1985) applied the title, "genetic similarity theory," to describe the effects of perceived genetic relat-

edness on various aspects of sociality, such as altruism, friendship, and group formation.

Silverman (1986; 1987), however, has argued against this position, maintaining that the influences of genetic relatedness in
interpersonal relations are limited for the most part to direct kin.
The premise for Silverman's demurrer resides in the prominent
function of intra- and intergroup alliances in hominid evolution.
Silverman contended that natural selection would have favored
the ability to form the most *effective* alliances; that is, to find allies
best suited to meet the specific goals of specific endeavors, either
cooperative or competitive. Further, the formation of effective
alliances would be enhanced by plasticity, meaning the capacity to
forge the most beneficial allegiances for a given set of circumstances and to shift allegiances as circumstances changed. (As a
contemporary case in point, the most reviled enemies of World
War II have become mutually esteemed economic and political
partners within several decades.) Plasticity, defined in this manner, will be naturally constrained by invariant commitments to a
specific class of "others" based on genetic factors; thus, ethnic
nepotism would have been a maladaptive characteristic.

The question then naturally arises as to why ethnocentrism, if it
is maladaptive, appears ubiquitous in human affairs. Silverman
proposed that ethnic prejudices, particularly at the intergroup
level, serve mainly as rationalizations—means of preserving self-
images of fidelity and fairness in the face of the perennial pursuit
of situationally optimal affiliations. An observation consistent
with this analysis was described in elegant manner by Wilson
(1978, 163), as follows:

> Human beings are consistent in their codes of honour but endlessly
> fickle with reference to whom the codes apply. The genius of human
> sociality is in fact the ease with which alliances are formed, broken and
> reconstituted, always with strong emotional appeals to rules believed
> to be absolute.

With regard to the question of why self-deception of this nature
would have been adaptive, Silverman referred to Alexander's
(1979) explanation that it enhanced the ability to deceive others.

Silverman described several sources of support for his argument, including a review encompassing three classic means by
which groups seek to increase their fitness at the expense of others: warfare, slavery, and famine. His conclusion was that, in con-

trast to conventional wisdom, these events tended throughout history to involve racially exogenous rather than endogenous groups. Silverman acknowledged that it is plausible from the standpoint of resource competition that conflicts will more likely occur between proximate groups, which would tend also to be genetically similar. He maintained, however, that the sheer fact that oppression does not generally follow racial lines, "does, nevertheless, suggest that, from a world view, the role of genetic communality is meagre and subordinate to pragmatic considerations, at best."

In contrast, Vanhanen (1991) concluded from a historical study of India, based on Van den Berghe's concept of ethnic nepotism, that more than 90 percent of violent social conflicts occurred between "clearly different ethnic groups."

The present chapter presents two further studies on the issue. The first was a laboratory investigation using an original, self-report method devised to measure the relative salience of ethnocentric vs. pragmatic motives. The second examined the competing theories described above as they apply to two current international conflicts, both generally described in the media as "ethnic wars" and "ethnic cleansing" movements.

A Self-Report Study of Ethnocentrism vs. Pragmatism

In psychological studies with animals, a common method of ascertaining the relative strengths of motives is to put them in opposition, for example, assessing by means of a T-maze whether a parturitional animal will go first to a food source or to the cries of her offspring. This paradigm was broadly adapted for the present purpose by means of a survey designed to evaluate the potency of motives based on ethnocentrism when confronted by pragmatic considerations. Various hypothetical scenarios were presented to subjects, for which they were required to decide whether they would favor a member or members of their own, self-defined, ethnic group or some other ethnic group, under conditions whereby: (1) there was no cost or risk to the subject whatever the choice (NCR); (2) there was a minimal cost or risk to the subject if his or her own ethnic group was favored (MCR); and (3) there was a substantial cost or risk to the subject if his or her own ethnic group was favored (SCR).

Survey directions

The survey was in written form and began with the following directions:

TO ALL RESEARCH PARTICIPANTS:
The study in which you are about to take part is designed to evaluate how peoples' ethnic group identifications may influence their decisions in various circumstances.

You will be presented with eight, brief scenarios. Each involves a person or persons called ALPHA and another person or other persons called BETA. Each is followed by a series of questions asking you to decide between the ALPHAS or the BETAS. Let ALPHA represent *your own ethnic group* and let BETA represent *some other ethnic group*. (These concepts are explained below.)

"Your own ethnic group" means however you define it for yourself. It may be in terms of religion, race, nationality, or any combination of these, for example, Jewish, Italian, Hispanic, Irish Canadian, White Anglo-Saxon Protestant, etc. Decide how you generally define your ethnic group and write this below. Use this definition to represent ALPHA throughout.

I DEFINE MY ETHNIC GROUP AS _____

"Some other ethnic group," can mean a particular one—any that you choose for any question—or you can let it refer to some non-specific group. BETA should be your answer, however, if there is *any* ethnic group that you would choose over ALPHA in a given situation.

Some of the scenarios will seem very improbable to you, but try to imagine yourself in each one, and give as authentic answers as possible. If you feel that you would want to know more about the ALPHAS or BETAS, or about the situations depicted in the scenarios, assume that all the information that is given is all the information that you would have in the actual situation. If you feel very undecided about some questions, pretend, again, that you are actually in the situation and *must make a choice*. There is space for comments you might wish to make about your answers on the last page, and we would very much like to see these, but please answer each question as directed.

Your responses will, of course, be completely anonymous and used for research purposes only. It would be useful for any analyses, however, if you would give the brief information requested about yourself on the last page.

Thank you for your cooperation and for contributing your self-insights to this project.

Survey items

When subjects had completed reading the directions, their individual questions were answered. Then they responded to the eight items of the survey, reprinted below, by writing either "A" for ALPHA or "B" for BETA in the space following each question. Prior to beginning the items, they were requested, again, to "Please give one or the other answer no matter how certain or uncertain you may feel about your choice."

1. THE HARDWARE STORE
   You need some hardware items and you have a choice of two stores, one owned by an ALPHA family and the other by a BETA family. Which would you go to if:
   a) They are similar in price, selection and distance from you?
   b) They are similar in price and selection but the ALPHA store is a little further away (50 yards further to walk) and there is a severe winter storm occurring?
   c) Both stores have similar prices and selections but the ALPHA store is quite a distance further away (a quarter of a mile further to walk) and there is a severe winter storm occurring?

2. THE RELIEF AGENCY PROGRAM
   You wish to join a relief agency program whereby you contribute ten dollars per month to help needy people. You have a choice of two such agencies, one of which assists ALPHAS and the other, BETAS. Both groups to be helped are equally needy and both are receiving about the same amount of assistance. Which would you contribute to if:
   a) Both agencies have the same overhead costs, and eight of your ten dollars per month would go directly for assistance?
   b) The ALPHA agency has slightly larger overhead costs and $7.50 of your ten dollars per month, rather than eight, would go directly for assistance?
   c) The ALPHA agency has considerably larger overhead costs and five of your ten dollars per month, rather than eight, would go directly for assistance?

3. THE BANQUET HALL
   You own and manage a banquet hall. Two requests for your hall arrive simultaneously in the mail, both for the same

evening. One is from an ALPHA group and the other from a BETA group. Which would you accept if:

a) They are both for the same arrangements, and the profit for you in either case would be about $500?

b) The BETA request is for slightly more expensive arrangements and the profit for you would be about $50 more?

c) The BETA request is for considerably more expensive arrangements and the profit for you would be about double; that is, $500 more?

4. THE EMERGENCY FOOD SUPPLY TRUCK

You are the driver and sole passenger of a truck bringing emergency food supplies to disaster victims in a remote area. You learn of two groups, equally desperate but in opposite directions from you, one composed of ALPHAS and the other, BETAS. Which would you go to if:

a) You have sufficient gasoline to make a trip to only one of the groups and return safely?

b) You have sufficient gasoline to get to the BETAS and return safely, but the ALPHAS are a little farther from you and there is a slight chance, about 1 or 2 percent, that you will become stranded in a dangerous area attempting to return?

c) You have sufficient gasoline to get to the BETAS and return safely, but the ALPHAS are considerably farther from you and there is a significant chance, about 40 to 50 percent, that you will become stranded in a dangerous area attempting to return?

5. THE PURCHASE

You are about to make a household appliance purchase of about one thousand dollars, and you have a choice of two brands. One is manufactured by a company owned by ALPHAS, and the other by BETAS. Which would you buy if:

a) They are equivalent in quality, service, price and every other relevant aspect?

b) They are equivalent in every relevant aspect except that the ALPHA's product is about $30 higher in price?

c) They are equivalent in every relevant aspect except that the ALPHA's product is about $150 higher in price?

6. THE NUCLEAR ACCIDENT

A nuclear accident has occurred in your region, and dangerous levels of radioactivity are expected. You have a shelter, how-

ever, in which you plan to stay with your family for an anticipated three-week period until it is safe to leave. You have sufficient facilities and oxygen for one other person, but you learn of
two in the vicinity, either of whom you can contact, who are in
need of shelter. One is an ALPHA and the other is a BETA.
Whom would you invite if:

a) You know that neither of the two has been near the site of
   the accident; thus neither poses any threat of having been
   contaminated and, consequently, of contaminating others in
   your group?

b) You know that BETA has *not* been near the site of the accident
   but ALPHA has for a few seconds, and you calculate that
   there is a remote chance, perhaps one in a hundred, that he
   or she has become contaminated?

c) You know that BETA has *not* been near the site of the accident
   but ALPHA has for several minutes, and you calculate that
   there is a significant chance, perhaps one in four, that he or
   she has become contaminated?

7. THE DESERTED ISLAND
   You have decided, for some good reason, to live the rest of your
   life on a deserted island that you own, and you advertise for a
   mate with the intention of raising a family there. There are two
   applicants, one an ALPHA and the other, a BETA. Which would
   you choose if:

   a) They are, overall, similar in attributes that may be important
      to you, such as age, state of health, attractiveness, intelli-
      gence, etc.?

   b) They are, overall, similar in attributes that may be important
      to you except that there is a history of a serious genetic
      disorder in ALPHA's family, with a very small chance,
      about one in 80, that it will become manifest in any one of
      your children?

   c) They are, overall, similar in attributes that may be important
      to you except that there is a history of a serious genetic
      disorder in ALPHA's family, with a significant chance,
      about one in three, that it will become manifest in any one of
      your children?

8. THE FLOOD
   You are escaping from a flood. There are two available boats
   waiting to leave, each with one space. There are also two other
   people trying to escape, one an ALPHA and the other a BETA,

each approaching one of the boats. Thus, you can enable ALPHA to escape by taking the boat BETA is headed for, or help BETA to escape by taking the boat ALPHA is headed for. Whom would you help to escape if:

a) You are assured of reaching either boat before the other person?
b) There is a slight chance; about one in 25, that you will not reach the boat BETA is headed for before BETA does? (Thus, if you try to help ALPHA to escape you may be stranded yourself.)
c) There is a significant chance; about one in three, that you will not reach the boat BETA is headed for before BETA does?

We considered that the use of nonspecific ALPHA and BETA designations allowed subjects to respond to scenarios in terms of self-defined ethnic identities and also controlled for biases they may have held toward specific ethnic groups.

Some scenarios were necessarily fanciful in order to include a range of costs and risks. Items 2, 3, and 5 dealt with monetary costs; 1 involved loss of comfort; 4 and 8 were related to risks of personal safety; 6 to safety of the person and his or her family; 7 was associated with health risks to future progeny.

In pilot studies we included a response category of "no preference" and found that this was, overall, the most frequent answer in the NCR condition. When we converted to a forced choice between ALPHA and BETA, however, more than 90 percent of responses to NCR were ALPHA, suggesting that "no preference" responses were largely prompted, consciously or otherwise, by considerations of social desirability. Thus, the forced-choice method was retained.

Subjects' written and verbal comments generally suggested that the scenarios did evoke self-examination. Some subjects complained that the survey was "too personal" or probed "too deeply." Others spoke positively of the self-insights they had gained.

Supplementary data

At the close of the survey, subjects were asked to indicate age and sex, which were assessed in terms of their relationships to ethnocentrism scores. Assessments were performed also on the relationship of ethnocentrism scores to subjects' own ethnic groups.

Procedure

The subjects, 339 volunteers from undergraduate and graduate courses at York University in Canada, were administered the survey in groups of approximately 20 to 40. Eleven subjects were excluded because they either failed to respond or inappropriately responded to more than two items. (A response was deemed inappropriate by virtue of its implausibility if the subject moved from BETA to ALPHA at any point between conditions, suggesting that the subject would not aid a member of his or her own ethnic group when there were lesser costs or risks involved but would when these were greater.) Resultant Ns were 214 females and 114 males, which was consistent with the sex ratio in the population from which they were solicited.

Scoring

The question of the salience of ethnocentric vs. pragmatic motives in interpersonal affairs was evaluated in terms of percentages of ALPHA responses for each item in each condition, across subjects.

For the analyses of interindividual correlates, an ethnocentrism score was derived for each subject in terms of the mean number of ALPHA responses per items answered. This yielded a theoretical range of scores of zero to three, from low to high ethnocentrism.

Factor analysis of survey items

A principle components analysis was conducted for ethnocentrism scores between items, across subjects. Based on a minimum criterion of eigen value greater than one, just one factor emerged (EV=2.89), demonstrating that the scale measured a unitary dimension. Individual item loadings on the factor were between 0.57 and 0.69, with the exception of Item 2, "The Relief Agency Program," which loaded at 0.44. Item 2 also showed a divergent pattern of responses between cost/risk conditions, described below.

Findings: ethnocentrism vs. pragmatism

Table 18.1 shows percentages of ALPHA responses in each cost/risk category by item and sex of subject.

For both sexes, more than 90 percent of responses in the NCR condition were ALPHA, suggesting that the scenarios did generally evoke ethnocentric motives when costs or risks to subjects

Table 18.1. Percentages of ALPHA Responses in No Cost/Risk (NCR), Minimal Cost/Risk (MCR), Substantial Cost/Risk (SCR) by Item and Sex of Subject[1]

	NCR		MCR		SCR	
Item	F	M	F	M	F	M
Hardware store	94	93	11	20*	2	4
Relief agency	88	91	60	68	26	36*
Banquet hall	93	89	27	43**	4	7
Supply truck	91	91	28	40*	9	17*
Purchase	93	95	18	31**	4	9*
Nuclear accident	92	91	23	26	6	11
Desert island	89	88	39	37	12	13
Flood	90	88	21	26	15	17

[1] Ns for items ranged between 209–14 for females; 112–4 for males.
* p at or >0.05   ** p>0.01.

were nil. There were no significant sex differences or trends of this nature in this condition.

Consistent with the propositions underlying this study, ALPHA responses across items decreased radically in the MCR condition. Item 2 (which was, as noted above, deviant in its factor loading), however, showed a markedly lesser decrease. Excluding this item, percentages of ALPHA responses ranged from a low of 11 for females on Item 1 to a high of 43 for males on Item 3. Thus, subjects tended to become largely pragmatic with anticipation of the most minimal costs or risks to themselves.

Sex differences were evident in the MCR condition with males showing higher percentages of ALPHA responses, significant or closely approaching significance for four of the eight items. In interpreting intergroup differences, however, we need to be aware that ethnocentric responses may be confounded with tolerance for costs or risks. In fact, the observation that sex differences were not observed in the NCR condition may suggest that tolerance for costs and risks was more likely the basis for sex differences in the MCR condition.

On the other hand, group differences in the NCR condition may readily have been subject to a ceiling effect. Moreover, the sex differences in MCR involved one item dealing with physical danger, compared to two items dealing with financial costs and one dealing with loss of convenience. If tolerance for costs and risks was the critical determinant, we might expect higher percentages of ALPHA scores for males to appear primarily when risks of physical danger are involved. Thus, in all, interpretation of the sex differences data in terms of greater ethnocentrism on the part of males seems favored.

ALPHA responses continued to decline in the SCR condition. Excluding Item 2, which was again deviant, percentages ranged from a low of 2 for females on Item 1 to a high of 17 for males for both Items 4 and 8. Again, sex differences in the direction of higher percentages for males were observed, significant or closely approaching significance for Items 2, 4, and 5.

Similar to MCR, two of the items showing sex differences concerned financial costs compared to one involving physical danger, suggesting again that ethnocentrism was the primary factor.

Though consistent with its lower factor loading, it is not readily apparent why Item 2 showed markedly lesser effects of costs and risks than the others. There was a difference in form between this item and the others in that costs were indirect; that is, subjects' projected monetary contributions were the same in all conditions though less would have been used for actual aid to the needy. In theory, costs should be perceived the same by subjects whether they are paid directly or indirectly. People may, however, respond to such situations concretely (perhaps in life as well as in our survey), calculating costs solely in terms of sums paid out. On the other hand, there may be some aspect of contributing to relief agency programs that increases ethnocentrism.

Correlates of ethnocentrism scores

There were no trends in the data between age and ethnocentrism scores, either for males or females, though it should be noted that the students comprising the sample represented a fairly restricted age group. The mean age was 24.56 (SD=6.57), and sexes were equivalent.

As indicated by the data of Table 18.1, sex differences in ethnocentrism scores were significant. Means were 1.41 (SD=0.49) and 1.30 (SD=0.42) for males and females respectively (t=2.01; p<0.05).

Mean ethnocentrism scores by racial/ethnic groups are shown in Table 18.2, in descending order from lowest to highest. The categories of WASP (White Anglo-Saxon Protestant), Italian, and Jewish represent verbatim self-descriptions. Other categories comprise consolidations of self-descriptions, which were necessary to render minimum Ns of 15 per group. Thirty-one subjects were not included because their descriptions could not be incorporated

Table 18.2. Mean Ethnocentrism Scores by Subjects' Ethnic Group

Group	N	Mean	SD
WASP	126	1.22	0.43
Asian	15	1.29	0.34
Italian	36	1.38	0.35
Other European	31	1.38	0.59
Black	15	1.52	0.33
Jewish	38	1.64	0.41

within one of the larger groups, and twenty others did not respond to the question.

A one-way ANOVA between groups was significant (F=5.91; p<0.001). The sole significant simple effect at p<0.05 by a Tukey Test was between the WASP and Jewish groups, though other comparisons may well have reached this level with increased Ns. Again, it should be considered that these differences may, to some extent, represent tolerance for costs and/or risks rather than ethnocentrism.

Reconciling Laboratory and Life:
An Inquiry into "Ethnic Wars"

To the extent that the ALPHA/BETA survey elicited valid projections of subjects' probable behaviors, the conclusion of this study is that ethnocentrism is a generally weak motive, readily relinquished when confronted with utilitarian considerations. Thus, it seems fallacious to regard ethnic nepotism as the root cause of human intergroup conflict. The thesis underlying the present study—that intergroup contests are primarily driven by pragmatics, and that ethnocentric rationales by protagonists are, in fact, rationalizations—appears more feasible.

Though profoundly tragic, the profusion of supposed "ethnic wars" and exercises in "ethnic cleansing" of the last several decades may provide a natural laboratory for this issue. Offhand, these events appear consistent with the notion of ethnic nepotism. We took a closer look at two of the most violent and genocidal of these wars, however—in the former Yugoslavia and in the nations of Rwanda and Burundi—focusing on three aspects in order to test between the ethnic nepotism theory and Silverman's alternative perspective. These were: (1) the relative degree of genetic relatedness of the protagonists; (2) the course of racist attitudes toward each other prior to the conflict and after its onset; and (3) pragmatic considerations that might represent the essential cause of the confrontation.

Genetic relatedness of the protagonists

The former Yugoslavia. The three protagonists in this region, Croats, Serbs, and Muslims, are of Slavic origin, and the only identifiable difference among them is religion. Croats are Catholic, Serbs are Orthodox, and Muslims follow Islam. The groups have lived together for about four centuries, speak the same language, and have intermarriage rates that seem relatively high for neighboring ethnic groups. For example, 26 percent of Bosnian residents are of mixed heritage; 29 percent of Serbs living in Croatia who married in the 1980s took Croatian partners; 62 percent of married Croats living in Serbia have non-Croatian partners (Denitch 1994; Djilas 1991; Rusinow 1988).

Rwanda and Burundi. This war is between the Hutus and the Tutsis, who have lived side by side in the region of both countries for at least four centuries. The origins of these tribes remains a mystery. In terms of physical attributes, it is said that Tutsis are taller, with higher foreheads and narrower features, but these differences are not reliably discernible (Lemarchand 1994; Shoumatoff 1994), suggesting that intermarriage was customary in their history.

The tribes share a common religion, language, and social organization. Zuure (1931), a missionary who served in Burundi for 17 years, concluded that it was futile to try to identify cultural, attitudinal, or behavioral distinctions between them. It has been argued, in fact, that whatever differences do exist relate to caste more than ethnicity (Lemarchand 1993; 1994; Shoumatoff 1994). This is evidenced, for example, by the fact that one can be regarded as both a Hutu and Tutsi. Lemarchand (1994, 10) writes: "Thus a Tutsi cast in a role of client vis-à-vis a wealthier patron would be referred to as a Hutu, even though the cultural identity remained Tutsi. Similarly, a prince was a Hutu in relation to a king, and a high ranking Tutsi was a Hutu in relation to a prince."

The course of ethnocentric attitudes

Although the tendency of the media has been to cite historical antagonisms as evidence for the ethnic nature of the conflicts in both the former Yugoslavia and Rwanda/Burundi, scholars tend to feel that this is a misguided view. Malcolm (1994, xxii) makes the point in regard to Bosnia, where the most vicious fighting in the former Yugoslavia has occurred, as follows:

> Of course it is easy to go through the history of a country such as Bosnia picking out instances of regional divisions, violence and ungovernability. The evidence is there ... But the political history of the late twentieth-century Bosnia had not been determined by what happened in the thirteenth or eighteenth centuries. Commentators who like to give some hastily assembled historical authority to their writings can always pick out a few bloody episodes from the past and say: "It was ever thus." One could perform the same exercise with the history of France, picking out the religious wars of the sixteenth century, the barbarity of the St. Bartholomew's Day massacre, the frequent regional rebellions, the Fronde, the brutal treatment of the Huguenots in 1685, the appalling violence and mass murder which followed the French Revolution, the instability of the nineteenth-century politics, even the whole history of collaborations and resistance in the Second World War. But if a number of foreign backed politicians and military commanders began bombing Paris with heavy artillery tomorrow, we would not sit back and say that it was an inevitable consequence of "ancient French hatreds." We would want to look a little more closely at the real nature and origins of this particular crisis.

The three Yugoslavian groups appear to have lived in relative harmony for all of their coexistence until the period of World War II, when they developed opposing alliances with the warring blocs and came into violent confrontation with each other (Denitch 1994; Duncan and Holman 1994). Despite this period, there was little indication of intense ethnic identifications during the decades prior to the present conflict. In fact, there seemed to be an obverse trend. Census figures reveal that the number of individuals identifying themselves as Yugoslavs rather than by ethnic label increased between 1971 and 1981 by five times in Croatia, four times in Serbia, and eight times in Bosnia (Rusinow 1988). Further, it was no easy task for any of the factions to marshal their forces in the initial stages of the struggle; for example, 85 percent of reservists in Belgrade failed to respond to a call-up (Denitch 1994). Once the war had begun, the rationalizations for it needed to be fueled continuously and relentlessly by ethnic hate-mongering on the part of Serbia's leader, Milosevic, and Tudjman, his equally powerful, neo-Stalinist counterpart in Croatia (Ignatieff 1994). Further evidence that ethnic attitudes were more an outcome than a cause of the conflict emanates from a poll of Croats (Siber 1992), first conducted in 1986 and repeated in 1990 when separation of the states of the region was imminent. The poll presented a list of group attributes headed by the question, "To what degree is the following central in defining your nation?" Regrettably for the present purpose, "genetic similarity" was not included, but the survey did list "religion," on which ethnicity was based, and "culture," which is often a euphemism for ethnic communality. In 1986, 13 percent of respondents considered religion and 10 percent deemed culture as "absolute" criteria, compared to 45 percent and 62 percent, respectively, in 1990. No other categories rose nearly as dramatically.

Regarding Hutus and Tutsis, according to the oral history dating to the turn of the century, they had always lived together without dissension of note (Vansina 1985). There were rivalries among ruling factions in the modern era, but before the inception of the present conflict in the mid-1960s, these did not involve Hutu-Tutsi differences. During the Burundi independence movement of the 1950s, two dominant parties arose, neither of which held particular affiliations with either tribe, and the election of 1961 resulted in a landslide victory for Prince Rwagasore, who was highly popular with both groups (Lemarchand 1993).

Practical factors influencing the wars

Economic conditions were generally poor in the region of the former Yugoslavia in 1990, as were prospects for becoming competitive in new free-world markets, and this was particularly true of Serbia. Then, in 1991, Slovenia, which represented 8 percent of the population yet produced 25 percent of the region's gross national product, declared its independence. Croatia and Bosnia prepared to follow suit, with apparent intentions to renew propitious economic partnerships with Germany and Austria. Serbia's traditional alliances had been with Russia, which could scarcely offer succor at this point in history. Thus, impending new affiliations by its present economic partners threatened to cast Serbia into economic isolation and increased poverty.

It was then that Serbia began its military mobilization and aggression. The rationale was ethnocentric; this step was required to protect the rights of the Serbian minority in the seceding states. The apparent true motives, however, were pragmatic: to prevent an imminent, adverse shift in alliances in the region and to gain territorial and economic resources (see Denitch 1994; Duncan and Holman 1994; Glenny 1992).

Rwanda and Burundi were also poor, and economic resources were inequitably distributed, with the majority of clerical, managerial and other relatively secure and high-salaried positions in the hands of the Tutsi minority. Seeking to alter this situation, Rwandan Hutus staged a successful rebellion in 1966, driving thousands of Tutsis into Burundi. Burundian Tutsis, fearing a similar upheaval, turned on the Hutus, and the conflict escalated from that point (Lemarchand 1993).

Conclusion

Studies of the ultimate origins of molar social variables, such as ethnocentric attitudes and human warfare, necessarily suffer somewhat in precision; hence, there probably are viable, alternative interpretations of our findings. Nevertheless, there are patterns in both our laboratory and historical data that appear contrary to the explanation of ethnocentrism based on ethnic nepotism or genetic relatedness, and that support the alternative perspective that human group alliances are pragmatic in their source and that ethnocentric attitudes are outcomes rather than antecedents of group conflict.

First, if ethnocentrism represents ethnic nepotism—an evolved extension of familial nepotism—we would expect the motivation for its expression to show a relatively high degree of salience and potency. The data of our laboratory study does not, however, sustain this assumption. Subjects' own ethnic groups were chosen in more than 90 percent of the cases in which no costs or risks were involved, but were favored in less than 30 percent of cases with minimal costs or risks, and less than 10 percent with substantial costs or risks. These conclusions are congruent to earlier social psychological theories and data emphasizing the functional nature and malleability of social attitudes, including racial prejudices (e.g., Campbell 1958; Silverman and Shaw 1973).

If ethnocentric motives are foregone in the face of the most minor costs or risks, how can they account for deadly warfare? Our analyses of two of the most virulent of the contemporary, so-called, ethnic wars suggest that they do not. In both wars, protagonists were highly similar if not identical in racial characteristics; had lived together in relative harmony for four centuries; shared the same language, social organization, and political structure; and intermarried freely. Clearly, it could not have been predicted on the basis of ethnic nepotism that two of the most brutal, so-called ethnic wars of this era would occur among these groups. It might readily have been predicted, however, based on the economic conditions and power politics of the regions.

References

Alexander, R. D. (1979). *Darwinism and human affairs*. University of Washington Press, Seattle.

Campbell, E. Q. (1958). Some social psychological correlates of direction of attitude change. *Social Forces*, **36**, 335–40.

Dawkins, R. (1976). *The selfish gene*. Oxford University Press, Oxford.

Denitch, B. (1994). *Ethnic nationalism: The tragic death of Yugoslavia*. University of Minnesota Press, Minneapolis.

Djilas, A. (1991). *The contested country: Yugoslav unity and the Communist revolution 1919–1953*. Harvard University Press, Cambridge, Mass.

Duncan, R. W. and Holman, G. P., Jr. (1994). *Ethnic nationalism and regional conflict: The former Soviet Union and Yugoslavia*. Westview Press, Boulder, Colo.

Glenny, M. (1992). *The fall of Yugoslavia: The third Balkan war*. Penguin, London.

Hamilton, W. D. (1964). The genetical theory of social behaviour (I). *Journal of Theoretical Biology*, **7**, 1–16.

———. (1975). Innate social aptitudes of man: An approach from evolutionary genetics. In *Biosocial anthropology* (ed. R. Fox), pp. 133–55. Wiley, New York.

Ignatieff, M. (1993). *Blood and belonging: Journeys into the new nationalism*. Viking, Toronto.

Lemarchand, R. (1993). Burundi in comparative perspective: Dimensions of ethnic strife. In *The politics of ethnic conflict regulation* (ed. J. McGarry and B. O'Leary), pp. 151–71. Routledge, London.

———. (1994). *Burundi: Ethnicide as a discourse and practice*. Cambridge University Press, New York.

Malcolm, N. (1994). *Bosnia: A short history*. Macmillan/Papermac, London.

Rushton, J. P., Russell, R. J. H., and Wells, P. A. (1984). Genetic similarity theory: Beyond kin selection. *Behaviour Genetics*, **14**, 179–93.

———. (1985). Personality and genetic similarity theory. *Journal of Social and Biological Structures*, **8**, 63–86.

Rusinow, D. I. (1988). *Yugoslavia, a fractured federalism*. Wilson Center Press, Washington, D.C.

Shoumatoff, A. (1994). Flight from death. *The New Yorker*, June, 44–55.

Siber, I. (1992). The structure and dynamics of the Yugoslav political environment and elections. In *The tragedy of Yugoslavia: The failure of democratic transformation* (ed. J. Seroka and V. Pavlovic), pp. 141–72. M. E. Sharpe, Armond, New York.

Silverman, I. (1986). Inclusive fitness and ethnocentrism. In *The sociobiology of ethnocentrism* (ed. V. Reynolds, V. Falger, and I. Vine), pp. 112–7. Croon Helm, London.

———. (1987). Race, race differences, and race relations: Perspectives from psychology and sociobiology. In *Sociobiology and psychology: Ideas, issues, and findings* (ed. C. Crawford, M. F. Smith, and D. Krebs), pp. 205–22. Erlbaum, Hillsdale, N.J.

Silverman, I. and Shaw, M. E. (1973). Effects of sudden, mass, school desegregation on interracial interaction and attitudes in one southern city. *Journal of Social Issues*, **29**, 133–42.

Symons, D. (1979). *The evolution of human sexuality*. Oxford University Press, New York.

van den Berghe, P. L. (1981). *The ethnic phenomenon*. Elsevier, New York.

Vanhanen, T. (1991). *Politics of ethnic nepotism: India as an example*. Sterling, New Delhi.

Vansina, J. (1985). *Oral tradition as history*. University of Wisconsin Press, Madison, Wis.

Wilson, E. O. (1978). *On human nature*. Harvard University Press, Cambridge, Mass.

Zuure, B. (1931). *L'ame du Murundi*. Beauchesne, Paris.

PART VI

❧

INSTITUTIONAL MECHANISMS

CHAPTER NINETEEN

IDEOLOGY, INDOCTRINATION, AND NONCOGNITIVE FOUNDATIONS OF BELIEF IN LEGITIMACY

A BIOBEHAVIORAL ANALYSIS OF LEGITIMATE VIOLENT SOCIAL ACTION

Gebhard Geiger

Introduction

In the social animal species, including humans, physical force is a frequent means of the resolution of conflict within and between social groups. Moreover, recent findings in ethology and sociobiology suggest that the observable variation in human aggressive behavior is, to some considerable extent, adaptive in the sense of Darwinian evolutionary theory (Huntingford and Turner 1987; Silverberg and Gray 1992). However, in the sociocultural contexts of human decision-making, one also has the problem of how to legitimize (justify) violent social action. Thus, it is specific of political institutions such as states that their administrations lay claim to the legitimate use of forceful sanctions as a routine means of social control. Similar questions of the ultimate foundation of rights and duties arise when military force is employed in international politics.

Substantive conceptions of legitimate social action have been the subject of philosophical speculation in Western moral and political thought for more than two thousand years. However, there are constraints on human society that render the legitimacy of social action a practical problem as well. For instance, cooperation in human groups usually involves division of labor and hierarchical organization. Hence, in complex sociocultural systems individuals may be expected to act in ways that do not necessarily accord with their own interests. Similarly, in large-scale societies conflicts of interest are always likely, especially under the conditions of ecological and economic scarcity. Modes of conflict resolution are thus required that are valid and generally accepted independently of subjective interests.

Table 19.1 lists various such modes of social action that are not necessarily guided by the self-interests of interacting individuals or groups, but nonetheless may be voluntary. The order in which they are listed is toward increasing degrees of the enforcement involved in their causation. According to this classification, legitimacy is understood as a nonselfish motivation to voluntary social action. A more comprehensive characterization of legitimacy from a combined sociological and biobehavioral perspective will be given below. However, the following points should be emphasized. In the analysis, the concept of legitimate action is used exclusively in the functionalist and subjectivist sense of empirical social science (Weber 1972, 1). In particular, legitimacy is an attribute that the social actors themselves assign to their actions and that is thus the intent of subjective attitudes and beliefs rather than a property of social interactions as such. Furthermore, the types listed in the table need not be mutually exclusive. Of course, there may be legitimate self-interests or legitimate institutional power, coercion, and so forth.

The following sections concentrate on the possible relationships between the legitimacy and the violent enforcement of social action. These relationships are indeed constitutive of political institutions, especially those of war. If physical force is to be employed in the resolution of political conflicts in a routine and organized fashion, a number of obvious functional requirements must be fulfilled concerning coherent social action and its motivational bases. These requirements include professional training and discipline as an attitude of prompt and habitual obedience on the part of the executive staff of political organizations, including the

Table 19.1: Various Types of Non-violently and Violently Enforced Social Action

Action	Particular Motivation	Motivation Type
Voluntary	Subjective utility	SELF-INTEREST
Voluntary	Moral attitudes Emotions Ritualized cues	LEGITIMACY
Traditional	Custom, habit, learning	
Discipline: professional, military, and other Obedience to positive law, political rule	Violent enforcement	SANCTIONS

armed forces. But among the individuals engaged in organized conflicts there must also be a minimum of voluntary readiness to apply physical force. Moreover, this readiness must be independent of the self-interests of the interacting individuals and groups because otherwise the organization would be costly, unstable, and inefficient. An efficient army is wholly dedicated to fighting the enemy rather than disciplining deserters and mutineers within its own ranks. Clearly, in any kind of planned and purposely organized mass action, especially under the stressful conditions of intergroup conflict, it is an absolute functional requirement to avoid intragroup conflict between individual interests and collective goals.

In the following, I therefore look at legitimacy as a motivation distinct from self-interest and kin altruism that can release violent social action. I do so by combining perspectives from epistemology, evolutionary biology, and sociology. First, I introduce the concept of ideology as a noncognitively induced belief, or "subjective epistemic attitude." Then, I establish close and subtle relationships between ritualized dominance-submission interactions as studied by ethologists on the one hand, and charismatic authority as the ultimate source of legitimate domination on the other hand. Eventually, I look at beliefs in the legitimacy of social actions as the possible outcomes of ideological indoctrination.

Indoctrination and Indoctrinability

In Table 19.2 various dispositions of knowledge and belief are listed together with the cognitive and noncognitive processes by which such attitudes may be motivated. Beliefs that are ultimately founded on empirical evidence and that are methodically confirmed typically arise in empirical science (Fetzer 1981). Since they are essentially hypothetical and open to revision in the course of the research process, they tend to involve degrees of conviction less than 100 percent.

Ideology is characterized as a noncognitively induced strong conviction and as such implies dogmatism. This notion is certainly compatible with the various accounts and criticisms of ideology and dogmatism that can be found in the history of epistemology and in modern sociology of knowledge (Bell 1960; Mannheim 1965; Riegel 1973). Observe, however, that contrary to many philosophical and scientific criticisms of ideology, the definition in Table 19.2 makes no reference to concepts of truth. The critical point rather is whether in our beliefs we take into account that human cognition may be fallible, as is explicitly admitted in the distinction between science and ideology in Table 19.2.

There may also be heuristic, pragmatic, or even cynical attitudes of belief that arise from noncognitive processes, but that are distinct from ideologies to the extent that they remain self-critical. This kind of attitude is illustrated beautifully in Table 19.2 by a quotation from Henry IV of Navarra, who, as a Protestant,

Table 19.2: Various Types of Cognitively and Non-cognitively Induced Beliefs ("Subjective Epistemic Dispositions")

Type of belief	Degree of conviction	Foundation
Logical	100%	Proof
Scientific	< 100%	Cognition, methodical confirmation
Intuitive	0–100%	"Anything goes"
Ideological	100%	Noncognitive interactions
Instrumental	> 0%	Pragmatism, cynicism (i.e., noncognitive processes; "Paris vaut une messe")

adopted the Roman Catholic faith in 1593 in order to confirm his position as king of France.

Examples of ideologies and noncognitive foundations of beliefs are given in Table 19.3, including the important case of indoctrination. This means teaching by pretending evidence or proof, for instance, by means of rhetoric, propaganda tricks, or "institutionalized persuasion" (see Salter, this volume).

Again, the various types of noncognitive processes listed in Table 19.3 need not be mutually exclusive. In real social interactions they rather tend to be correlated and reinforce each other. Thus, the prestige or authority a person has gained in his or her group may make him or her an effective "opinion leader" within that group, even in fields where the person has no experience or knowledge (Barkow 1989). Similarly, the success of indoctrination in the form of pretense of proof or evidence is sensitive to noncognitive interactions suitable for reconfirming human attitudes and convictions that may be challenged by counterevidence or otherwise subject to doubt. Accordingly, indoctrination often conveys simplified and stereotyped views and propagates them in highly repetitive and exaggerated ways, in order to make them appear self-evident. Where this can be achieved, indoctrination proves effective in shaping the social attitudes of individuals, especially emotional ones such as bonding, group attachment, and readiness to joint action (Eibl-Eibesfeldt 1984, 745, 837).

In view of the broad empirical significance of indoctrination and its effectiveness in changing attitudes and behaviors, a number of questions arise concerning the indoctrinability, or disposi-

Table 19.3: Examples of Non-cognitively Founded Beliefs

Ideologies:

- Holy books and traditional dogmas of the world religions
- Dogmatic theories of morality, politics, "natural right," etc.

Non-cognitive Foundations:

- Tradition, cultural transmission
- Imitation
- Gossip
- Authority
- Religious revelation
- Indoctrination, propaganda tricks, teaching by pretending evidence or proof
- Ritualized communication

tion to dogmatic belief, of the human individual. What precisely constitutes indoctrinability, how can its causes and constraints be explained, and how is this property conferred on the individual?

According to social science methodology, dispositions are hypothetical properties—or inferred "latent" variables in observed behaviors (Nowak 1977)—which, under experimentally controlled conditions, lead to particular observable responses, but which can be assigned to a person even if the test conditions do not prevail. Familiar examples are intelligence (as measured by I.Q.), economic preferences, and attitudes of risk acceptance, which can be meaningfully attributed to a person even in situations in which he or she is not engaged in cognitive problem-solving, economic activities, or decision-making under risk.

Problems of the origins and constraints of indoctrinability have been treated in human ethology within the framework of ritualized communication (Eibl-Eibesfeldt 1984). Since the present analysis aims at an evolutionary account of authority relations, I shall concentrate on ritualized dominance as a source of human indoctrinability.

Ritualized Dominance

By ritualization sociobiologists mean the adaptive evolution of previously noncommunicative traits into signals (Wilson 1975; Krebs and Davies 1981; Eibl-Eibesfeldt 1979). In animal dominance conflicts, morphological traits and expressive movements indicating an animal's age, sex, competitiveness, or experience are the typical signals suitable for ritualization. Once displayed, they help the contestants to estimate realistically the likely outcome of the conflict in case of further escalation, thus providing "cues" for less competitive individuals to retreat "voluntarily," that is, to settle the conflict by submitting, with an expected minimum loss in fitness. Here the critical point is that an individual's lower social status gets established or reinforced not through overt demonstrations of, but through this individual's ritualistically induced "belief" in, his opponent's superior physical and emotional dispositions to control the actions of the other group members.

Reference to the ritualization of dominance behavior is a central point in my argument. Theorists in the tradition of Western moral, legal, and political thought have tried to ultimately justify human action by philosophical reasoning. Whatever this may mean, reason implies intelligibility. Thus, according to this tradition, the legitimacy of an action is ultimately established by cognitive processes (Johnson 1966; von Kutschera 1982; Goldman 1988). While the traditional approach has largely remained speculative, modern positivism and empirical social science have always had great difficulties explaining nonselfish behavior that is not enforced, including voluntary obedience in dominance relations (Mansbridge 1990). I try to remove these difficulties by linking the ethology of ritualized dominance with Max Weber's famous sociology of legitimate domination (Weber 1972; Glassman and Swatos 1986).

Charismatic Authority

Weber distinguishes three "pure types" of authority—charismatic, traditional, and legal—as forms of legitimate domination, as opposed to coercive or economic power. Each of these three is roughly characterized as an effective, though nonviolently reinforced, claim to obedience. But only the first of these types ultimately constitutes the validity of social norms, whereas the latter two are historical and institutional (bureaucratic, economic, depersonalized, routinized, etc.) transformations of the former (Weber 1972).

To Weber, legitimacy is an individual's subjective belief in the normative preference order of social actions. This belief need not, but can, be sanctioned in a given social group and is generally held independently of subjective interests, notably economic ones. Originally, it is motivated by charismatic revelation on the part of a political or religious leader, where charisma is a person's capacity to gain a specific kind of recognition ("authority") by others— namely, the emotional stimulus to voluntary submission under the command of a person who is believed to possess extraordinary (magic, supranatural, heroic, etc.) qualities (Weber 1972).

Evolutionary Foundations of Charismatic Legitimacy

There are a number of connotations of charismatic authority that make this concept broadly susceptible to analysis and interpretation in ethological terms (Geiger 1993). First, legitimacy ultimately depends on the judgment of the leading individual in a social dominance relationship, with the validity and historical origins of legal norms being explicitly included in this explanatory scheme (Weber 1972).

Second, Weber defines the concept of charismatic legitimacy without any reference to the contents of the norms rendered legitimate. Thus, any kind of behavior may appear legitimate to a social actor motivated by charismatic authority, including actions as "base" as "passion for vengeance, plunder and the spoils of office" (Weber 1977, 63). However, this possibility is perfectly consistent with the observed, broad sociocultural variability of moral views and attitudes with which moral and legal philosophers and the proponents of "natural right" have never come to grips.

Third, charismatic reinforcement is conceptually distinct from the coercive sanctioning of behavior, although empirically the two modes of social control often concur. Where this is not the case, that is, where there is no additional support to authority by economic incentives or any institutional means of control, charisma is inherently unstable and needs to be continuously reconfirmed through demonstrations of the extraordinary qualities of the leader, signs of his or her magical powers, heroic deeds, and other proofs of "success." In ethological terms, this demonstration is a mode of signaling and exchange of ritualized "cues"—adaptive emotive agents or "releasing mechanisms"—of dominance-submission interactions in the social animal species (Krebs and Davies 1981; Eibl-Eibesfeldt 1986).

Eventually, charismatic legitimacy is an irrational belief, for subordinate individuals in a genuinely charismatic relationship tend to act in complete and unconditional devotion to their leader's will, which they perceive as their duty, rather than mind their own (e.g., economic) interests (Weber 1972).

Dominance hierarchies and the distribution of social rank and status within them are difficult to explain in evolutionary terms since they imply a considerable loss of fitness for subordinates. The situation is similar to the problem of irrational behavior in charismatic authority relations. In both cases, patterns of non-selfish behavior tend to occur that apparently "pay off" neither for those who adopt them nor for their descendants or any other close relatives. The evolutionary success of these control modes is due to the fact that low status in social groups, although disadvantageous in terms of lowered fitness (compared to the dominant), prevents the much greater loss of fitness on being ejected from the group. For group-living species, solitary living risks complete loss of fitness through death or failure to mate (Wittenberger 1981, 591). Submitting to a stronger individual is thus a fitness-conserving alternative to fleeing.

Since in the social animals, especially primates, social status is generally not an inherited but rather an acquired trait, continued face-to-face exchanges of status signals are necessary to establish or reconfirm rank orderings in these species (Walters and Seyfarth 1987). The same situation arises in charismatic interactions in human societies since charismatic status is, according to Weber, a face-to-face relationship and is not culturally inherited. Primarily for these two reasons, Weber's observation that charisma requires continued emotive signaling is perfectly compatible with the ethological pattern of manipulative cues in animal dominance behavior (cf. Krebs and Davies 1981; Eibl-Eibesfeldt 1986).

An overview and summary of the close correspondences between ritualistic signaling from the biobehavioral perspective, and charismatic authority from the point of view of Weber's sociology of legitimate domination is given in Table 19.4 (after Geiger 1993). The parallels extend to details of phenomenology, motivational and manipulative mechanisms, and functions of charismatic authority. Theoretically, these correspondences can be explained as the result of a functional change from an adaptive social pattern into nonadaptive expressions arising in the course of the cultural development of charismatic social relations (Geiger 1993). "Preadaptive" functional changes of this kind are adequately conceived by the notion of ritualized submission as an evolved behavioral disposition that, in sociocultural applications, constitutes indoctrinability. As such it may prove functional under the constraints of cultural history, which can be quite different from the "test conditions" under which it once evolved in human natural history.

Conclusion

A number of conclusions can be made from the foregoing, which can be summarized as follows. What people have believed to be legitimate in society and cultural history *need* not and, after all, *can* not be conceived in terms of moral cognitivism. It is the institutional transformations of face-to-face authority that motivate us to act in prescribed ways, at least insofar as we do so voluntarily. This notion of the ultimate reason of legitimacy is compatible with

Table 19.4: Correspondences Between Charismatic Authority and Ritualistic Signaling

Attached to:	Attributes of "Genuine" Charisma As Described by Max Weber	Ritualistic Status Signaling According to Ethology and Sociobiology
Social relation	Authority-obedience relation	Manipulation of submissive responses
	Emotional stimulus to coherent social action	Emotional stimulus to coherent social action
	Face-to-face	Face-to-face
	Asymmetric	Asymmetric
	Not restricted to any particular domain of authority	Multifunctional manipulative trait
	Unstable; continued emotive signaling required	Social status individually acquired; to be controlled by recurrent status signals
Leading individual	Non-violent status reinforcement	Ritualistic displays as against overt dominance aggression
	Signs of extraordinary ("charismatic") qualities	Movements and displays expressing superior abilities
	Focus of attention	Focus of attention
Subordinates	Voluntary obedience	Non-violently motivated compliance
	Subjective belief in charismatic quality	Assessment of ritualistic dominance signals
	Obedience perceived as duty	Emotionally motivated submission
	(Economic) irrationality of obedience	Loss in fitness

the findings of empirical sociology on the one hand, and the evolutionary biology of social dominance on the other. It also helps explain why ideological indoctrination often works so effectively in mobilizing organized mass action. Indoctrination may indeed make large-scale collective behavior look legitimate if it is reconfirmed by charismatic interactions or institutional authority ultimately derived from charisma.

Eventually, one can see indoctrination, charisma, and legitimacy as purposely and carefully designed stimuli promoting voluntary compliance with collective social action. This noncoercive way of motivating nonselfish behavior is a kind of "biotechnology," that is, the instrumental, effective mobilization and use of biobehavioral dispositions for purposes such as large-scale organized conflict—functions for which they were not originally selected by Darwinian evolution. Sociobologists sometimes seem to feel obliged to emphasize that biological (physiological, genetic, ecological) factors may indeed contribute to adaptive variation in human individual aggressiveness, but that these effects are small compared to those of social and cultural circumstances. "So if we seriously want to reduce levels of aggression in society, we should look to sociological, economic and political solutions and not to biology" (Huntingford and Turner 1987, 364). However, this conclusion is beside the point if we really want to understand organized violent behavior in society. Rather, the point is that the social, economic, and political solutions to which people should look may be reached by suitable biobehavioral means and strategies, including violent sanctions in case of conflict. Precisely the fact that there may be no biological reasons for physical force in politics and society is a powerful motivation for making such force look legitimate.

References

Barkow, J. H. (1989). *Darwin, sex, and status*. University of Toronto Press, Toronto.

Bell, D. (1960). *The end of ideology*. Free Press, Glencoe, Ill.

Eibl-Eibesfeldt, I. (1979). Ritual and ritualization from a biological perspective. In *Human ethology* (ed. M. von Cranach, K. Foppa, W. Lepenies, and D. Ploog), pp. 3–55. Cambridge University Press, Cambridge.

———. (1984). *Die Biologie des menschlichen Verhaltens*. Piper, Munich. Engl. transl.: 1989, *Human ethology*, de Gruyter, Hawthorne.

———. (1986). *Grundriß der vergleichenden Verhaltensforschung* (7th edn). Piper, Munich.

Fetzer, J. H. (1981). *Scientific knowledge*. Reidel, Dordrecht.

Geiger, G. (1993). Evolutionary anthropology and the non-cognitive foundation of moral validity. *Biology and Philosophy*, 8, 133–51.

Glassman, R. M. and Swatos, W. H., eds. (1986). *Charisma, history and social structure*. Greenwood, Westport, Conn.

Goldman, A. H. (1988). *Moral knowledge*. Routledge, London.

Huntingford, F. and Turner, A. (1987). *Animal conflict*. Chapman and Hall, London.

Johnson, O. A. (1966). *Moral knowledge*. Nijhoff, The Hague.

Krebs, J. R. and Davies, N. B. (1981). *An introduction to behavioural ecology*. Blackwell, Oxford.

Mannheim, K. (1965). *Wissenssoziologie*. Luchterhand, Neuwied.

Mansbridge, J. J. (ed.) (1990). *Beyond self-interest*. University of Chicago Press, Chicago.

Nowak, S. (1977). *Methodology of sociological research*. Reidel, Dordrecht.

Riegel, K.-G. (1973). Ideologie. In *Handlexikon zur Politikwissenschaft* (ed. A. Görlitz), pp. 154–60. Rowohlt, Reinbek.

Silverberg, J. and Gray, J. P., eds. (1992). *Aggression and peacefulness in humans and other primates*. Oxford University Press, Oxford.

von Kutschera, F. (1982). *Grundlagen der Ethik*. de Gruyter, Berlin.

Walters, J. R. and Seyfarth, R. S. (1987). Conflict and cooperation. In *Primate societies* (ed. B. B. Smuts, D. L. Cheney, R. S. Seyfarth, R. W. Wrangham, and T. T. Struhsaker), pp. 306–17. University of Chicago Press, Chicago.

Weber, M. (1972). *Wirtschaft und Gesellschaft* (5th edn). Mohr, Tübingen. Engl. transl.: 1968, *Economy and society*, Bedminster, New York.

———. (1977). *Politik als Beruf* (6th edn). Duncker und Humblot, Berlin. Engl. transl.: 1946, Politics as a vocation. In *From Max Weber: Essays in sociology* (ed. H. H. Gerth and C. W. Mills), pp. 77–128. Oxford University Press, New York.

Wilson, E. O. (1975). *Sociobiology: The new synthesis*. Harvard University Press, Cambridge, Mass.

Wittenberger, J. F. (1981). *Animal social behavior*. Duxbury, Boston.

CHAPTER TWENTY

INDOCTRINATION AS INSTITUTIONALIZED PERSUASION

ITS LIMITED VARIABILITY AND CROSS-CULTURAL EVOLUTION

Frank Kemp Salter

indoctrinate *v.tr.* 1. teach (a person or group) systematically or for a long period to accept (esp. partisan or tendentious) ideas uncritically
Concise Oxford Dictionary

I am a little girl, I play and sing;
I don't know Stalin, but I do love him.
Soviet school song introduced under Stalin

[Y]ou must really love people. You must "love-bomb" them. Onni has a staff of about twelve people who are the best "love-bombers" in the whole world.
"Moonie" cult member

Introduction

The argument of this paper leads to the conclusion reached by Eibl-Eibesfeldt (1982) that humans possess an evolved capacity to be indoctrinated into identifying with some group. But I take a different route to Eibl's bottom-up evolutionary approach based in ethnography and selection processes. Instead, I begin by identifying common aspects of indoctrination techniques found in diverse contemporary settings. The questions are then posed: if indoctrination is so valuable a tool of social control, why are the methods for achieving it so limited? What has constrained cultural experimentation, in so many other ways a source of rich variation, in the case of indoctrination? Not only is Eibl's trait hypothesis supported, but the indirect argument offers some further details of what indoctrinability is at the behavioral, emotional, and cognitive levels. But let me begin with definitions and a little history.

As the dictionary definition quoted above indicates, indoctrination has two distinct meanings related to the *method* of instruction and the *content* of the lesson. Indoctrination has not always carried negative connotation. Religious and secular educators alike assumed that a degree of indoctrination was of positive worth. Military forces have, at least until recently, put raw recruits through training programs carrying that name. The decline in acceptability of indoctrination, or a particular meaning of the term, can be traced in part to the progressive education movement led by John Dewey in the early part of the twentieth century (Raywid 1980).

The present volume is concerned primarily with indoctrinated changes to self-identity and group values. Of particular interest are processes leading an individual to favor a group with which he or she has been brought to identify. Indoctrination is not just any process resulting in the inculcation of group identity and values. An outcome of group identification does not prove that indoctrination was a contributing cause, unless it is further shown that some directed, systematic effort was involved on the part of an indoctrinating agent. In the absence of such effort the process is more appropriately called informal socialization, which includes spontaneous imprinting, the polar opposite of indoctrination. Indoctrination is organized socialization, whose political version has been defined thus: "Narrowly conceived, political socialization is the deliberate inculcation of political information, values, and practices by instructional agents who have been formally charged with this responsibility" (Greenstein 1968, 551).

To put this in ethological parlance, indoctrination is a superfluous catalyst in a process by which a subject irreversibly learns an attachment or other response after minimal exposure to a specific releasing stimuli. Wiessner (this volume) makes a similar point regarding traditional initiation: kin loyalty develops naturally; it is loyalty to a wider community that requires concerted effort at indoctrination. The criterion of effort means that the indoctrination concept does not apply to values that are taken up with little exposure to relevant symbols or ideas, since the concept implies systematic inculcation through repetition. The more stubborn the subject in resisting a doctrine, the more indoctrination is needed to effect change. And the exertion needed to effect indoctrination seems to be inversely related to the permanency of inculcation. In this way as well, indoctrination lies at the opposite extreme to imprinting, which not only occurs spontaneously without deliberate effort, but is usually irreversible. For example, according to Greenstein (1968), indoctrination ("civic training") enters the stream of deliberate government policy when there is a perceived need to forge a community, that is, when it is not forging itself. Hence, there was a rise in intensity of civic training in the United States around the turn of the century when large-scale immigration was underway, but less of this formal political socialization in Great Britain, which was less an immigrant society.

These definitional remarks lead to an interesting prediction concerning the relationship between indoctrination and indoctrinability. We should expect the most easily indoctrinated people, those possessing "high indoctrinability," *not* to be salient targets of indoctrination. For them, informal socialization should be sufficient to forge group identity. It is low indoctrinability connected to sensitive social behavior that should be targeted by elaborated sociocultural traditions of indoctrination. In this regard, it is interesting that the most rigorous indoctrination processes target young males and both sexes in the adolescent years (see section below regarding traditional initiation; and Wiessner this volume). Could it be that teenagers exhibit the least indoctrinability? Certainly this group is perceived cross-culturally to be the most disruptive and rebellious. A functionalist interpretation might apply. The extra effort directed at this group might have evolved culturally due to the payoffs gained from successfully harnessing adolescents to group goals, focused at points where it has been most profitable or cost-avoiding for achieving social goals, such as stability and mobilization for group tasks.

The argument to follow builds on a theory of social control belonging to the interdisciplinary field of political ethology (Tiger and Fox 1989/1971; Reynolds 1973; Milgram 1974; Caton 1988;

Geiger 1988; Salter 1995). A definition of political ethology offered by Caton (1983/1994) is succinct and heuristic for this purpose:

> Political ethology describes behaviors used for combining individuals into political aggregations and keeping them there. It presupposes a description of hunter-gatherer behaviors, and it assumes that such behaviors are the only material available for combining men into larger aggregations.

Caton notes that behavior can be "stretched" to achieve organizational goals. However, a sufficient condition of stable social engineering is that hunter-gatherer behaviors can be decoupled from their evolved small-group context and recombined into functional complexes (see also Eibl-Eibesfeldt 1972/1970; Caton 1988, Introduction; Salter 1995, Chs. 1 and 12). The decoupling is due to changes to a society's economy and demography, but the recombination is due to techniques of control that build up in cultural traditions and in the more formalized frameworks of institutions.

Cross-cultural universals of institutional techniques of control emerge from psychological, anthropological, and ethological studies of organizations. These techniques work by keying in to innate behavior systems implicated in the giving and receiving of face-to-face directives. Two such behavior systems are dominance and affiliation. It is possible to distinguish the assemblages of control techniques specific to these systems. In *Emotions in Command* (1995) I suggest as names for these assemblages "dominance infrastructures" and "affiliation infrastructures."

The evidence strongly indicates that the match of institutional control techniques and human universals of behavior is in large part the outcome of control techniques being adapted, over time, to fit human behavior. That is, control techniques are devised and, over time, culturally evolve to match relatively immutable human motivational and interactional characteristics. This complements the common sociological view that social structure determines individual social behavior. Structures can change the behavior of those who enter them, both in macro patterns such as routines and time allocation and in micro patterns of interpersonal style. And structure, as well as individuals strategizing on their own behalf, influences which affective behaviors among the human repertoire are emitted. But whether at work or leisure, in urban or rural societies, human social behavior is drawn from a limited functional set associated with particular physiological and environmental releasing conditions (Eibl-Eibesfeldt 1972/1970; 1989). In that case, *all* command hierarchies work on a limited set of social behaviors, because they are "jerrybuilt" around innate elements of the human biogram, to use E. O. Wilson's phrase (1975, 548). This is the core of what I call the infrastructure theory of social control.

The argument of this paper works within the framework of infrastructure theory, working backwards along that analysis in relation to indoctrination. As with dominance and affiliation, if the social infrastructure and behaviors involved in *indoctrination* correspond in a universal manner, that will be evidence that *indoctrinability* is typical of the species. However, if it is found that given techniques have diverse effects, or that "indoctrination infrastructures" do not overlap—i.e., that techniques are not drawn from a relatively invariant set across cultures and eras—that will be evidence against Eibl-Eibesfeldt's (1982) notion that there is an evolved trait of indoctrinability. In a broader context, evidence that social technologies are not constrained by human nature would undermine the very notion of human nature as a relatively invariant set of discrete behavioral systems and psychological traits. Conversely, the broad empirical base of the neo-Darwinistic model of human nature is a reason to have confidence in infrastructure theory and the concept of indoctrinability.

Some Indoctrination Techniques

Is there a universal behavioral or psychological process of indoctrination to group identity and affiliation? Does it have relatively stable, definable releasing conditions? In particular, which behaviors and relationships are common to *effective* indoctrination? The examples to be considered include extreme types of coercive indoctrination as well as voluntary methods. The examples also traverse doctrines that are attractive to the initiate, as well as those that are not. Communist ideology was not compatible with most Western victims of brainwashing. By contrast, nationalist ideas are taken up readily by many individuals. In sampling these several substantial literatures I aimed to tap mainstream, uncontroversial findings. The review is most thorough where coercion was salient, a counterintuitive factor for securing group identification, and relatively cursory with regard to well-known types of indoctrination, such as that practiced by totalitarian regimes and by advertisers.

Communist Chinese methods of brainwashing

Summary. This method is highly effective in inculcating ideological identification in opposition to strong resistance from mature Westerners holding firm beliefs and self-identities.

Brainwashing is a method of indoctrination with many precursors. The form to be discussed in this section was developed by the Communist Chinese initially for use against Chinese nationals, such as captured nationalist officers during the Civil War of the 1930s and 40s, then against Western residents of China, and finally in a much less intense form against American and other prisoners of war captured during the Korean War of the early 1950s. Somit (1968, 138) gave a good definition of brainwashing as "the enforced but real conversion of political belief and/or the sincere confession of guilt for crimes of which one is actually innocent." The point of sincerity requires emphasis. Lifton (1956) interviewed twenty-five European and American civilian residents of China who had undergone "thought reform" and who had then been released by the Communists to Hong Kong. He noted the "remarkable results" of the process: "Western civilians released from Chinese prisons, repeating their false confessions, insisting upon their guilt, praising the 'justice' and 'leniency' which they have received, and expounding the 'truth' and 'righteousness' of all Communist doctrine" (173).

The persistence of indoctrinated attachments and emotional responses must also be emphasized. This was not at all clear at first sight. Lifton followed up his twenty-five subjects three to four years after the initial interviews in various Western countries, and found that brainwashing had failed to sustain conversion to communism. Only one subject was still fully converted at that time. Indeed, most had developed harsh sentiments toward communism, usually harsher than before being brainwashed. This is not surprising, considering the powerful pressures to conform to prevailing anti-Communist ideas in Western society of the 1950s. Also, many subjects, such as the priest and the businessman, would have been under group pressure from work colleagues to reevaluate any Communist leanings. Nevertheless, Lifton found that their "deprogramming" was far from complete, that they "were still grappling with the powerful emotions and ideas implanted by the Chinese Communists" (Lifton 1989/1961, 237).

In particular, subjects experienced recurring cycles of fear, guilt, and relief. Lifton identifies residual fear and guilt as the most destructive long-term effects. There were also therapeutic effects including a sense of being emotionally strengthened, greater sensitivity to others' feelings, and more flexibility and trust in forming relationships (238). A lasting emotional effect was separation grief on leaving China. Lifton considers the factor of his subjects' long-term residence in China as missionaries or businessmen, but adds: "Some were mourning the loss of a very special intimacy of the thought reform group—the delight in total exposure and sharing" (226).

Schein (1956b) makes the significant point that the Communist Chinese invented no new method of indoctrination. Early assertions that the technique was a *sui generis* invention based on Pavlovian psychology (Meerloo 1957) do not fit the historical record of a buildup of methods over time and of those methods' lack of originality (Schein 1956b). Lifton's (1956, 193; and see 1989/1961) informants maintained that the basic methods were Soviet in origin, that is, part of the Marxist-Leninist political approach, but were adapted during the Civil War and honed during the Yenan period of 1937 to 1945 in the indoctrination of intellectuals joining the movement. In Schein's view, the novelty of brainwashing lay in the combination of many methods of persuasion deployed over a relatively brief period. A less intense form of thought reform was used on the whole Chinese population, a process in which most remained out of prison. The pressures used in the Cultural Revolution of the 1960s and 1970s is graphically described by Chang (1991).

Brainwashing in its full form as applied against prisoners is a benchmark against which other methods of indoctrination can be compared. Drawing on the case studies of Lifton (1956; 1989/1961), the full, coercive brainwashing process can be summarized thus:

(1) After a dramatic arrest involving weapons, the victim is blindfolded and/or bound, but without clear charges being stated. From that point on almost all the information received is controlled by the captors. The victim enters a regime of total "milieu control" in which "the prisoner's every word, action, or show of feeling becomes quickly known to the officials; and their subsequent manoeuvres can be immediately conveyed

back to him, magnified by overwhelming group pressures" (Lifton 1956, 191–2).

(2) A series of emotional assaults is made involving interrogation without clear charges, demands for confession of unspecified crimes, and binding. During this period the victim is deprived of sleep and is badgered night and day by interrogators (calling themselves "judges" or "instructors") and by cellmates who are working in concert with the interrogation team. Sympathetic interactions are allowed with other prisoners when the interrogators know they will advise cooperation. Eibl-Eibesfeldt (1972, 152) has referred to the regression to infantilism induced by extreme dependency, such as that found in brainwashing victims. This is not a new phenomenon. The Nazis degraded and tortured political prisoners to the point where they regressed to an infantile state in which they were in awe of their jailers and tended to identify with them, adopting their standards of behavior around the barracks (Bettelheim 1943, cited by Schein 1956b, 171; see also Caton's analysis, this volume).

(3) Physical and psychological breakdown are induced. The poor hygiene, poor quality food, inadequate sleep, isolation, unnatural surroundings, torture, and interrogations lead to a state in which the prisoner is "guilt-ridden, demoralized, and depressed, frequently to the point of being suicidal or experiencing transient psychotic symptoms" (Lifton 1956, 179).

(4) Leniency is shown when the prisoner reaches the breaking point. Calculated acts of kindness and some lifting of conditions are shown, often by someone other than the torturer. All prisoners reported that this had an immense impact on them. They felt gratitude toward the kind official, identified with his viewpoint, and were eager to comply to requests, even anticipating his wishes. The interrogator and prisoner began to work together toward a common goal (Lifton 1956, 180). This crucial stage in thought reform conforms with experimental research reported above indicating that perceived persuasiveness is increased by nonverbal evidence that the speaker likes the listener and is signaling moderately less status than warranted by the speaker's actual status (Mehrabian and Williams 1969).

(5) All the foregoing is aimed at making the prisoner confess, a word that is repeated *ad nauseam* during every interrogation. The "reformed" prisoner is expected to compile all previously written confessions into a final document. The indoctrinating mechanism at work may be the same as that in psychological experiments

conducted in the United States by Nuttin and colleagues (1987), in which subjects adopted beliefs and attitudes merely by being exposed to them in a state of arousal, in the absence of external arguments. In one experiment, students were asked to prepare and deliver a speech in favor of an almost universally hated exam system. At the end of the experiment, the students had undergone an extraordinary conversion from adamant opposition to a neutral or even supportive position. Based on other experiments, Nuttin concludes that attitude change is strongly affected by the conditions under which subjects evince their views. Once stated, a person tends to retain an attitude, in what Nuttin calls "response contagion." Nuttin was not sanguine about the "remarkable resistance to change of a once emitted 'attitude' response" (173), concluding that human behavior is less complex than most psychologists have thought.

(6) The confession is the starting point for denunciation of others, which is a required stage in the brainwashing process.

(7) Confession also serves as the basis of humiliation and self-denunciation, which can go on twelve hours per day. The victim must repeatedly rehearse his crimes, analyze them from the Communist viewpoint, and criticize himself for them.

There is a striking resemblance between these confessional procedures and those used in the Spanish Inquisition (Lifton 1956, 191). Jesuit priests who had experienced brainwashing told Lifton that the procedure resembled, in its criticism and self-criticism, their own training within the Church. One priest suggested that the method could have originated with Bolsheviks trained as youths in Russian Orthodox seminaries (191, n. 31). Lifton also points out brainwashing's similarity with Western psychiatry. Both emphasized the therapeutic aims of "help," "analysis," and "insight." Frank (1970) extended Lifton's suggestion by comparing the experience of a trainee psychoanalyst with that of the brainwashing victim. Both are authoritarian approaches to breaking down "resistance" to received doctrine. One might add that in both cases the divulging of intimate details has potentially subordinating and degradational effects. The connection between Freudian psychiatry and Soviet brainwashing techniques is made more palpable by recent scholarship. Freud observed around 1910 that his ideas had been most enthusiastically received in Russia. More to the point, his disciples rose to political prominence following the Bolshevik revolution (Etkind 1995, as reported by Chamberlain 1995). In no other country were psychoanalysts so powerful. In one of those extraordinary historical correlations, almost all leading Russian analysts were also important Bolsheviks, concentrated in Trotsky's wing of the Party. With the rise of Stalin, this circle experienced the suppression of Western-style analysis; many practitioners escaped to Hungary, Czechoslovakia, Germany, and further afield. Those who remained did so under the temporary protection of Trotsky, an enthusiast of Freud. The reform movement incorporated Pavlovian conditioning theory to produce a behavioral tool designed to indoctrinate children, starting in kindergarten, with sexual liberalism and other "progressive" ideas. So *Homo sovieticus* appears to have received a good dose of modern medicine from Freud and Pavlov. It would thus not be strange if Chinese Communist methods had a whiff of ether about them, given the importance of Soviet advisors to the early Chinese Communist Party. The psychiatry-brainwashing connection has reemerged in recent times with concern being expressed about the "psychiatric casualties" produced by certain group therapies which employ techniques reminiscent of Chinese thought reform (Hochman 1984; Singer and Ofshe 1990).

(8) Reeducation follows thought reform, and consists of study groups and individual instruction. Instructors get to know their charges intimately, developing close personal relationships and discovering salient aspects of their past.

Schein's (1956a) case study of twenty repatriated American prisoners of the Chinese Communists in Korea basically agrees with Lifton's account, though most soldiers experienced less intense treatment than did Lifton's civilians and reverted ideologically soon after release and reintegration into American society.

Somit (1968) presents a functional classification of methods that clarifies aspects of the chronology given above. *Total control* puts every aspect of the prisoner's life under strictly enforced rules. *Uncertainty* as to the nature of the charges nurtures anxiety. The victim is *isolated* from news, family, and friends. Continuous interrogation and sleep deprivation lead to *physical debilitation and exhaustion*, which, combined with *humiliation*, make the victim more vulnerable to the instructor's apparent *certainty of his guilt*. Somit's enumeration of psychological mechanisms underlying indoctrination through brainwashing agrees with those of Lifton and Schein. Prisoners come to *identify* with the chief interrogator, especially if he is less brutal than his subordinates. This can involve *emotional involvement*. Prisoners suffer *decreased intellectual capacity*, becoming *disoriented* due to solitary confinement. They become more susceptible to *suggestion,* which is exploited by *repetition* on the part of the instructors. *Guilt feelings* are elicited by forced self-analysis, contributing to *ego destruction* or humiliation and degradation. The prisoner becomes *conditioned* to compliance. Many are emotionally overwhelmed by the experience and show *nonrational behavior in the face of sudden stimulus.* Finally, the prisoner is manipulated by the *alternation of fear and hope.* Somit evaluates the Chinese brainwashing method as irresistible when fully applied, but very costly to any regime wishing to apply it on a large scale. Somit's view that brainwashing is irresistible when focused on individuals is consistent with Schein's view that the Chinese were not successful in brainwashing large numbers of prisoners of war, while being successful with singled-out individuals.

Criticism can be leveled at the overly cognitive interpretations made by Lifton, Schein, and other early analysts of brainwashing. Even Sargant (1957), whose approach was ostensibly physiological and based on Pavlovian theory, assumed that conversion behavior followed the acquisition of conversion beliefs (see critique by Richardson and Kilbourne 1983). Yet the descriptions summarized above suggest the reverse temporal order: victims are coerced or led into degrading rehearsals of conversion behavior, and the beliefs follow.

The coercive and intimidating component of brainwashing tends to be underplayed by analysts seeking to draw parallels with cults. Singer and Ofshe (1990) state that "the effectiveness of thought reform programs did not depend on prison settings, physical abuse, or death threats." However, they and others agree with central elements of the Lifton-Schein description, including coercion and induction of fear (Singer and Ofshe 1990, 188).

The following sections draw parallels between these techniques and other forms of indoctrination.

Totalitarian indoctrination of civil populations
(fascist and Communist)

Summary. These techniques are effective, though mostly with doctrines and values compatible with informal socialization.

Some regimes of the twentieth century earned the label "totalitarian" by applying indoctrination methods of great thoroughness. The documentation of such political methods in fascist and Communist states is on such a scale that I can only report snapshots here. It appears that some similar principles were deployed in both cases.

The society that has been subjected to the most sustained totalitarian persuasion is the former Soviet Union, beginning with Russia after 1917 and ending in the late 1980s. A useful, though somewhat dramatic, account of the institutional techniques deployed by the Bolsheviks from Lenin to the 1980s is Heller's *Cogs in the Soviet Wheel* (1988). Heller identifies elements of Soviet state indoctrination similar to those developed in fascist Italy and Nazi Germany: strategic use of intimidation, ritual denunciation of an enemy, and mass rehearsal of reverence and love for the "great leader." Totalitarian regimes are suspicious of independent associations such as trade unions and adopt systematic approaches to monopolizing the loyalties of citizens. The Communists in Russia and China aggressively undermined competitors for the masses' loyalties by persecuting alternative political parties and the church and, for a time, by attempting to subvert traditional patterns of authority and fidelity within the family. Significantly for the present analysis, Heller ascribes the function of "infantilization" to this assemblage of techniques.

In Heller's view, fear is the main tool of state indoctrination, followed by fostering of hatred of out-groups and affiliation with the leader-indoctrinator. Fear was the weapon used to destroy existing attachments as a prelude to remolding human consciousness to form the "New Soviet Man."

Control of information was given high priority. Bolshevik education policy prescribed ideologically correct curricula. Humanities subjects were infused with ideological messages, whether in schools, universities, the media, or the arts. A Lenin cult was developed which amounted to worship. Ritual praise and expressions of love were directed by teachers, textbooks, and students toward Lenin and present leaders. Lenin's image and that of Stalin in his time were difficult to avoid since their faces and names were omnipresent in school. Heller reports that the first word learned in school was "Lenin." Lenin and Trotsky sought to establish a "Communist ritual" to replace that of the church, the latter leader declaring that "the workers' state has its own feast days, its own parades, its own symbolic spectacles and its own theatricality" (Trotsky 1976, *Les questions du mode de vie*, 75, cited in Heller 1988, 204). The taking over of religious rituals was accompanied by the forcible closure of churches and persecution of the clergy, isolating the population from alternate sources of leadership.

The public realm invaded the private. One temporary focus of the Bolshevik assault was the traditional family. Strategies included female liberation in the form of equal rights. Another was "free love" combined with liberal abortion laws. Another was easy divorce in which either partner could unilaterally annul the contract. These measures were explicitly aimed at destroying the "bourgeois family" (Heller 1988, 200). The Freudian critique of and therapy directed at conventional sexuality was most influential within the Party during this period (Etkind 1995). By the late 1930s the Stalin regime reversed all but the first of these reforms because, Heller argues unconvincingly, the Party had achieved its aim of reconstructing society. A more likely reason is that the social dysfunctions fostered by the reforms prompted a renewed appreciation of stable family units.

Heller's dramatic presentation backfires when he describes elements of the Soviet system that the reader is meant to find odious, but which are in fact normal in many democracies. Female equality in marriage is an example. Indoctrination can be seen as one of the main attractions of universal public education as provided by the modern state, whether for purposes political (Counts 1978/1932) or economic (Lott 1990; and see Salter 1995, 463–5). Heller's stark portrayal asserts a disjunct between totalitarian and open societies. Yet everywhere in the modern world, indoctrinating symbols are pushed, or pulled, across the private-public divide. The modern technology of mass communication has achieved in some ways the insertion of symbols and ideas into all social niches, including the family, without resort to particular government warrant. This is especially clear with regard to national symbols. Hobsbawm (1990, 141–3; and see Johnson 1987; Billig 1995) points out the ways in which the press, cinema, radio, and television bring, without centrally controlled design, the symbols and rituals of the nation into the everyday lives of the people, in their homes and workplaces, where once these symbols and rituals had been restricted to particular places or particular days.

However, to say that indoctrination takes place in democracies does not invalidate the analysis of indoctrination in one-party states, since the study of extreme cases can help elucidate general principles. Heller's description tallies with the large critical literature on Soviet political methods, some of which it incorporates. The tactics of the radical Lenin-Trotsky years resemble to some degree the microcosm of Chinese brainwashing. To that extent, this brief look at totalitarian methods of indoctrination confirms the suggestion made in the previous section that indoctrination draws on a limited repertoire of techniques, namely intimidation, information control, severance of previous relationships of authority and loyalty, and ritual hatred of an enemy.

Recruitment for cults—the case of the Unification Church

Summary. The success rate is poor if one takes as a base line the number of people approached in the street. But of those who show sufficient interest to attend a weekend-long workshop, 5–13 percent joined at the height of Moonie success in the 1970s.

Caution must be exercised in drawing parallels between methods of persuasion used by cults and those of brainwashing (Richardson and Kilbourne 1983). Nevertheless, some similarities emerge from descriptions of cult methods for inducting new members.

Galanter (1983) reports observations of the five stages by which the Unification Church (the "Moonies") recruit and induct new members. (1) Typically, a street proselytizer who is "witnessing" for the Church invites passers-by to attend a workshop. (2) The initial workshop lasts two days and is usually held in a secluded rustic setting. The schedule runs from 8 A.M. to 11 P.M. and involves alternating 90-minute lectures with 90-minute small group discussions. The discussions are more conceptual than emotional, though there is a good deal of investigation of individuals' attitudes and experiences (perhaps exploiting the "response-contagion" effect discussed by Nuttin 1987). Lectures and group discussion are complemented by group activities, such as singing, athletics, and acting games. Guests are invited to continue with a seven-day workshop.

(3) Each day of the seven-day workshop begins with breakfast at 8 A.M., followed by lectures and other organized activity until the midevening. The guests are asked to fill out a "reflection notebook," entries which they may choose to discuss next day (note the resemblance with written self-analysis used in Chinese brainwashing). At each stage a number of guests drop out or are asked to leave. In Galanter's sample, only 17 percent of the original cohort remained after the second workshop.

(4) The remaining inductees move on to a 21-day workshop, which includes one week of fundraising and one week of "witnessing" or recruiting. In this phase, the schedule becomes more rigorous; guests arise at 6 A.M. and go to bed some time before

midnight after a session of "sharing" and filling out reflection notebooks. Daytime activities mostly involve intensive fundraising and recruiting.

(5) At the end of this period, guests are asked to move permanently into a Church residence. Often this entails moving to a distant part of the country to continue Church activities. In Galanter's sample, only 9 of the original 104 guests elected to continue on with the process. Four months later, three of these had left, one returning to his family, one being abducted by "deprogrammers," and one being expelled for a bad attitude. This left a success rate of 5 to 6 percent. Recall that this small but significant success rate refers to people who had already been sufficiently attracted by the Moonies to attend a weekend-long workshop. The retention rate over the whole recruitment process, based on the number of people approached in street contacts, is much smaller.

Barker (1984, 284-5) cites figures provided by Unification Church officials that agree with Galanter's figures: 13 percent of individuals who attended seven-day workshops in late 1975 joined and remained members until 1984. Considering that before the seven-day workshop there was a dropout rate of 50 to 75 percent, the success rate of Moonie indoctrination even after an initial display of interest, was between 3 and 6 percent during this period, when the reaction against the Moonies had not set in and recruitment success was high (284). Galanter extended this analysis to a comparative study of charismatic groups, adopting an explicitly sociobiological and ethological orientation (1989), though one employing pre-Hamilton assumptions about the causal agency of "survival of the species" (Hamilton 1964). His findings, however, are consistent with the existence of a trait of indoctrinability being activated out of the context in which it evolved.

Galanter's account is basically confirmed by Barker (1984), who states that Moonie recruitment methods include environmental control, deception, and fostering of affiliative relationships. Methods include "love-bombing" (constant affection and touching between groups of people), sleep deprivation, protein withdrawal, sugar-buzzing (increasing the blood-sugar level so that the brain becomes muddled), repetitive lectures, familiar music with "restored" lyrics, and other seemingly innocent but insidious devices (*Daily Mail*, 29 May 1978, quoted by Barker 1984, 121). Barker takes pains to argue that this sort of manipulation is not coercive, answering popular critics of cults who have accused them of brainwashing youngsters using methods essentially the same as the Communist Chinese. Certainly, the coercive element is weak. But as we saw above, brainwashing also contains an important affective element shared by Moonie and other cult practices, a point well made by Lofland and Stark (1965) and acknowledged by Barker (1984, 181; see also Lofland and Skonovd 1984).

A relatively benign view of cult methods is held by analysts such as Young and Griffith (1992), who find no significant differences in coercive persuasion between cults and certain mainstream religious organizations, such as the Opus Dei (part of the Roman Catholic Church). "We maintain that such religious ritual inherently possesses elements that are more or less subtly coercive and that diminish the individual's capacity to exercise judgment freely.... Yet no one now complains about ... the baptism of infants, the pressure felt when children reach the expected age for first communion or confirmation, and even the routine element of subtle compulsion involved when everyone rises row-by-row for holy communion" (92). This view does not deny that cults use manipulatory methods of indoctrination. The only point of contention is whether such methods are also part of mainstream religions.

An antagonistic position is taken by analysts such as Singer and Ofshe, who maintain that cult methods are more sophisticated than brainwashing's old tools of "group pressure, modeling, accusations, and confessions." Only hypnosis was not identified by Lifton (1956b) or Schein (1956) as a brainwashing method, although it was discussed by others (e.g., Hunter 1956, 232–7).

> [Cult] programs often incorporate technical advances in influence production, such as hypnosis to intensify recalled or imagined experiences, emotional flooding, sleep deprivation, stripping away of various psychological defense mechanisms, and the induction of cognitive confusion. (Singer and Ofshe 1990, 189)

While disagreeing over the degree of coercion and loss of control induced within cults, apologists and critics agree on some descriptive elements. Based on these, the main similarities between cult recruitment tactics and brainwashing appear to be: (1) authoritarian control of procedure in which the initiate does not influence content or structure; (2) milieu control, including isolation from other sources of information and deception; (3) disruption of normal routines with long hours, disorientation accelerated by group pressure in the form of prolonged discussion, and self-revelation; (4) severance of the initiate from other attachments, including family and friends; and (5) devices for eliciting bonding between potential recruit and cult members (for a similar conclusion see Taylor 1983).

Key differences between brainwashing and cults appear to be a lack of coercion, intimidation, and overt degradation. There is also a large difference in the latter's success at effecting conversion, cultists being poor performers compared to brainwashers. Since the main difference in method is the cults' lack of coercion, it is reasonable to conclude that this is the cause of different success rates.

Deprogramming from cults

Summary. This is an effective form of indoctrination. Solomon (1983, 182) cites reports of a 90 percent success rate. However, note that ex-inductees are in a way self-selected since they are drawn from the small minority that proved susceptible to cult doctrines and/or methods in the first place.

Bromley (1988, 185-6) states that the reaction against cults came primarily from families who felt they had lost contact with a young adult child. Cult indoctrination techniques do in fact sever initiates' bonds with their family and friends. The family backlash created a market for professional "deprogrammers" whose activities flourished in the United States during the 1970s but fell away in the 1980s. Bromley (1988) provides little detail on the actual methods used, but notes the consensus among analysts as to the process involved. Victims (who saw themselves as such, at least at first) were abducted, taken to a secluded place, and held for a time ranging from a few hours to many weeks. The aim was to have the victim disavow cult membership. Techniques included:

> eliciting *guilt* for having rejected family members and educational plans, expressing *love* and concern about the dubious future the individual had charted, *refuting* the group's doctrines, revealing esoteric beliefs and practices that were not known to the individual, challenging the *motives* and *sincerity* of the group's leaders, providing *testimonials* by former members that they had been brainwashed ..., and *threatening* that the individual would be released only on the condition that membership in the group was renounced. (Bromley 1988, 193–4, emphases added)

Deprogramming could involve any combination of professional deprogrammers, family, friends, and former cult members. The use of group pressure, interpersonal affiliation, guilt, the undermining of personal bonds with cult members, testimonials by authoritative sources, and self-examination implies a great overlap in methods between the cultist and the deprogrammers (Solomon 1983 makes the same point).

There was also a significant difference between the two in success rate. Bromley compiled statistics on deprogrammings aimed at members of the Unification Church from 1973 to 1986, involving 397 cases. He found that 64 percent were successful, which concurs with another analysis (1988, 199). He notes that the rate was so high because attachment to the Moonies was low. The Church experienced a high turnover, so that at any given time most members were either in the process of joining or leaving. The strongest predictor of success in deprogramming an individual was length of membership. While 96.3 percent of individuals who had joined less than two months previously were successfully deprogrammed, only about one-third of four-year or longer members succumbed (Bromley 1988, 201). Success also fell away as age increased between 18 and 26 and over. Interestingly, females were somewhat more prone to deprogramming than males (60.8 percent success rate with males; 67.8 percent with females).

Since cult recruiters had to deal with the same individuals as the deprogrammers, and during the same historical period, we are faced with a natural experiment that controls most variables excluding the methods deployed by the two sides. Cults had dramatically lower success rates than deprogrammers. The difference might have been due to the latters' greater use of coercion, perhaps combined with the strong emotional bonds of family members and friends.

Initiation in primitive societies

Summary. Effectiveness is difficult to assess. The process signifies, and contributes to, a transition of identity and involves rehearsal of obedience and experience of extreme fear, often with physical deprivation and loneliness, as preludes to transmission of secret knowledge.

The success rate of traditional initiation is unknown because of the difficulty of separating out effects of informal socialization and the subsequent interdependence of inductees that tends to deter defection from the group. It is applied in its more coercive mode to all young males of a community and is usually directed to intensify the effect of informal socialization. Occasionally, initiates are directed away from previously socialized values, for example, in extending group loyalties from a small natal group to a wider community (see Wiessner this volume).

Eibl-Eibesfeldt (1989, 603-4) draws a parallel between male initiation in many societies and brainwashing. The point of similarity is "infantilization," a state of dependency created in the initiate or prisoner. This entails segregation from normal society, deprivation, whether voluntary or forced, and near total reliance on the instructor. The example given by Eibl-Eibesfeldt is that of Bushman boys, whose initiation involves them tolerating cold and hunger, as well as being frightened and intimidated at night. The scarification that is inflicted is painful and presumably frightening. Eibl-Eibesfeldt concludes that the intimidation and infantilization found in initiation ceremonies function to indoctrinate often rebellious young men into the larger social group and imprint a group ethic that extends beyond immediate family. Scholars of Communist brainwashing techniques similarly conclude that artificial infantilization creates a readiness to be instructed.

Descriptions and interpretations supporting Eibl-Eibesfeldt's analysis are available in the ethnography of initiation (e.g., van Gennep 1960; Haddon 1971; Tuzin 1982). Van Gennep reviewed initiation rites in several primitive societies. His descriptions of the rites of Australian Aborigines, some Native American tribes, the natives of Zaire and the Gulf of New Guinea, have in common a period of exclusion, often dietary restrictions, beatings, and often scarification. Treatment is more severe for boys than for girls. In Zaire the novice is "taken into the forest, where he is subjected to seclusion, lustration, flagellation, and intoxication with palm wine, resulting in anesthesia. Then comes the transition rites, including bodily mutilation" (81). Instruction from elders or tribal magicians is often timed to coincide with disorientation of the initiate, partly caused by physical weakening and partly by social isolation and intimidation (Haddon 1971, 210).

The intimidating potential of ritual violence is well expressed by Tuzin (1982, 337) in his description of initiation among the Ilahita Arapesh of the Sepik River area in Papua New Guinea.

What cannot be conveyed in a short space is the full emotional force of this violence: it is one thing to be thumped on the head or to have your penis lacerated, but when these attacks are staged in a dramatic atmosphere of weird costumery, unearthly sounds, and frenzied stomping, screaming, and singing by scores, perhaps hundreds, of armed warriors, each of whom seems madly intent on your destruction, the experience is transformed into one of nightmarish horror.

For the argument presented here to be valid, it is not necessary that *every* initiation involves the rigors or affiliations described above. But it is necessary that initiations indoctrinating rebellious young men with a group ethic entail a subset of the elements found in other effective indoctrinations. These include the induction of negative emotions connected narratively with the identity to be rejected and positive emotions connected to the achievement of test criteria as a measure of manhood identity, all conducted against a background of preexisting strong interpersonal relationships with group members.

Propaganda—political advertising

Summary. This is the weakest form of indoctrination considered so far. Yet it usually has the widest reach. Propaganda works by keying into existing beliefs and predispositions, focusing group identification but not changing it.

Propaganda has acquired derogatory connotations. The *Concise Oxford Dictionary* notes this, but offers a neutral definition of "an organized programme of publicity, selected information, etc., used to propagate a doctrine, practice, etc." A morally neutral meaning of the term is also adopted by Welch (1995), who points out that propaganda can be used to good or evil effect, can resort to rational case-making as well as to various degrees of deception, and can key into affiliative as well as to aggressive emotions. Welch, quoting Aldus Huxley (1936), contends that propaganda has limited capacity to sway people. It is most effective when it seeks to channel and focus existing sentiments and ideas.

Thus at the outset, propaganda can be described as a weak form of indoctrination when strong indoctrination is taken to be the *changing* of ideas and loyalties. Usually, Welch argues, propaganda is a method for reinforcing existing "trends and beliefs" (5). However, the power of political advertising increases dramatically when combined with control of competing messages, usually achieved by coercive means but conceivably through media monopolies or homogeneous journalistic ideology, as argued by Herman and Chomsky (1988). Nazi propaganda assumed its legendary power when, after 1933, Goebbels found himself in charge of the technical means of mass communication (Reut 1993; Welch 1995). But the use of coercion to silence opponents is distinct from propaganda, however much the combination increases the latter's effectiveness. Hence, propaganda can be treated as a means of political advertising, whether practiced as a monopoly in an authoritarian state, or in the face of competition as can occur in democracies.

Advertising experts can provide only tentative advice to practitioners beyond the perennial wisdom of rhetoric and such obvious findings as that attention-getting and repetition are important in getting a message through. The traditional skills of rhetoric are the stock-in-trade of the modern advertising industry, as they have been for indoctrinators through the ages (Murphy 1974; McArthur 1992). Not much has been learned since Lenin and Hitler plied their trade. Hitler attributed much of his knowledge to British propaganda during World War I and to Austrian socialist methods. He appears to have contributed ideas as well. Padgett and Brock (1988, 187-9) refer to Hitler's anticipation of research on one- versus two-sided arguments and his research on environmental effects of persuasive communications. Based partly on the example of Hitler, they conclude that successful propaganda tends to operate at a nonverbal level and can be effective even though little verbal content is being understood by the receivers. The chapters in this volume by Deutsch and Sütterlin support this contention.

Emotion has emerged as an important variable in theories of advertising effectiveness (e.g., Cafferata and Tybout 1989). A central hypothesis of this research is that people buy products they associate with good feelings rather than, or in addition to, having good reasons for doing so. It follows that a successful advertisement creates a positive mood and through repetition associates this with a symbol of the product (e.g., Calder and Gruder 1989). In a political context, some support for this hypothesis comes from research indicating that positive emotional responses to candidates are more influential than negative responses (Marcus 1988). However, predicting which behaviors will elicit a positive mood is not a simple matter. Cultural and sex differences produce different responses to the same nonverbal behaviors (Masters 1991). A further complication is that supporters respond positively to anger/threat displays from politicians, while antagonistic viewers respond negatively (Masters et al. 1986). And among neutral viewers there is a sex difference, with males indicating greater support to politicians who show friendly displays but females directing their support to anger/threat displays (Englis 1994).

As a general hypothesis, the effectiveness of "mood advertising" is uncertain. Indeed, recent findings contradict the long-held assumption that persuasiveness is increased when the receiver of a message is in good humor. On the contrary, recent experimental results indicate that depression and fear, both low-rank emotions, can increase suggestibility to advertising stimuli (Gardner 1994; and see discussions in Cafferata and Tybout 1989). Gardner induced positive and negative emotions by having subjects read stories. Subsequently, they read print advertisements, and their attitude toward the product was evaluated by questionnaire and interview. The finding was that negative affect increases advertisement effectiveness. This seems to contradict the view that positive mood increases receptivity, though in Gardner's research negative mood was not generated by the salesperson's (or politician's) own behavior.

Positive emotional enhancement of advertising tallies with aspects of more intensive indoctrination involving affiliative ties with the instructor. And negative emotional enhancement is consistent with descriptions of coercive persuasion involving fear, guilt, and humility induced in the victim by individuals other than the instructor. Arguably, the role of negative affect will remain largely academic knowledge for propagandists operating in the open marketplace, and will be useful mainly to those with captive audiences. Where consumers are free to "switch off" an indoctrinator, the best predictor (though still a poor one) of an advertisement's effectiveness will probably remain its "likeability," a construct compatible with attention-holding and memorableness (Leather et al. 1994).

Conclusion

The great transferability of indoctrination methods across cultures and eras is remarkable. Not only have they been passed on or reinvented between diverse cultures, they have been used across cultural interfaces: Jesuit priests experienced *déjà vu* at the hands of Chinese brainwashers; a Korean mystic won converts in California; a Western anthropologist understands the terror and disorientation induced in traditional initiates. It is tempting to compare similar indoctrination methods in contrasting cultures as biologists treat similar adaptations between different species. The parallels, in which the method or characteristic of interest has been reinvented or reevolved to meet recurring challenges, are sometimes analogous. The most common elements of indoctrination probably arose independently by borrowing from universals of the species' social behavior: all cultures carry models of dominance and training on which a would-be indoctrinator could draw (Whiting 1968; Eibl-Eibesfeldt 1989). Techniques can also be homologous, adopted through imitation or training. Whether due to analogy or homology, the capacity to be transferred across cultures indicates a continuity of human nature, in particular that part comprising the capacity to be indoctrinated. It confirms Eibl-Eibesfeldt's evolutionary case for a species-typical trait of indoctrinability (1982). Left at this point, this analysis is consistent with indoctrinability being innate in the weak sense of having a fixed external form but weak internal differentiation. It is possible that the ways to get indoctrinated are many, that there are more than one or a few necessary experiential pathways, which are replicated across cultures and eras. But such a possibility looks decidedly bleak in light of the foregoing review.

All of the methods reviewed above appear to draw on a limited number of specific mechanisms. Table 20.1 breaks them down into relatively pure constituent elements. The multipronged nature of most methods is evident. As noted, recourse is taken to more techniques—and more coercive ones—by indoctrinators attempting to overcome already held beliefs and loyalties. Dominance and control of information invariably enter the picture when a whole group is to be indoctrinated and high success rates are required, as with brainwashing of prisoners or persuasion of whole populations.

There appears to be a relationship between the intuitive appeal of a doctrine and effective means for its indoctrination. The more attractive an idea or group identity to an individual, the less extreme the methods needed to inculcate it. The Chinese Communists used a mix of methods including torture, isolation, and group pressure to temporarily overcome strongly held beliefs and loyalties in mature individuals. At the other extreme, national and religious symbols can cue a degree of patriotic and religious sentiment merely on repeated presentation together with a dose of collective "response contagion" or self-persuasion following the evincing of a belief. Unforced national and religious indoctrination can be effective even in competition with countervailing symbols and the "noise" of the mass media. Nevertheless, the success of coercive methods such as brainwashing is remarkable considering that the inductees were not self-selected, as they often are in the case of nationalism, religions, and cults. Indoctrination in the absence of coercion appears to be most successful with a fraction

Table 20.1: Behavioral Techniques of Indoctrination in Different Approaches

Behavioral Tactic	Approach						
	1	2	3	4	5	6	7
Physical coercion and restraint	•	•	•				
Routine obedience	•	?			•		
Milieu control	•	•	•	•	•		
Isolation from information	•	•	•	•	•		
Severance of interpersonal bonds	•	•	•	•	•		
Intense peer pressure	•	•	•	•	•		
Interrogation	•						
Threat	•	•	•		•		
Ritual attack on outgroup	•	•	?	?	•		
Sleep deprivation	•	?	•	•			
Physical debilitation	•		•	?	?		
Shackles—made highly dependent	•		•				
Repetition of message	•	•	•	?	•		•
Rehearse petty compliance	•		•				
Accusation	•	•					
Mild degradation—self-revelation	•			•	?		
Intense degradation—confession/apology	•						
Punishment and reward	•						
Argumentation/statement of doctrine	•	•	•	•	•	•	•
Prestige testimonials	•	•	•	•	•		•
Intense affiliation	?	?	?	•			
Some compassion at point of collapse	•		•				
Effectiveness	H	H	H?	M	M	L	L

An attempt is made to rank techniques by order of effectiveness.
(Key: • = techniques used; ? = perhaps used)
Key: 1 = Full Brain-washing; 2 = Deprograming; 3 = Traditional Initiation; 4 = Moonies: From First Workshop; 5 = Leninist Bolshevism; 6 = Advertising; 7 = Moonies: At First Contact; H = High; M = Medium; L = Low

Table 20.2: Psychological Effects of Different Indoctrination Methods

Psychological Experience	1	2	3	4	5	6	7
Reduced mental function—confusion	•		?				
Interest/curiosity						?	•
Humor							•
Uncertainty	•	?	•				
Loneliness	•		?	?			
Guilt	•	•		?			
Mild anxiety and/or fear	•	•	•		•		
Intense anxiety and/or fear	•	•	•				
Depression/despair alternating with hope	•	?	•	?			
Affiliative bond with instructor-leader	•	?	•	•	?		
Intense relief upon conversion—euphoria	•	?	?	•			
Effectiveness	H	H	H?	M	M	L	L

An attempt is made to rank techniques by order of effectiveness.
(Key: • = techniques used; ? = perhaps used)
Key: 1 = Full Brain-washing; 2 = Deprograming; 3 = Traditional
Initiation; 4 = Moonies: From First Workshop; 5 = Leninist Bolshevism;
6 = Advertising; 7 = Moonies: At First Contact; H = High; M = Medium;
L = Low

of the population that is predisposed to some aspect of the doctrine or susceptible to the proselytizing method. In this light, we should pay special attention to any method that achieves high rates of success with essentially random samples of subjects—persons who have not sorted themselves according to susceptibility. This has been my reason for subjecting brainwashing to relatively close scrutiny.

An attempt is made in Table 20.2 to itemize the main psychological impacts of the indoctrination methods reviewed in this chapter. The number of question marks indicates the preliminary nature of this analysis.

Brainwashing and initiation deal with relatively random samples of the population, and any success they have at indoctrination is worthy of note. Cults might be effective at indoctrinating, but only with individuals whose particular life experiences and/or personalities predispose them for the limited array of techniques cults are able to mobilize in open societies. Also, their success appears more significant when one considers their limited tactical options, especially the unavailability of institutional coercion. Those tactical options will be definable as a subset of brainwashing's full species-typical repertoire should it be confirmed that the factors predisposing individuals to enter cult induction programs are those deliberately induced in coercive programs such as brainwashing, disorientation, isolation, guilt, and physical debilitation.

Repetition was the strongest nonaffective component shared by all persuasive regimes reviewed here. This makes sense if teaching is a necessary element of indoctrination. However, as argued in the Introduction, while learning is a necessary component of being indoctrinated, it is not sufficient. Furthermore, since repetition is present in almost all cases, it does not distinguish effective from ineffective indoctrination. A similar situation exists with argumentation/statement of doctrine, which is spread across effective and ineffective methods. Which constituent techniques are *unique* to effective indoctrination? Coercion and institutional control must be candidates, including associated features of hierarchy—routine obedience and threat. With some exceptions, the following techniques are also associated with successful indoctrination: rehearsed petty compliance, sleep deprivation, peer pressure, and affiliation. Perhaps effectiveness is not a matter of quality so much as quantity—a relatively large number of techniques combining to overwhelm resistance. In this regard, it is relevant to distinguish between necessary and sufficient causes of indoctrination.

My approach so far has been to search for a single element or cluster of elements associated with effective indoctrination, and to treat these as necessary causes. What of *sufficient* causes of effective indoctrination? Of course, it is more difficult to determine whether a set of conditions is sufficient to effect indoctrination under all circumstances. More examples need to be considered, and more refined descriptions compiled. It might be the case that many combinations of techniques are effective, and that the causal "bottleneck" we should be looking for is not some particular array of techniques but the behavioral and psychological effects leading to indoctrination. Table 20.2 addresses this issue. Certain mental states—confusion, intense fear and/or anxiety, and perhaps loneliness—are unique to highly effective indoctrination. However, taking into account the uncertain effectiveness of initiation, one could also treat guilt, depression/despair, and an intense bond with the indoctrinator as possible emotional precursors of indoctrination.

The foregoing discussion tends to confirm a version of Sargant's (1957) physiological interpretation of the success of brainwashing and other indoctrination techniques. He argued that inductees become suggestible after experiencing the profound emotional shock of fear, anger, or excitement. Sargant also identified guilt and conflict of loyalties in the case of brainwashing (135). The review of Lifton (1956; 1989/1961), Galanter (1989), and others indicates that we should add dependent and affiliative relationships with the indoctrinator to the list of effective mechanisms.

Finally, I want to consider two factors that recurred in this study—coercion and routine obedience. Both entail dominance, varying from aroused intimidation to routinized command-obedience interactions as found in schools and other hierarchical institutions. These factors were salient in effecting indoctrination against the resistance of subjects. Dominance is useful for teaching large groups by virtue of its ability to hold subjects in place and direct their attention, and to do so in more predictable and lengthier periods than entertainments. Dominance also appears able to increase the persuasiveness of a message. The literature on hunter-gatherer teaching methods helps show how this might work. Storytelling and answering questions, as well as imitation, are the main teaching tools in hunter-gatherer societies. J. W. M. Whiting (1941) provided a description of teaching behavior among the Kwoma of New Guinea. In Whiting's analysis it is clear that aggressive as well as affiliative emotional systems are activated, largely going from parent or other older family members to children. Interestingly, many elements of informal teaching are evident in the more successful cases of indoctrination. Taking the most extreme, Chinese brainwashers taught from a position of authority analogous to parents or other elders, and used combinations of just those behaviors described by Whiting, including positive and negative motivation as well as pure instruction. The recurring description of infantilization induced by indoctrinators accords with Geiger's (1993; and this volume) argument that the dominance component is crucial in making authority figures sources of group norms.

The importance of institutional dominance to effective indoctrination also confirms the view expressed at the beginning of this chapter that the process of indoctrination differs in important respects from imprinting. The need to hold subjects in place to allow for repetition and emotional manipulation suggests that many of the doctrines so inculcated are not readily taken up, that their acceptance requires more than one exposure to a releasing stimulus. And it suggests that *indoctrination,* as a process, is often considered socially desirable precisely where *indoctrinability,* as a predisposition, is weakest.

This chapter can be summarized thus. Methods of indoctrination employ a subset of specific techniques found in the highly successful method of "thought reform" or "brainwashing" developed by the Chinese Communists from the 1930s to the 1950s, which was used to convert prisoners to the Red Chinese viewpoint. The only method not clearly found in brainwashing is "love bombing," an affiliative tactic used by some cults, although a hallmark of intensive thought reform was a close, personal relationship with the instructor. The most successful approaches to indoctrination challenge self-identity and induce a common set of psychological states that sway individuals toward identifying with a leader, group, or doctrine. The process induces intense emotions of fear, depression, guilt, and loneliness combined with a state of dependency on the instructor. These combine to drive the subject into an affiliative bond with one or more representatives of the indoctrinating group. It is this bond, combined with the instructor's authority and the subject's altered physiological and psychological state, that increases the likelihood of a new identity and set of loyalties being embraced. This pathway appears to be a common denominator of highly effective indoctrination. Furthermore, the behaviors, emotions, and relationships that it evokes all belong to the species-typical repertoire, that is, they are innate universals. The lack of variety of effective paths to indoctrination, especially at the functional level of cognition and emotion in the subject, confirms the hypothesis that the means for indoctrinating humans, no matter how technically developed, are constrained by the necessity of keying in to the human sensory and behavioral apparatus. This apparatus is a product of hominid and primate phylogeny stretching back over geological epochs. As such, it and the principles by which it is manipulated, are unlikely to change much in the foreseeable future.

Acknowledgments: I wish to thank Hiram Caton for helpful comments and a lively debate on the subject. Pete Richerson kindly passed on the reference to Nuttin (1987).

References

Barker, E. (1984). *The making of a Moonie. Choice or brainwashing?* Basil Blackwell, Oxford.

Bettelheim, B. (1943). Individual and mass behaviour in extreme situations. *Journal of Abnormal and Social Psychology*, **38**, 417–52.

Billig, M. (1995). *Banal nationalism*. Sage, London.

Bromley, D. G. (1988). Deprogramming as a mode of exit from New Religious Movements. The case of the Unification Movement. In *Falling from the faith: Causes and consequences of religious apostasy* (ed. D. G. Bromley), pp. 185–204. Sage, Newbury Park.

Brown, P. and Levinson, S. C. (1987). *Politeness: Some universals in language use*. Cambridge University Press, Cambridge.

Cafferata, P. and Tybout, A. M., eds. (1989). *Cognitive and affective responses to advertising*. Lexington Books, Lexington, Mass.

Calder, B. J. and Gruder, C. L. (1989). Emotional advertising appeals. In *Cognitive and affective responses to advertising* (ed. P. Cafferata and A. M. Tybout), pp. 277–85. Lexington Books, Lexington, Mass.

Caton, H. P. (1983/1994). Descriptive political ethology. Unpublished manuscript, Griffith University, Brisbane, Australia.

———. (1988). *The politics of progress: The origins and development of the commercial republic, 1600–1835*. University of Florida Press, Gainesville.

Chamberlain, L. (1995). Freud and the eros of the impossible. Review of A. Etkind, 1995, Eros Nevozmozhnogo. Istoria psikhoanaliza v Rossii. *Times Literary Supplement*, no. 4821, August 25, 9–10.

Chang, J. (1991). *Wild swans: Three daughters of China*. Flamingo, New York.

Counts, G. (1978/1932). *Dare the schools build a new social order?* Southern Illinois Press, Carbondale, Ill.

Eibl-Eibesfeldt, I. (1972/1970). *Love and hate: The natural history of behaviour patterns* (trans. G. Strachan). Holt, Rinehart and Winston, New York (Original German edition 1970, R. Piper, Munich).

———. (1982). Warfare, man's indoctrinability and group selection. *Ethology (Zeitschrift für Tierpsychologie)*, **60**, 177–98.

———. (1989). *Human ethology*. Aldine de Gruyter, New York.

Englis, B. G. (1994). The role of affect in political advertising: Voter emotional responses to the nonverbal behavior of politicians. In *Attention, attitude, and affect in response to advertising* (ed. E. M. Clark, T. C. Brock, and D. W. Stewart), pp. 223–47. Lawrence Erlbaum, Hillsdale, N.J.

Ervin-Tripp, S. (1976). Is Sybil there? The structure of some American English directives. *Language in Society*, **5**, 25–66.

Etkind, A. (1995). *Eros Nevozmozhnogo. Istoria psikhoanaliza v Rossii* (The eros of the impossible. The story of psychoanalysis in Russia). Meduza, St. Petersburg.

Frank, J. D. (1970). *Persuasion and healing*. Schocken Books, New York.

Galanter, M. (1983). Group induction techniques in a charismatic sect. In *The brainwashing/deprogramming controversy* (ed. D. G. Bromley and J. T. Richardson), pp. 183–93. Edwin Mellen Press, New York.

———. (1989). *Cults: Faith, healing and coercion*. Oxford University Press, New York.

Gardner, M. P. (1994). Responses to emotional and informational appeals: The moderating role of context-induced mood states. In *Attention, attitude, and affect in response to advertising* (ed. E. M. Clark, T. C. Brock, and D. W. Stewart), pp. 207–21. Lawrence Erlbaum, Hillsdale, N.J.

Geiger, G. (1988). On the evolutionary origins and function of political power. *Journal of Social and Biological Structures*, **11**, 235–50.

———. (1993). Evolutionary anthropology and the non-cognitive foundations of moral validity. *Biology and Philosophy*, **8**, 133–51.

Gennep, A. v. (1960). *The rites of passage* (trans. M. B. Vizedom and G. L. Caffee). University of Chicago Press, Chicago.

Goffman, E. (1956). Embarrassment and social organization. *American Journal of Sociology*, **62**, 264–71.

Greenstein, F. I. (1968). Political socialization. In *International encyclopedia of the social sciences* (ed. D. L. Sills), pp. 551–5. Macmillan and Free Press, New York.

Haddon, A. C. (1971). Initiation. In *Reports of the Cambridge anthropological expedition to Torres Strait*, vol. 5 (ed. A. C. Haddon), pp. 208–21. Cambridge University Press/Johnson Reprint Corporation, Cambridge/New York.

Heller, M. (1988). *Cogs in the Soviet wheel. The formation of Soviet Man*. Collins Harvill, London.

Herman, E. S. and Chomsky, N. (1988). *Manufacturing consent: The political economy of the mass media*. Pantheon Books, New York.

Hobsbawm, E. J. (1990). *Nations and nationalism since 1780: Programme, myth, reality*. Cambridge University Press, Cambridge.

Hochman, J. (1984). Iatrogenic symptoms associated with a therapy cult: Examination of an extinct "new psychotherapy" with respect to psychiatric deterioration and "brainwashing." *Psychiatry*, **47**, 366–77.

Hunter, E. (1956). *Brainwashing. The story of men who defied it*. Farrar, Straus and Cudahy, New York.

Huxley, A. (1936). Notes on propaganda. *Harper's Magazine*, **174**, 39.

Johnson, G. R. (1987). In the name of the fatherland: An analysis of kin terms usage in patriotic speech and literature. *International Political Science Review*, **8**, 165–74.

Leather, P., McKechnie, S., and Amirkhanian, M. (1994). The importance of likeability as a measure of television advertising effectiveness. *International Journal of Advertising*, **13**, 265–80.

Lenin, V. I. (1929). *Agitation und Propaganda*. Verlag für Literatur und Politik [original in Russian], Berlin.

Lifton, R. J. (1956). "Thought reform" of Western civilians in Chinese Communist prisons. *Psychiatry*, **19**, 173–95.

———. (1989/1961). *Thought reform and the psychology of totalism. A study of "brainwashing" in China*. University of North Carolina Press, Chapel Hill.

Lofland, J. and Skonovd, N. (1984). Conversion motifs. In *Of gods and men: New religious movements in the West* (ed. E. Barker). Mercer University Press, Atlanta, Ga.

Lofland, J. and Stark, R. (1965). Becoming a world-saver: A theory of conversion to a deviant perspective. *American Sociological Review*, **30**, 871.

Lott, J. R. J. (1990). An explanation for public provision of schooling: The importance of indoctrination. *Journal of Law & Economics*, **33**, 199–231.

Marcus, G. E. (1988). The structure of emotional response: 1984 presidential candidates. *American Political Science Review*, **82**, 737–61.

Masters, R. D. (1991). Individual and cultural differences in response to leaders' nonverbal displays. *Journal of Social Issues*, **47**, 151–66.

Masters, R. D., Sullivan, D. G., Lanzetta, J. T., McHugo, G. J., and Englis, B. (1986). The facial expression of leaders: Towards an ethology of human politics. *Journal of Social and Biological Structures*, **9**, 319–43.

McArthur, T., ed. (1992). *The Oxford Companion to the English Language.* Oxford University Press. Oxford/New York.

Meerloo, J. A. M. (1957). *Mental seduction and menticide: The psychology of thought control and brainwashing.* Jonathan Cape, London.

Mehrabian, A. and Williams, M. (1969). Nonverbal concomitants of perceived and intended persuasiveness. *Journal of Personality and Social Psychology,* **13**, 37–58.

Milgram, S. (1974). *Obedience to authority. An experimental view.* Harper & Row, New York.

Murphy, J. J. (1974). *Rhetoric in the Middle Ages: A history of rhetorical theory from St. Augustine to the Renaissance.* University of California Press, Berkeley.

Nuttin, J. M. (1987/1975). *The illusion of attitude change: Towards a response contagion theory of persuasion.* Leuven University Press, Leuven, Belgium.

Padgett, V. R. and Brock, T. C. (1988). Do advertising messages require intelligible content? A cognitive response analysis of unintelligible persuasive messages. In *Nonverbal communication in advertising* (ed. S. Hecker and D. W. Stewart), pp. 185–203. Lexington Books, Lexington, Mass.

Raywid, M. A. (1980). The discovery and rejection of indoctrination. *Educational Theory,* **30**, 1–10.

Rescher, N. (1966). *The logic of commands.* Routledge and Kegan Paul, London.

Reut, R. G. (1993). *Goebbels* (trans. Krishna Winston). Harcourt Brace & Company, New York.

Reynolds, V. (1973). Ethology of social change. In *The explanation of cultural change: Models in prehistory* (ed. C. Renfrew), pp. 467–78. Duckworth, London.

Richardson, J. T. and Kilbourne, B. (1983). Classical and contemporary applications of brainwashing models: A comparison and critique. In *The brainwashing/deprogramming controversy* (ed. D. G. Bromley and J. T. Richardson), pp. 29–45. Edwin Mellen Press, New York.

Salter, F. K. (1995). *Emotions in command. A naturalistic study of institutional dominance.* Oxford University Press, Oxford.

Sargant, W. (1957). *Battle for the mind.* Doubleday, New York.

Schein, E. H. (1956a). Distinguishing characteristics of collaborators and resisters among American prisoners of war. *Journal of Abnormal and Social Psychology,* **55**, 197–201.

———. (1956b). The Chinese indoctrination program for prisoners of war. A study of attempted "brainwashing." *Psychiatry,* **19**, 149–72.

Selznick, P. (1952). *The organizational weapon: A study of Bolshevik strategy and tactics.* Free Press, Glencoe, Ill.

Singer, M. T. and Ofshe, R. (1990). Thought reform programs and the production of psychiatric casualties. *Psychiatric Annals,* **20**, 188–93.

Solomon, T. (1983). Programming and deprogramming the Moonies: Social psychology applied. In *The brainwashing/deprogramming controversy: Sociological, psychological, legal and historical perspectives* (ed. D. G. Bromley and J. T. Richardson), pp. 163–82. Edwin Mellen Press, New York.

Somit, A. (1968). Brainwashing. In *International encyclopedia of the social sciences* (ed. D. L. Sills), pp. 138–43. Macmillan and Free Press, New York.

Taylor, D. (1983). Thought reform and the Unification Church. In *The brainwashing/deprogramming controversy: Sociological, psychological, legal and historical perspectives* (ed. D. G. Bromley and J. T. Richardson), pp. 73–90. Edwin Mellen Press, New York.

Tiger, L. and Fox, R. (1989/1971). *The imperial animal*. Henry Holt and Company, New York.

Tuzin, D. F. (1982). Ritual violence among the Ilahita Arapesh: The dynamics of moral and religious uncertainty. In *Rituals of manhood. Male initiation in Papua New Guinea* (ed. G. H. Herdt and R. M. Keesing), pp. 321–55. University of California Press, Berkeley.

Welch, D. (1995). *The Third Reich: Politics and propaganda*. Routledge, London and New York.

Whiting, J. W. M. (1941). *Becoming a Kwoma: Teaching and learning in a New Guinea tribe*. Yale University Press, New Haven.

———. (1968). Socialization: Anthropological aspects. In *International encyclopedia of the social sciences* (ed. D. L. Sills), pp. 545–51. Macmillan and Free Press, New York.

Young, J. L. and Griffith, E. E. H. (1992). A critical evaluation of coercive persuasion as used in the assessment of cults. *Behavioural Sciences and the Law*, **10**, 89–101.

CHAPTER TWENTY ONE

ON THE EVOLUTION OF POLITICAL COMMUNITIES

THE PARADOX OF EASTERN AND WESTERN EUROPE IN THE 1980S

Roger D. Masters

Introduction: Analyzing Political Institutions from a Biological Perspective

The existence of centralized governments (or "the state") is more of a problem than it first appears. For over 99 percent of hominid evolution, our species has lived in face-to-face groups of at most 50 to 100 members. Our nearest primate relatives—chimpanzees, orangutans, and gorillas—form bands of the same size. Even in industrial societies, working groups in offices, schools, armies, and factories rarely exceed this scale. Humans may tolerate impersonal crowds going to and from work or while watching entertainment and sporting events, but only rarely do we invest time and energy assisting anonymous strangers. Governments create benefits—punishing criminals, developing an economic infrastructure, defending against foreign threats—that are "collective goods" shared by all members of a community numbered in the millions, and the obstacles to such institutions are important to recognize and understand.

The centralized state, particularly in the form associated with a market economy and cooperation among anonymous "citizens," has been an enigma since the dawn of systematic political theory. As the Sophists in ancient Greece pointed out, whatever benefit could be gained by obeying the state's laws could be increased by openly appearing to conform while secretly cheating. It's well to pay your taxes, but better to fool the tax collector. Heroes die for their country, but the clever get draft deferments and make money on the home front. In terms of contemporary economic or choice theories, the calculus of cost and benefit should lead a self-interested individual to be a "free-rider" on collective goods, gaining all the benefit of the community while paying none of the costs.

Paradoxically, however, observation shows that humans are remarkably easy to indoctrinate. Children imitate each other and the adults around them. Groups spontaneously elaborate fads and styles of dress, behavior and art. Shamans, priests, and rulers establish doctrines and rules of the most exotic variety, sometimes with puzzling speed. How can it be that, despite evolutionary principles that seem to favor defection from collective norms, humans so readily adopt them? And why do methods of indoctrination that successfully produce cohesive or aggressive societies in some cases fail completely in others?

Evolutionary theory leads to the prediction that the extent of the groups in which humans cooperate is constantly changing—and that the reasons for these changes can be understood (Masters 1989; Schubert 1989; Gruter 1991). If so, we should be able to analyze the growth or collapse of political, social, and economic institutions by discovering the causes of human attachments to varied groups. These causes are in turn related to the changing costs and benefits of nepotism, reciprocity (whether direct or indirect), legally enforced obligations toward others, and pure altruism. Psychology—the emotionally charged perception of self-interest and social belonging—can be rationally explained even when (and perhaps most especially when) the individuals involved seem wildly irrational to those around them.

In this chapter, I develop a model to explain the ease and paradoxical fragility of large-scale communities into which humans have often been indoctrinated. To test this model, the recent collapse of Soviet control over Eastern Europe, followed by the upsurge in nationalism and ethnic conflict from the Soviet Union to Yugoslavia, makes an excellent case study. During the 1980s, why should Western Europe have been moving, however slowly and cautiously, toward economic, social, and political community at the same time that, in the East, parochial attachments were challenging and destroying broader political ties? Within countries, whether in Eastern or Western Europe, why do some groups have xenophobic reactions to expansions of the political community that are welcomed by other citizens? Although the events in the West seem predominantly economic while those in Eastern Europe originally focused on political institutions, can an evolutionary model explain why attitudes toward the social and political units have varied so markedly within states as well as between them?

With Whom Can I Cooperate? Recognition Markers, Optimism about the Future, and Social Groups

All social animals have developed, through natural selection, mechanisms for distinguishing those members of their own species with whom cooperation is likely to be beneficial. Similarly, animals evolve the capacity to identify both predators and threatening rivals of their own kind. In some species, the cues for identifying friend and foe are individually learned; in others, they are instinctive or imprinted by experiences in the first hours of life; often, there is a complex integration of innate and acquired factors (Lorenz 1970–71). Whatever the process, the specific cues indicating that another individual is likely to reciprocate if helped or to attack if approached too closely are called *recognition markers*.

Humans are social animals with an exceptionally large variety of mechanisms for recognizing others. The infant distinguishes its mother from others within hours of birth through such "proximate mechanisms" as odor, face, and voice; mothers—and fathers—use similar recognition markers to distinguish their offspring from others. Even in identifying kin, however, these cues are supplemented by linguistic and cultural factors: the complex and varied kinship systems studied by anthropologists define who it is that we call "the sisters and the cousins" and whether we "reckon up by dozens" and include "aunts" (as Gilbert and Sullivan put it). Perceptions of visible cues of face, speech, movement, dress, or even odor are thus combined in humans with symbolic recognition markers that can be learned and modified in adulthood.

We are all aware of course of flags, uniforms, and passports. Such symbols of community define states and, often, elicit the emotions of patriotism and nationalism. But how do these cultural abstractions translate into day-to-day behavior? Language—especially dialect, accent, and speech patterns—provides a quick way to identify where someone comes from. Clothing, style, and manners tell us much about social class and likely behavior. Facial expressions and other nonverbal cues communicate intentions to help or harm, providing instantaneous information of whether another is likely to be cooperative (Frank 1988; Masters 1989).

For example, a recent study shows that when viewers in the United States were shown silent videotapes of unknown French, German, and American politicians, they responded very differently to the sight of their own nation's leaders. When asked to rate the leaders by using a scale from 0 to 100 ("thermometer") known to predict voting choices, the viewers' average rating of an unknown, silent American was around a neutral rating of 50. But even though the foreign leaders were not identified on the videotapes, American viewers rated them negatively, with average thermometer ratings of around 41. Cognitively defined traits (honest, powerful, active, etc.) and warmth of emotion felt while watching the French and German leaders were also negative compared to similar reactions to American politicians (Table 21.1). In short,

Table 21.1: Differences in American Viewers' Responses to Political Leaders from the United States, France, and Germany

| | Nationality of Leaders | | |
	American	French	German
Average Cognitive Rating (3 Dimensions of Osgood's Semantic Differential)	6.44*	2.01*	-1 .21*
Average "Net Warmth" of Emotional Response (Positive Emotions minus Negative Emotions)	1.66*	-.29*	-.48*
Average Overall Attitude (0–100 "Thermometer" Rating)	50.3**	42.3	41.0

Average responses of experimental sample of 84 American adults (42 males, 42 females) after watching image-only excerpts of low-status leaders, selected from month-long sample of TV news in three countries.
Source: Warnecke, Masters, and Kempter, 1992
* Variation across three nationalities significant (p < .001).
**Average rating of American leaders significantly different from ratings of French and German leaders (p < .05); mean ratings of French and German leaders not significantly different.

something about the "looks" and body movement of an individual elicits a predictable difference in our responses to fellow countrymen (Warnecke, Masters, and Kempter 1992).

Nonverbal behavior is one of the many recognition markers by which we distinguish those who seem comfortable as partners in cooperative behavior. (Frank 1988). Such cues, which have evolved from similar displays in nonhuman primates but are used in somewhat different ways by each human culture, are especially effective in contemporary politics because they allow leaders to use television as a means of triggering powerful feelings in a mass audience (Masters 1989; Sullivan and Masters 1988).

Other recognition markers included not only the verbal or grammatical aspects of language, but the rhythms of speech (Treeck, Bente, and Frey 1989), voice accent (Mehler 1986), and social spacing (Hall 1959). These cues provide subtle but important information about where others are "from" and what they are likely to do. Compared to nonhuman animals, therefore, humans may well use a greater variety of markers permitting us to distinguish cooperators from competitors (Schubert and Masters 1991). Somehow, the brain integrates or averages the information from these multiple cues so that, while different individuals usually respond to a particular person or event in different ways, humans show a general tendency to prefer to cooperate with those identified as the "in group" (Falger, Reynolds, and Vine 1987).

Because humans use so many cues of group membership, our species seems specialized in shifting not only allegiances within groups, but the definition of social units themselves. In an important recent study, Shaw and Wong (1989) classified five main categories of these recognition markers: kinship (presumed common descent); phenotypic similarity (visible resemblance of facial or bodily configuration, movement, or dress); language (mutually intelligible speech); religion (shared beliefs and rituals); and territory (shared residence). Some societies, such as primitive tribes without centralized governments, base cooperative groups on those who share markers for all five traits. In such cultures, because shared language, religion, and territory coincide with presumed kinship and perceived physical resemblance, there is often extremely intense in-group cooperation and out-group hostility. At the other extreme are multilingual, multiethnic states or empires, like the traditional Austro-Hungarian Empire, whose members shared a common territory but little else (Shaw and Wong 1989).

The evolution of diverse recognition markers and their multiplicity in humans helps explain why issues of inclusion or exclusion from the group are so emotional and seemingly irrational. Anyone who has suffered from racial or religious prejudice knows this at first hand. Hence it is hardly surprising that shifts in the scope of social, economic, and political institutions are often accompanied by strong emotions and surprisingly weak rational justifications.

What Is the State—and Why are Centralized Governments Fragile?

Evolutionary biology establishes principles of social cooperation and competition, based on strategies of nepotism, direct or indirect reciprocity, helping and altruism (see above). Among most social mammals, the costs and benefits of these strategies prevent the emergence of large social systems like the centralized nation-state (Wilson 1975; Alexander 1987; Masters 1989). Unlike other animals, however, humans can shift social behavior in response to the environment, using an extraordinary array of recognition markers as cues of likely cooperation or competition. When common territory and language are the primary cues defining social cooperation, the centralized state can arise because group membership is no longer limited to those of the same kin or ethnic group. If states are constituted more narrowly on presumed homogeneity of ethnic descent, physical appearance, and/or religion, as well as on territory and language, the passion of individual commitment can be increased; if those benefiting from the state's laws and security are defined merely by territorial residence, as in ethnically, linguistically, and religiously heterogeneous empires, population size can be increased.

According to some thinkers, states arise due to external threat and competition; for other theorists, economic and social cooperation made possible by common legal and social institutions can account for the state. The evidence suggests, however, that the costs of indirect reciprocity and indiscriminate helping are so high that *both* of these processes probably had to interact under the guidance of exceptional leaders for human populations to form centralized states (Masters 1989). And even then, the success of a state quite typically breeds the seeds of its own downfall.

The problem can be illustrated concretely by considering the funding of public education in a model community.[1] Imagine a town of 4,000, only 3,000 of whom are couples with children of school age. If it costs $1,000 a year to educate each child in school and there are 2,000 school-age children in town, the town's school budget would be $2,000,000. A tax of $1,000 per family or $500 per adult would fund the schools. But why should it be paid by the families whose children are already grown or too young for school, not to mention those who are childless or unmarried?

Simple reciprocity—paying for educating the other citizens' children in return for the eventual schooling of one's own—will not explain the taxpayers' behavior. Not only do some people always have fewer children than others (or no children at all), but the rational "free-riders" would not move into the town until their children were starting school, and then would leave for a community without schools as soon as their youngest graduated. This is, in fact, precisely what many American families do, following a residence pattern that has produced significant problems in suburban towns whose older middle-class citizens leave for retirement communities after their children have grown.

To be sure, a good educational system improves labor productivity and thus provides benefits for all. However great these advantages, even greater gains arise for those who avoid paying taxes for these collective goods (Olson 1965; Margolis 1982). Without some form of civic pride in having a fine school system, therefore, compulsion seems the only means to generate tax revenues. Such uses of force are, in turn, costly for those in power. Hence political systems tend to provide only those services whose benefits exceed not only the costs to the public but the expense of tax collection and enforcement.

In many premodern states, composed of heterogeneous populations, the principal benefits to subjects were protection from external attack, minimal infrastructure for trading, and occasional legal recourse in dispute settlement. Since the costs of such a state

1. This example is intentional, since the provision of free public education became the hallmark of the modern nation-state in the late nineteenth and early twentieth centuries. Prior to that epoch, centralized states rarely provided education as a free good. The correlation between the emergence of highly trained, literate labor force (a key to the development of a fully industrial society) and national "self-determination" as a basic political principle (enshrined in Wilson's rhetoric during and after World War I) is too easily forgotten by those critics of all forms of "government" action who take the infrastructure of the market economy for granted.

were relatively small, as were the benefits, tax payments—while usually dependent on the use of force—were less problematic. In the imaginary town of 4,000 serving as our model, a tax of $125 per adult would fund a $40,000 police force—and since all would gain from the security, a police department would be less vulnerable to free-riders than the public schools. Compulsion is thus more likely to work as a means of securing obedience to a state that is providing limited benefits to its subjects. In contrast, some form of ideological, mythical, or religious legitimacy becomes necessary as the state provides more extensive possibilities for cooperation and larger collective goods.

Limiting the state's members or identity to a single ethnic or cultural group is a way of justifying the support of governmental institutions that provide great potential benefits to the citizens but are vulnerable to free-riding. When the growth of the market economy, technological innovation, and industrial production promised hitherto unknown economic prosperity after the middle of the eighteenth century, national states began to replace the multicultural monarchies or local principalities that had dominated Europe for centuries; by the first quarter of the twentieth century, the concept of the nation-state had become the norm or expectation (with all of the attendant contradictions observed to this day). The contemporary nation-state, based on common language, shared culture, and defined territories, is thus not as "natural" as is generally presumed. Quite the contrary, it is a historically conditioned device for adjusting recognition markers to facilitate the intensification of economic and social cooperation in a highly competitive international system.

Why Communities Expand and Contract: Present Satisfaction and Hope for the Future

To this point, I have illustrated how an evolutionary approach can *describe* the history of social and political institutions by relating them to the changing scope of cooperative groups. The human ability to shift behavioral strategy by expanding or contracting the recognition markers for friends and enemies provides a plausible mechanism for such events as the recent explosion of nationalism and ethnicity in Eastern Europe. This focus on the psychological foundations of politics can be useful: it is risky to ignore the unconscious behaviors, emotions, and beliefs about ourselves or others that lead humans to vote, pay taxes, protest, revolt, or lapse into political apathy. But a scientific theory needs to do more.

To develop a comprehensive theory of the rise and fall of states, the principles outlined above need to be formalized in a way that could ultimately be measured and tested. Just as behavioral ecologists have been able to analyze variations in social structure among other species, economists have developed models to explain variations in human behavior (Hirshleifer 1987; Getty 1989). A problem arises when extending such theories to humans, however: we construct symbols, perceive the world through myths, scheme, deceive ourselves, and otherwise transform the costs and benefits of our material world. What follows is an attempt, necessarily preliminary and imperfect, to show how these apparently ineffable factors can lead to paradoxes like the unification of Western Europe and the disintegration of the Eastern Bloc under the impact of the same socioeconomic process.

The evolutionary study of social cooperation rests on a simple cost-benefit relationship (Wilson 1975; Alexander 1987). Animals generally help others when to do so improves long-run reproductive success as measured by the individual's genetic contribution to future generations. Helping behavior is defined as an act whose costs exceed its benefits to the actor; such behavior is often called "altruism," but the latter term is perhaps best reserved to a specific case of helping—namely, the human motivation or desire to provide extensive help to strangers without tangible rewards and, in the pure case, without being observed. From a neo-Darwinian perspective, natural selection normally eliminates all forms of gratuitous helping, since animals who benefit from assistance without reciprocating will, on average over the long run, have more offspring than those who provide the assistance.

The most general exception to this premise, called "inclusive fitness" by Hamilton (1964), occurs when helping is directed to kin: if the recipient of helping behavior is a close relative, then costs to the helper greater than direct benefits can be incurred as long as the resulting benefits to the recipient increase the net reproductive success of that helper's *genes*. Evolutionary theorists (e.g., Barash 1982) formalize this relationship as:

$$K > 1/r \tag{1}$$

where K = ratio of the recipient's benefit to the helper's cost
r = coefficient of relatedness of the recipient and helper

Whereas a self-interested individual does not tend to do things if the cost is greater than the personal benefit, such a costly behavior that assists the helper's full-sibling or an offspring (either of whom has a coefficient of relatedness of .5, sharing one-half of the helper's genotype) would be performed if its benefits to the recipient were twice the cost to the helper (K = 2). This same action would not be undertaken for the benefit of a single grandchild or first cousin (coefficient of relatedness of .25) unless it had a benefit to cost ratio of 4; toward a distantly related member of the group (a coefficient of relatedness of .01), only very "inexpensive" helping (K = 100) would be predicted. In economic terms, one can think of this relationship as discounting the benefit a rational actor would gain from helping another by the extent to which they are kin.

The basic assumption of inclusive fitness theory can be extended to the total of an individual's cooperative and helping behavior as it relates to all other members of the group. To do so, one needs to sum the benefit/cost ratio of the actor's behavioral repertoire and consider the total number of beneficiaries, each discounted by his/her coefficient of relatedness. Averaging the coefficient of relatedness for all those who benefit from helping,[2] this gives an expression for the equilibrium level of social cooperation.

$$\Sigma K = 1/ (n) (r') \tag{2}$$

where r' = average coefficient of relatedness
n = size of group benefiting from cooperation

Substituting terms and solving for the number of those who cooperate:

$$n = \frac{\Sigma C}{\Sigma B (r')} \tag{2a}$$

For example, an individual engaging in helping behavior that averages a net benefit/cost ratio of 4 would have to help eight grandchildren or first cousins in order to gain the predicted level of inclusive fitness, whereas if the beneficiaries were barely related ($r = .01$), the same action would only be done if it provided simul-

2. Technically, this average might not be exact for small groups: helping two second cousins and one brother may be different from helping three first cousins (though in each case $r = .25$).

taneous benefits to 25 others. And, of course, those 25 others would be genetic rivals, many or all of whom would not be likely to reciprocate.

As this example shows, it is little wonder that the hunter-gatherer bands characterizing most of human evolution, like groups of chimpanzees, gorilla, baboons, or vervet monkeys, tend to be extended kin groups of limited size; when helping is extended beyond lineal descent, as it is in mating with outsiders, reciprocity based on individual recognition is typically involved (Trivers 1971). Although horticulturists and pastoral tribes form larger populations, even there the effective community is typically a village or band of less than 100 individuals. Since expansion beyond this size is vulnerable to free-riders, how can populations in the millions governed by a centralized state come into existence? The use of indoctrination to inculcate shared beliefs or customs in an extensive population must necessarily reduce the average genetic relatedness within the group—and hence the likelihood of refusals to pay taxes, not to mention to serve and die in the army.

The key, setting humans apart from other primates, seems to be our capacity to name things and to plan for the future. The larger cerebral cortex of *Homo sapiens* makes it possible to conceptualize time, to imagine myths or symbols, and to defer present gratification in return for future benefits. Try telling your dog that if he sits still for 15 minutes, he will have a bone; unless the dog has been trained to sit on command without limit, he will be up and off at the first temptation. Yet even a fifteen-year-old boy can understand and obey a request to wait 15 minutes or more for an ice cream cone ... and do so even knowing the condition of getting the ice cream is that he share with his sister.

Linguistic communication and planning for the future make it possible for humans to calculate—however vaguely and imprecisely—in terms of the future benefits of their children and kin. As analysis of time preference and interest rates indicates (Rogers 1990), such planning never *replaces* the assessment of current costs and benefits; rather, it adds a complexity to such a calculus. To see how this might work in the formation, expansion, or contraction of political communities, let us return to the example of funding the public schools of our imaginary town, this time using the formalizations of inclusive fitness theory as it applies to humans who create myths and symbols.

Recall the model: a town with 4,000 adult citizens, of whom 1,000 do not have school-age children: suppose the remainder form 1,500 families of which 250 have one child in school, 1,000 have 2 children, and 250 have 3 children. Public education costs $1,000 a year per child, which can be taken as the level of direct benefit to the families with children. While families without children do not gain directly from schools, public education is also a collective good insofar as it provides an educated labor force and increases property values in the community. Assume that this collective benefit (shared by all in town as long as each is certain that free-riders will be caught and punished by the town government) is worth 20 percent of the cost of education.

Table 21.2 converts the basic principle of inclusive fitness theory (Formula 1) into the benefit per adult depending on the number of children in school. As will be obvious, there are differences of self-interest: families with children in school—and especially those with two or more offspring—stand to gain by taxation to pay for public schools, whereas the childless lose. Unless it is easy to coerce these people, the logic of self-interest dictates against the formation of a political community and the provision of government services, even when they can produce collective benefits that are otherwise unobtainable.

Now imagine that the town fathers explain to the citizens that they are all related as descendants of a distant ancestor or create some ideology with a comparable effect.[3] The fictive relationship is slight ($r = .0002$)—far less than could be recalled by the experience or recognition markers that humans share with other animals. But it is enough to justify tax paying by all (Table 21.3). By the same token, because families with children gain substantial benefits, migration into the town would be attractive; hence, the mythic recognition markers associated with common descent will also be used to keep newcomers out. It is easy to think of real life illustrations at the local level, such as ethnic bias in real estate markets or prior residence requirements as a condition for eligibility for welfare and other public services. In the modern nation-state, the expansion of public goods available to all citizens coincided with the invention of passports, immigration quotas, and other restrictions on population movement.

The situation of our model community in Table 21.3 represents the expansionist or optimistic phase of state development. The net surplus for everyone with children creates incentives for increasing family size, investment, and economic growth. Even with con-

3. The classic example, of course, is the "noble lie" in Book III of Plato's *Republic*.

Table 21.2: Short-Term Costs and Benefits of Education in Model Town (No Cultural Kin Recognition Markers)

Number of Children in school	Benefit to Parents		Collective Good (@ 20%)		Cost per Adult		Net Gain per Adult
3 (n=500)	$1,500 ($1,000x3x.5)	+	$200	—	$500	=	$1,200
2 (n=2000)	$1,000	+	$200	—	$500	=	$ 700
1 (n=500)	$ 500	+	$200	—	$500	=	$ 200
none (n=1000)	none	+	$200	—	$500	=	– $ 300

Assumptions: All families with children have two parents who share equally in the payment of taxes; all children are legitimate offspring of their parents. Adults are not related to each other. Of the 1,000 adults with no children in school, subsequent versions of this model assume 300 have preschool children, 300 have adult children, and 400 are unmarried, celibate, or childless.

trols on newcomers, these advantages are also likely to produce illegal immigration. Given the human ability to plan and the penchant of some for optimistic assessments of the future, a new school building and other long-term investments in the community's infrastructure will be proposed. Despite the difficulty of generating support for collective goods among competing individuals, the human capacity to think ahead makes this possible. Historically, in fact, the optimistic investments at this stage often overshoot the actual needs or real benefits, leading to the boom and bust cycles that marked the nineteenth century (particularly

Table 21.3: Short-Term Costs and Benefits of Education in Model Town (Fictive Kin Recognition Markers)

Number of Children in school	Benefit to Parents		Collective Good		Fictive Kin Benefit		Cost per Adult		Net Gain per Adult
		Plus		Plus	(=0002)	Minus		Equals	
3	$1,500	+	$200	+	$299.40	—	$500	=	$1,499.40
2	$1,000	+	$200	+	$299.60	—	$500	=	$ 999.60
1	$ 500	+	$200	+	$299.80	—	$500	=	$ 499.80
none	none	+	$200	+	$300.00	—	$500	=	none

Assumptions same as in Table 21.2 except that all citizens are convinced that residence in town creates a "fictive kinship" equivalent to a coefficient of relatedness of .0002 in the development of the United States). To see why this is so, let us return to the imaginary community.

The citizens of our model town can make a calculation of their long-term gains from capital investments in schools or other collective goods, taking the annual costs and benefits in Table 21.3 and projecting them over future generations. To illustrate, assume the adults plan as far ahead as the completion of the education of their grandchildren: say, roughly, 40 years (five years of preschool for children in the first generation, thirteen years of schooling, nine years before these children have offspring of their own in school, and thirteen years of school for the grandchildren). To make the most conservative estimate of the effects of fictive kinship, let us assume that all of the citizens interested in having families not only optimistically plan to emulate their contemporaries with three children, but expect that each of these offspring will in turn have three children. If prices remain stable, all citizens would gain substantial benefits even if they paid the total costs of education for the 40-year period in advance, financing the investment by borrowing at 5 percent (and paying off capital at the rate of $1,000 per year), as illustrated in Table 21.4.

The presumed benefits due to fictive kinship with other citizens' offspring are so large that even adults without children would think they have an interest in investing in public education, borrowing enough in advance to pay their share of the community's education for the coming 40 years. Some such calculus seems to explain why citizens pay taxes to support the infrastructure of a growing state. All evidence of state formation—especially in the so-called "pristine" centralized states emerging for the first time—indicates heavy investment in infrastructure during an early growth phase: irrigation systems, communal buildings, walls, roads, and monuments all have the character that they promise future benefits that are some mixture of pure collective goods, indirect benefits to the offspring of other members of the community, and direct benefits to one's own descendants (Masters 1989, Ch. 5–6).

The imaginary town of 4,000 illustrates why, in this optimistic phase, population grows rapidly. Human history shows that the emergence of the state has had just this effect. The enormous benefits *perceived* to flow from collective enterprises also generate important differences in wealth (symbolized in the simplified model by the substantial inequalities in the last column of Tables 21.3 and 21.4). Again, historical evidence confirms that the growth

Table 21.4: Long-Term Costs and Benefits of Education in Model Town (Fictive Kin Recognition Markers)

Number of Children in school	Benefit to Children	Benefit to Grand-children	Collective Good	Fictive Kin Benefit (r=.0002)	Cost per Adult	Net Gain per Adult
Adults with Children (n = 3600)	$18,000	$27,000	$8,000	$77,760	$81,000	$49,760
Adults without Children	none	none	$8,000	$77,760	$81,000	$ 4,760

Assumptions: All citizens borrow $40,000 at 5 percent per year to pay taxes of $1,000 per year for coming 40 years; total interest over life of loan is $41,000. Benefit to children of citizens is $1,000 per year times 12 years of schooling times three children per adult, discounted by the coefficient of relatedness (0.5); benefit to grandchildren computed the same way for average of nine grandchildren each with a coefficient of relatedness of 0.25.

of states coincided with the emergence or accentuation of status and class differences. Governmental authorities are needed to administer and plan communal projects, to collect taxes, and to punish those who do not pay: recall that the premise of the entire model is the belief that those who attempt to be free-riders will be identified, punished, or excluded. A police force or army is needed, not only to keep order but, above all, to protect the community's resources from outside attack.

It is not difficult to find historical examples of the way fictive kinship actually functioned in the emergence of the modern nation-state to produce effects like those described in the model:

> Allons enfants de la patrie / Le jour de gloire est arrivé ... Aux armes, citoyens ...[4]

The "citizens" called to "arms" in the *Marseillaise* were "children" of the "fatherland" whose motto—*liberté, égalité, fraternité*—openly proclaimed fictive kinship. The resulting spirit of these phrases can be explained by means of a simple relationship between the assessments of present and future benefits. As has

4. A literal translation of these lines of the *Marseillaise* would be: "Go, *children* of *the fatherland*, the day of glory has come ... To arms, citizens ..." (italics added).

been emphasized, humans differ from other animals in the ability to think, to plan, and to deceive others (or ourselves) about the future. This ability seems to be the foundation of the phenomenon of investment in collective goods of a sort that other sexually reproducing mammals do not create, which were developed along with the formation of settled communities and centralized governments only in the last 15,000 years or so (after over 2 million years of hominid evolution in small bands), and which periodically collapse after a time of success. In this view, it is the ability to think simultaneously about the future and the present that underlies the expansion and contraction of states.

This psychological phenomenon can be represented formally by a simple ratio. Assume that humans are aware, however intuitively, of the net value of all material goods accessible to them, including not only direct personal benefits but those derived from indirect reciprocity with others in the community and from collective goods (e.g., summing the benefit columns in Tables 21.3 or 21.4). Let V_p stand for the net value of these benefits in the present, and V_f for the value at some future time (the number of generations projected into the future being itself an important variable). The ratio V_f/V_p then stands for the relative assessment of the future as compared with the present.

When V_f/V_p approaches unity, such that the present value of material resources is roughly equal to its future value, one can predict the maximum of competition for control over these resources. In contrast, as V_f/V_p declines below 1 and approaches 0, individuals will tend to consume resources at their disposal but

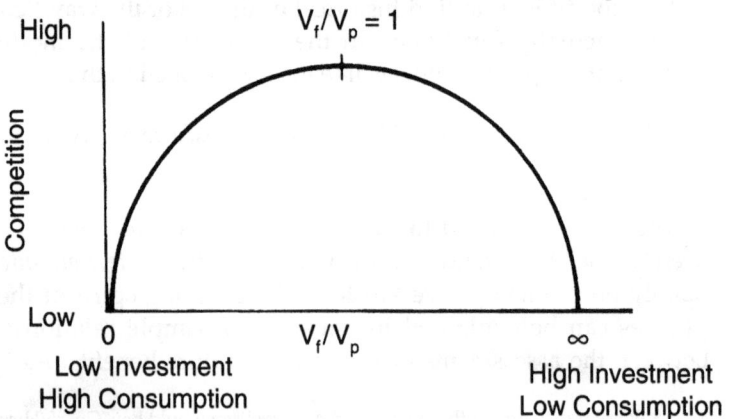

Fig. 21.1 V_f/V_p *Ratio and the Propensity to Consume, Compete, and Invest*

not to defend any excess or to invest. Conversely, as V_f/V_p exceeds 1 and increases toward infinity, it becomes more rational to invest and ultimately to cooperate rather than to consume or compete. This relationship is presented in Fig. 21.1.

If the only value of a resource is its immediate consumption (V_f very low compared to V_p), organisms will consume as much as they can and allow others to use what remains. Such situations can arise in environments of abundant resources. When an animal cannot defend a large chunk of resources, such as a deer killed by a single animal, the resulting form of behavior can be seen as "tolerated theft" rather than true sharing (Blurton-Jones 1991). If future values are as great as present ones—because a good can be stored, defended, or exchanged—rivals will compete for it; for many animals, most resources are in this category insofar as the only measure of future value is present physical benefit and, without language and forethought, there is no other way to compute V_f. For humans, however, it is possible to calculate or estimate future values—and, as we have just seen, this capacity seems to be related to the emergence of cultural, political, or religious communities that create collective goods.

A newborn baby with no capacity to conceive of future values—a ratio of V_f/V_p approaching zero—consumes without competing. A monk, religious ascetic, or political revolutionary for whom the future has infinite value whereas present material goods are worthless—a ratio of V_f/V_p approaching infinity—gives of himself unstintingly while limiting personal consumption and competition with others; in these cases, the investment of resources and energies tends to focus on broader and less precisely defined social groups—for the Christian or Buddhist holy man, the entire human species. Although most human situations fall between these extremes, there is obviously a wide variation in the way individuals and groups assess their present satisfaction and their future hopes.

It is important to consider the political implications of situations in which V_f greatly exceeds V_p. If the future value of resources is likely to be much greater than that at present, it makes sense to invest and to defend material goods, even at great cost to oneself: consider the motivation of the Europeans who settled the North American frontier from the sixteenth to the nineteenth centuries. Although such investments can originate in an individualist calculus of benefits to one's own kin, the logic of very high ratios of V_f/V_p, particularly if based on an extension of V_f to future generations, will favor investment in collective goods such as the social infrastructure symbolized by the schools of the imaginary town in Tables 21.2 through 21.4. The reason for this bears emphasis, since it is directly related to the creation, expansion, or contraction of the symbolic recognition markers for fictive kin.

If I plan to enhance long-term reproductive success by transmitting resources to my children—or even my grandchildren—high ratios of V_f/V_p can give rise to strategies of nepotistic investment. But projecting the future to the fourth, fifth, or nth generation has a paradoxical effect: with each generation, my coefficient of relatedness to each direct descendant comes closer to that of any randomly chosen member of the group. The difference between fictive kin and either direct descendants or collateral kin becomes progressively smaller as one calculates farther into the future (Table 21.5).

If one is planning four or five generations into the future, moreover, it becomes difficult to predict which of one's offspring or grandchildren will themselves have great-grandchildren in whom it is worthwhile to invest. Hence, as V_f is extended into the very distant future, if V_f/V_p is high, it is rational to invest in collective goods (which will be shared by anyone carrying one's genes) rather than to attempt to control the fates of reproductive lottery by investing in individuals. It is no accident that the very wealthy make large bequests to universities, museums, and other

Table 21.5: Generational Depth, Descent, and Fictive Kinship

Generation	Relation	Coefficient of Relatedness	Ratio to Fictive Kin (r = .0002)	Relation	Coefficient of Relatedness	Ratio to Fictive Kin
1	Self	1.0	5000	Cousin	0.25	1250
2	Child	0.5	2500	Cousin's child	0.125	625
3	Grandchild	0.25	1250	Cousin's grandchild	0.0625	312
4	Great-grandchild	0.125	625	Cousin's great-grandchild	0.0312	156
5	Great-great-grandchild	0.0625	312	Cousin's great-great-grandchild	0.0156	78

charities once they feel their offspring are well-provided for—
especially if, in so doing, their family name is given to a building
or public monument.

Fictive kinship—the extension of recognition markers to the
large population of the nation-state—serves to encourage mythical references to past and future. Leaders speak of both progress
ahead ("les lendemains qui chantent") and of a common heritage:
patriotism, the flag, culture, history, and the bond of fellow citizens. But—and it is an essential "but"—these appeals and the psychology they reflect are never abstracted from the flow of events.
Whereas an economist might look at Fig. 21.1 in terms of the shape
of the curve at a moment in time, an evolutionary perspective
needs to emphasize the *changes* in present and future values of
material resources.

Only now is it possible to test the model by examining the
paradox from which we began. If V_f/V_p has been very high, citizens will be encouraged to work hard, invest, and devote themselves to the improvement of the political community. Marxism as
an ideology extended the principle of fictive kinship to a direct
reciprocity with all proletarians throughout the world ("Workers
of the world, unite! You have nothing to lose but your chains"). In
the Leninist-Stalinist phase of "building communism," the present was sacrificed to make possible a better future, and the enormous disproportion between V_f and V_p supported the
replacement of previously distinct recognition markers for cooperation: nationality, religion, ethnicity, language, and territory
were submerged by ideological commitment to the recognition
markers of communism and party membership.

Over the last generation, the value of material goods presently
available (V_p) has *increased* in Eastern Europe. Paradoxically, it is
this improvement in material living conditions that destroyed
institutionalized communism: as V_p increased, people began to
consider the assessment of both V_p and V_f in a more "realistic"
manner. Inconveniences or shortages in supply that appeared necessary a generation earlier came to be seen as the result of human
error or avoidable inefficiency. Future goals were scaled back as
ideology was replaced by the discovery of corruption and
self-interest in the elite. The need for technical expertise, requisite
for the improvement of material conditions, extended the ability
to make more realistic assessments of the future as well as of the
present. Hence, increases in V_p led to declines in V_f and a shift

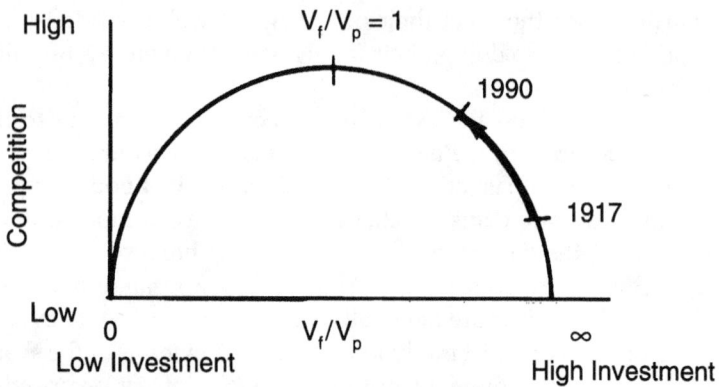

Fig. 21.2 *Hypothetical Change of V_f/V_p Ratio in Eastern Europe*

in the ratio of V_f/V_p from the Leninist values (approximating infinity) to those of a competitive situation (1), a change symbolized in Fig. 21.2.

The universalistic recognition markers associated with communist ideology and typical of very high V_f/V_p ratios are now psychologically untenable. Investments in cooperation can be supported only if directed to a community whose fictive kinship is narrower and more believable. Historical antecedents—one is tempted to say *any* historical antecedents—will do. And so ethnic and national attachments that seemed suppressed or dormant, religion (Polish Catholicism supported by a Polish Pope, East German Lutheran pastors, the Russian Orthodox Church), language, and even forgotten symbols of ethnicity—older recognition markers associated with narrower groups and less excessive appeals to immediate self-sacrifice—gain immense power as if by magic. It is no accident that renaming Leningrad as St. Petersburg became a critical issue at a time when attempts were being made to extend the scope of the market economy and reform the bankrupt communist state. The change is represented in Fig. 21.2.

In Western Europe, by contrast, the development of the EEC from 1945 to 1990 reflects a slow growth phase of cautious optimism. In the aftermath of World War II, the historical pessimism of the 1930s has slowly given way to greater self-confidence. The future for which many French, English, or Italians planned in 1945 was next Saturday's dinner; four decades later it was the twenty-first century. As V_p increased, V_f increased to keep pace—and, insofar as values of present material benefits meet the hopes

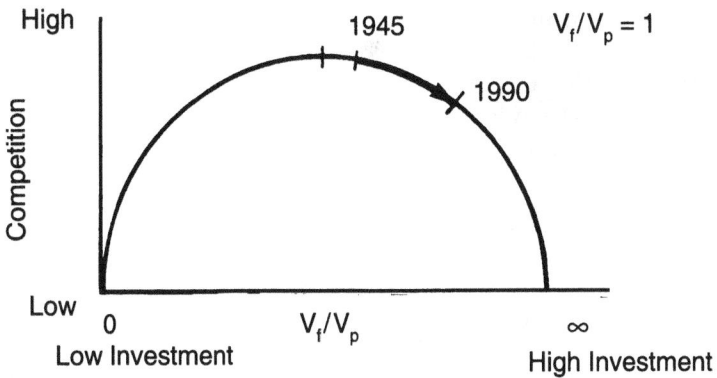

Fig. 21.3 *Hypothetical Change of V$_f$/V$_p$ Ratio in Western Europe*

of the current generation, self-confidence can be directed to enhanced future wealth and prosperity. This change is represented in Fig. 21.3.

Figs. 21.2 and 21.3 have been drawn to illustrate how the same value of V$_f$/V$_p$ can arise as a result of a movement from either a higher ratio (Eastern Europe) or a lower one (Western Europe). In the first case, the recognition markers for the most important political communities will shrink; in the second, they will expand. In both cases, however, the actual recognition markers are equally symbolic, if not mythical: "Europe" is as much or as little a fiction as "Lithuania" or "Croatia."[5] A common psychological process can thus be discerned under the apparently contradictory events of the last decade.

The model presented here needs, of course, to be subjected to empirical testing. Evidence of a very preliminary analysis, comparing assessments of the present and the future in Eurobarometer opinion polls from nine Western European countries in 1977 and 1988, is consistent with predictions (see Appendix). This measure of V$_f$ and V$_p$ does seem to reflect psychology rather than such features of each country as wealth or GNP (Inglehart 1990, Ch. 7).

Not only was the trend toward greater unification between 1977 and 1988 paralleled by increases in this measure of V$_f$/V$_p$, but the average value for all nine Western European countries rose from .65 (1977) to 1.51 (1988). Perhaps more intriguing, V$_f$/V$_p$ ratios in 1988 were consistent with the outcome of three national

5. Lest this seem an exaggeration, it needs to be recalled that in the Middle Ages, Europe—the *Republica Christiana*—was as much or more of a cultural unity than were any of the current "nationalities."

referenda on the Maastricht Treaty in 1992. Even though much changed in the interim, the 1988 Vf/V_p ratio for Denmark (whose voters rejected the treaty) was .77, whereas the 1988 ratio in both Ireland (1.42) and France (2.10)—countries in which a vote for the treaty in 1992 was in doubt—exceeded the midpoint of Figs. 21.1–21.3.

Conclusion

Political observers, journalists, and national leaders all professed astonishment at the sudden changes that led to the end of Soviet domination in Eastern Europe. Unexpected reversals of such massive importance suggest that beneath the apparently solid facts of economic statistics, military power, or political institutions lie deep but imperfectly understood emotions and feelings. More specifically, the myths and symbols that humans construct seem to play a more important role in determining the scope of the political and economic communities than has generally been understood by economists and political scientists.

In this essay, I have sought to show that evolutionary theory is particularly relevant to an understanding of these processes. It is not typical for mammals, or even for humans, to help strangers indiscriminately; the institutions of the centralized state, which require such helping behavior of the citizen, taxpayer, and soldier, are relatively recent and surprisingly fragile events in the broad scope of human history. Only when this fact is fully understood do we realize how mythical recognition markers—such as the fictive kinship of the modern nation—serve as a basis for the development of economic and social infrastructures on which large scale markets depend.

Assessments of the future, along with those of the present, have been made possible by the development of human intelligence and consciousness. But these transformations of the proximate mechanisms by which other primates establish varied behavioral strategies and social structures do not come without cost. Myths and symbols make it possible for humans to develop hitherto unparalleled material wealth and control over environmental contingencies. But these same myths and symbols also make it possible for humans to deceive themselves and others to a hitherto unparalleled degree. Whether our civilization will continue to prosper—or collapse as a result of overextended hopes and excessive coercion—remains the major issue of the coming century. Perhaps the outcome will be more favorable if we can understand the paradoxical expansion of Western European institutions under the influence of factors that, in the same historical epoch, have led to the disintegration of Eastern Europe.

Appendix: Testing the Model of V_f/V_p in Western Europe (1977–1988)

The model predicts that the extension of the European Economic Community over the last decade should have been accompanied by increases in the ratio of V_f/V_p in Western Europe. Prior to the recent expansion of the community, the model is consistent with ratios at or below 1.0 (since each society is consuming without bitter competition with the others), but ratios should have increased to well over 1.0 during the prosperity of the 1980s (reflecting a disposition to expand the effective political community). Moreover, the model predicts that these measures of social attitude should not be correlated with either V_p alone (psychological assessments of the value of the present) or objective measures of output and material wealth (such as GNP, etc.).

To test the model, data were used from Eurobarometer polls that have routinely been taken by representative samples throughout Western Europe (Inglehart 1990). In two years (1977 and 1988), the same respondents were asked to rate both how "satisfied" they were with the present and how "satisfied" they expected to be in five years. Responses were weighted to form comparable scales, which were then used to compute the V_f/V_p ratio; the results are in Table 21.6.

In 1977, data from nine European countries (France, Belgium, the Netherlands, Germany, Italy, Luxembourg, Denmark, Ireland, and Great Britain) show values of V_f/V_p between .28 (Belgium) and 1.31 (Italy); eleven years later, the range is between .77 (Denmark) and 3.27 (Great Britain). In 1977, only Italy had a ratio above 1.0; by 1988, six countries had ratios above 1.0, with only Denmark, Luxembourg, Germany, and the Netherlands below that mark. *The relevant figure for Western Europe as a whole—the average value of V_f/V_p—rose from .65 (1977) to 1.51 (1988).*

A number of statistical details suggest that this measure of popular attitudes reflects subjective dispositions associated with social cooperation rather than objective social characteristics. Con-

Table 21.6: Ratio of V_f/V_p in Nine Western European Countries (1977 and 1988)*

	1977	1988
France	0.44	2.10
Belgium	0.28	1.55
Netherlands	0.43	0.92
Germany	0.80	0.88
Italy	1.31	1.75
Luxembourg	0.31	0.89
Denmark	0.43	0.77
Ireland	0.81	1.42
Great Britain	0.79	3.27
Average for 9 Countries	0.65	1.51

*Source: Computed on the annual Eurobarometer polls administered to national samples of approximately 1,000 per country (for methods and general interpretation, see Inglehart 1990). In most years of this survey, respondents have been asked: "On the whole, are you very satisfied, fairly satisfied, not very satisfied or not at all satisfied with the life you lead?" The options are: "Very Satisfied; Fairly satisfied; Not very satisfied; Not at all Satisfied; Don't Know." In 1977 and 1988, a similar question was also asked concerning expectations of satisfaction in five years. Ratios were computed from data made available by the Inter-University Consortium for Political and Social Research.

sistent with Inglehart's findings at the individual level, neither a country's average V_p (the value of the present, as represented by a weighted measure of satisfaction with the present) nor its V_f (the value of the future using a similar measure of expected satisfaction) is significantly correlated with an objective measure of a country's economic wealth like GNP (1977: $r^2 = .19$; 1988: $r^2 = .02$, not significant). Inglehart (1990) hypothesized that religion might be a cultural factor associated with assessments of the present, and although neither the percent Catholic nor the percent reporting either religious practice or nonpractice was significantly associated with V_p, the percent Protestant was marginally correlated (1988: $r^2 = .25$, $p = .09$). The assessment of the future (V_f) is also not correlated with GNP (1977: $r^2 = .03$; 1988: $r^2 = .01$, not significant), and is not associated with any of the religious characteristics of the sample in each country.

In contrast, population size—a variable known to relate to social cohesion—is associated with subjective evaluations of the present. Consistent with the hypothesis that cooperation and reciprocity are favored in smaller groups unless there is an element of fictive kinship to support an expansion of the community, the overall population of a society has a negative correlation with V_p for 1977 ($r^2 = .55$) but not for 1988 ($r^2 = .043$, not significant). In neither year is V_f associated with population size (1977: $r^2 = .09$; 1988: $r^2 = .03$, not significant).

These findings suggest that measures of subjective assessment of the present and future do reflect what people are actually feeling—and the ratio V_f/V_p reflects the extent to which the future is perceived as more favorable than the present. If so, this ratio might well provide a useful measure of changing psychological dispositions to cooperate that are neither reducible to the country's objective characteristics nor an artifact of the way these questions are asked. Needless to say, however, better measures, longer time series, and more extensive data are needed to test the theory more fully.

Acknowledgments: Thanks are due to Michael T. McGuire, Martin Shubik, Will Masters, Seth Masters, Carol Barner-Barry, and Nelson Kasfir for helpful comments on earlier drafts, and to David Chang for research assistance in the Appendix.

References

Alexander, R. D. (1987). *The biology of moral systems.* Aldine de Gruyter, New York.

Barash, D. (1982). *Sociobiology and behavior.* 2d ed. Elsevier, New York.

Bente, G., Frey S., and Treeck, J. (1989) Taktgeber der Informationsverarbeitung. *Medien Psychologie,* Heft **2**, 137–60.

Blurton-Jones, N. (1991). Tolerated theft: Suggestions about the ecology and evolution of sharing, hoarding, and scrounging. In *Primate politics* (ed. G. Schubert and R. D. Masters), pp. 170–87. Southern Illinois University Press, Carbondale, Ill.

Frank, R. (1988). *Passions within reason.* Norton, New York.

Getty, G. (1989). The hunt for r: One-factor and transfer theories. *Social Science Information,* **28**, 385–428.

Gruter, M. (1991). *Law and the mind.* Sage Publications, Newbury Park, CA.

Gruter, M. and R. D. Masters, eds. (1986). *Ostracism. A social and biological phenomenon.* Elsevier, New York.

Hall, E. T. (1959). *The silent language.* Fawcett, Greenwich, Conn.

Hamilton, W. D. (1964). The genetical evolution of social behavior: Parts I and II. *Journal of Theoretical Biology,* **7**, 1–52.

Hirshleifer, J. (1987). *Economic behaviour in adversity.* University of Chicago Press, Chicago.

Inglehart, R. (1990). Subjective well-being and value change: Aspirations adapt to situations. In *Culture shift in advanced industrial society*, pp. 212–47. Princeton University Press, Princeton, N.J.

Lorenz, K. Z. ([1931–63] 1970–71). *Studies in animal and human behaviour*. 2 vols. Harvard University Press, Cambridge, Mass.

Margolis, H. (1982). *Selfishness, altruism, and rationality*. Cambridge University Press, Cambridge.

Masters, R. D. (1989). *The nature of politics*. Yale University Press, New Haven.

Mehler, J. (1986). Language comprehension: The influence of age, modality, and culture. Paper presented at the 37th Annual Meeting of the Orton Dyslexia Society, Philadelphia, Pa., November 1986. Inglewood, Calif.: Audio-Stats Educational Services, tape #916R-21.

Olson, M., Jr. (1965). *The logic of collective action*. Harvard University Press, Cambridge, Mass.

Orbell, J. and Dawes, R. M. (1991). A "cognitive miser" theory of cooperators' advantage. *American Political Science Review*, **85**, 515–28.

Reynolds, V., Falger, V. S. E., and Vine, I., eds. (1987). *The sociobiology of ethnocentrism*. Croom Helm, London.

Rogers, A. (1990). Birth, death, and the evolution of initial time preference. Unpublished manuscript.

Schubert, G. (1989). *Evolutionary politics*. Southern Illinois University Press, Carbondale, Ill.

Schubert, G. and Masters, R. D., eds. (1991). *Primate politics*. Southern Illinois University Press, Carbondale, Ill.

Shaw, R. P. and Wong, Y. (1989). *Genetic seeds of warfare*. Unwin & Hyman, Boston.

Sullivan, D. G. and Masters, R. D. (1988). "Happy warriors": Leaders' facial displays, viewers' emotions, and political support. *American Journal of Political Science*, **32**, 345–68.

Trivers, R. L. (1971). The evolution of reciprocal altruism. *Quarterly Review of Biology*, **46**, 35–57.

Warnecke, A. M., Masters, R. D., and Kempter, G. (1992). The roots of nationalism: Nonverbal behavior and xenophobia. *Ethology and Sociobiology*, **13**, 267–82.

Wilson, E. O. (1975). *Sociobiology: The new synthesis*. Belknap Press of Harvard University Press, Cambridge, Mass.

Note Added in Press. Two recent books provide important empirical evidence of factors associated with state formation, expansion, and collapse. For the complex ecological and historical configurations that have given rise to centralized states, see Jared Diamond, *Guns, Germs and Steel: the Fates of Human Societies* (New York: W. W. Norton, 1997). On the economic and psychological factors underlying long-term changes in Western economic, social, and political institutions since the late middle ages, see David Hackett Fischer, *The Great Wave* (New York: Oxford University Press, 1996).

INDEX OF PERSONS

SUBJECT INDEX